Turning Science into Business

PATENTING AND LICENSING AT PUBLIC RESEARCH ORGANISATIONS

OECD

ORGANISATION FOR ECONOMIC CO-OPERATION AND DEVELOPMENT

ORGANISATION FOR ECONOMIC CO-OPERATION AND DEVELOPMENT

Pursuant to Article 1 of the Convention signed in Paris on 14th December 1960, and which came into force on 30th September 1961, the Organisation for Economic Co-operation and Development (OECD) shall promote policies designed:

- to achieve the highest sustainable economic growth and employment and a rising standard of living in member countries, while maintaining financial stability, and thus to contribute to the development of the world economy;
- to contribute to sound economic expansion in member as well as non-member countries in the process of economic development; and
- to contribute to the expansion of world trade on a multilateral, non-discriminatory basis in accordance with international obligations.

The original member countries of the OECD are Austria, Belgium, Canada, Denmark, France, Germany, Greece, Iceland, Ireland, Italy, Luxembourg, the Netherlands, Norway, Portugal, Spain, Sweden, Switzerland, Turkey, the United Kingdom and the United States. The following countries became members subsequently through accession at the dates indicated hereafter: Japan (28th April 1964), Finland (28th January 1969), Australia (7th June 1971), New Zealand (29th May 1973), Mexico (18th May 1994), the Czech Republic (21st December 1995), Hungary (7th May 1996), Poland (22nd November 1996), Korea (2th December 1996) and the Slovak Republic (14th December 2000). The Commission of the European Communities takes part in the work of the OECD (Article 13 of the OECD Convention).

Publié en français sous le titre :

Des débouchés commerciaux pour la science
LA GESTION DE LA PROPRIÉTÉ INTELLECTUELLE PAR LES ORGANISMES PUBLICS DE RECHERCHE

FOREWORD

This publication has emerged from a year-long project at the OECD, "The Strategic Use of IPRs by Public Research Organisations", undertaken at the request of the Committee on Scientific and Technological Policy in 2001 and carried out by the Working Group on Innovation and Technology Policy (TIP), to : *i)* document and assess the legal and regulatory frameworks for commercialising IP generated with public research funds; *ii)* to measure and analyse the patenting and licensing activities of PROs in member and selected non-member countries; and *iii)* to identify areas for policy action.

The project involved a survey of national laws and regulations concerning the ownership and exploitation of IP at universities and other public research organisations (PROs), a survey of patenting and licensing activities at PROs, addressed to technology transfer offices or similar contact points, and finally, a series of case studies. The OECD surveys of IP policy and of patenting activity at PROs have mapped for the first time and for a number of OECD countries the state of affairs regarding IP policies and activity at publicly financed research organisations, while 13 case studies provide the "policy stories behind the figures".

Part I, based on the OECD surveys and written by Mario Cervantes and Benedicte Callan of the OECD Secretariat, examines policies and trends in the management of intellectual property generated at universities and other public research organisations (PROs) in OECD countries. It presents international data on the patenting and licensing of PROs, covering such issues as the size and structure of technology transfer offices, the size of patent portfolios and number of new patents, the types of licensing agreements concluded with firms, as well as the policies for owning IP and allocating royalties from licensing activity. Sandrine Kergroach was responsible for the statistical work.

The cases studies in Part II provide insight into how countries such as Canada, France, Germany, Denmark, Korea and Russia are reforming legal frameworks or implementing new policies governing the ownership and exploitation of IP arising from publicly funded research as well as an insider's look at the strategies of major research organisations for improving technology transfer through strategic licensing or the creation of spin-offs while dealing with issues specific to industries such as ICT and biotechnology. In-depth examples of IP management and policies at PROs in Belgium, Germany, Korea, the Netherlands, Spain, Switzerland and the United States provide practical lessons while highlighting the trade-offs involved in commercialising academic inventions.

The case studies in this volume were co-ordinated by an editorial team comprised of Pim den Hertog of Dialogic, Utrecht (the Netherlands) under contract to the Netherlands Ministry of Economic Affairs, Thomas Gering of Ventratec, the venture and business development arm of the Fraunhofer Patent Centre in Germany and Mario Cervantes of the OECD's Science and Technology Policy Division. The overall project would not have been possible without the active involvement of the national experts and authors of the case studies. Marianne van der Steen at the Netherlands Ministry of Economic Affairs and Kathryn Sullivan at the United States Department of Commerce Technology Administration provided overall leadership for this project. The Netherlands Ministry of Economic Affairs further co-organised with the OECD a workshop on "The Strategic Use of IPRs and Public

Research Organisations" in The Hague on 17 October 2002 to debate the initial findings of the surveys and case studies.

This report is published on the responsibility of the Secretary General of the OECD.

TABLE OF CONTENTS

PART I. FINDINGS FROM THE OECD SURVEY OF PATENTING AND LICENSING AT PUBLIC RESEARCH ORGANISATIONS

Executive Summary... 9

Chapter 1. Legal and Regulatory Frameworks for Intellectual Property at Public Research
Organisations 21

Chapter 2. Technology Transfer Structures and Public Research Organisations............................ 37

Chapter 3. Trends in Patenting and Licensing across OECD Countries 49

Annex 1. Notes on the Methodology of the OECD Survey of Patenting and
Licensing Activity on PROs 75

Annex 2. Glossary of Terms 79

Annex 3. OECD Questionnaire on the Patenting and Licensing Activities of Public Research
Organisations.. 81

References 89

PART II. CASE STUDIES

Introduction

Chapter 4. Introduction and Overview
by Pim Den Hertog, Thomas Gering and Mario Cervantes... 95

Government Policies for Managing Intellectual Property at Public Research Organisations

Chapter 5. Policy on Title to Intellectual Property under Crown Procurement
Contracts in Canada
by Jeanne Inch, with Donovan Vernon, Elizabeth Blackburn and Michel Grenier...... 113

Chapter 6. Changing IPR Regulations for Researchers in Denmark
by Sven Milthers... 129

Chapter 7. French Technology Transfer and IP Policies
     by Alain Gallochat 139

Chapter 8. Legal Regulation of Protection and Commercialisation of Intellectual Property
     Created by Russian Public Research Organisations
     by Natalia Zolotykh 153

Putting IP Policies into Practice

Chapter 9. Management of Intellectual Assets by German Public Research Organisations
     by Thomas Gering and Ulrich Schmoch 169

Chapter 10. University Technology Transfer in Switzerland: Organisation, Legal Framework,
     Policy and Performance
     by Patrick Vock 189

Chapter 11. The Evolution of Knowledge Management Strategies in PROs:
     The Role of S&T Policy in Spain
     by Clara Eugenia García and Luis Sanz-Menéndez 203

Leveraging IP for Biotechnology

Chapter 12. Intellectual Property in the German Biotechnology Sector
     by Oliver Werner 225

Chapter 13. Regulatory Regime Governing Management of Intellectual Property of
     Korean Public Research Organisations: Focus on the Biotechnology Sector
     by Mikyung Yun 237

Chapter 14. Development of a Policy to Ensure the Sharing of Unique Biomedical Research
     Resources in the Research Community
     by Theodore J. Roumel 253

Channels for Transferring IP to Industry

Chapter 15. IP-based Spin-offs of Public Research Organisations in the Dutch
     Life Sciences and ICT Sectors
     by Rudi Bekkers and Marianne van der Steen 263

Chapter 16. Trends in the ICT World and the Impact on IPR: The Case of IMEC
     by Johan Van Helleputte and Kristin Robeyns 291

PART I

FINDINGS FROM THE OECD SURVEY OF PATENTING AND LICENSING AT PUBLIC RESEARCH ORGANISATIONS

Part I presents the findings from the OECD survey on patenting and licensing at public research organisations. It contains information on the national laws and policies for owning and exploiting intellectual property at universities and other public research organisations; information on the characteristics of technology transfer offices; and new data on the amount of patenting and licensing activity in OECD countries.

EXECUTIVE SUMMARY

Introduction

Protection of intellectual property by public research organisations is increasing...

Intellectual property (IP) rights – of which patents, industrial designs, copyrights and trademarks are among the most widespread – reward investment in R&D and innovation by granting inventors and creators market power over competitors. Over the past decade in many OECD countries, universities, national laboratories and other research organisations receiving significant public research funds (hereafter referred to as "public research organisations – PROs") have become more aware of the value of their intellectual property. In large part, this awareness reflects the recognition by governments that, in some cases, placing the outputs of publicly funded research in the public domain is not sufficient to generate social and economic benefits from research.

...driven by legislative reforms but also by closer interaction with industry...

This awareness and demands to generate more economic benefits from public support to R&D have focused policy makers' attention on the laws and rules governing the ownership and exploitation of IP at PROs. In 1980 the Bayh-Dole Act in the United States gave university contractors of federal research the right to take out patents on inventions and license them to firms. Although patenting at US universities was occurring before 1980, it has since increased sharply. Between 1993 and 2000, US universities were granted some 20 000 patents. Over that period, some of these academic patents had generated millions of dollars in licensing revenue and have spurred the creation of over 3 000 new companies, according to the Association of University Technology Managers. Consequently, in other OECD countries and beyond, the Bayh-Dole Act has been widely viewed as a catalyst for increasing the social and economic benefits from public research funding.

...against a background of a strengthening of IPRs in the knowledge-based economies.

PROs have also been encouraged to protect their academic inventions and creative works by a general strengthening and broadening of intellectual property protection to new areas such as databases, ·genetic inventions, software or new materials that are closer to basic research. The results of publicly financed research have thus become more valuable to the research community and to firms. The rise of universities and new biotechnology firms as sources of commercially valuable know-how for the pharmaceutical and agricultural sectors illustrates this point.

This is creating opportunities for both governments and PROs.

For governments, granting PROs rights to IP generated with public funds can lead to better use of research results that might otherwise remain unexploited as well as to the creation of academic spin-offs or start-ups that create employment. For PROs the benefits may include increased licensing and royalty revenues, more contract research and greater cross-fertilisation between entrepreneurial faculty and industry. Equally important, however, are the intangible benefits to an institution's reputation and to the quality of its research that closer interaction with the private sector can generate.

A more active IP stance by PROs, however, raises a number of policy issues.

A more active IP stance at PROs, however, raises a number of policy issues about the costs of these activities and their impact on PRO missions. Does a more strategic IP policy: *i)* raise significant funds from licensing; *ii)* limit access to publicly funded research results; *iii)* affect the cost and efficiency of research; *iv)* reorient research towards more lucrative fields; and *v)* lead to conflicts of interests? As such questions are raised, many governments are trying to strike a balance between the research and commercial missions of PROs. In some OECD countries, observers point to a backlash against the commercialisation of public-sector research, fuelled by a perception that PROs have become overly influenced by market objectives and that the public interest requires safeguards against potential excesses.

The OECD Survey of Patenting and Licensing and Case Studies in IP Management at PROs

The lack of empirical evidence has clouded the policy debate.

To clarify the debate and to help countries address some of these issues, the OECD's Committee for Scientific and Technological Policy (CSTP) asked its Working Group on Innovation and Technology Policy (TIP) collect empirical evidence on the amount of patenting and licensing activity at PROs in OECD countries as well as information on the legal and regulatory frameworks that govern IP at PROs.

The OECD survey and case studies provide new information...

Few OECD countries, however, with the exception of Australia, Canada, the United States and the United Kingdom, regularly collect data on IP activity in the public research sector. Consequently, in 2001 the OECD launched the first international survey of patenting and licensing at PROs. A series of country case studies in IP management at PROs complement the survey by providing the "policy stories" behind the figures. This publication presents the findings of the survey and case studies.

...but the results should be viewed as an experiment.

The results of the OECD survey should be viewed as an experiment, albeit a revealing one that should be repeated. The data refer to patents assigned to PROs. In many countries, universities either do not automatically retain title or cede title to the inventors or the firms that sponsor the research. Therefore, the data on institutionally owned patents may understate the total amount of PRO patenting. The data also do not allow for full comparability across countries. Responses to variables such as full-time equivalent staff or research expenditures at PROs were submitted by only a few countries. This limits the ability to normalise responses using a common denominator. The data also cover patenting and licensing activity for the last calendar or fiscal year (2000 or 2001) and thus do not provide time-series information. Not all responding countries surveyed individual universities and non-university PROs; some provided only aggregate data, others provided disaggregated data only for universities or only for non-university PROs. Still, the survey has generated a substantial amount of useful information and raises new questions for further research.

Trends in intellectual property policies at public research organisations

Policies on ownership of IP are changing across OECD countries...

Across OECD countries, laws and policies governing the ownership of IP generated with public research funds are being re-examined with a view to encouraging ownership of inventions by the institution performing the research. In the European Union, there is concern that different national laws regarding the ownership and exploitation of IP from PROs, especially at universities, may create barriers to international collaborative research. Austria, Denmark, Germany and Norway have recently introduced new legislation to grant universities title to IP resulting from publicly funded research. In Finland, proposals are afoot that would, under certain conditions, give universities title to inventions. In Japan and Korea, recent reforms in funding regulations have given universities more control over the IP generated by their researchers. These policy trends echo the landmark US Bayh-Dole Act of 1980.

...to promote institutional ownership of IP.

However, whereas the Bayh-Dole Act modified the IP rules for federally funded research in the United States, most legislative moves in European Union countries have focused on changing employment laws so that university professors are no longer exempted from legislation that gives employers the IP generated by employees. A rationale common to both types of reforms is that ownership by institutions, as opposed to title by individual researchers, provides greater legal certainty for firms interested in exploiting research results, lowers transaction costs for partners and encourages more formal and efficient channels for knowledge and technology transfer.

IP policies are not well disseminated at PROs, including among students.

Despite changes in national legal frameworks, policies at the institutional level do not appear well disseminated among faculty and researchers at PROs. Similarly, rules on ownership of IP by students and other non-faculty at university-based PROs are either lacking or unclear in several countries. In addition, policies on ownership of non-patented IP, including copyrightable works, such as software or databases, are not well established or diffused at PROs in a number of OECD countries.

Most reforms focus on ownership but lack of incentives remains a problem.

Much of the focus of the reforms to legal frameworks has been on the issue of transferring ownership of IP to the performing institution. However, in several countries where PROs have owned the IP, patenting activity by institutions has nevertheless been weak. Part of the reason is that PROs have not had sufficient incentives, beyond legal requirements or institutional policies, to disclose, protect and actively commercialise IP.

Non-IP related rules can be a barrier.

In many OECD countries, non-IP related laws and regulations such as public-sector pay scales that make it difficult for PROs to recruit qualified technology transfer personnel can be a barrier to capacity building in technology transfer offices (TTOs). Fiscal rules that prevent PROs from receiving and retaining royalty income from licences – such as those recently lifted in the United Kingdom and Korea – can also weaken incentives for technology transfer.

Legislation is not the only policy option however. Funding guidelines can help...	The experience of OECD countries suggests that while legislation may sometimes be necessary to create the incentives for PROs to protect and commercialise IP, new laws are not the only action that can be taken. As an alternative, some governments have implemented "codes of practice" or general guidelines on IP ownership and management to foster greater transparency and coherence. Both the Canadian and Irish governments have sought to improve management of IP at PROs by reviewing or clarifying IP policies among the various performers of government research.
...and new legislation has raised awareness of IP at universities and other PROs.	Nevertheless, in countries that have implemented policies by legislative or other means, one of the main impacts has been to raise awareness of and support for technology transfer from universities and other PROs, especially within the administration of the organisations and among scientists/researchers and graduate students.
Greater coherence in national rules might induce cross-border harmonisation.	While greater compatibility – if not harmonisation – of the policies and practices of PROs within particular countries has the potential to improve technology transfer by reducing transaction costs, it can also help induce cross-border harmonisation and thus facilitate international collaborative research.

Technology transfer structures

Managing IPR requires institutional, financial and human resources.	A direct consequence of policies to grant PROs title to inventions and requirements for disclosure and exploitation has been the creation of TTOs or similar licensing offices to file patents and to enter into licensing agreements with third parties. Managing IPRs, however, requires institutional, financial and human resources.
Technology transfer offices are recent and generally have fewer than five full-time staff.	The OECD survey revealed a number of trends in the organisation and practice of technology transfer. There are several institutional models. Some TTOs have an arm's-length relationship to the PRO and may manage technology for several organisations. The majority, however, appear to be dedicated on-site institutions and integrated into the university or research institution. The TTOs are typically young structures; in Japan over 90% were established after 1990. Even in the United States their median age is 12 years. They are relatively small structures; in most cases, they have at most five staff (in full-time equivalent).
Countries are experimenting with regional or sector-based technology transfer offices	Denmark, Germany, Korea and the United Kingdom are experimenting with TTOs that are regional or sector-based according to field of research/technology and manage technology transfer activities for many PROs. Potential economies of scale might be realised by spreading fixed costs over a large number of inventions and perhaps exploiting the benefits of portfolio diversification. A potential drawback of regional approaches and "central broker" technology transfer models more generally is the difficulty of developing close working relationships with faculty/employees of individual PROs, relationships which are often valuable for stimulating invention disclosures, writing patent applications, and finding licensees.

The most important channel for licensing PRO patents is researcher contacts.

Indeed, the OECD survey shows the channels most often used by TTOs to seek licensees are informal relations and networks of researchers. This testifies to the importance of involving scientists in the further development and licensing of an invention. The networks or contacts of the TTO are also an important channel. Advertising or technology broker networks are used less frequently or not at all.

There is no "one size fits all" approach to technology transfer.

There are, however, are important differences among PROs that shape TTO structures and affect patenting and licensing strategies. Universities, fundamental research organisations, government labs and contract research organisations play different roles in innovation systems, generate different types of knowledge for different clients and therefore require different IP management processes. A contract research organisation such as IMEC in Belgium will differ in its approach to patenting and licensing from a basic research organisation, such as Germany's Max Planck Society. A university with research groups in different technological fields and a different type of staff (including students) may need yet another IP management strategy.

Governments are providing more support to academic patenting and licensing in many countries.

In line with legislative reforms to create incentives for IP management at PROs, governments in Denmark, Japan, and Germany are providing direct and indirect support, on a time-limited basis, to help universities and other PROs cover the costs associated with patenting and commercialising inventions. Indirect support takes the form of reduced patent application costs for universities as well as informational and awareness creation measures. Without leadership from senior university or research management, however, public support for IP activities at PROs is likely to have a limited impact – increasing the number of patents filed but not necessarily the transfer of technology.

International evidence of patenting activity by PROs

The size of patent portfolios is larger at non-university PROs.

The size of patent portfolios or the stock of currently active patents varies widely across and within OECD countries, depending on whether the PRO is a university or a national laboratory. Total active patents in portfolios ranged from 692 in Japan, 991 in the Netherlands, 1 184 in Switzerland to more than 5 000 in Germany (at non-university PROs only) and over 9 000 in Korea (both universities and non-university PROs). On average, individual TTOs manage between five and 50 patents. Here again, differences by type of PRO are apparent. In Italy only 18% of universities manage up to 50 patents whereas 80% of non-university PROs surveyed reported managing between ten and 50 patents. There are several explanations for differences in patent portfolio by type of PRO. For one, universities in several OECD countries have only recently either obtained the right to patent or established TTOs. Furthermore, non-university institutions, especially in European OECD countries, have had a longer tradition of protecting and commercialising IP.

New patents granted range from the low to high hundreds.	Total number of patents granted in the last year (2000 or 2001) ranged from several hundred in Germany (747) and Korea (832), to the low hundreds in Japan (163), Netherlands (167) and Switzerland (112).
PROs file less than ten new patent applications per institution but applications are likely to increase.	New patent applications per PRO ranged from an average of less than ten in almost half of the countries surveyed to several dozen. However, low patenting may also reflect PRO strategies: some apply for patents after a thorough examination and selection process while others may file for patents automatically each time an invention is disclosed. Public funding requirements that PROs protect and exploit the IP arising from research can also affect patent application rates. As several OECD countries have recently implemented new requirements for PROs, patenting applications are likely to increase in the near future.
Invention disclosures are indicative of potential patenting.	The number of "invention disclosures" – the document submitted by inventing scientists to their TTO – is another indication of the potential for new patents. The countries where PROs reported the greatest number of invention disclosures are the United States (16 286 at both universities and federal labs), Germany (948 at non-university PROs), Japan (489 at universities), Korea (418 at all PROs) and Switzerland (280 at all PROs) followed by Belgium (Flanders only) (230 at all PROs).
PRO patenting is not limited just to biotechnology and health fields…	While much of the increase in academic patenting has been attributed to the expansion of biotechnology, the OECD survey finds that even if patents in health and information technology predominate for some countries (Belgium, Germany, Netherlands and Switzerland), academic patenting is also significant in production, food and energy technologies. Patenting outcomes are likely to be associated with a country's R&D and industrial specialisation. In Korea for example, where IT is important in business value added, over 70% of universities declared having filed a patent in IT and electronics.
…and there is significant protection of IP by PROs in foreign jurisdictions.	TTOs may be small, but their approach to protecting PROs' IP seems to take a geographically broad view. Patents are filed first and foremost at national level, but almost all TTOs reported that they also filed abroad. PROs in Germany, the Netherlands and Switzerland were more likely (over 50% of institutions surveyed) to seek protection at European-wide level, in the United States and Japan than were PROs in Spain, Norway or Russia and Italian universities.
The IP activity of researchers has a greater influence on earnings than on careers.	While PROs are adapting human resources policies to give greater recognition of IP activity in recruitment and career advancement, licensing revenues provide strong incentives for researchers to explore the commercial applications of research. The survey finds that the effects are greater on researcher earnings than on career advancement.

Summary results of the OECD survey on patenting and licensing activities

		Patents					Licences			Start-ups and spin-offs
		Total patent stock	Patent grants		Patent applications		Total number of active licences	Total number earning income	Gross income	Total number created in last year
			Number granted in last year	% total stock	Number filed in last year	% total stock			EUR (000)	
Australia (2000)	All	-	498	-	834	-	417	491	99 525	47
	Univ	-	219	-	586	-	234	-	79 834	32
	PRO	-	279	-	248	-	183	-	19 691	15
Belgium (Flanders) (2001)	All	506	57	11.3	121	23.9	46	4	240	15
	Univ	-	-	-	-	-	-	-	-	-
	PRO	-	-	-	-	-	-	-	-	-
Germany (2001)	All	-	-	-	-	-	-	-	-	-
	Univ	-	-	-	-	-	-	-	-	-
	PRO	5 404	747	13.8	1 058	19.6	555	1 188	66 368	37
Italy (2000)	All	-	64	-	190*	-	36*	84	-	36
	Univ	-	34	-	102*	-	27*	12	-	27
	PRO	-	30	-	88*	-	9*	72	-	9
Japan (2000)	All	682	163	23.9	567	83.1	89	324	1 397	6
	Univ	-	-	-	-	-	-	-	-	-
	PRO	-	-	-	-	-	-	-	-	-
Korea (2001)	All	9 391	1 018	10.8	1 692	18.0	247	132	3 822	56
	Univ	404	186	46.0	244	60.4	44	22	1 032	19
	PRO	8 987	832	9.3	1 448	16.1	203	110	2 790*	37
Netherlands (2000)	All	991	167	16.9	212	21.4	368	93	11 400	37
	Univ	394	64	16.2	111	28.2	250	-	-	27
	PROs	597	103	17.3	101	16.9	118	-	-	10
Norway (2001)	All	-	-	-	-	-	-	-	-	67
	Univ	-	-	-	-	-	-	-	2 000*	16
	PRO	114	28	24.6	43	37.7	22	39	7 700*	51
Spain (2001)	All	781	64	8.2	133	17.0	125	136	961	11
	Univ	-	-	-	-	-	-	-	-	-
	PRO	-	-	-	-	-	-	-	-	-
Switzerland (2001)	All	1 184	112	9.5	175	14.8	475	77	5 650	68
	Univ	914	59	6.5	132	14.4	200	61	2 800	56
	PRO	270	53	19.6	43	15.9	275	16	2 850	12
United States (2000)	All	-	5 103	-	8 294	-	-	-	-	-
	Univ	-	3 617	-	6 135	-	4 049	8 670	1 297 452	390
	PRO	-	1 486	-	2 159	-	3 007	484	69 600	-
Russia (2001)	All	-	349	-	171	-	206	8	1 375	15
	Univ	-	-	-	-	-	-	-	-	-
	PRO	-	-	-	-	-	-	-	-	-

Australia: Data from the *National Survey of Research Commercialisation*, Australian Research Council 2000. Gross income in USD.
Italy: number of patent applications and number of licences granted are estimates.
Korea: One licence reported is not included in total number of active licences and total gross income. Gross income in USD.
Netherlands: Gross income is an estimate.
United States: Total number of income earning licences for federal labs is probably understated, as data are collected as earning "running royalties" and licences can earn income in other ways. Gross income in USD.
Russia: total number of patent granted and patent applications are estimates.

Licensing strategies of public research organisations

Two-thirds of PROs negotiate less than ten licences per year...but many licences are for copyright and other non-patented IP.

The majority of PROs negotiate a very small number of licences (often less than ten) a year. One-third negotiate between 15 and 46 licences each year. Surprisingly, a large share of licence agreements in Italy, Japan, the Netherlands and Switzerland were concluded for patent-pending inventions or non-patented inventions (*e.g.* biological materials or know-how), as well as for copyrighted materials. The importance of non-patent licensing seems to support other evidence that PROs tend to license early-stage technologies requiring further development by firms.

Licensing revenue varies greatly across PROs and countries...

One of the most sought-after pieces of information is the amount of revenue that PROs generate from the licensing of intellectual property. There is enormous variation across OECD countries and even among PROs within a country. In absolute terms, US universities generated the largest amount of income from licences, over USD 1.2 billion followed by Germany at EUR 6.6 million (PROs only). Per institution gross licensing income ranges from the thousands to the low millions: United States (USD 7.7 million); Germany (EUR 2.3 million); Switzerland (EUR 269 000); Korea (USD 537 000); and Japan (EUR 93 000).

and is highly skewed, as a few licences generate most of the revenue.

Data on licensing revenue per licence reveals the skewed nature of income from technology transfer. While some PROs in the United States generate several million USD from licences, the average value of each licence in 2000 was USD 150 000. A large percentage of licences never generate any income and only a small percentage earn high income. Japan, which has fewer licences and less aggregate revenue, generated EUR 139 000 per licence. In Switzerland, the average revenue per licence is EUR 45 000. This shows that some licences are more valuable than others and that a high number of licences does not necessarily mean high revenue or *vice versa*.

The number of new spin-off companies created to commercialise inventions is small but the phenomenon is widespread...

In general, PROs prefer to license to existing companies but they may also license IP to a spin-off or start-up company. The number of spin-offs per TTO created in 2000/2001 is low, yet spin-off activity is widespread across OECD countries. In most cases, PROs create less than one spin-off or start-up a year, except in the United States where the average in 2000 was two per university PRO. Licensing and spin-offs are two sides of the same technology transfer coin, however. PROs often license their technology to a spin-off to retain greater control and access to the IP.

...and the numbers are influenced by PROs' licensing strategies.

In many ways, the number of spin-offs is influenced by the licensing strategies of PROs as well by the pool of entrepreneurial managers and access to seed capital. The field of technology also matters, and inventions arising in areas of non-core research may be spun off. Case-study research suggests that so-called "platform" inventions, those that may lead to a wide range of applications, are more likely to be licensed to spin-offs than to existing firms.

Small companies obtain slightly more licences than large ones and licensing overseas is common.

Evidence on licensing by firm size is inconclusive in the aggregate, but in several countries small firms appear to obtain more licences than larger ones. Non-university PROs tend to license to small firms (in Germany, Korea and Switzerland). In Belgium (Flanders) and Japan (universities) most licensees are large firms. Some 80% of Swiss PRO licensees are foreign firms. Similarly, Dutch universities are more likely to license abroad than at home, possibly owing to the international nature of Dutch research as well as the limited national market for IP.

Small firms do not obtain more exclusive licences than large firms

One of the concerns of the scientific community and policy makers is that the exclusive licensing of patents to single firms will limit the diffusion of knowledge generated with public funds. Yet firms, especially small firms and academic start-ups/spin-offs for which IP constitutes a main asset, generally demand exclusive licences in order to offset the risks involved in developing academic inventions further. Contrary to expectations that start-up firms are especially reliant on exclusive licences, data from the OECD survey show that small firms (fewer than 500 employees) do not obtain exclusive licences more frequently than large firms.

Licences negotiated by PROs often contain clauses that protect public interests.

About half of the PROs include clauses in their agreements which require the licensee to make good-faith efforts to exploit the invention. Licences often include some form of limited exclusivity (*e.g.* by territory or field) so that the technology may be used by more than one firm. Less common but still important are clauses in licensing agreements that grant the PRO reach-through royalties or rights of first refusal on future inventions. There is, however, a good deal of variation among countries as to how common such clauses are.

Fears of crippling legal costs for PROs seem unsubstantiated.

Despite the upswing in PRO IP activities, they have not to date been heavily involved in infringement litigation. In fact, PROs are slightly more likely to sue a third party for infringement than to be sued.

Conclusions

Legal action can stimulate the "transfer" of publicly funded research.

In most OECD countries some sort of legal action has been necessary to stimulate the "transfer" of publicly funded research, although there is no single template for how such legislation should look like. Differences in national contexts may call for different solutions, even if most OECD countries are moving in the same direction. Harmonisation – or at least compatibility – of national rules regarding IPR at PROs may also facilitate international collaborative research by reducing transaction costs.

But laws are not sufficient; a change in mindset is needed.

Legal instruments are important but not enough: in many countries a change in the culture and mindset of researchers is also needed. TTOs also need to be free to hire high-quality technology transfer specialists with industry experience, and governments may need to modify legal regulations to facilitate this.

Countries are still learning about the costs and benefits of various types of TTOs.

There is no one model for a technology transfer office. Individual countries and organisations are still learning about the costs and benefits of various approaches. Several countries are experimenting with regional or sectoral TTOs, recognising that many individual PROs do not have the scale of research necessary for local TTOs.

Close relationships with inventors and labs are necessary for technology transfer.

However, to the extent that close relationships with inventors and labs are necessary to the technology transfer process, the geographic proximity offered by on-campus TTOs may be important. Since few TTOs are likely to generate positive net revenues, at least in their early years, some sort of cross subsidisation by PROs might be desirable.

Licensing safeguards can help PROs balance research and commercial goals.

PROs are best suited to negotiate the terms of licensing agreements with firms. However, policy safeguards such as those recommended by funding agencies can help balance the research and commercial goals of PROs. Individual PROs can set their own judicious guidelines. Finally, the licensing strategies of PROs can be used to maintain access to IP so that it is not lost should, for example, a "spin-off" company fail.

Regular surveys would benefit PROs and policy makers.

Regular surveys of patenting and licensing activities – undertaken by national governments, multilaterally, or by PROs themselves – are needed to provide input to policy makers but also to help PROs benchmark performance and learn from one another. It is important to remember that for many institutions, reporting of IP activities is new. The US experience shows that the ability of PROs to respond to such surveys improves over time.

Although the OECD project was limited to assessing IP rules at PROs and collecting empirical and anecdotal evidence of patenting and licensing at PROs in OECD countries, it has resulted in substantial insight into the increase in IP activity at PROs, and the challenges facing research administrators and policy makers.

Main Policy Recommendations

I. Make national IP policies more coherent

Policies for IP ownership should be coherent across universities, other PROs and funding agencies:

In many OECD countries, legislative action has been taken to ensure that both universities and non-university PROs have a common basis for allocating ownership of IP to institutions (or contracting parties). This helps reduce transaction costs, increases transparency and facilitates exploitation of IP by third parties.

Government funding agencies may also foster coherence through non-legislative means such as "codes of practice" or government policy guidelines which clarify ownership and exploitation requirements for universities and other PROs.

II. Encourage the development and implementation of IP policies at the institution level

Policies on the ownership of patented inventions as well as copyrightable works such as software should be better disseminated among faculty, research staff and students

Regulations and policies requiring research staff to disclose and report inventions allow for greater oversight by universities and PROs. National funding laws or regulations can promote this by requiring PROs to report IP to funding agencies. But requirements should be backed by control mechanisms and incentives.

Design and disseminate conflict of interest rules

Universities and other PROs should develop clear guidelines on conflict of interests. Governmental funding agencies can help set the standard by promoting national guidelines.

Permit exclusive licensing while protecting public research interests

Universities and other PROs should be free to negotiate exclusive licences but should design guidelines to ensure that IP that is not commercialised by licensees is not lost. For example, minimum royalty and milestone requirements could be used to create pressures to cancel the exclusive licence if the licensee fails to exploit the IP. Field-of-use restrictions on exclusive licences can also be used to ensure that the IP is made available for future research as well as other firms.

Designing licence agreements to share liability and responsibility for protecting against infringement with licensee firms could help reduce the potential costs of litigation to the PROs.

III. Enhance IP management capacity at PROs

IP management must become an integral part of research management

Presidents and directors of universities and PROs should make IP management part of their research management plans. One way to accomplish this is by having heads of technology transfer operations report directly to university presidents and/or research directors.

PROs should have greater freedom and resources for hiring and training technology transfer managers

The success of PROs in commercialising IP depends strongly on human resources, in particular technology transfer professionals with both a scientific and industrial background. In many countries, rigid public pay regulations limit PROs from hiring professional technology transfer staff. Relaxing such regulations should be encouraged.

Universities should also invest in specialised educational programmes to train engineers, scientists and lawyers in technology transfer. This can build awareness of IP among future science graduates as well create a pool of talent from which TTOs can develop their skills base.

Government support to TTOs should be limited

Insofar as the goal of TTOs is to facilitate the commercialisation of publicly funded research where social returns might exceed private returns, there is an argument for subsidising the creation of technology transfer structures, at least in the early stages. Support should be limited and focused on building greater *incentives* for IP management rather than simply reducing operating costs. In some cases, direct government subsidies to TTOs may be incompatible with national and supra-national legislation on government aid as well as with competition laws.

National patent offices should be mobilised to diffuse information on IP management to universities

In some OECD countries, national Patent Offices are providing educational and internet-based services to help universities become more aware of IP. Such good practices should be emulated in other countries.

IV. Improve data collection and share good practices

Governments and PROs should promote better monitoring of IP activity

Requirements by government funding agencies for invention disclosures and reporting by PROs can create incentives for greater data collection.

Associations of universities or research organisations can help PROs to regularly collect and share information on IP activity, including good practices.

Chapter 1

LEGAL AND REGULATORY FRAMEWORKS FOR INTELLECTUAL PROPERTY AT PUBLIC RESEARCH ORGANISATONS

Introduction

This chapter presents the results of the OECD survey on the legal and regulatory frameworks that govern the ownership, management and exploitation of intellectual property (IP) developed at public research organisations (PROs) in OECD countries. The results are based on responses to a survey of policies of government ministries responsible for PROs, as well as responses to the OECD survey of patenting and licensing at PROs. The objective of this chapter is to describe the current situation in OECD and selected non-member countries with respect to legal and regulatory frameworks for the ownership and exploitation of IP. Also, in light of the findings of the OECD surveys, it seeks to draw out implications for policy makers as to how laws and regulations can be improved to create greater incentives for PROs to protect and exploit IP resulting from publicly funded research.

Why should OECD governments be concerned about the legal and regulatory frameworks for intellectual property at PROs?

There are several reasons why governments should be concerned about the creation, ownership and exploitation of intellectual property emerging from publicly funded research organisations. First, there is now evidence, as well as greater awareness, that results of scientific research, particularly research from the public sector, in the form of publications and intellectual property that can be protected through patents and copyright, contributes to technological innovation and economic growth. Second, governments are important funders – the most important in some OECD countries – of public research; as such, they have the responsibility to ensure that the IP generated is diffused broadly and contributes to economic and social development. Third, the conduct of basic and applied research involves closer collaboration with industrial firms, with other PROs and with entities in other countries where IP regimes may differ. Given the growing complexity of financing and performing research, governments have a role in ensuring legal and regulatory frameworks for IP which can support both the education and research missions of PROs and innovation.

Governments are also interested in understanding how differences in national legal frameworks affect international scientific co-operation and cross-border technology transfer. At the EU level, for example, the European Commission is concerned that differences in legal frameworks for IP at PROs may slow, impede or raise the costs of trans-European co-operation in research and technology transfer. To illustrate: in some countries university researchers own the IP arising from government funded research, in others ownership devolves to the institution and in still others the government owns title to invention. A better understanding of the legal and regulatory framework in OECD countries is important to address concerns about the potential for negative effects on research arising from the heightened patenting activity of PROs. Are existing laws, regulations and practices sufficient to ensure the ability of PROs to balance research and teaching missions with commercialisation goals? Finally, both governments and institutions wish to identify best practices for supporting IP management at PROs and to share experience with other countries.

What is the legal basis for ownership and exploitation of IPR at PROs in OECD countries?

Legal frameworks for IP at PROs are complex and involve a combination of general intellectual property legislation (*e.g.* patent and copyright laws) and specific laws (Figure 1.1).

Figure 1.1. Legal frameworks for IP policy at PROs

Generally, the legal framework for IP at PROs is determined by:

- *National legislation for intellectual property.* National legislation on intellectual property such as patents, trademarks and copyright (see Box 1.1) sets the terms for the kinds of IP that may be protected and the terms and length of that protection. Some national patent laws may include clauses for particular categories of authors of creative works and inventions, such as public employees, or for contracts of publicly funded research agencies.

- *International intellectual property rights regimes.* International and supra-national treaties and agreements (*e.g.* TRIPs, EU directives, etc.), by exerting pressures for changes to national IP regimes, also influence the legal framework in which PROs and inventors act.

- *Employment laws* play an important role in determining the extent to which individual researchers can or cannot own and commercialise the IP generated in the context of their employment. Employment law, however, may differ between researchers that are public or civil servants and those that are private employees. Also, certain categories of employees, such as university professors, may, for various reasons, be exempt from employment laws concerning ownership of creative works by employees.

- *Research funding regulations.* At national level, there may be specific laws and rules that govern the ownership and use of the intellectual property created by PROs according to source of research funding (*e.g.* the PRO's own funds, national or regional government funds). The historical and national context in which PROs operate also affects the legal arrangements for IP protection and commercialisation.

- *Contract law.* As industry funds more academic research than in the past, defining the IP provisions for co-operative research agreements or industrial research contracts with firms becomes important. Many public research funding agencies, universities and public research labs have standard or model contracts. Contract law is especially important in defining the terms for licensing of IP from or to PROs.

The scope or applicability of the laws to PROs depends on a variety of factors and differs across OECD countries. Table 1.1 summarises the main legislation for allocating rights to IP arising from researchers or other employees of public and private research institutions. In some countries, provisions for ownership of IP by researchers at PROs are found in patent legislation, in others they are the result of employment law governing inventions by employees. Rules of government funding agencies (Canada, Germany, the United Kingdom) stipulate the rights of government contractors to the IP generated by the research or service contract. Regulations on research funding may contain explicit provisions regarding the ownership and transfer of IP, but again there are important differences among countries. In some countries, the provisions take the form of recommendations or are institutionalised in procedures and practices, leaving room for interpretation and exceptions.

What are the national laws or policies on the ownership of IP emerging from PROs

Table 1.2 summarises the current situation regarding the allocation of intellectual property rights (IPR) at PROs in OECD countries. In most, ownership of IPR at non-university PROs generally devolves to the institution. Several European countries have a dual system whereby title is granted to the professor (inventor) at universities, while the institution retains title at non-university PROs. For example, in Norway (until 2003) and Finland, the employees of non-university PROs do not retain title to patented inventions, but in these same countries a professor employed by a university does. This was also the case in Germany until 2002.

In many countries, university systems are rather autonomous from national/central governments, and this may explain in part why within a country, IP ownership differs between non-university-based PROs, which are generally state-run institutions, and universities. For example, IP ownership policies at Canadian universities vary among the provinces. Swiss universities, which are under cantonal jurisdiction, usually retain title to inventions, but rules can vary; in contrast, inventions by employees of the Swiss federal institutes of technology and federal research organisations systematically belong to the institution.

Is institutional ownership of IP a "best practice"?

The issue of institutional ownership of IP arising from public research at PROs, in particular patentable inventions, has recently generated debate in countries where professors (inventors) have traditionally held this right, owing to particularities in employment law. In theory, granting title to researchers should provide greater incentive for disclosing and commercialising inventions. In practice, applying for patent protection is expensive, especially outside one's national jurisdiction. The legal costs of protecting against patent infringement can also be prohibitive for individual owners. This is perhaps one of the reasons why individual inventors in the United States have historically received a small share of total patents issued. In absolute numbers, patenting by individual inventors in the United States has remained broadly stable since the 1920s with less than 25 000 patents issued a year compared to over 100 000 issued to firms and organisations (Schwartz, 2002).

Table 1.1. Legal basis governing the ownership of IP at PROs in selected OECD countries

	IP-related legislation	Employment-based laws	Government research regulations
Austria	Austrian Patent Law grants ownership of employee inventions to the employer. In the case of universities, the employer is the Austrian government represented by the Ministry of Science.		A new university law in 2002 assigned title of inventions at universities to the institution.
Belgium	Federal Law on Industry Property and Intellectual Property. Universities fall under competence of "community" governments. In Flanders all IP from university researchers belong to university. Since 1998 universities in the Walloon region can own the results of research that is fully funded by the region.		1999 Decree on Education was adopted to create a framework for IP at universities. Decree regulates rights and responsibilities of researchers and universities. A special decree was introduced regarding IP arising from research at public labs granting them title and requiring them to agree up front on the ownership of IP in collaborative research with universities.
Canada	The Patent Act (R.S. 1985, c. P-4) requires that government Crown employees who, acting within the scope of duties and employment, invent any invention in instruments or war munitions, can be required by the Defence Ministry to assign rights to benefits of the invention and of any patent obtained or to be obtained for the invention subject to compensation. Copyright Act (R.S. 1985, s.c. C-30, s. 1) states that, in the absence of any agreement, employers retain copyright to works created under a contract of service or apprenticeship. Authors of articles or similar contributions to a newspaper, magazine or similar periodical shall, in the absence of any agreement to the contrary, reserve a right to restrain the publication of the work.		1991 Crown Procurement Policy stipulates that IP resulting from Crown procurement contracts remain with the contractor. In 2000, the policy was revised to re-affirm its application to all government contracts for goods and services, remove ambiguities and include a mechanism to deal with complex IP ownership situations by identifying the rights and obligations of all parties involved.
Denmark	Act on Inventions at Public Research Institutions (2000) grants title to PRO but allows inventor right of first refusal. Consolidated Act on copyright regulates ownership of literary and artistic works. Copyright at PROs is governed by rules that govern copyright ownership in private enterprises.		
France	Article L.6111-6 of the French Intellectual Property Code stipulates that inventions made by salaried employees, both in the public and private sector, in the context of the employee's functions shall belong to the employer but the employee has a right to additional compensation.		
Germany		2001 Reform of Employee Law has rendered university inventions "service inventions" which means they now belong to the university.	New federal regulations grant PROs title to inventions arising from government funded research, 1998.
Ireland		Employment law provides for employers to retain title to inventions by employees except as otherwise agreed in contracts.	
Italy	Article 7 of National Law No. 383 of 18 October 2001 assigns title of inventions at universities to researchers.		
Japan	1998 Technology Transfer Act; Article 15 Copyright Act grants employer [legal person] authorship rights for works by employees made public under the name of the employer [legal person] unless otherwise stipulated by contract.		Invention committees at national universities decide whether the government or the university inventors retain title to invention. Government regulations on contract research between national universities and firms give the latter the right to retain up to half of the IPR.

Table 1.1. Legal basis governing the ownership of IP at PROs in selected OECD countries (cont'd.)

	IP-related legislation	Employment-based laws	Government research regulations
Korea	General Patent Law.		Directive for the National R&D Programme.
Netherlands	Dutch Patent Act grants PROs title unless agreed otherwise by contract.		
Norway	General Patents Act 1967.	Act on Employers Right to Commercialise Inventions Made by Employees, 1970.	
Russia	The Patent Law, amended on 7 February 2003, establishes that IP developed with state funds belongs to the PRO if a state contract does not stipulate ownership by the Russian Federation on behalf of a state client represented by a ministry. Executive and legislative decrees oblige government ministries to claim ownership of patented and non-patented IP but in the framework of a state contract and do not establish in which cases the government ministries can assign their IP rights to a PRO	The Patent Law establishes that right to a patent for an invention, utility model or industrial design, created by an employee (author) in connection with execution of his duties or a specific assignment, belongs to the employer if not otherwise specified by an agreement.	The Law on Science and State S&T Policy establishes that the use of results of scientific research of the Russian Academy of Sciences, conducted with federal budget resources is determined by legislation of the Russian Federation. The legislation does not contain any special standards, regulating relations with respect to ownership by the Russian Academy of Sciences of the IP created with the use of state budget.
South Africa			No IP legislation for funding.
Spain	Article 12-20 of the Spanish Patent Law (1986) regulates ownership of inventions in companies and public organisations. It indicates that universities will apply for patents resulting from the research of professors.		
Switzerland	Federal laws concerning patents, copyrights, design, trademarks, plant varieties and integrated circuits are applicable for all organisations, but public rules can complement and modify ownership rights.	The Federal employer law grants IP rights for patents, design and plant varieties to the employer. This rule is generally not applicable to the public sector, unless public rules specifically refer to it.	Swiss National Science Foundation grants IP ownership to researcher respectively to their employees; Federal Research Law does not specify IP ownership rights.
United Kingdom	1977 Patent Act and 1988 Copyright Act indicate that IP generated in the normal course of employment shall belong to the employer. Recent guidelines by the UK Patent Office reaffirm that IP generated in publicly funded research should generally be vested in the organisation that does the research.		Health Service Circular (HSC1998/106) of the National Health Service Trust (NHS) stipulates that IP arising from R&D funded by the R&D Levy normally resides with the organisation (e.g. university, commercial organisation, NHS body) carrying out the R&D and capable of exploiting the resulting IP. A new framework and guidance document has been established for hospital employees and other health workers (www.innovations.nhs.uk)
United States	The Bayh-Dole Act allows individuals (researchers, scientists, etc.), whose work resulted in the creation of an invention and was financed partially or completely through federal funds, to own their inventions; 35 USC (United States Code) 202 applies this policy to non-profit organisations, including universities, and small business firms and allows them to retain title to invention; 35 USC 210(c) applies this policy to others, i.e. large businesses; and E.O. 10096 applies to federal government workers.		The 1980 Stevenson Wydler Innovation Act (and subsequent amendments to the Act) authorised federal laboratories to conduct co-operative research and development agreements (CRADAs) with private firms and to allow licences to these firms.

Source: OECD Questionnaire on the Patenting and Licensing Activities of PROs, results; European Commission (2003).

Because most academic inventions involve multiple researchers, there is a risk that individual ownership may lead to fragmentation of property rights. Firms may hesitate to license a technology from a PRO when several individuals have claims on one invention. Joint owners may not agree on licensing terms or may not be willing to share legal expenses relating to patent infringement with licensee firms. Another potential problem for countries is that the researcher who owns the IP can commercialise it abroad, thus reducing national benefits from the public investment in research.

Table 1.2. Ownership of IP at PROs in OECD and non-member countries

	Universities			Non-university PROs		
	Institution	Inventor	Government	Institution	Inventor	Government
Australia	♦			♦		
Austria	♦			♦		
Belgium	♦			♦		
Canada[1]	♦	♦		♦		
Denmark	♦			♦		
Finland		♦		♦		
France	♦			♦		
Germany	♦			♦		
Iceland		♦		♦		
Ireland	♦			♦		
Italy		♦			♦	
Japan[2]		♦	◊	♦		
Korea	♦			♦		
Mexico	♦			♦		
Netherlands	♦			♦		
Norway	♦			♦		
Poland	♦			♦		
Russia			♦			♦
South Africa	♦			♦		
Spain	♦			♦		
Sweden		♦		♦		
Switzerland	♦	◊		♦		
United Kingdom	♦			♦		
United States[3]	♦	◊	◊	♦	◊	

♦ = Legal basis or most common practice; ◊ = allowed by law/rule but less common.

1. In Canada, ownership of IP at universities generated through institutional funds varies, but IP generated through Crown procurement contracts devolves to the institution performing the contract research.
2. In Japan, the president of a national university or inter-university institution decides upon the right to ownership of inventions made by a staff member of the university/institution on the basis of discussions by the university invention committee.
3. In the United States, universities have the first right to elect title to inventions resulting from federally funded research. The government (*e.g.* federal agency) may claim title if the performer does not. In certain cases, the inventor may retain rights with the agreement of the university/federal partner and the government.
Source: OECD Questionnaire on the Patenting and Licensing Activities of PROs, results; OECD (2002); European Commission (2003).

Consequently, the granting of ownership of IP to the research organisation and ensuring that benefits (royalties) are shared with inventors has emerged as common practice in a number of OECD countries (OECD, 2002). Ownership gives PROs control over their IP, provides legal certainty and fosters technology transfer and public/private research partnerships. Ownership by PROs also allows governments to channel support for technology transfer and the commercialisation of public research more effectively.

Box 1.1. Ownership of copyright at PROs

Unlike ownership of patented inventions, ownership by PROs of copyright works, such as coursework, scientific manuals, journals, research papers and other educational materials as well as software and artistic works, has received little attention from policy makers. Yet PROs generate a large share of their IP in the form of literary and artistic works that can be protected by copyright. For PROs, national copyright laws, in line with international conventions and treaties, have provided authors with basic protection against unauthorised reproduction, translation, performance or distribution of their works for a limited time. However, at universities in many countries there is a long tradition of transferring or waiving rights to copyrightable works by faculty and research staff created, either fully or partially, on employer time and resources, in particular as regards academic publications. A survey of the top 135 US universities (in terms of licensing revenue) found that ownership of copyrightable books belonged to the author, not the university, while title to software inventions was retained by the university (Thursby *et al.*, 2001).

National copyright laws limit to some extent the rights of employees to copyright work executed on behalf of employers, including universities, but legislation differs widely. In the Netherlands, the copyright of particular works of literature, science or art belong to the author-employee rather than the employer, unless otherwise agreed by the contracting parties. Because the definition of particular works is subject to interpretation and debate, Dutch universities try to avoid problems of ownership by including university copyright in collective bargaining agreements. In France, software inventions at universities, although copyrightable, must be disclosed by researchers and registered. The executive decrees and legislative acts of the Russian Federation which grant the state claims on the IP created by PROs with public funds also apply to copyright and non-patentable IP. The United States (via the Office of Management and Budget Circular A 110) allows university grantees to own copyright, while the Federal Acquisition Regulation requires federal authors to request permission to copyright.

Ownership of copyright for publicly funded databases at universities and other PROs has become an important issue because there are increasing demands by firms and the public for access to such databases. OECD governments do not have specific legislation for universities and other PROs concerning the ownership and protection of databases at PROs. Instead, protection falls under general copyright right law and, in the case of specialised databases, *sui generis* database rights in countries with such rights. The European Union adopted a database directive in the 1990s. The United States does not provide statutory protection for databases or industrial designs. In Japan, national copyright law governs ownership of databases developed at universities or non-university PROs.

The increased digitisation of copyrightable materials produced by PROs and their distribution over the Internet has increased the channels through which such works can be copied and distributed and thus the risks of copyright infringement. Consequently, PROs, particularly in the United States and the United Kingdom but also in Ireland and France, are paying more attention to clarifying copyright ownership of works created by their employees.

PRO policies on the ownership of IP at the institution level

Results from the OECD survey of TTO managers show that, despite the existence of national laws regarding ownership of IP, there remains some confusion at institutional level in terms of the ownership of IP (Table 1.3). This confusion may arise from an interpretation of the term "ownership" which can be taken to mean any claim or partial claim on IP by the various stakeholders. For example, the majority of Danish respondents to the TTO survey reported that the institution owned the IP, in line with the new Danish law on university inventions. At the same time, over half also noted that the researcher "owns" the IP. This may be because Danish researchers in fact have the right of "first refusal"; universities must decide whether to take title to the invention or leave it with the researcher. At non-university PROs in Germany, all respondents reported that the institution owned the IP, but a small percentage also reported that either researchers or funding agencies owned it. Concerning ownership by students and non-faculty employees, see Box 1.2.

One implication of the discrepancy between institutions' views on ownership and national laws is that policy makers may need to encourage greater coherence between laws and rules at universities, funding agencies and other PROs. Institutions for their part may need to disseminate PRO policies on IP among faculty, researchers and non-employees more effectively. As IP activity has increased at PROs, some institutions publish their policies on Web sites as well as disseminate them among newly hired research staff and other employees.

Table 1.3. University or other PRO policies towards ownership of intellectual property

As a percentage of respondents

Country	Type of responding Institution	Institution owns IP	Researcher owns IP	Funding agency owns IP	Government owns IP
Belgium (Flanders)	All	86	14	57	0
Denmark	Universities	80	44	33	0
	Other PROs	80	60	0	0
Germany	Non-university PROs only	100	10	43	0
Italy	Universities	75	46	29	0
	Other PROs	80	60	40	0
Japan		82	41	47	23
Korea	Universities	75	25	13	13
	Other PROs	74	37	16	11
Netherlands	Universities	95	0	58	0
	Other PROs	100	11	44	0
Norway	Universities	11	67	11	0
	Other PROs	80	44	44	8
Russia	All	21	4	14	0
Spain		94	11	61	0
Switzerland	Universities	71	20	40	0
	Other PROs	89	33	11	0

Source: OECD (2002).

Ownership of IP resulting from research sponsored by industry

The evidence available from responses to the OECD questionnaire suggests that in most OECD countries ownership of IP arising from research at PROs that is jointly funded by industry is shared according to the following principle: ownership of the patented invention remains with the PRO while the firm funding the research retains the right (or option) to license the patent on an exclusive basis. When a firm funds more than 50% of the research, firms may claim title to the IP. In cases where the sponsored research addresses a particular application that is specific for the contracting firm, the PRO may relinquish title to the invention in return for financial compensation, such as research costs plus a share of PRO overhead and staff costs.

The Netherlands and several other countries responded that IP from sponsored research is shared between the firm and the PRO. In many cases, it was unclear whether this reflects actual joint ownership of a patented invention or a contract that requires the PRO to license a patent on an exclusive basis to the sponsoring firm or, inversely, that requires the university to retain a non-exclusive licence to the invention (Arundel and Bordoy, 2002).

What incentives exist to encourage researchers and PROs to disclose and exploit inventions?

Disclosure of IP

A necessary counterpart to governmental legal or funding rules on ownership is a requirement that a researcher report or disclose his/her IP to the PRO. Most US universities require disclosure, in particular in order to comply with regulations to disclose IP to federal agencies that funded the research. Flemish universities in Belgium require inventors to disclose inventions. In Denmark, disclosure of IP is obligatory at universities, hospitals and other PROs. A Canadian survey found that 26 out of 81 research universities did not require researchers to disclose their patentable inventions and that only 29 did; for copyright, disclosure was even less common, with half of the universities surveyed reporting that researchers were not required to report software- or database-related IP (Gu and Whewell, 1999). Japanese researchers in national universities are not obliged to disclose inventions to technology licensing offices (TLOs) but are encouraged to so. Japanese inventors at national universities, however, may be required to assign title to the state government if the university president, according to certain criteria, determines that the invention should belong to the state. Kneller (2000) argues that this system discourages Japanese academic inventors in national universities from disclosing inventions to the presidents of their universities as there are great incentives for academics to avoid classification of their inventions and instead assign title to companies in exchange for compensation. However, recent data on TLO patenting in Japan show an increase in patents granted and invention disclosures. This suggests that Japanese academic inventors may be disclosing inventions and relying more on formal channels of technology transfer.

Government or research funding requirements for disclosure Disclosure requirements for PROs	No disclosure requirements
Austria (universities), Belgium (Flanders), Canada, Denmark, Germany (universities and other PROs), Spain, United Kingdom, United States	Ireland, Japan

Requirements for working inventions

With ownership rights comes the obligation or responsibility to make use of the IP. In many countries, laws and regulations governing the patenting of inventions by PROs require that the invention must be worked and/or that the invention must be used for national benefit. Funding agencies may also have specific exploitation requirements. There are no laws stipulating that PROs must exploit their IP in Ireland, Japan and Norway, but Denmark, Germany and Korea have laws requiring an invention at a PRO to be worked. Since 1999, PROs in Germany that receive federal research grants can elect title to any IP generated in the course of research, but they are obligated to file for a patent and actively market the invention to industry. In addition, PROs must file an exploitation plan when filing research grant applications. The US Bayh-Dole Act requires universities to commercialise inventions, and the government may step in if the inventing organisation does not take responsible steps to do so.

Legal or administrative requirements to work IP	No legal or administrative requirements to work IP
Australia, Belgium (Flanders), Canada (for IP resulting from Crown Procurement Contracts), Denmark, Germany, Korea, United Kingdom, United States	Ireland, Japan, Norway, South Africa

National exploitation requirements are often geared towards fostering national economic benefits. The programmes of Australia's Research Council require recipients of funding to adhere to a set of national principles for managing IP, with the aim of ensuring that IP is used to maximise benefits to Australia. When a contractor owns the IP in Canada, the Crown may require it to be exploited in Canada and/or within a specific time frame. In Germany, transfer of IP to non-EU countries by PROs is authorised but requires prior consent from the funding authority. In addition, German PROs can be obliged by administrative regulation to grant non-exclusive licences to domestic firms if they fail to take active measures to exploit their IP. A general problem with rules on national economic benefits is a tendency for different stakeholders to interpret them very differently and the fact that compliance is rarely monitored (OECD, 2002). At institutional level, PROs may have their own policies for ensuring due diligence. Licensing agreements are commonly designed to ensure that the licensee firms are committed to exploiting a PRO invention. For example, PRO may require licensee firms to make minimum royalty payments. If the firm is prepared to spend a considerable amount of money to maintain exclusive rights, it is more likely to fulfil its commitment to commercialise an invention.

Providing incentives through benefit sharing

When the institution owns the IP, it is the sole beneficiary of royalties from licences. However, sharing of royalty revenues is common and is increasingly seen as a way to provide incentives not just to individual researchers but to research teams. Royalty sharing is determined by institutions but governments set the stage. Countries such as Denmark, Germany, Italy, Japan, Norway and the United States have either national laws or institutional guidelines for allocating royalties from patents and licences. The US Bayh-Dole Act, for example, stipulates that royalties from licensing are to be shared with the inventors and that remaining income, less payment of expenses, is to be used to support research and education at the university. While the Bayh-Dole Act does not specify a percentage, a common practice in US universities is to grant royalties subject to meeting a certain revenue threshold. With regard to US federal labs, 15 USC 3710c requires that the first USD 2 000 of royalties received by the US government from licensing go to the inventor(s) and at least 15% of gross royalties thereafter.

In Denmark, the Ministry of Science, Technology and Innovation approves local rules on royalty sharing. In Japan, government guidelines determine the sharing of royalties at national universities. The Japan Science and Technology Corporation (JST), to which university inventions are transferred, grants 80% of royalties to the inventors (researchers) if the patent is successfully commercialised. At German universities, inventors receive up to 30% of royalties from licences but the share varies at non-university PROs. In France, the decree of February 2002 grants inventors at universities 50% of net royalties paid to institutions up to a certain threshold (currently EUR 60 000 per year), after which the share drops to 25%. It is quite common for French universities to engage in co-ownership of patents between research establishments, as much research is carried out in partnership by universities and national research labs such as the CNRS (*Centre National de la Recherche Scientifique*). At Spanish PROs, revenues from the exploitation of IP are shared equally between the institution, the inventors and the Board of Directors of the institution. In Italy until 2001, the policy at the *Consiglio Nazionale delle Ricerche* (CNR), one of Italy's largest PROs, was to give the institution 80% of the gross licensing revenues and the inventor the remaining 20%. Since the new law, inventors can retain all revenue but generally negotiate with the PRO or company assisting them in commercialising the invention.

This diversity in approaches to the sharing of licensing revenues highlights two main policy trends. On the one hand, some countries, via research ministries or funding agencies, determine more or less directly the sharing of royalties at PROs. Others, while encouraging sharing or compensation in principle, tend to let the institution decide the actual amounts. Most countries that have recently changed their legislation on ownership of IP at PROs have taken the latter approach, recognising that PROs need some level of autonomy and flexibility to respond to demands from industry but also their own researchers.

The influence of IP activity on researchers' careers

PROs use other incentives besides royalties to reward researchers' contribution. Increasingly, PROs include researchers' patenting and licensing or spin-off activities among the criteria for career advancement. The OECD questionnaire found that personnel policies at PROs, including recruitment criteria, take the IP activities of candidates and researchers into account in Denmark, Germany and Japan but not in Korea or Norway. In Germany, Italy and Japan, the IP activities of researchers are also taken into account for recruitment, career advancement and salaries. Denmark considers IP activities in recruitment decisions and for applications to Science Councils. At the level of PROs themselves, respondents to the survey of TTO managers reported that, by and large, licensing activities had a higher impact on salary and wages than on career/tenure prospects (Figures 1.2-1.7). In Germany and the Netherlands, the influence of licensing on salaries/wages is greater than the influence of IP activity *per se*. In Korea, despite the absence of IP criteria in personnel policies, IP activity has a strong influence on career/tenure prospects, perhaps owing to the fact that public research has generally been more applied in Korea. In Japan, the influence of IP is rather muted. While these preliminary results confirm what would be expected intuitively, they also provide empirical evidence that IP activity has a positive influence on the recruitment and careers of researchers and a strong influence on earnings.

Figure 1.2. Impact of IP on Dutch researchers

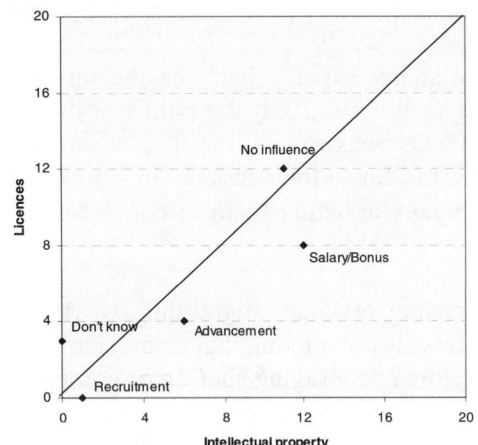

Figure 1.3. Influence of IP on German researchers

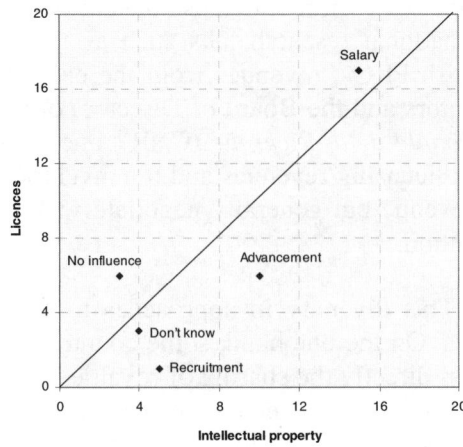

Figure 1.4. Impact of IP on Italian researchers

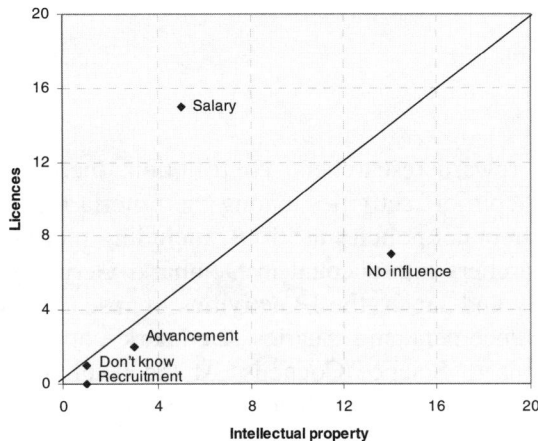

Figure 1.5. Impact of IP on Japanese researchers

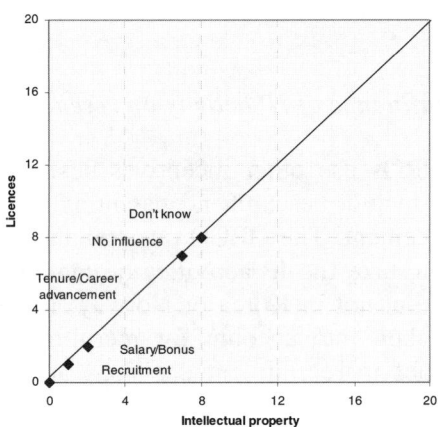

Figure 1.6. Influence of IP on Korean researchers

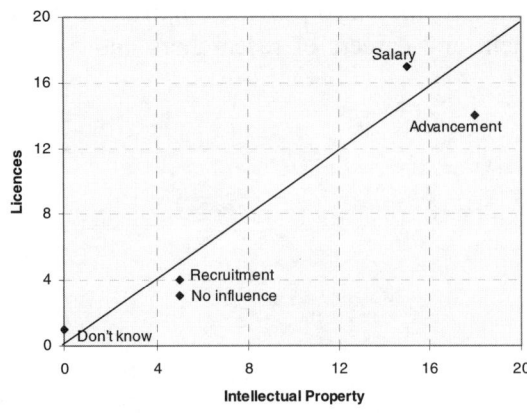

Figure 1.7. Influence of IP on Norwegian researchers

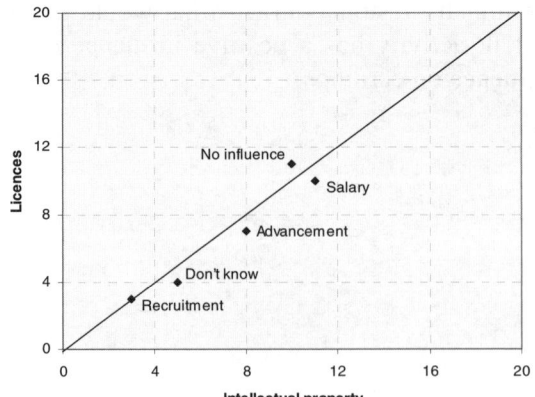

Managing conflicts of interests

The increase in patenting and licensing activities, along with greater co-operation with industry, has led to the development of regulations to avoid or manage potential conflicts of interest between the researcher's obligations and the more entrepreneurial activities such as patenting inventions, carrying out contract research or working on a start-up or spin-off. Conflict of interest involves "a situation in which an official's private interests – not necessarily limited to his/her financial interests – and the official duties in his/her public function are in conflict (actual conflict of interest), could come into conflict, or could reasonably appear to be in conflict (potential conflict of interest) (OECD, 2002). Conflicts of interest do not just exist among researchers, but also among non-faculty such as graduate students. Guidelines for dealing with individual conflicts of interest vary but there are common elements such as disclosure of all relevant financial interests and activities outside the framework of employment or disclosure of financial interests related to non-government sponsored research.

National guidelines	Institution or funding agency guidelines
Denmark, Germany	Canada, France, Ireland, Netherlands, United Kingdom, United States (*e.g.* NIH)

In the replies to the OECD survey, only Denmark and Germany reported that their government had developed national guidelines concerning conflicts of interests involving research staff and IP activities. In the United States, there are no federal policies with regard to employment that directly encourage researchers to produce IP, but PROs may have institution-based practices that encourage and recognise IP activity of new or existing employees. With regard to conflict of interest rules concerning the IP activities of researchers, countries did not report specific national rules but rather rules of institution or funding agencies. For example, the US National Institutes of Health has promulgated a policy that applies to grant recipients. Non-government entities such as the American Association of Universities and the American Association of Medical Colleges have issued conflict of interest guidelines. In France, the Charter for IP management at Universities stipulates provisions to avoid conflicts of interests.

Do countries need "Bayh-Dole Act" legislation to foster commercialisation of public research results?

The lack of institutional ownership among some categories of PROs, notably universities in certain OECD countries, has focused the attention of policy makers on US experience with the Bayh-Dole Act, which gave research contractors title to inventions and allowed them to license patents on an exclusive basis to firms. However, the law also helped create incentives for institutions that perform government-funded research to protect, manage and exploit IP. In other words, the issue of institutional ownership is only one, albeit important, aspect of the Bayh-Dole Act.

In many OECD countries, the issue is not that institutional ownership of IP by PROs is lacking, but rather that the current legal and regulatory frameworks offer too few incentives for disclosing, protecting and exploiting IP generated with public funds. Mandatory disclosure of IP and rules on benefit sharing or reporting of IP to funding agencies are crucial if universities and other PROs are to have incentives to engage in IP management. In both the US and Danish reforms, elements of these requirements are similar but not identical, reflecting specific national policy-making objectives (Box 1.3).

Another outcome of Bayh-Dole was the emergence of a coherent and consistent policy on federally funded research. Prior to the law, there was no government-wide policy regarding ownership of inventions made by government contractors and grantees under federal funding. Inconsistencies in policies and practices among the various funding agencies resulted in a very limited flow of government-funded inventions to the private sector. Related to the lack of consistency for federally funded research was the fact that government would retain title to inventions and make them available through non-exclusive licences. Companies thus did not have exclusive rights under government-owned patents and were thus reluctant to invest in and develop new products if competitors could also acquire licences and then manufacture and sell the same products (Lita, 2001).

Box 1.3. Key provisions of the Danish and US legislation on patented IP from PROs

The US Bayh-Dole Act	Danish Act on Inventions at Public Institutions
(Public Law 96-517, The Patent and Trademark Law Amendments Act enacted 1980 and amended in 1984).	Act No. 347 of 2 June 1999 (applicable to inventions made after 1st January 2000)

Scope: The provisions apply to all inventions conceived or first actually reduced to practice in the performance of a federal grant, contract or co-operative agreement. Provisions do not apply to federal grants that are primarily for the training of students and post-doctoral scientists.

Ownership rights: The university must decide on taking title to the invention within two years after disclosing the invention to the (federal) agency. If the research results must be published, the time period for claiming title is at least 60 days before the end of the statutory period. Federal agencies may claim title if the university does not. The university must file a patent application within one year, or prior to the end of any statutory period in which valid patent protection can be obtained in the United States. Universities may not assign their ownership of inventions to third parties, except to patent management organisations.

Disclosure: The university is obligated to have written agreements with its faculty and technical staff requiring disclosure and assignment of inventions. The university has an obligation to disclose each new invention to the federal funding agency within two months after the inventor discloses it in writing to the university.

Licensing regulations: The university must provide the government, through a confirmatory licence, a non-exclusive, non-transferable, irrevocable, paid-up right to practice or have practiced the invention on behalf of the US throughout the world. Under certain circumstances, the government can require the university to grant a licence to a third party, or the government may take title and grant licences itself (these are called "march-in rights"). Universities must give preference to small business firms (fewer than 500 employees), provided such firms have the resources and capability for bringing the invention to practical application. However, if a large company has also provided research support that led to the invention, that company may be awarded the licence.

Royalties: Universities must share with the inventor(s) a portion of any revenue received from licensing the invention. Any remaining revenue, after expenses, must be used to support scientific research or education.

Exploitation requirements: Manufacturing by a company holding an exclusive licence to an invention must substantially manufacture the product in the United States. Waivers of this rule may be granted by the federal funding agency under certain conditions.

Reporting requirements: The university must submit periodic reports regarding the utilisation of the invention as requested by the funding agency, but not more often than annually.

Source: OECD based on, "The Bayh-Dole Act: A guide to the law and implementing regulations", Council on Government Relations (1999).

Scope: The law applies to patentable inventions made by an employee as part of his work at the university, the government research institution, the public hospital or the health research institution under the county authorities or the Copenhagen Hospital Corporation.

Ownership rights: The right to inventions made by an employee at an institution shall be accorded to the employer. The institution shall, within the limit prescribed by law or agreed upon with the employee, decide on the claim of transfer of the right or on whether the employee maintains the right in exchange for compensation. Institutions may order the employee not to publish or have the disposal of an invention for up to two months from receipt of notification or longer if agreed with the employee. The institution may, for projects completed in co-operation with or are financed, in full or in part, by a party not covered by the Act, on its own and the employee's behalf, upon prior agreement with the party concerned, renounce, in full or in part, the right to the inventions made in the project.

Disclosure: The employee must notify the institution in writing without undue delay and provide the institution with all necessary information in accordance with the provision of the institution. Institutions may lay down specific rules concerning how notification may take place. The employee must not publish or have the disposal of an invention before the institution has confirmed receipt of notification in writing. The institution is under an obligation to send confirmation as soon as possible.

Exploitation requirements: If the rights attached to an invention have been transferred to the institution with a view to commercial exploitation, the institution is at the same time under an obligation actively to seek exploitation of the rights. Within two months from the date of notification, the institution shall have had carried out an evaluation of the possibility of exploiting the invention and of protecting the rights to the invention and, with the employee, shall have considered how rights to the invention may be exploited commercially.

Royalties: The employee who made the invention is entitled to a reasonable payment from the institution. If the right to an invention, as agreed with the institution, is exploited commercially by the employee who made it, the institution is entitled to a reasonable payment. The institution shall lay down the rules for calculation of payment. The rules must be approved by the Minister of Science, Technology and Innovation. Revenues from the transfer of rights to inventions are to be used by the institutions for activities within the mission of the institution.

Equity: An institution may receive revenues in the form of profit by transferring its right to a limited company against payment in the form of shares in the company in question. Similarly, the institution may accept to receive payment in the form of shares in a limited company. The institution must not obtain the same connection to the company as that of a parent company to a subsidiary under the Danish Companies Act.

Source: OECD based on Chapter 6 in the present volume.

While research shows that major US research universities were patenting before the passage of the Bayh-Dole Act in 1980 (Mowery and Sampat, 2001), the strong increase in university patenting has nevertheless focused the attention of policy makers in other countries on the legal basis for encouraging their own universities and labs to patent and license technologies. Several European OECD countries have recently reviewed or modified ownership rules for employees of universities. Denmark enacted a new law in July 1999 (effective from 1 January 2000) and Germany changed its employee invention law in 2001 (effective in 2002) to grant universities (as well as hospitals and other PROs in the case of Denmark) title to employee inventions.

Despite the trend to grant title to institutions, legislation in many countries permits inventors some pre-emptive rights and allows institutions to waive title in favour of inventors. In Denmark, the law grants an inventor the right of first refusal. Even in the United States, under certain conditions, inventors at universities and federal agencies may be allowed to retain property rights. In Canada, the 2000 IP Policy on Crown Procurement allows the Canadian government to retain ownership in some cases. The IP policy also contains provisions that allow the government to license contractor-owned IP and *vice versa*.

In Italy, in contrast to the general trend in European countries, the government passed legislation in 2001 granting IP ownership to researchers at universities. By the middle of 2002, however, proposals were presented in parliament to transfer this right back to universities in conjunction with measures to support the development of technology transfer offices (TTOs). In Norway, a new bill on the commercial exploitation of inventions entered into force in January 2003 which, under certain conditions, transfers the right to commercialise an invention from the researchers to the institution.

In early 2001, the Russian Patent Office and the Ministry of Industry, Science and Technology drafted policy recommendations indicating that the government should only retain ownership of IP from public research relating to defence and national security and that in all other cases ownership rights should be transferred to the organisation performing the research. Later that year, the State Duma adopted several resolutions to introduce changes or amendments to the Russian Patent Law to limit the rights of state ownership of IP resulting from public research.

The experience of OECD countries suggests that while legislation may be necessary to create incentives for PROs to protect and commercialise IP, it is not the only policy option. Both the Canadian and Irish governments have sought to improve coherence and clarity for managing IP at PROs by modifying or clarifying existing policies among the different stakeholders. In countries that have implemented policies by legislative means or otherwise, one of the main impacts has been to raise awareness of and support for technology transfer, especially within the hierarchy of PROs and among researchers and graduate students.

Chapter 2

TECHNOLOGY TRANSFER STRUCTURES AND PUBLIC RESEARCH ORGANISATIONS

Introduction

The transfer of ownership of intellectual property (IP) from governments or researchers to institutions has given PROs incentives to develop technology transfer or licensing offices (TTOs or TLOs) to manage the transfer or sale of IP from universities to third parties, mainly firms. For the purpose of the OECD survey, technology transfer offices were defined as "those organisations or parts of an organisation which help staff at PROs to identify, protect, exploit and defend intellectual property". This chapter presents the main results of the survey on the characteristics of TTOs in OECD countries, their organisation, activities and functions, and discusses the role of government in supporting TTO operations.

Characteristics of technology transfer offices in OECD countries

Technology transfer offices have existed in significant numbers since the mid-20th century. Germany's Fraunhofer Society's TTO was founded in 1952. In the United States, the University of California system founded an office for technology transfer in 1926. Nevertheless, most TTOs in the United States and elsewhere are very recent; their mean age in the United States is 12 years (Figure 2.1). While the US government did not require (or provide direct funding for) universities to establish TTOs or TLOs, the fact that universities had an exclusive right which allowed them to generate revenue forced them to establish the administrative and legal structures necessary to fulfil their obligations under the Bayh-Dole Act. Indeed, the creation of specialised TTOs or TLOs became essential to the management and exploitation of IP. Most US research universities and public labs have TTOs and their numbers continue to rise.

Age of TTOs

In Norway, half of the TTOs surveyed were set up before 1996 and 11% were established after 1997. In Italy, more than 40% of university TTOs were established in 2000-01, just before the law on employee ownership changed to grant title to inventors rather than institutions. Among non-university Italian PROs, 60% declared that their offices were created between 1975 and 1985; only one office was created recently (in 1999). This finding is not surprising if one considers that, in the Italian system, the mission of labs has traditionally placed greater emphasis on applied research (Pammoli and Donadio, 2002). In the Netherlands, 77% of universities had a TTO before 1997, compared to only 33% of non-university PROs. In other words, Dutch universities have had access to an office responsible for patenting and licensing for longer than other PROs. The same pattern is found in Switzerland, where around 60% of university TTOs were established between 1990 and 2000, and slightly more than half of TTOs of non-university PROs were established between 2000 and 2002. Most TTOs at non-university PROs in Germany were created in the late 1980s and early 1990s.

Figure 2.1. Most TTOs are less than ten years old and have fewer than five staff (FTE)

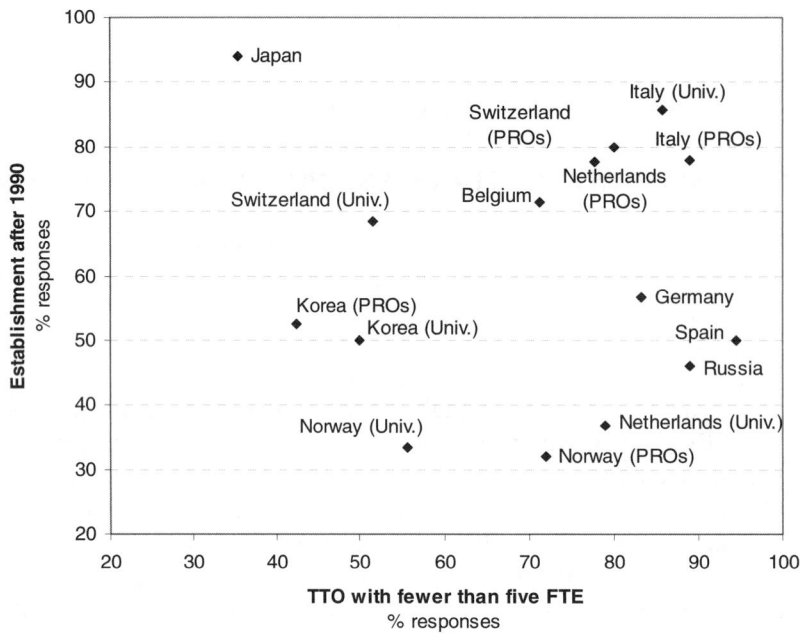

Note: Belgium: Flanders only.

Staff at TTOs

The staff at TTOs are at the forefront of technology transfer. Their role includes liaising with scientists and patent attorneys. In most OECD countries, TTOs are small operations with fewer than five full-time employees. Results from the OECD survey show that for most countries TTOs are small but growing. In Norway for example, only about one-fifth of survey respondents reported having more than one full-time equivalent (FTE) staff dedicated to technology transfer issues. In the United States, the number of TTO staff is somewhat larger, with a mean of 3.3 for staff devoted to licensing issues and 3.5 for other staff (Table 2.1).

Table 2.1. Employment at TTOs at US universities (full-time equivalent), 2000

	Licensing staff in FTE	Other TTO staff
Total	562.5	586.5
Mean	3.3	3.5
Median	2.0	1.8
No. of responding universities	168	168

Source: US Technology Administration, Department of Commerce, based on AUTM FY 2000 data.

The OECD survey did not allow for determining the functional skills of TTO staff, but evidence from the case studies shows that many of these professionals are generalists who specialise in a given technological field or managerial function, in which they develop specialised knowledge and expertise. This expertise makes them indispensable for constructing a wide variety of relationships between university research and industry (see Chapter 15 in this volume). Technology officers also play a role in preventing potential conflicts of interest that may occur as a result of personal interests of individuals involved in the research or corporate interests when companies are funding research programmes.

Structure of technology transfer offices

Previous OECD work has identified a typology of institutional arrangements for exploiting IP at PROs: *i)* dedicated TTOs (on-site or off-site); *ii)* administrative departments of PROs whose main mission is not IP management; and *iii)* external (private or public) providers of IP management services (Figure 2.2).

Figure 2.2. Most TTOs are an integral part of universities but many are not exclusively devoted to technology transfer

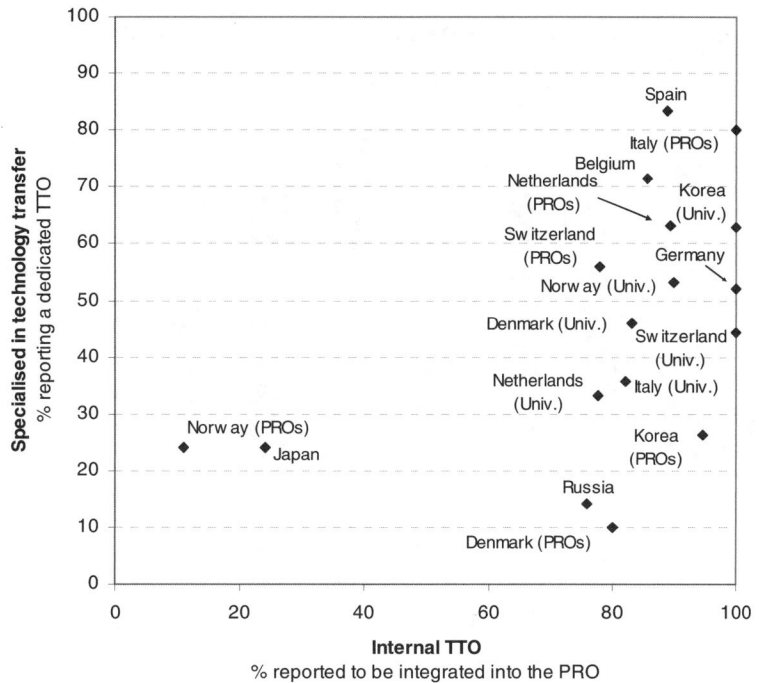

Note: Belgium: Flanders only.
Source: OECD.

Results of the OECD survey found that by and large in the Netherlands and Korea university-based TTOs are quite institutionalised in their organisation of IP. In Italy, in contrast, only 35.7% of universities rely on a dedicated technology transfer or licensing office, while 46.4% delegate such activities to other offices for which technology transfer is not the main mission. In Germany, in both Danish universities and research labs, as well as in Russia, TTOs in non-university-based PROs tend to be organised as a division of the PRO that is not dedicated to TTO. The question arises of whether there is an optimal institutional arrangement for organising TTOs.

The answer is not altogether clear, as the relation of a TTO or similar body to the PRO depends on several factors. One is the legal environment; PROs that can claim title to inventions have a greater incentive to develop such structures. Another is the university's or PRO's degree of institutional autonomy and the existence of laws and regulations (*e.g.* fiscal status of PROs) that require the PRO to adopt alternatives to in-house operations. To illustrate, many US public and state-chartered universities have established arms-length institutions (*e.g.* foundations) because they generally benefit from the immunity from prosecution granted to state governments. In Japan, national universities are not autonomous and there as well TLOs have been established as separate and private entities. In Israel, the TTOs at the Weizmann Institute (Yeda) and at the Hebrew University (Yissum) were established as fully owned subsidiary companies to allow PROs to earn revenue and hold equity in spin-off companies. Until recently, rules in many European countries prohibited (public) universities from having equity participation in spin-offs. The United Kingdom changed a law prohibiting universities from keeping revenue from commercialisation; previously, licensing revenues were transferred to the Treasury. Korea amended its legislation in 2001 to allow TTOs in public universities to become legal entities, thus making it possible for them to appropriate financial returns from licensing. The appropriateness of one institutional arrangement or another depends on the context in which the PRO operates: its status as a private or public institution; the amount of government funding it receives; the size of its research portfolio and fields of specialisation; its geographical proximity to firms and insertion in innovation networks; and its funding capacity (OECD, 2002b).

Figure 2.3. Types of IP activities carried out by TTOs in OECD countries

Percentage share of responses

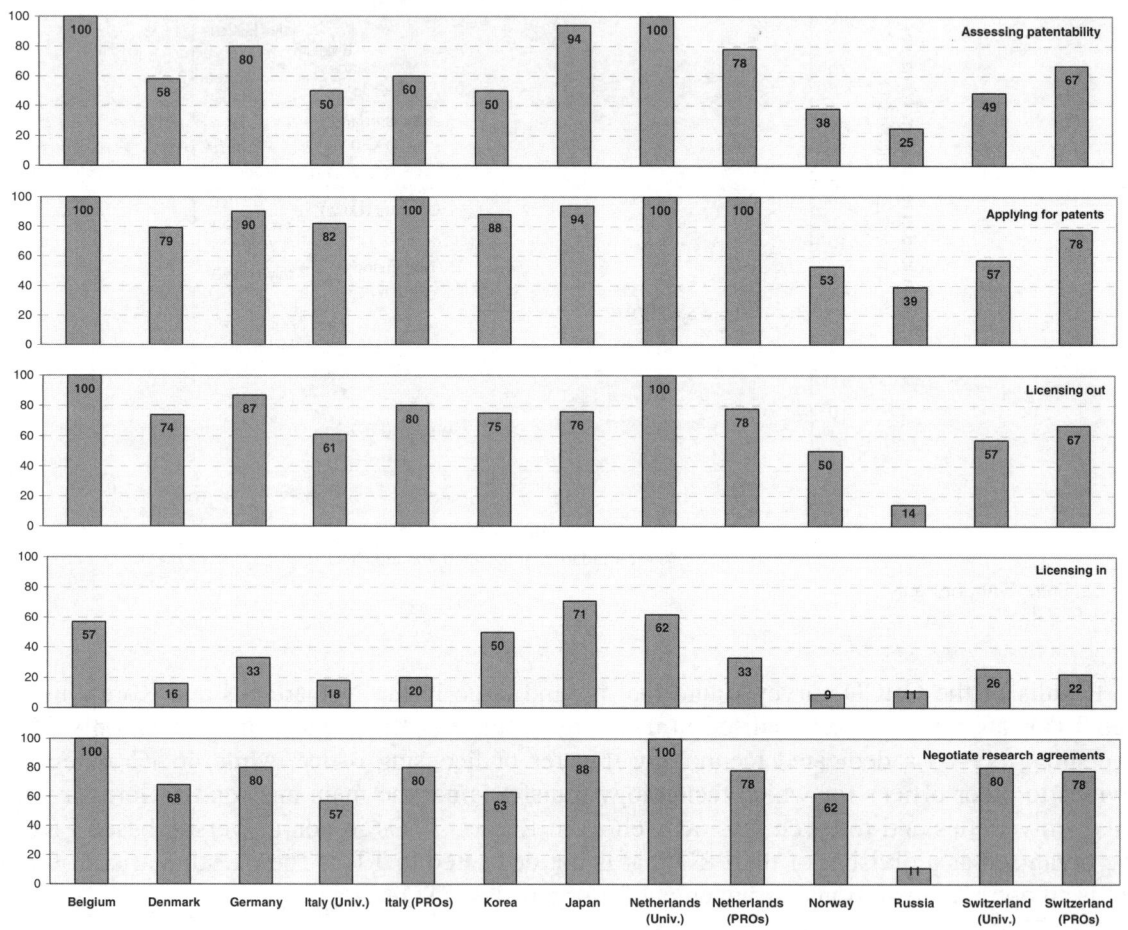

Activities of TTOs

TTOs are perhaps better understood in terms of their mission, which is to assess and protect IP and make it available to industry. Among responding countries, TTOs in Germany (non-university PROs), Japan and the Netherlands provide more IP services than TTOs in other countries. In the countries surveyed, with the exception of Japan, TTOs do not usually "license in" technologies from companies or other PROs. This is also the case for Switzerland. Overall, TTOs tend to be oriented towards managing patent and licensing, especially licensing contracts and research agreements with firms (Figure 2.3). However, in several countries such as Italy, Norway, or Russia TTOs appear less

40

equipped to assess the patentability of new inventions. This may be due to the relative young age of TTOs in these countries and hence, their limited scientific and legal expertise or weak incentives to patent.

TTO management

The share of IP activities managed by the TTO for its host institution varies across OECD countries. In other words, the degree to which IP activities are concentrated in a TTO or administrative unit of the PRO tells much about the TTO's formal organisation and capacity. In Japan, 35% of PROs claim to manage 100% of IP for their institution, while 23% claim to manage between 25% and 75%; this reflects the use of separate or independent TLOs to manage IP for national universities. The figures for the Netherlands are 66% for universities and 91% for non-university PROs. Only 38% of Norwegian PRO report that they manage 100% of the IP and nearly 30% report that IP is managed by other actors, namely the researcher, a central PRO or research managers. This undoubtedly reflects the fact that in Norway individual researchers own the IP; hence, the responsibilities for managing IP are more informal and diffuse. At Swiss university-based TTOs, 34% report that they manage up to 100% of the IP for their institution in contrast to 56% for TTOs at non-university PROs. In Germany, management of IP at non-university PROs is highly formalised and concentrated; two-thirds of PROs mange IP in a single office and 81% manage over 75% of their own IP (Figure 2.4). Other players that manage IP in many of the countries surveyed include individual research departments/institutes and researchers themselves.

Figure 2.4. Share of IP managed by non-university PROs in Germany

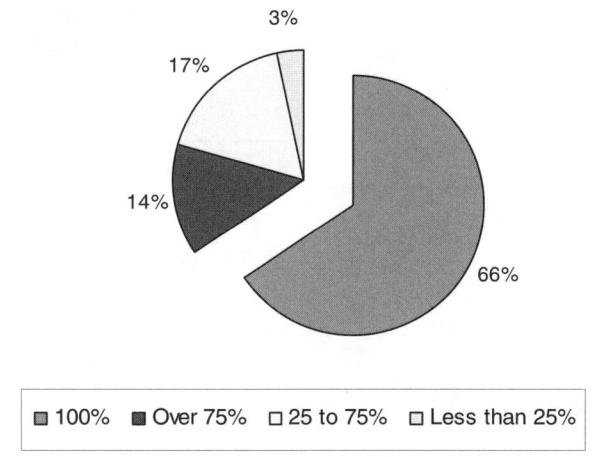

Making the transfer of IP work: the role of informal relations

One of the main challenges facing TTO managers involves the strategies to use to diffuse and commercialise a PRO's inventions (Figure 2.5). Most TTOs surveyed, however, stress the importance of both the TTO's and the researchers' informal relations. In Denmark and Italy, researchers' informal networks were used more often than the PROs' informal networks or advertising campaigns. In Italy, 61% of Italian universities did not use Internet-based intermediaries or advertising to promote their IP portfolios; 75% used informal contacts between researchers and inventors with a success rate of 24%.

Figure 2.5. Channels used for licensing

Percentage share of responses

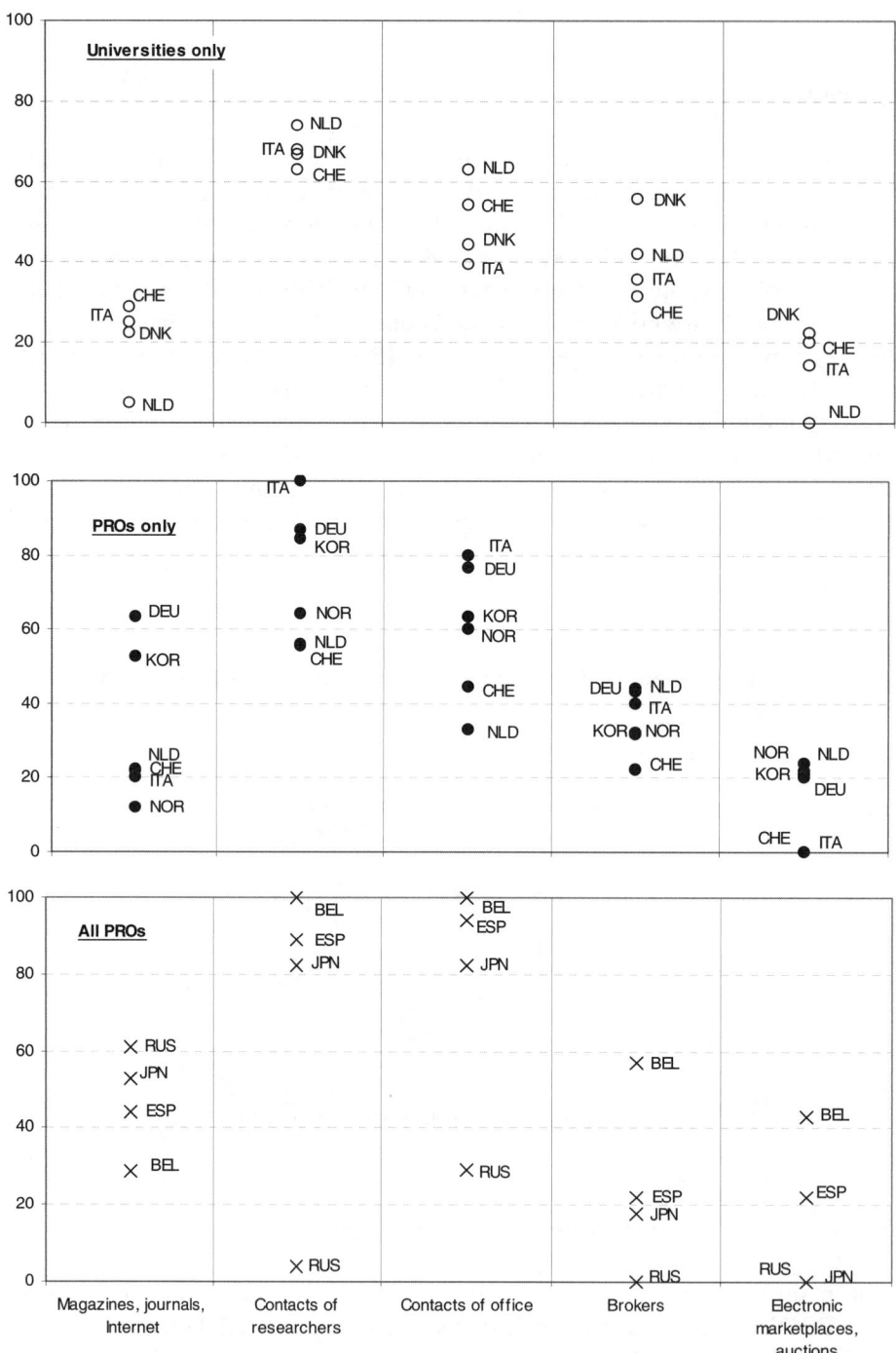

The low incidence of use of technology brokers and intermediaries or Internet-based channels, combined with lower performance in licensing than in patenting in many countries (see Chapter 3), may indicate a "passive" rather than a strategic approach to the exploitation of IP at many TTOs. Box 2.1 reviews the experience of Germany's Fraunhofer Society's centralised TTO, which illustrates the shift from traditional IP administration to the strategic management and exploitation of IP.

Box 2.1. Patenting and licensing at Germany's Fraunhofer Society

Basic characteristics

The *Fraunhofer Patentstelle (*Fraunhofer Patent Centre*)* was founded in 1955. As an institute of the Fraunhofer Society, it does not perform any basic or applied research but deals only with transforming inventions into patents and licences. It acts as a service organisation, serving not only the Fraunhofer institutes, but also universities and individual inventors. All clients of the Fraunhofer Patent Centre have access to the full services offered, such as the acquisition and the evaluation of intellectual property rights (IPR), inventions and technologies, the filing of intellectual property applications, technological consulting, strategic planning, negotiation and issuance of licences, collecting of royalties and much more. The institution is by far the biggest intellectual asset management (IAM) institution in Germany working almost exclusively for PROs. It currently employs more than 70 full-time equivalent staff and has total annual royalty income of more than EUR 20 million and receives more than 2 000 invention disclosures a year, most of them from outside the Fraunhofer organisation.

IP management approach

Until recently the most common path to commercial exploitation was to collect licence fees and royalties from industry. In some cases, however, the creation of a start-up company offers an alternative for effective commercialisation of IPR. The Fraunhofer Patent Centre has experimented with a number of mechanisms aimed at increasing the likelihood that a licence for its IPR will become commercially successful. Some of these mechanisms are:

♦ The development of prototypes showing the technical feasibility of patented inventions.

♦ Sponsoring IPR applications of company founders based on agreements that provide for sharing benefits if the start-up enters the market.

♦ Supporting start-up entrepreneurs through consultancy, including the provision of services under the federal innovation programme INSTI.[1]

In 2000 it launched support schemes for start-up entrepreneurs by forming its own start-up company, Ventratec GmbH. When Ventratec takes on a project, it also acquires an equity stake in the start-up.

In parallel, the Fraunhofer Board of Management established a Venture Group under the supervision of the central legal department. The Venture Group is specifically responsible for consulting employees at Fraunhofer institutes who may have plans to become self-employed. The Fraunhofer Board of Management and the Venture Group have also been instrumental in setting up a new Venture Capital Fund that is intended to become operational by the end of 2002.[2]

Assessment

The multitude of technology transfer activities at Fraunhofer have led to a substantial presence in IAM in the German PRO landscape, a fact that is underlined by the questionnaire findings submitted to the OECD by the Federal Ministry of Education and Research. However, a closer look into Fraunhofer IAM practices reveals internal inconsistencies that so far seem to limit its effectiveness.

Almost none of the institutes plans IAM strategically, as the Fraunhofer financing model has led them into a strong dependency on domestic collaborative grants and direct contracts,[3] and both the institutes and the central administration regularly provide inroads for industry in the form of cheap access rights to Fraunhofer results and IP.

One consequence of this practice can be seen when IPR prosecution costs are compared with royalty income. Here, Fraunhofer shows only a minor surplus. In fact, only one of the 54 research institutes generates substantial royalty income;[4] virtually all other institutes lose money on their patents, claiming that these are needed to remain attractive to co-operation partners in industry.[5] This practice not only has a detrimental effect on royalty income, it is also a systematic problem with regard to start-ups. Here, exclusive rights to intellectual assets are almost always needed to secure third-party investment.

The Fraunhofer Patent Centre is the major player in IAM for German PROs, but because of the inconsistencies this know-how does so far not seem to be systematically used by Fraunhofer research institutes.

---

1. INSTI – *Innovationsstimulierung in der deutschen Wirtschaft* (Stimulation of Innovation in the German Economy), a support programme launched by the federal government in 1995 which administered a wide array of stimulation measures particularly in the field of IPR.
2. http://www.venturecommunity.fraunhofer.de/news.php3?sessionid=54425e4cb3378afdfe2a7913c3ae57d0
3. With project partners in industry.
4. In an area where the institute deliberately reserved the IP without granting rights to collaborative project partners while at the same time building an impressive IPR portfolio over a period of almost ten years.
5. While at the same time not using some form of a benchmarking system in order to support this theory.
Source: Gering *et al*. (2002).

43

Government support for IP management and technology transfer

Governments shape the legal framework for IP management at PROs. They can also influence the institutional infrastructure that enables and encourages technology transfer and commercialisation of public research.

Support for the creation of TTOs/TLOs in other OECD countries

One of the challenges that institutions and governments face, especially in countries where most PROs are government or public institutions, is sustaining the viability of technology transfer operations. Even in the United States, few TLOs generate sufficient licence income to exceed expenditures (Nelsen, 1998). Those that have become profitable have done so after five to ten years of operation and with long-term investments in management and marketing (Kneller, 2001). While some non-university PROs in Europe, such as the United Kingdom's Medical Research Council (MRC), Germany's Max Planck Society and Belgium's IMEC, are quite successful in terms of patenting and licensing, technology transfer operations at universities, partly owing to the legal restrictions described above, are more recent and are being spurred by government support. In early 2002, the German Ministry of Research and Technology (BMBF) launched a multi-million euro programme to assist universities in hiring external services for licensing and prosecution of IP (Gering *et al.*, 2002). In France, the Innovation Law of 1999 provides for the strengthening of TTO structures at universities, notably through the creation of departments for commercial and industrial service activities (*Services d'activités industrielles et commerciales – SAIC*). Since 1998, the Japanese government has subsidised the newly created TLOs, which now number 27, to provide university inventors with IP management and commercialisation services.

Governments also support technology transfer at PROs by sponsoring the establishment of one-stop IP centres or networks to serve several smaller PROs that lack the resources or critical mass to build their own TTO. Belgium's Interuniversity Institute for Biotechnology (VIB) for example, manages IP and technology transfer in biotechnology for nine universities. To strengthen capacity in TTOs, the Flemish government is providing EUR 1.25 million a year over five years to help six PROs (of which three are universities) develop, implement and evaluate annual work plans for technology transfer. In Denmark, as part of the government's implementation of the new law, a grant of EUR 8 million was set aside for the period 2000-03 to help universities and other PROs protect and market their inventions. The grant is used to help PROs cover the external costs of patenting and marketing (up to EUR 20 000 per invention) as well as for helping PROs establish joint TTOs or networks along geographic/sectoral lines (*e.g.* in the life sciences). The concentration of IP management aims to address the lack of PROs' financial and managerial resources to sustain individual patenting and licensing operations. In the United Kingdom, some PROs, with government support, have developed a partnership to pool resources and increase the rate at which they market their IP in the health and life science fields (Box 2.2). However, the success of such an approach often depends on extensive and good relations between staff in the TTO and in the PROs who interface with researchers and faculty.

Subsiding patent costs

The low incentive to patent or license is reinforced by the high costs of patenting and licensing, and the uncertainty over potential revenue from licensing. Governments encourage PRO patenting activity by lowering or subsidising the costs of patent protection. Patent costs are lower in the United States and Japan than those for filing a patent at the European Patent Office (EPO) with protection in several European countries.[1] In Germany, a university pays EUR 3 000-4 000 for application and attorney fees to file a national patent claim, while a European Patent Convention (EPC) patent costs EUR 50 000. The OECD survey shows that European PROs tend to file most of their patents in their home country and that fewer academic patents are filed at European level or overseas. This likely reflects the importance of filing within home jurisdictions first, but there are concerns that subsequent patenting at EU level could be deterred by the costs of an EPC patent. The higher costs, however, may also act as a litmus test: if the potential commercial value of the invention is high, the incentive to seek protection in foreign markets may also be high, despite the higher patenting costs. Nevertheless, the advent of a single, cost-efficient European patent could help widen the market for commercialising PRO inventions in Europe.

Box 2.2. UK regional partnerships for managing IP from hospitals and other health bodies

A network of hub organisations is being established across England to manage IP coming out of hospitals (NHS trusts) and other health organisations responsible for providing primary care (Primary Care Trusts, PCTs). These hub organisations receive public funding from the Department of Trade and Industry (DTI) (through the PSRE Fund), by the Department of Health, the English Regional Development Agencies and others. These hub organisations will cover NHS Trusts and PCTs in the nine local government regions. Concentrating expertise in a hub, which can be centred in one or more locations in each region, allows for efficient management of IP through the concentration of resources and recognises that most NHS organisations are too small to justify a dedicated activity. Hubs will normally be found close to university medical schools and will work closely with university TTOs. This is important in terms of sharing knowledge and expertise and when dealing with IP resulting from joint research between hospitals and universities.

The prototype of this kind of partnership was a network centred around Manchester, where three NHS Trusts (Central Manchester, Salford Royal, South Manchester) worked in partnership with four universities (Manchester, UMIST, Salford, Manchester Metropolitan). Their MANIP partnership (Manchester Intellectual Property) received funding from the DTI's Biotechnology Exploitation Platform (BEP). IP is identified, evaluated and an exploitation route agreed. Much of the IP arises from joint work between the NHS Trusts and the universities, and the route to exploitation is managed by the partner university's TTO, including the Manchester Bioscience Incubator, or by one of the partner Trusts.

This NHS partnership has now expanded to cover all NHS organisations in the Northwest, and it is now the northwest hub, TrusTECH. In addition to the other sources mentioned above, TrusTECH is supported by another BEP. Many of the BEPs funded by DTI have NHS Trusts as partners.

Source: DTI, *White Paper on Science and Technology* (2000).

In Japan, the 1998 Technology Transfer Law exempts "acknowledged" TLOs *(nintei TLO)* from paying patent application fees and annual patent and examination fees. With respect to "authorised" TLOs *(shonin TLO)*, universities and university researchers, the application, examination and annual fees are reduced by 50% for three years.[2] In the United States, the United States Patent and Trademark Office (USPTO) offers reduced patent fees to small entities with fewer than 500 employees. It also lowered patent application fees across the board in 1999, although costs have recently risen. In addition, it has implemented an on-line electronic filing system and lowered the average processing time. Since 1995, the USPTO also permits a provisional patent application which is particularly useful for universities and small firms, as it allows them to obtain early protection on an invention (without preventing the researcher from publishing the results[3]). This is important if protection is to be sought in foreign jurisdictions with first-to-file patent systems. Finally, research councils or funding agencies in some countries allow grant recipients to use research grants to pay IP-related costs. For example, research grant applications by PROs to the German BMBF must include an exploitation plan and applicants can include the projected patenting costs in the grant application. The European Union also allows patent costs to be included in the indirect research expenditures eligible for Community Framework grants.

Support for legal training of TTO staff

Well-trained staff at TTOs are not only essential to the efficiency of technology transfer but can also help to limit conflicts of interest with researchers. One of the main challenges facing PROs is to attract and retain the human resources to manage TTOs and interact with scientists. In recent years, OECD governments have, either through direct schemes or via national patent offices, supported IP training at PROs. Since 1998, the German government sponsors training schemes at universities. The UK patent office actively promotes awareness of IP management at universities and other PROs and diffuses information on good practices. Switzerland's Network for Innovation sponsors training on IP matters and the government indirectly sponsors the IP activities of PROs such as the federal institutes of technology. Enterprise Ireland provides short training seminars on technology transfer and IP-related matters through its Campus Company Programme. The USPTO and the Japan Patent Office also offer regular training courses on IP management to small businesses and organisations.

Government support for the creation of TTOs and the costs of patenting and licensing activity has increased in Japan and in European countries in parallel to changes in the legal framework. The long-term viability of technology transfer operations remains an issue in most countries. However, anecdotal evidence from successful TTOs suggests that as IP operations develop, TTOs expand their operations beyond patenting and licensing to developing contract/sponsored research and providing technology consulting services, thus broadening their revenue base and generating more research for PROs.

NOTES

1.   While there is not yet a single European Community Patent, the European Patent Convention (EPC) states that "a European patent shall, in each of the Contracting States for which it is granted, have the effect of and be subject to the same conditions as a national patent granted by that State, unless otherwise provided in the Convention".

2 .   Acknowledged TLOs (*nintei TLO*) are those that may engage in transfer of patent or patent rights owned by the government and result from the research results of national universities, inter-university institutions, test and state government research establishments and independent administrative institutions. Authorised TLOs (*shonin TLO*) are those that are authorised by both the Minister of Education, Culture, Sports, Science and Technology and the Minister of Economy, Trade and Industry to transfer patents or patent rights owned by entities other than the state government but resulting from the research results of national universities and inter-university institutions.

3.   The US patent system allows inventors a "grace period" of 12 months for disclosure, allowing them to publish their results and still apply for a patent. Since 1995, the USPTO has offered inventors the option of filing a provisional application for patent. It allows filing without a formal patent claim or an information disclosure statement. It was designed to provide a lower-cost first patent filing in the United States and to give US applicants parity with foreign applicants under the GATT Uruguay Round Agreements. A provisional application for a patent has a pendency of 12 months from the date it is filed. The pendency period cannot be extended.

Chapter 3

TRENDS IN PATENTING AND LICENSING ACROSS OECD COUNTRIES

Introduction

This chapter discusses new data concerning the intellectual property activities of technology transfer offices (TTOs) affiliated with public research organisations. The data presented are based on responses received from TTO managers to the OECD questionnaire about the size and nature of their intellectual property (IP) portfolio; the licences they have negotiated and the types of clauses typically included in them; and the income and expenditure associated with the protection and exploitation of IP. Their responses should help policy makers understand which innovations are being commercialised, under what conditions, with what safeguards for the research missions of public research organisations (PROs) and with what economic repercussions for the PRO and the economy more generally. The responses are grouped into three broad areas:

- The intellectual property portfolio of the TTO:

  - What is the patent portfolio under management, in what technical fields and where are the patents exploited?

  - What non-patent intellectual property is also under TTO management?

- Licensing practices:

  - What were the number, type and value of licences negotiated in the last year and to whom were they granted?

  - Which type of clauses (*e.g.* to protect the research capacity of the PRO or to ensure exploitation) were included in these licences?

- Licensing income:

  - What was the licensing revenue generated, by which types of intellectual property and how was that income divided and shared?

  - Does income cover the expenses incurred by the TTO for its technology transfer activities?

The survey questions that touch on the intellectual property portfolio of PROs borrowed heavily from the annual survey of the Association of University Technology Managers (AUTM), as well as from recent Canadian surveys of PRO IP activity. The intention was to make responses from countries that newly surveyed their PROs and those that used existing surveys as comparable as possible. However, the questions on licensing practices and licensing income, as well as those about non-patent IP, are new. They represent an effort to understand the full range of IP activities at PROs and their success at exploiting IP commercially (the OECD questionnaire can be found in Annex 3).

Thirteen countries submitted data regarding their patenting and licensing activities. The countries are: Australia, Belgium, Denmark, Germany, Italy, Japan, Korea, the Netherlands, Norway, Russia, Spain, Switzerland and the United States. The United States responded to the questionnaire with aggregate data from the AUTM survey. Australia submitted data from a recent survey of IP at PROs rather than on the basis of the OECD survey; for the purposes of this report, data were also drawn from Australia's *National Survey of Research Commercialisation Year 2000*. The remaining countries administered the OECD survey to their PROs in the winter and spring of 2002.

Aggregated country data are presented here, but it is important to note that the information does not presume to benchmark individual country performances. Rather, the data are meant to give the reader a sense of the range of responses received and the broad trends evident in OECD member countries.

TTO intellectual property portfolios

While many OECD countries have some evidence that the patenting activities of their PROs are on the rise, few have surveyed the entire PRO sector to obtain a global picture of patenting activity and the number of active patents under management by PROs. The approximate number of patents applied for and granted in a year, as well as the total number of patents granted still under management, is important in estimating the TTO's potential costs and revenues.

Moreover, since there are concerns that growth in patenting at PROs may negatively affect the orientation of research and the missions of PROs, data on the size of patent portfolio is useful to help ascertain the likelihood that IP activities are distorting research or education missions. Knowing in what technological fields patents are most often applied for also helps identify those sectors where commercialisation is deemed most likely and in which the impact on primary missions may be felt most strongly.

Patenting data are of primary concern because this is the category of intellectual property that has been the target of most recent policy reforms aimed at fostering greater commercialisation by PROs. However, the survey also explored the other types of intellectual property activities in which a TTO may be involved, such as securing protection for copyright, industrial designs and plant breeder's rights. The IP activities of TTOs may extend beyond the protection of formal IPR. TTOs may also receive invention disclosures and be responsible for deciding which innovations and creative works to protect and how to do so. They may also be involved in negotiating contracts that stipulate how IP is to be used or revealed.

Patent portfolios of currently active, technically unique patents

The most basic questions asked about the TTOs' IP portfolios were: *i)* what is the total stock of patents for which the TTO is currently responsible; and *ii)* what was the number of patents granted to the institution in the past year? These questions ask specifically about "currently active, technically unique patents". "Currently active" means that the patents are still the property of the PRO: they have not expired, been allowed to lapse or been sold. "Technically unique" means that patents for a single invention filed in multiple jurisdictions [*e.g.* European Patent Office (EPO) and Japanese Patent Office (JPO)] should not be double (or multiple) counted as separate patents. The objective is to understand how many unique patented inventions are under management by the organisation.

It was easier for respondents to identify how many patents they had been granted in the past year than to report the stock of patents in their portfolio. The stock of patents at TTOs ranges from less than five to a few dozen (Figure 3.1), although in a couple of exceptional cases, the stocks were in the hundreds. Around 70% of the Swiss and Italian universities and 40% of the Korean ones reported managing fewer than 50 active patents. For non-university PROs, portfolio sizes do not exceed ten patents in 50% of these institutions in Germany and over 20% in Norway, Korea or Italy. Over 50% of all PROs in the Netherlands, Spain and Belgium also manage portfolios of fewer than 50 patents. Japanese PROs are a notable exception. In addition, very large portfolios should be considered with care, as at least one country noted that PROs had counted non-patented inventions in their stock.

Figure 3.1. The stock of active, technically unique patents in TTO portfolio, by PRO type

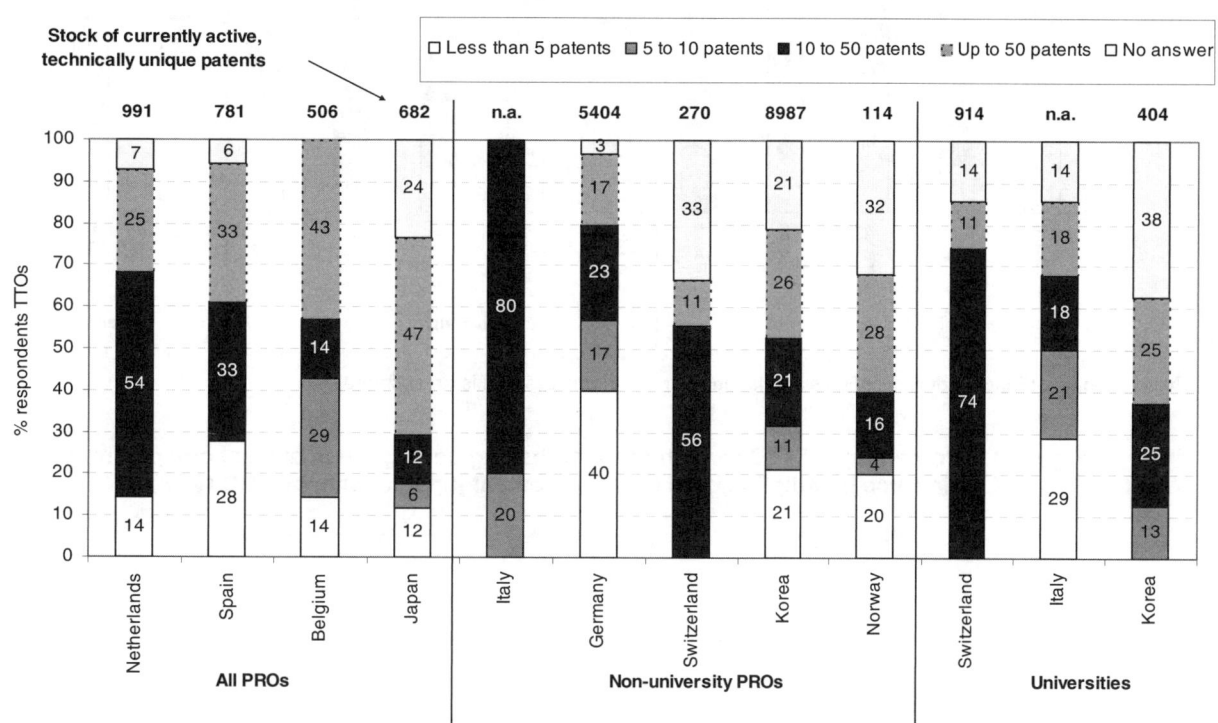

Note: For the Netherlands and Switzerland, upper percentages refer to TTOs that have reported stocks with fewer than 50 patents (rather than from 10 to 50). Belgium: Flanders only.

TTOs varied across countries in terms of the average number of patents their institutions were granted in the past year (Figure 3.2). It is not uncommon for 20-30% of TTOs not to obtain a single patent in a given year. With the notable exception of Italian PROs, the majority of TTOs received on average fewer than five patents a year. In the United States, which has the longest record of monitoring patent grants, the average university was granted 22 patents in 2000. Only Korea claimed a more prolific record. Non-university PROs seem to be slightly more active in patenting: in Switzerland and Italy, for which data by type of PRO could be compared, the share of non-university PROs declaring having been granted more than five patents in the last year was substantially larger than that of universities.

TTOs were also asked in what jurisdictions their patents had been granted – their own country, the US Patent and Trademark Office (USPTO), the EPO, the JPO or some other jurisdiction. Respondents were simply asked to say whether any of their patents had issued from each of these patent authorities.

51

Figure 3.2. The number of patents granted to TTOs in the last year, by PRO type

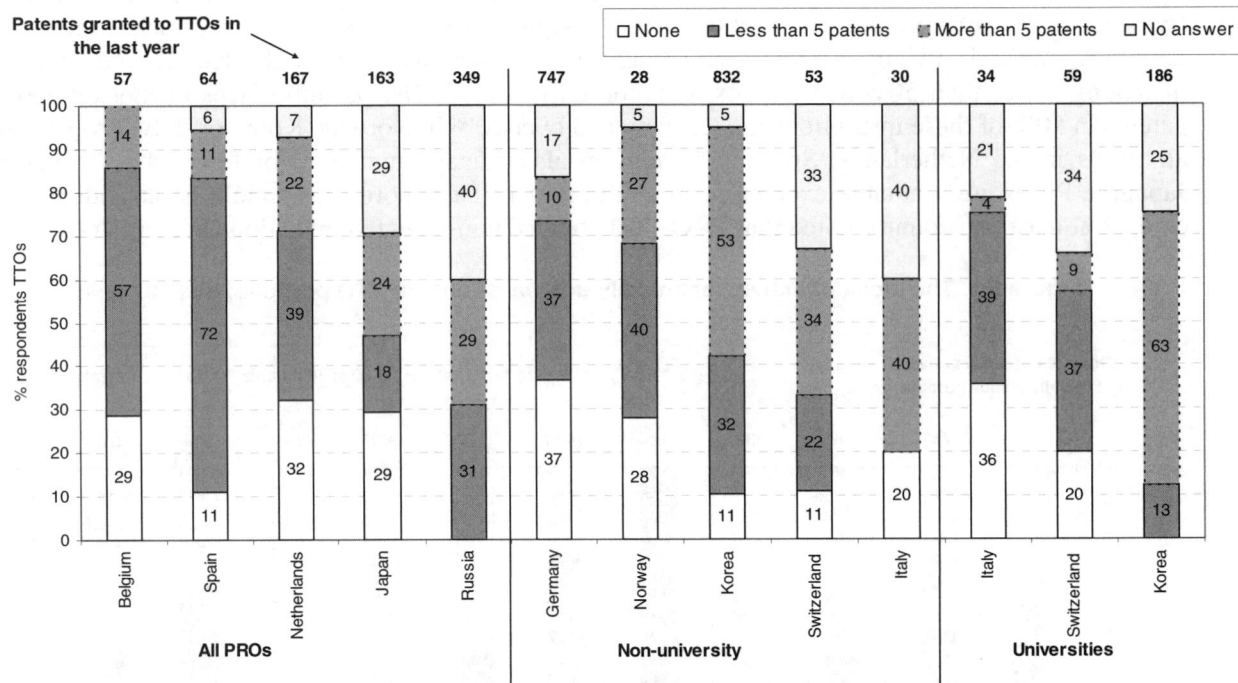

Note: Belgium: Flanders only. For Russia, total number of patents granted is an estimate.

Figure 3.3. Percentage of TTOs which reported having been granted at least one patent in their home jurisdiction or in the major patent jurisdictions, by PRO type

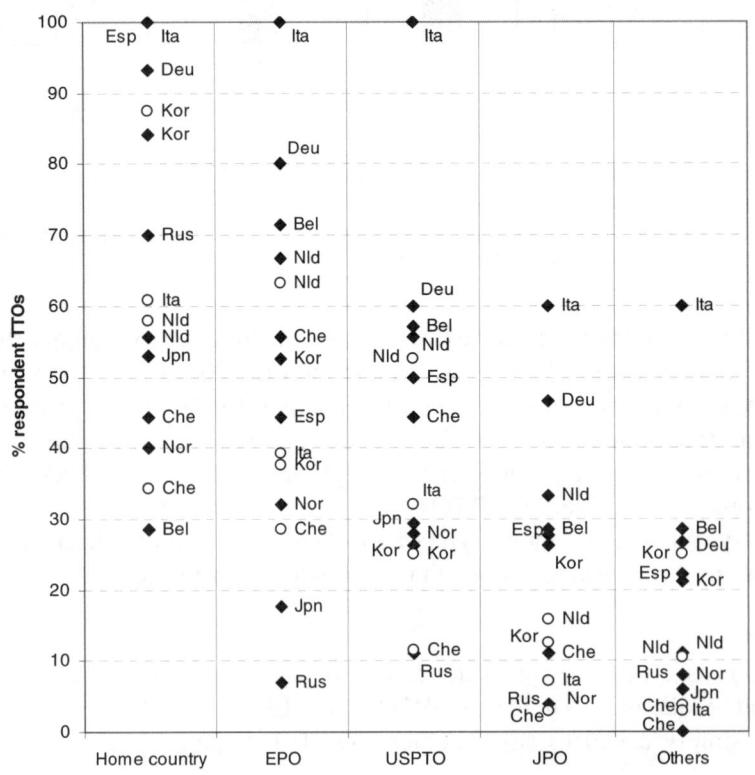

Not surprisingly, patents are obtained most frequently in the home country (Figure 3.3). The only exception was the Netherlands, where TTOs received more EPO grants than grants from the Dutch patent authority. However a significant proportion of PROs have been granted patents in multiple offices. Over 60% of PROs in Belgium, Spain and Korea (both universities and non-university PROs) and 80% in Germany reported having received patents from at least three out of the four major patent jurisdictions. Typically, grants from the EPO were second most common, followed by the USPTO and the JPO. The geographic location of the countries surveyed probably explains the over-representation of the EPO as compared with the USPTO or other national authorities (for example, those of Australia, Canada, Israel, Singapore, South Korea) (Figure 3.4). While the home country is the most popular place to apply for and receive protection, overseas patents are clearly very important to public research bodies and they frequently obtain protection from all the major jurisdictions.

Figure 3.4. Percentage of TTOs reporting having been granted at least one patent in other patent jurisdictions

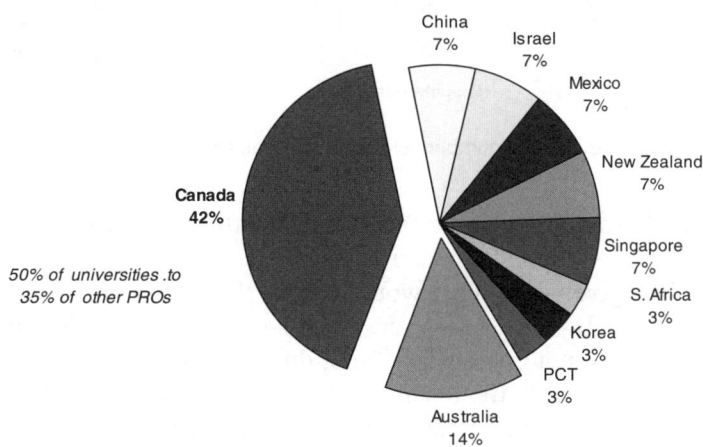

Patent applications – number per institution and by technical field

TTOs were asked not only how many patents they were granted, but also the number of patents they had applied for in the last year (Figure 3.5). In general, TTOs reported applying for more patents than the number of granted patents they received in the last year. Patent applications are in fact likely to be more numerous than grants as not all patent applications pass the tests of novelty, inventive step and utility. It should be remembered that the patents and grants are reported in the same year, so that they are not for the same inventions, as there is often a lapse of a couple of years between the date of application and the date of grant.

The number of patent applications per TTO ranged from an average of less than ten a year to several dozen. Some TTOs in Spain, Italy, Norway and Switzerland reported no applications over the last year. In exceptional cases, the US federal laboratories for example, organisations reported a couple of hundred patent applications. However, the size of the PROs must be taken into account when comparing these figures.

Figure 3.5. Number of patent applications per TTO, by PRO type

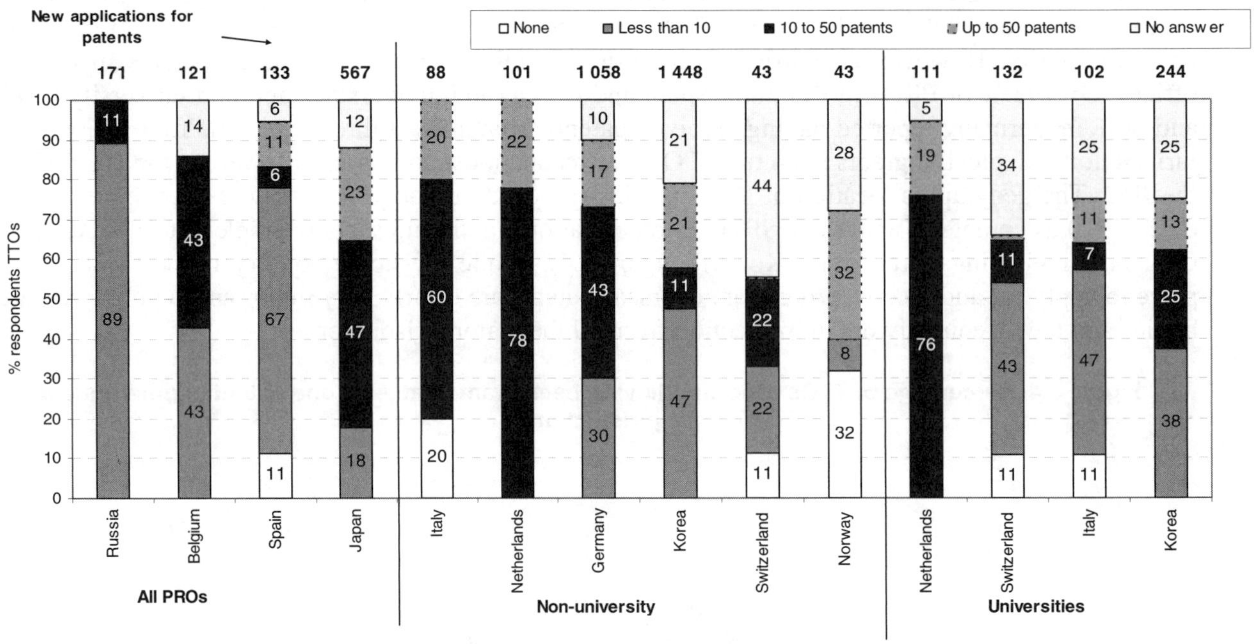

Note: Belgium: Flanders only. For Italy and Russia, total numbers of patent applications are estimates.

A more comprehensive understanding of how PROs manage their patent portfolio can be gained by comparing the number of patents applied for and granted, as well as the total number of active patents still owned by a PRO in a given year. One would expect the number of patent applications to be larger than the number of eventual grants. However, a cross-country study (Figure 3.6) shows that the number of applications and grants in a given year do not differ greatly. This may be because PROs applied for more patents in prior years, with the result that their grant numbers are higher. However, if patent applications are relatively stable, an alternative explanation might be that a high proportion of patent applications are actually granted. Information about application and grant rates over time would help interpret these figures. A second notable finding of the study was that, in universities, the stock of patents under management is several times the size of patents granted in a year, which suggests that PROs retain ownership of patents for a long period of time and do not sell them or let them lapse. Experts do not yet know what is an ideal, or best practice, ratio of patent applications, grants and stock (Vock and Jola, 2002).

While the average number of patent applications and grants per PRO suggest a rough range of normal IP activity, it would be more valuable to control for the size and research intensity of the PRO, as this would give comparisons of PRO IP productivity more meaning. The Netherlands was able to do so by normalising responses with the respect to the number of research personnel at each PRO (Table 3.1). The Dutch study concludes that "patent applications at universities exceed patent grants by almost two to one, which could be indicative of future growth in patent grants (given a rate of approval for patent applications of over 58%)" (Arundel and Bordoy, 2002). At non-university PROs, in contrast, the number of patent applications approximately equals the number of grants, which could presage a drop in patent grants. Concerning the productivity of universities and other PROs, as measured by the number of patent applications and grants per 1 000 full-time equivalent (FTE) staff, the report concludes: "Universities are more productive than [other PROs] for patent applications (11.0 versus 5.8 patent applications per 1 000 FTEs).... The rate is similar for patent grants, at 6.3 per 1 000 FTEs for universities and 5.9 per 1 000 FTEs at [other PROs]." An important improvement to consider in future surveys is the normalisation of IP outputs by research expenditures or research staff size.

Figure 3.6. Cross-country comparison of patent applications, grants and total portfolio size

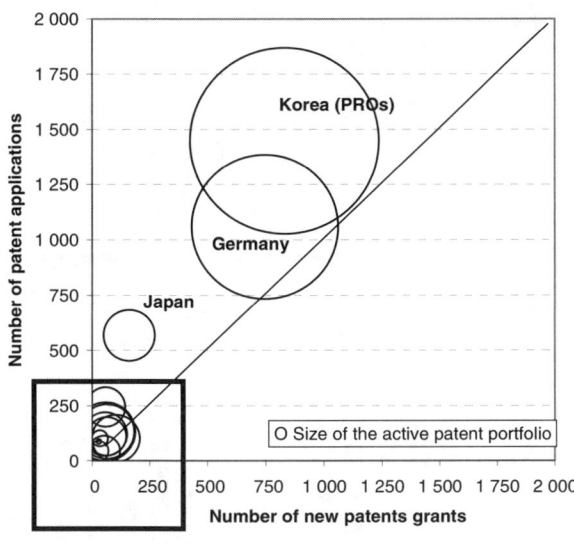 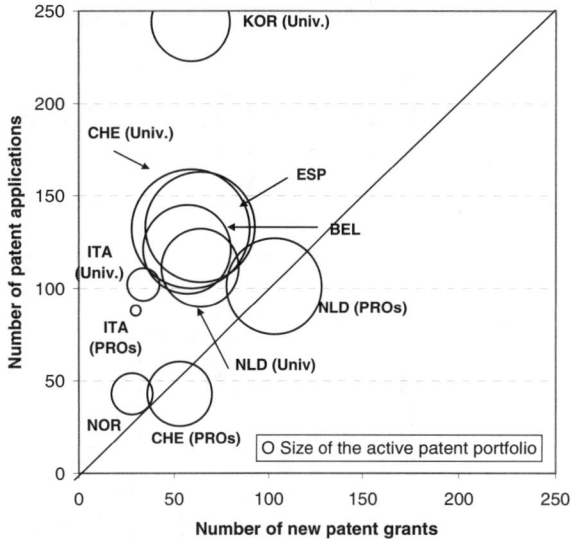

Note: Belgium: Flanders only.

Table 3.1. Dutch patent output and productivity

	Universities		Public research institutes		Total
	Total	FTE (000)[1]	Total	FTE (000)[2]	
Total number of valid patents[3]	394	41.4	597	34.0	991
Patents granted in last year[4]	64	6.3	103	5.9	167
Patent applications in last year[4]	111	11.0	101	5.8	212

1: Patents per 1 000 FTEs in 1998 in science, agriculture, technical, and health faculties in all 13 universities.
2: Patents per 1 000 FTEs in 1998.
3: Employment at non-respondent institutes is not included in the calculation of total patents per 1 000 FTEs.
4: The expected number of applications and grants at non-respondent institutes (less than 5% of the total number of patents) is estimated using regression techniques.

TTOs were asked to identify the fields of technology in which they had applied for patents (Figure 3.7). Across OECD member countries, health technologies, information technologies and production technologies ranked the highest. For the last year, TTOs reported more applications in these fields than in the food or energy sectors. While energy, environment and transport technologies are important to Germany, Norway and Japan, they did not rank as high as health, information technology and production technologies. Health technologies, however, did not rank as high as initially expected. The explosion of patenting, and especially of PRO patenting, is often attributed to the rise of biotechnology and other medical sciences as commercially relevant fields. One might have expected this boom to be reflected more widely across countries. TTOs applied for health patents to a greater extent in Belgium, Germany, the Netherlands and Switzerland. The dominant patent application fields may reflect countries' industrial make-up, but there are slight discrepancies; when one compares the share of a given technological sector in total business value added, the match between output and academic patents varies.

Figure 3.7. Percentage of TTOs reporting patent applications filed in various fields of technology

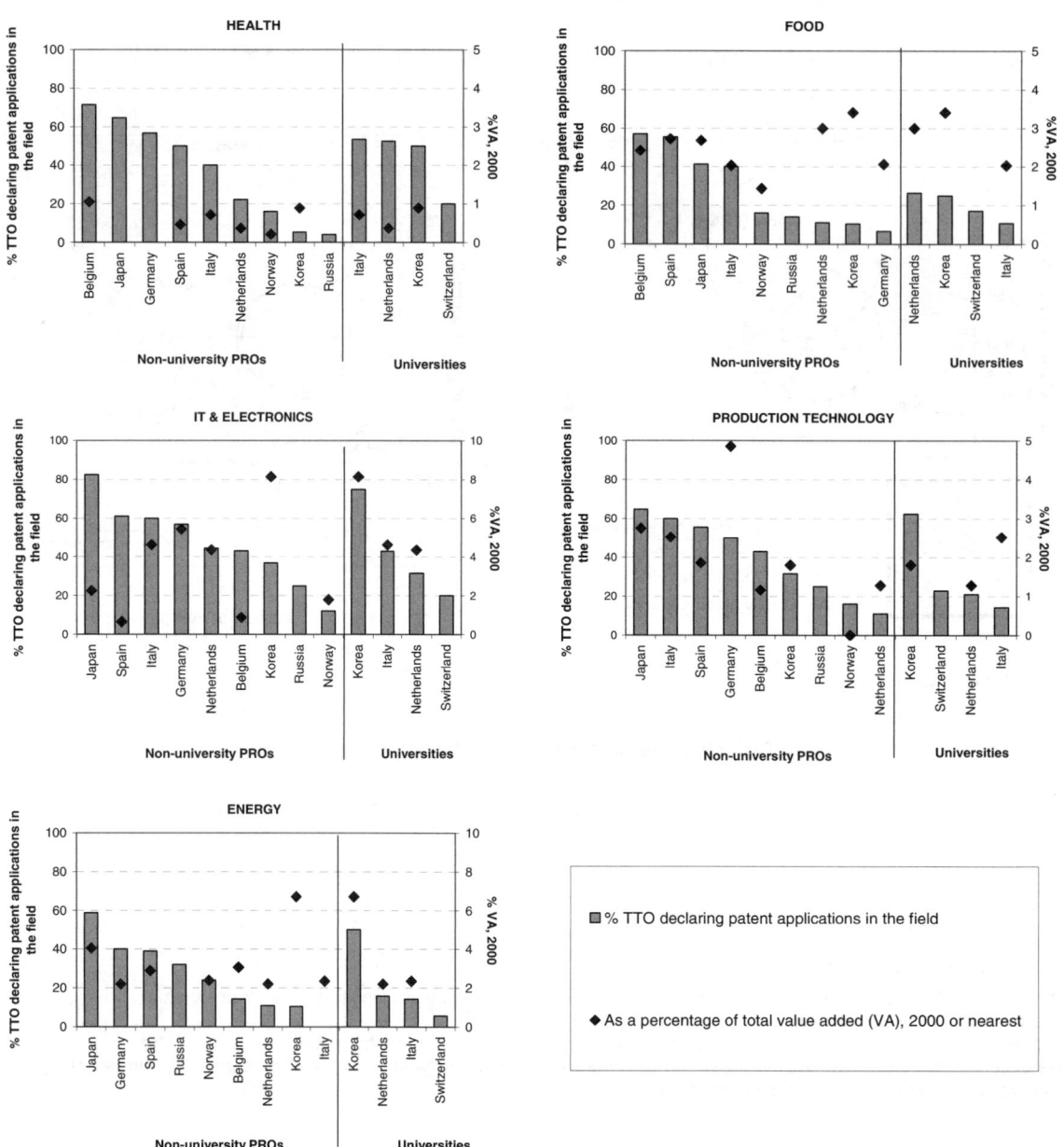

Note: Belgium: Flanders only.

Non-patent IP actions

Applying for patents is only one of a range of actions that TTOs can take to help protect and exploit their institution's intellectual property. A first step may be to receive "invention disclosures" from researchers detailing innovations that may be ripe for formal intellectual property protection. If the TTO decides a disclosed invention is patentable, the TTO may proceed to file a patent application based on the invention disclosure or it may decide to protect and exploit it using other means.

Some TTOs are also involved in registering copyright to protect creative works such as software, databases, educational materials (papers, books, courses) and multimedia works (*e.g.* on-line courses, digital textbooks). Whether the TTO is involved in copyright registration may have to do with laws and rules regarding ownership of copyrighted material. It is only recently that universities in some countries have begun to claim rights to copyrighted works. Two sorts of *sui generis* protection – industrial design registration and plant breeder's rights – might also be managed by the TTO.

Finally, for patented and non-patented inventions alike, TTOs may be involved in negotiating agreements or contracts regarding the confidentiality of research results, including promises not to disclose resultant intellectual property for contract or joint research, especially R&D contracts that stipulate how existing and future IP will be treated by the PRO and its contractual partner.

The questionnaire asked TTOs to identify what non-patent IP actions they had engaged in over the last year (Table 3.2). Many TTOs had difficulty answering this question, with response rates at less than 50% in many cases. However, the answers do seem to indicate that TTOs engage to some extent in all of these activities. TTOs generally obtain invention disclosures from inventors and are involved in negotiating non-disclosure and confidentiality agreements. In many countries, a moderate number of TTOs are also involved in copyright registration for creative works. TTOs were rarely involved in protecting industrial design and plant breeder's rights. Other types of IP actions reported included registration of trademarks, brand names and domain names on the World Wide Web, and the negotiation of materials transfer agreements.

Table 3.2. Number of TTOs reporting having undertaken various types of IP actions

	BEL	DEU	ITA	JPN		KOR		NLD		NOR		ESP	CHE	
	PRO	PRO	Univ	PRO	Univ	Univ	PRO	Univ	Total	Univ	PRO	Univ	Univ	PRO
Invention disclosures	5	15	6	2	9	4	8	2	3	0	3	3	17	4
Copyright registration for:														
Software & databases	0	4	3	2	1	4	5	>4	0	0	3	8	11	3
Education materials	0	2	1	1	0	1	1	-	0	0	1	2	11	2
Multimedia	0	1	1	0	0	2	2	-	0	0	1	1	9	3
Industrial design reg	1	4	0	0	2	1	4	0	0	0	1	1	9	2
Plant breeder's rights app.	1	0	0	1	1	1	0	-	0	0	0	0	5	2
Non-disclosure, confidentiality	6	14	7	4	4	2	2	12	4	0	3	6	12	5
Other	0	0	0	1	0	0	0	-	0	0	1	0	7	1
Total TTOs surveyed	7	30	28	5	17	8	19	19	9	9	25	18	35	9

Note: Belgium: Flanders only.

TTOs were also asked to report or estimate the number of non-patent actions undertaken in the last year in order to know how frequently these were undertaken (Table 3.3). Again, obtaining invention disclosures and negotiating non-disclosure and confidentiality agreements ranks first by far. However, in some cases (Korea, Switzerland, and to a lesser extent Spain and Italian PROs), TTOs were also involved in a significant number of copyright registrations.

In theory, to gain a more accurate sense of the importance at TTOs of patenting relative to other forms of IP protection, the number of patents applied for by PROs could be compared to the number of invention disclosures received, copyrights registered and non-disclosure and confidentiality agreements negotiated. In rare cases, TTOs are heavily involved in copyright registration (as in Norway) or the protection of other forms of IP such as plant breeder's rights and industrial design (as in Korea).

Table 3.3. Approximate number of IP actions by all responding TTOs

	AUT	BEL	DEU	ITA		JPN	KOR		NLD		NOR	ESP	CHE.		USA		RUS
	PRO	TTO	PRO	Univ	PRO	Univ	Univ	PRO	Univ	PRO	PROs	TTOs	Univ	PROs	Univ	PROs	All
Invention disclosures	62	230	948	62	21	489	274	144	n.a.	n.a.	11	20	241	39	12 075	4 209	64
Copyright registration for:																	
Software & databases	--	0	11	4	3	4	1 487	21	49	-	0	20	14	3	--	--	24
Education materials	--	0	3	2	2	0	10	5			100	3	24	0	--	--	8
Multimedia	--	0	1	2	0	0	31	5			3	1	9	1	--	--	0
Industrial design reg.	--	3	9	0	0	2	111	5	n.a.	n.a.	2	1	28	0	--	--	0
Plant breeder's rights app.	--	5	0	0	1	3	0	3	n.a.	n.a.	0	0	0	0	--	--	0
Non-disclosure, confidentiality	--	1 345	311	30	16	92	21	14	413	27	9	21	157	153	--	--	38
Other	--	60	10	0	5	0	0	0	-	-	0	0	67	13	--	--	0
Total	62	1 643	1 293	99	48	590	1 934	197			125	66	540	209	12 075	4 209	134

Note: Belgium: Flanders only.

Spin-offs as a form of technology transfer

An increasingly popular channel for technology transfer from public research is the formation of new, technology-intensive firms. Two types can be distinguished. A spin-off is a company that includes among its founding members a person affiliated with a PRO (*e.g.* a professor or researcher). A start-up is a firm that is not founded by a staff member of the PRO but is developing technology originating at a PRO (*e.g.* a technology licensed from the PRO).[1] Many PROs do not yet monitor the formation of spin-offs or start-ups, despite their political and potential economic importance. Response rates to this question were typically low (often up to 70% of the respondents did not know or did not answer the question).

Nevertheless, the number of spin-offs reported per PRO were in line with previous estimates of spin-off and start-up activity published by the OECD (OECD, 2001). Table 3.4 shows the total number of spin-offs and start-ups reported by the TTOs. In half of the reporting countries, the average number of new spin-offs or start-ups reported is under one a year. This includes all the TTOs reporting the creation of no firms of this type but not those that did not answer the question or did not know.

At the upper end of the spectrum, the United States reports that universities on average saw the creation of two start-ups in 2000, a figure which has remained stable since the end of the 1990s according to the Association of University Technology Managers (AUTM, 2002).

It would be highly desirable to be able to relate these average figures to PRO research expenditures or to staff FTEs. Also a correlation of the number of start-ups and spin-offs with a PRO's patenting would be an interesting indicator. A recent attempt was made to give a sense of the number of start-ups and the amount of licensing income generated by US universities as a percentage of their research expenditures. Australia's *National Survey of Research Commercialisation Year 2000* presented data for Australia, Canada and the United States on commercialisation activity (number of

US patents issued, number of licence agreements executed, amount of licence income and number of start-ups formed) relative to research expenditure and GDP.

Table 3.4. Number of spin-offs and start-ups per TTO reported in the last year

		Spin-offs		Start-ups		Total	
		Total	Per TTO	Total	Per TTO	Total	Avg. per TTO
Australia	UNIV	-	-	-	-	32	-
	PRO	-	-	-	-	15	
Belgium	All	11	1.83	4	0.67	15	1.25
Germany	PRO	28	1.12	9	0.36	37	0.74
Italy	Univ	14	0.50	13	0.46	27	0.48
	PRO	9	3.00	0	0.00	9	1.50
Japan	All	1	0.10	5	0.45	6	0.28
Korea	Univ	10	2.50	9	2.25	19	2.38
	PRO	30	3.00	7	0.70	37	1.85
Netherlands	Univ	23	1.77	4	0.36	27	1.07
	PRO	3	0.33	7	1.00	10	0.67
Norway	Univ	15	5.00	1	0.50	16	2.75
	PRO	24	1.71	27	1.59	51	1.65
Spain	All	8	0.67	3	0.30	11	0.48
Switzerland	Univ	39	1.77	17	1.06	56	2.33
	PRO	7	1.17	5	1.00	12	2.00
United States	Univ	-	-	390	2.00	-	2.00
Russia	All	8	1.33	7	1.75	15	1.54

Note: Belgium: Flanders only.

Notable points regarding TTO IP portfolios

Survey responses suggest that TTOs are involved in a broad range of IP activities. TTOs do far more than simply ensure the protection of patentable inventions. They are often involved in protecting and exploiting innovations in a number of technological fields. Given the small average size of TTOs, this finding is somewhat surprising. The geographical extent of their patenting activities is also impressive. Most survey respondents seem to have an international focus when it comes to the protection of patentable inventions.

Some responses need clarification. The relation between the stock of patents reported by TTOs and the flow of new patents granted seems skewed. While the number of patents granted is less than the total stock of patents under management, it seems large by comparison for most countries (except Switzerland). There are many possible explanations. TTOs may not have good records of stocks. Alternatively, PROs may prefer to sell the rights to their patents outright or, if no buyers are found, they may allow patents to lapse, so that the number of patents owned by a PRO is in fact quite small.

Clarification of this apparent anomaly would be useful in understanding PRO patenting and licensing strategies.

TTO licensing practices

Patents and other forms of intellectual property are an important means of transferring technology to third parties. The survey explored the licensing practices of TTOs by asking what technologies are licensed, to whom and with what sort of stipulations. To date, there has very little public information available about the licensing practices of PROs. The information collected in the survey thus represents a first attempt to provide international data on PRO licensing activities.

Policy makers' interest in PRO licensing stems from two competing concerns. On the one hand, the licensing of intellectual property creates commercial value. Policy makers would like to know how much income PROs can reasonably expect from the exploitation of their knowledge base. Many governments are providing infrastructure support or subsidies for the creation of TTOs in the hopes that they will eventually be financially autonomous and perhaps a source of extra revenue for the PRO. Data on licensing activities can help them understand what percentage of which technologies are likely to generate income and who will pay for the privilege of using the intellectual property. Licensing information is likely to be a better indicator of technology transfer activity than intellectual property rights alone.

On the other hand, policy makers are also interested in licences because the terms of the contract negotiated between a PRO and a third party can be constructed so as to achieve non-commercial goals. For example, clauses can be included to ensure that technologies are broadly disseminated or exploited domestically. Alternatively, it can be stipulated that PROs can continue using the intellectual property, thus safeguarding against fears that commercial ties will interfere with advances in research.

Licences granted by TTOs in the past year

TTOs were asked how many licences had been negotiated in the last year and what types of intellectual property were licensed. Licences can be granted for the use of patented technologies, for technologies with a patent pending, for unpatented technologies (*e.g.* biological materials or know-how) for which no formal form of protection has been or will be sought, for innovations covered by a *sui generis* form of protection, (*e.g.* plant varieties), or to creative works covered by copyright.

Countries appear to be divided into two broad categories. Two-thirds report that their PROs negotiate less than ten licences a year (Table 3.5). The other third report that PROs negotiate between 14.7 and 45.8 licences a year.

However, when asked to break down their licences by type of innovation or type of intellectual property involved, TTOs generally reported more licences negotiated than the total reported above. This disparity probably means that TTOs had difficulty answering the question as phrased or first focused on licences for patented technologies.

The breakdown of licences by type of intellectual property was surprising in several respects. Most interesting was the finding that patented inventions are not the most frequent object of licences. Korea was the only country where patented technologies topped the list of licences. In many countries, technologies for which patents are pending and non-patented innovations are more frequently the object of a licence. Licences for inventions with patent pending are especially significant, because they are an indicator that TTOs license early-stage technologies to firms that subsequently invest in their further development. The large percentage of licences for non-patented inventions in Italy, Japan, the Netherlands and Switzerland is interesting, as this runs counter to the axiom that licensees prefer to license "strong" forms of IP with guaranteed market exclusivity.

Table 3.5. Total and average number of licences negotiated by PROs last year

		Total no. of licences	Avg. per PRO	No. of responding PROs
Australia[1]	PRO	183	n.a.	n.a.
	Univ	234	7.1	33
Belgium (Flanders)	All	46	7.7	6
Germany	PRO	555	19.1	29
Italy	Univ	27	1.4	20
	PRO	9	2.3	4
Japan	All	89	5.9	15
Korea[2]	Univ	44	8.8	5
	PRO	203	20.3	10
Netherlands	Univ	250	14.7	17
	PRO	118	14.8	8
Norway	Univ	0	0.0	1
	PRO	22	1.4	15
Spain	All	125	7.8	16
Switzerland	Univ	200	9.5	21
	PRO	275	45.8	6
United States	Univ	4 049	24.1	168
Russia[3]	All	206	7.4	28

1. Australian university data from Australian Research Council (2002).
2. One PRO reported high numbers of licences anonymously. It was not included in the total.
3. Total number of respondents to the questionnaire was used; total respondents to this question not known.

Equally surprising was the number of countries for which copyright was an important category of licensed IP. Germany, the Netherlands, Norway, Spain, Switzerland and the Italian non-university PROs all reported that 25% or more of their licences involved copyright. In Norway, Spain, Russia and the Netherlands, the number of copyright licences far exceeded licences for patented, patent-pending and non-patented technologies. More information is certainly needed to understand which fields or activities are the object of copyright licences and why so few TTOs in most countries reported having been involved in copyright protection (Table 3.6). Finally, it appears that TTOs are rarely involved in licensing *sui generis* types of intellectual property, a finding which is consistent with the limited number of actions taken by TTOs to protect plant breeder's rights or industrial designs.

Exclusivity of licences on patented technologies

Licences are permissions granted by the owner of a piece of intellectual property to another party for the use of the invention or work. Licences can be granted on an exclusive basis, to a single licensee, thus guaranteeing a strong degree of market exclusivity. But licences can also be granted non-exclusively, to many parties, as is frequently the case for software. Finally, licences can be limited in some form or other, in order to create limited types of exclusivity. For example, licences can grant exclusivity for a limited time period (less than the life of a patent), exclusivity in a particular geographic territory or market (*e.g.* North America but not Europe), and exclusivity in a particular technological field or market type (*e.g.* animal but not human health).

Table 3.6. Total number and percentage of licences negotiated last year by type of IP protection

	Belgium (Flanders)		Germany		Italy				Japan		Korea			
	All		PRO		Univ		PRO		All		Univ		PRO	
	No.	%	No.	%	No.	%	No.	%	No.	%	No.	%	No.	%
Patented inventions	18	15.1	103	28.6	17	19.5	3	21.7	37	8.7	43	67.2	229	34.2
Patent pending	46	38.7	134	37.2	36	41.4	6	52.2	227	53.3	13	20.3	227	33.9
Non-patented	53	44.5	25	6.9	18	20.7	0	0.0	155	36.4	4	6.3	179	26.7
Copyrighted material	2	1.7	90	25.0	2	2.3	3	26.1	7	1.6	4	6.3	25	3.7
Industrial designs	0	0.0	2	0.6	0	0.0	0	0.0	0	0.0	0	0.0	10	1.5
Plant breeder's rights	0	0.0	6	1.7	0	0.0	0	0.0	0	0.0	0	0.0	0	0.0
Other	0	0.0	32	8.9	14	16.1	0	0.0	0	0.0	0	0.0	0	0.0
Total licences	119	100	360	100	87	100	12	100	426	100	64	100	670	100

	Netherlands				Norway		Spain		Switzerland				Russia	
	Univ		PRO		PRO		All		Univ		PRO		All	
	No.	%	No.	%	No.	%	No.	%	No.	%	No.	%	No.	%
Patented inventions	20	8.0	9	8.0	8	5.8	10	7.7	21	10.8	8	25.8	6	2.9
Patent pending	30	12.0	11	9.0	16	11.5	12	9.2	33	16.9	7	22.6	40	19.4
Non-patented	130	52.0	48	41.0	12	8.6	0	0.0	27	13.8	9	29.0	24	11.7
Copyrighted material	60	24.0	50	42.0	100	71.9	107	82.3	81	41.5	7	22.6	122	59.2
Industrial designs	0	0.0	0	0.0	3	2.2	0	0.0	9	4.6	0	0.0	14	6.8
Plant breeder's rights	3	1.0	0	0.0	0.0	0.0	1	0.8	1	0.5	0	0.0	0	0.0
Other	5	2.0	0	0.0	0.0	0.0	0	0.0	23	11.8	0	0.0	0	0.0
Total licences	250	100	118	100	139	100	130	100	195	100	31	100	206	100

Granting only limited exclusivity may help ensure that a technology is used more broadly than in the case of an exclusive licence to a single licensee. For this reason, some countries have tried to encourage their PROs to consider non-exclusive or limited exclusivity licences when granting access to publicly funded research results. However, a firm may require a exclusive licence in order to commit to the necessary further investments in commercialising a technology; this is often argued for spin-offs and start-ups whose future depends on the promise of a limited number of new technologies. Exclusive licences may also be granted if there is only one interested potential licensor.

Table 3.7 shows PROs that have granted at least one licence in the past year with the different types of exclusivity described above. In most cases, response rates to this question were above 50%, a sign that the question was relatively well understood. However, the extent to which PROs grant exclusive rather than non-exclusive licences varies widely from country to country. When asked whether TTOs had granted a fully exclusive licence in the past year, positive responses ranged from 11% to 80%. In other words, for some countries, exclusive licences are rarely granted, as in Japan and

Norway, while in others they are the quite common (Italian non-university PROs, the Netherlands, Japan and Belgium).

Table 3.7. Percentage of TTOs reporting concluding at least one licence agreement with various types of exclusivity

	Australia		Belgium		Germany		Italy				Japan	
	Univ	PRO	All		PRO		Univ		PRO		All	
	Yes	Yes	Yes	No	Yes	No	Yes	No	Yes	No	Yes	No
Fully exclusive	50	24	57	29	37	43	11	57	80	20	59	12
Time limited exclusivity	-	-	14	43	50	30	18	46	40	40	35	24
Geo. territory exclusivity	-	-	43	14	27	53	14	50	20	60	18	41
Field or mkt. exclusivity	-	-	29	29	37	40	4	61	20	60	12	41
Other exclusivity	-	-	14	43	13	63	4	61	0	60	12	41
Non-exclusive	50	76	57	14	63	17	21	50	20	60	35	24
Total respondents TTOs	-		7		30		28		5		17	

	Korea				Netherlands				Norway		Spain	
	Univ		PRO		Univ		PRO		PRO		All	
	Yes	No	Yes	No	Yes	No	Yes	No	Yes	No	Yes	No
Fully exclusive	50	13	26	42	64	-	50	-	12	40	28	39
Time limited exclusivity	50	13	21	37	91	-	33	-	12	28	28	28
Geo. territory exclusivity	38	13	21	37	64	-	33	-	8	32	22	33
Field or mkt. exclusivity	25	13	21	37	72	-	67	-	8	36	22	39
Other exclusivity	0	38	5	53	18	-	33	-	0	36	11	44
Non-exclusive	25	25	37	16	45	-	67	-	8	24	22	33
Total respondents TTOs	8		19		19		9		25		18	

	Switzerland				Russia	
	Univ		PRO		All	
	Yes	No	Yes	No	Yes	No
Fully exclusive	45	35	20	80	18	-
Time limited exclusivity	30	50	20	80	25	-
Geo. territory exclusivity	15	50	40	40	11	-
Field or mkt. exclusivity	45	45	60	40	4	-
Other exclusivity	15	45	0	60	42	-
Non-exclusive	40	30	80	0	-	-
Total respondents TTOs	20		5		28	

Note: Belgium: Flanders only. Totals of "yes" and "no" do not equal 100% owing to missing responses.

Nevertheless, PROs frequently limit the rights of their licensees in some way. All countries indicate that their PROs use time-limited, territory-limited, or market-/field-limited exclusivity to a certain extent. In Germany, the Netherlands and Norway, for example, these types of limited licences are relatively common, with over 50% of TTOs reporting their use in the past year. Most of the other countries report their use by one-third to one-quarter of their PROs.

The wide dissemination of technologies through non-exclusive licensing is reported as common practice by Australia, Germany, the Netherlands and by Swiss PROs. However, less than 50% of PROs in Italy, Japan, Korea, Spain and in Swiss universities report having issued any non-exclusive licences.

TTOs thus appear to vary across countries in the extent to which they limit the rights granted to licensees. The differences may have to do with the kinds of intellectual property being licensed, the fields of technologies involved or the type of licensee which typically contracts with PROs. Certainly, no best practice appears to have emerged about how to construct licensing agreements or how to balance the public good of broad diffusion of innovations with private desires for exclusive rights.

Licence requirements

In addition to limiting the exclusivity of licences, technology transfer activities can also be influenced by the inclusion of certain clauses in licensing agreements. TTOs were asked how frequently they negotiated licences with clauses to: *i)* encourage the use of publicly funded technologies; *ii)* ensure the broad diffusion of the research results; or *iii)* maximise their future IP revenue streams.

Requirements to work inventions are clauses which commit the licensee to make good faith efforts at commercialising a technology within a reasonable period of time. Requirements to work the invention can be territorially non-specific, allowing the IP owner to break the contract if the licensee fails to work the technology. In some cases, the licensee may be required to use the technology domestically. Such clauses usually have their origins in policies aimed at promoting national competitiveness.

Public research institutions may find that they are asked to delay publication of papers related to the invention that is being licensed to allow the licensee time to establish a market lead. While such clauses may have a sound commercial basis, many PROs find that publication delays run counter to their public research missions. As a result, some institutions make it a policy to avoid signing publication delay clauses, or limit permissible delays to three to six months.

Finally, some licence clauses attempt to secure future revenues from present technologies. For example, reach-through clauses make claims to royalties on future products developed with the aid of a licensed technology. Reach-through clauses are most common in the life sciences, and especially in the licensing of research tools which themselves may have low or no financial value but whose use could lead to profit-making diagnostics or therapies. In addition, research institutions may ask for the right of first refusal on licences to any patented products developed by a licensee. A right of first refusal is an option on the (potentially exclusive) use of a future product or process.

The survey asked PROs about the frequency with which they included such strategic clauses in their IP licences in order to get a sense of whether PROs use safeguards to protect their research missions or to maximise the broader economic impact of publicly funded IP. Table 3.8 gives the percentage of TTOs that indicated that all or some of their licences included such clauses. As with the previous question, not all countries were able to provide meaningful responses; the response rate was around 50%.

A large proportion of respondents indicated that they negotiated licences with stipulations to work the invention, to grant rights on future revenue or to give a first refusal option. A clause requiring the licensee to work the invention is most commonly included in contracts. Slightly fewer TTOs seem to specify that the invention should also be worked domestically. If one discounts the Australian data, which is derived from one PRO, Australia's Commonwealth Scientific and Industrial Research Organisation (CSIRO), no other licensing clause stands out as being particularly frequent.

There was a good deal of variation in responses concerning the inclusion of clauses on publication delays. At the low end of the spectrum, Norway and Russia report that only 4% of their PROs had negotiated such clauses. However, at the other end of the spectrum, the Netherlands and Belgium reported that 91% of universities and 71% of PROs limit permissible publication delays. PROs do not appear as yet to have a common policy approach on limiting publication delays.

Table 3.8. Percentage of TTOs for which some or all licences include various requirements

	Australia	Belgium	Germany	Italy		Japan	Korea	
		All	PROs	Univ	PROs	All	Univ	PROs
Require to work the invention	-	71	67	14	60	41	38	42
Require to work domestically	100	43	43	11	40	41	13	32
Right to delay publication	-	71	30	11	20	18	38	26
Reach-through clause	100	43	27	14	60	47	38	32
Right of first refusal	-	71	30	11	0	41	25	32

Note: Belgium: Flanders only.

Characteristics of the licensees

In some countries, policies to encourage the commercialisation of publicly funded technologies require universities and PROs to make efforts to license their technologies domestically, preferably to small companies, in order to encourage the formation of new firms. This question asked TTOs to report whether they had in the last year licensed a technology to a small firm, a large firm or another PRO. Response rates to this question were relatively low. Table 3.9 shows that in almost all countries, TTOs reported having more often negotiated licences with small than with large firms. Large firms are here defined as firms with more than 500 employees and small firms as those with fewer than 500. If one considers that large firms have far greater resources at their disposal to network with PROs, this is a somewhat surprising finding. In addition, the results show that licensing to other universities or public research bodies is rare.

Table 3.9. Percentage of TTOs that have licensed IP to small firms, large firms or another PRO

	Type of institution surveyed	Small firm	Large firm	University or PRO
Belgium	All	29	57	0
Germany	PRO	80	53	23
Italy	Univ	25	18	7
	PRO	80	20	20
Japan	All	41	59	0
Korea	Univ	50	13	0
	PRO	47	32	11
Norway	PRO	20	8	0
Spain	All	50	28	0
Switzerland	Univ	37	14	11
	PRO	56	22	22
United States	Univ	60	40	-

Note: Belgium: Flanders only.

PROs were also asked to report how many licences were negotiated with small firms, large firms and other PROs, and whether these licences were exclusive or not. The policy issue of interest here is whether small firms are more likely to require exclusive licences than large ones. An argument can be made that PROs should be able to negotiate exclusive licences. If not, governments run the risk of discouraging public-sector technology transfer to start-ups. The survey data on this issue is inconclusive. Small companies do not appear to obtain exclusive licences more frequently than larger firms.

However, this result may be skewed by the way company size was defined in the survey. Australia's National Survey of Research Commercialisation breaks down the percentage of university licences which are exclusive according to the size and age of the licensee. For start-ups, 86% of their university licences are exclusive, compared to 48% for small companies, 54% for medium-sized companies and 29% for large companies (Australian Research Council, 2002). The report concludes: "A significant proportion of licensing activity is focused on small companies. The very high proportion of exclusive licences executed to start-up companies suggests that the ability to grant exclusive licences is important to company start-up activity."

The survey asked whether licensees were domestic or foreign firms. While the data are incomplete, domestic licensees appear to be more common. However, there are exceptions. For example, Vock and Jola (2002) report that 80% of Swiss licences went to foreign firms, although the report from one university heavily influenced this result. Similarly, Table 3.10 shows that Dutch universities are slightly more likely to license abroad than at home. It would be important to take into account the size of the home market when analysing the propensity to license domestically versus abroad.

Table 3.10. Types of licences granted by Dutch PROs

	Universities	PROs	Total
1. Percentage of universities and PROs granting at least one licence to:			
Small firm with fewer than 500 employees	100	71	88
Large firm with more than 500 employees	80	57	71
University or public research organisation	20	14	18
2. Percentage of reported licences granted to:			
A small firm (< 500 employees)	46	61	51
A large firm (> 500 employees)	54	33	47
A university or other PRO	-	6	2
Total	100	100	100
3. Percentage of reported licences to licensees[2]			
In the Netherlands[3]	45	78	51
Outside the Netherlands[4]	55	22	49
Total	100	100	100

Infringement threats by and against PROs

The rise in patenting and licensing of PROs has caused some commentators to worry about a concomitant rise in litigation over the infringement of IPR. Indeed, the rights granted by IP can only be protected through litigation. This question asked PROs to indicate whether they had threatened to sue or actually sued a third party for infringement and whether the PRO had itself been threatened with an infringement suit. Table 3.11 shows that more than 25% of Belgian, Dutch and Russian PROs and more than 25% of Swiss non-university PROs report having sued a third party for infringement of IP in the last three years. The German, Belgian, Dutch, Russian and Swiss reports indicate that a little over 10% of their PROs have been sued for infringement. In almost all countries, the use of litigation by and against public research bodies remains unusual. It is slightly more common for PROs to sue infringers than for them to be sued. However, fears that IP activities would be legally costly have not yet appeared in countries that were able to respond to the litigation question.

Table 3.11. Percentage of PROs having sued or been sued for infringement of IP in the last three years

	Belgium	Germany		Italy	Japan	Korea	
	All	PRO	Univ	PRO	All	Univ	PRO
PRO sues unlicensed user	29	13	0	20	0	0	5
PRO is sued by third party	43	13	0	0	0	0	5

	Netherlands	Norway		Spain	Switzerland		Russia
	All	Univ	PRO	All	Univ	PRO	
PRO sues unlicensed user	36	0	4	0	0	33	25
PRO is sued by third party	11	0	0	0	11	11	11

Note: Belgium: Flanders only.

This latter observation may have to do with the "informal research exemption" which benefits PROs. In many countries, a research exemption allows non-commercial users of patented technologies to use the technology without a licence. The research exemption is sometimes "informal" in that even if a firm could prove infringement, suing a public research institution which generates no profits from the use of the patented technology would make very little business sense as no damages could be claimed. In many of the responding countries, litigation does not appear to have grown significantly with the patenting activity of PROs. The survey did ask whether PROs had experienced a notable change in litigation over the last three years, but few responded and the data are inconclusive.

Notable points regarding TTO licensing practices

Responses to the questions regarding licensing practices of TTOs confirm that, given the relatively small size of their IP portfolios, most TTOs negotiate few licences (often less than ten) a year. In most cases, the licences are for patented, patent-pending or non-patented inventions. Despite beliefs that firms prefer to license strong intellectual property rights, it would appear that early-stage technologies (patent pending) and know-how or materials (non-patented) are more frequently the object of licences than "stronger" patents. Moreover, those TTOs that have engaged in copyright management report negotiating many licences a year. Trends in some countries to give PROs ownership of certain types of copyrighted works developed by their faculty or staff could have an important impact on the number of licences TTOs negotiate. The role of TTOs in copyright protection and exploitation needs to be better understood.

Licensees are most likely to be small domestic firms, although large domestic firms do not trail far behind. PRO licensing to other PROs remains rare. PROs appear to be aware that the clauses they include in licences can accomplish non-commercial goals. For example, about half of the PROs include clauses which require the licensee to make good faith efforts to exploit the invention. The licences often include some form of limited exclusivity (*e.g.* by territory or field) so that the technology may be used in a non-rival manner by more than one firm. More rarely, PROs negotiate reach-through royalties or rights of first refusal on future inventions. However, there is a good deal of variation among countries as to how common such clauses are. It is not easy to identify good practices across countries.

Licensing revenues

Policy makers are greatly interested in revenues from publicly funded intellectual property rights. Because many OECD member countries have recently enacted reforms to encourage technology transfer and invested in TTO infrastructure, policy makers would like to know when these new TTOs will become self-sufficient. In addition, being able to anticipate the financial returns to a given IP portfolio would be very useful for both PROs and governments. At the moment, there is a belief among technology transfer professionals that licensing revenues are highly unpredictable because a small number of licences are responsible for most licensing revenues. When these patents expire or the licence ends, revenues can dip dramatically.

Better information on the percentage of IPR that results in licences and on the distribution of royalties and fees obtained from these licences should help policy makers understand why some PROs transfer technology more or less efficiently. Licensing information may eventually elucidate questions such as: *i)* Is a focus on encouraging patenting justified in the light of the licensing revenues from different sorts of IP?; and *ii)* How does licensing and spin-off formation compare in terms of returns to the PRO?

PROs were asked to report on their IP expenditures and licensing income. Many respondents had difficulty answering these questions. In particular, the costs associated with protecting and exploiting intellectual property are not well documented.

Percentage of active licences earning income in the last year

Not all patents are licensed, and not all licensed technologies earn income. Moreover, licences can generate income in different ways: some may ask for an up-front fee from the licensee, others for a percentage of royalties on sales, still others for a usage fee. Licences can also use some combination of these mechanisms.[2] PROs were therefore asked how many of their active licences actually earned income over the last year. Response rates for this question were above 50% in most countries, and the question was not perceived as being particularly difficult.

While there is a temptation to compare the number of licences negotiated in the last year (Table 3.5) with the number of licences earning income (Table 3.12), it is important to remember that licences may not immediately earn income, that their income-earning patterns may be erratic, and that licences that earn income probably do so over a number of years. Some countries have more licences that earn income than licences negotiated in a given year; others have negotiated more licences than they have income earning licences in the same year.

Table 3.12. Number of active licences earning income in the last year

	PRO type	Licences per TTO	
		Average	Median
Belgium	All	1.3	1
Germany	PROs	51.6	5
Italy	Univ	0.6	0
	PROs	14.4	5
Japan	All	21.6	3
Korea	Univ	5.5	4
	PROs	11.0	1
Netherlands	All	0.8	<5
Norway	Univ	0.0	0
	PROs	2.4	0
Spain	Univ	9.7	2
Switzerland	Univ	4.1	1
	PROs	5.3	5
United States	PROs	48.4	--

Note: Belgium: Flanders only.

Table 3.12 shows that, per TTO, there is a wide range in the average number of licences that earn income. In many countries, fewer than ten licences earn income. Germany, Japan and the United States reported a large number of income-earning licences per PRO in the last year. However, these high numbers are often skewed owing to one or two very active PROs with a great many licences. The median number of licences earning income at most TTOs is consistently quite low: often only one or no licences earn income in a given year. If one looks at the median number of income-earning licences, only German, Japanese and Spanish PROs, Italian non-university PROs and Korean universities report more than one income-earning licence per institution.

Figure 3.7 shows the distribution of the number of licences earning income at German PROs; 10% have no licences that earn income. About 50% reported that fewer than ten licences are income-earning. A large proportion (23%) did not answer the question.

Figure 3.7. Number of income-generating licences in German PROs

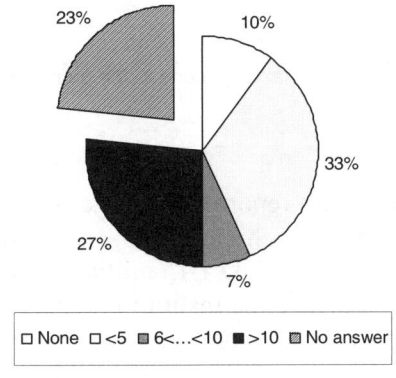

□ None □ <5 ▨ 6<...<10 ■ >10 ▨ No answer

With respect to gross income earned from intellectual property at a university or PRO in the last year, there is an enormous variation across countries and even across PROs within a country (Table 3.13). Gross income ranged from an average of a few thousand euros to a few million euros per institution.[3]

Table 3.13. PROs' gross income from intellectual property in the last year

	Belgium	Germany	Italy¹		Japan	Korea	
	All	PROs	Univ	PROs	All	Univ	PROs
	EUR	EUR	EUR		EUR	USD	
Gross income (000)	240	66 368	n.a.	n.a.	1 397	1 032	2 790
Income range (%)							
0	28.6	3.3	46.5	20.0	5.9	12.5	26.3
<50 K	0.0	30.0	-	-	11.8	12.5	15.8
50<…<100 K	0.0	6.7	14.3	40.0	11.8	0.0	0.0
100<…<500 K	14.3	13.3	10.7	40.0	29.4	12.5	5.3
>500 K	0.0	30.0	-	-	0.0	12.5	15.8
No answer	57.1	16.7	32.1	0.0	41.2	50.0	36.8
Avg. income/active licence (000)	80	55	-	-	139	47	25
Avg. income/TTO (000)	-	2 886	-	-	93	258	279

	Nether-lands²	Norway		Spain.	Switzerland		United States	Russia
	All	Univ	PROs	All	Univ	PROs	Univ	All
	EUR	EUR	EUR	EUR	USD	EUR	USD	EUR
Gross income (000)	11 400	2 000	7 700	961	2 800	2 850	1 297 452	1 375
Income range (%)								
0	18.0	11.1	28.0	22.2	22.9	11.1	n.a.	0.0
<50 K	-	0.0	0.0	38.9	-	-	n.a.	3.6
50<…<100 K	23.0	0.0	4.0	5.6	14.3	11.1	n.a.	0.0.
100<…<500 K	59.0	0.0	0.0	5.6	5.7	0.0	n.a.	0.0.
>500 K	-	11.1	28.0	5.6	5.7	22.2	n.a.	3.6
No answer	0.0	77.8	40.0	22.2	51.4	55.6	n.a.	92.9
Avg. income/active licence (000)	123	-	197	7	41	64	150	172
Avg. income/TTO (000)	760	-	428	69	165	713	7 723	688

Note: This table includes data only from institutions that responded to the question. Belgium: Flanders only.
1. Less than and up to EUR 92 000.
2. Less than and up to EUR 125 000.

The United States and Germany reported average gross licensing income of more than EUR 2 million per institution. Some very high earners skew the average. The mean income per university in the United States is closer to USD 1.15 million (EUR 1.24 million). Similarly, in Korea, which also reported high licensing income, one institution reported earnings of over EUR 240 million. If this institution is omitted – other responses indicate that it is very active in technology transfer – the average gross income for TTOs in the country remains high but is more in line with most of the other countries at EUR 232-258 million.

The proportion of public institutions earning no licensing income from intellectual property in any year tends to be rather high, in some countries as high as 60% of all reporting institutions. This may be due to the fact that a small number of PROs are big earners, or it may be due to the volatility of licensing income at any given PRO (so that licensing income an institution receives is not stable from year to year).

US university licensing income and research expenditures

Only a half dozen US universities to date manage to earn a significant percentage of their total research expenditures in licensing revenues. The high income earners – Dartmouth, Columbia, Florida State, and Brigham Young to name the most successful – generate 30% or more of their research budgets from IP. The vast majority of US universities, including Stanford and MIT, earn less than 10% of their research expenditures (which may run in the tens to hundreds of millions of USD) from IP commercialisation. Figure 3.8 shows the licensing income of US universities and the percentage of the research expenditure covered by this licensing income.

Figure 3.8. Licensing revenues and spin-offs at US universities, 2001

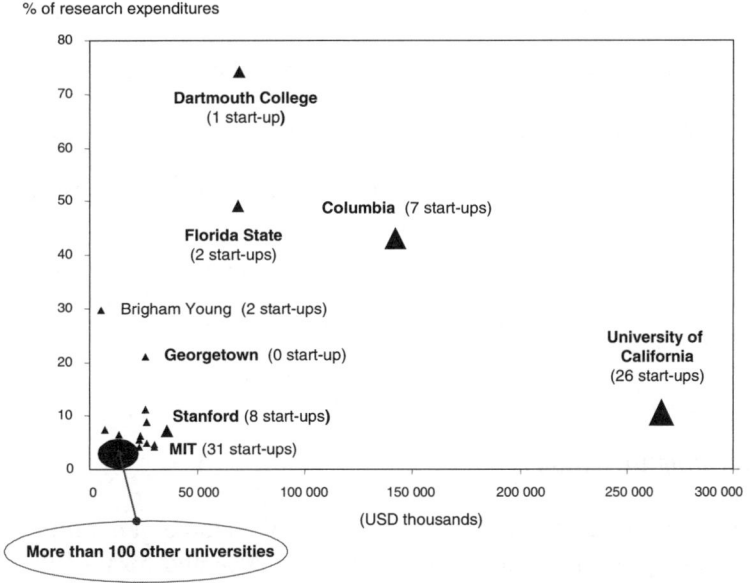

Source: OECD calculations based on data from AUTM (2002) and Chi Research, in *Technology Review University Research Scorecard* (2002).

These highly successful universities earn several million dollars in licensing income (the University of California system is an outlier but has ten campuses). The great majority of US universities earn far less. Nevertheless, even the most successful cannot rely on IP commercialisation to meet the bulk of their research budget needs. Licensing income, in all cases, is an extra benefit, not a replacement for the major public and private sources of R&D funding.

Percentage of patents licensed and earning income

Respondents were asked to identify how many patents in the total TTO portfolio are licensed and how many of these licences currently earn income. This information can give a measure of a TTO's successful commercialisation. Obviously, PROs prefer not to expend resources on patenting inventions that will not find buyers or licensees and therefore will not ultimately earn income for the public sector. However, the decision to patent is a gamble. No one knows with any certainty what proportion of patents can reasonably be expected to be licensed and earn income. A good measure of the productivity of commercialisation would be useful to both governments and TTOs in evaluating their performance.

Responses to this question were not high. In most cases, only 30% of TTOs responded. Table 3.14 shows that it is exceedingly rare for more than 50% of TTO patents to be licensed. Indeed, it would appear that somewhere between 20% and 40% of patents are licensed and only about half of these licences, or around 10% of the patent portfolio, earn income. There was a certain amount of variation across countries and types of PROs. This result needs to be confirmed through higher response rates and across more countries.

Table 3.14. Percentage of total patent portfolio ever licensed and earning income

	BEL	DEU	ITA		JPN	KOR		NLD		NOR	ESP	CHE	
	All	PRO	Univ	PRO	All	Univ	PRO	Univ	PRO	PRO	All	Univ	PRO
% ever licensed	7.3	31.4	>30.6	-	13.0	29.0	44.5	19.0	51.0	45.1	8.8	50.6	40.5
% currently earning income	4.7	21.5	>23.6	-	1.2	18.0	5.7	7.0	13.0	25.5	4.6	23.1	16.0
Total number of active patents (eligible responses)	343	5,038	n.a.	n.a.	682	283	209	277	247	102	692	-	-
Total number of active patents (stock reported above)	506	5 404	>n.a.	n.a.	682	404	8 987	394	597	114	781	914	270

Note: Belgium: Flanders only.

Highest income-generating inventions

Finally, to get an even better sense of the skewness of income-generating patents and licences, TTOs were asked how many of their patents accounted for 20% and 50% of their gross income from intellectual property. Reports from several sources indicate that a few inventions that earn high income often account for the majority of intellectual property income at public research institutions. For example, Australia's CSIRO reports that of 220 income-producing licences, six accounted for 55% of total gross income (AUD 11.62 million) and just over one-fifth of the licences accounted for 90% of the gross income (Australian Research Council, 2002).

Most PROs found it very difficult to identify the skewness of income-generating licences, and only a couple of countries were able to give meaningful responses. Even the Netherlands, which had one of the highest PRO response rates, only elicited answers from 50% of its population on this question. Table 3.15 shows answers from the Dutch survey as an example of the data that could be obtained. Half of the Dutch respondents claim that 20% of their gross IP income comes from two or fewer inventions. A quarter claim that just one invention accounts for 50% of their licence income.

This seems to confirm that income earned from licensed inventions is concentrated in a very small number of inventions, but is perhaps not as concentrated as the Australian data suggest.

Table 3.15. Share of Dutch licence income from x inventions: number of institutes reporting that x inventions account for 20% and 50% of licence income

	20% of licence income	50% of licence income
1 invention	31%	25%
2 invention	19%	6%
3 invention	-	13%
> 3 inventions	-	13%
Don't know/no answer	50%	44%
Total	100%	100%

It is quite likely that not only do a small number of licences account for a large part of a PRO's licensing income from IP, but also that a small number of PROs account for the majority of a country's total PRO licensing income.

Notable points regarding TTO IP income

There appears to be a great deal of variation among countries in terms of the average number of licences per PRO that earn income and in the gross income generated. The median number of licences per PRO that are active and income-earning, however, is relatively small in all countries, often between one and five. Differences in gross revenue, however, are large. At the extremes, the highest and lowest income-earning PROs can differ by a factor of 1 000. Of course, for such comparisons to be meaningful, the data should be corrected for the size and type of PROs involved in each country. However, it is probably safe to say that different TTOs in different countries have varying degrees of experience with technology transfer and that their objectives (*e.g.* income generation vs. local dissemination of knowledge) may account for such large disparities.

Policy makers would like to have a sense of the percentage of intellectual property rights likely to be licensed and earn income. While it is too early to model this, it would appear across all OECD countries that the percentage of active patents ever licensed is somewhere between 20% and 40% of the total, and that about half of these can be expected to earn income. Data on the concentration of income was not conclusive, but one or two countries seem to indicate that a relatively small number of licences earn a large proportion of the gross total licensing income at TTOs. There may be room for productivity improvement.

NOTES

1.   Both definitions are included because countries differ in their definition of spin-offs and start-ups.

2.   Other income from IP includes income from cashed-in equity and payments under options and termination payments.

3.   In this survey, gross income is not adjusted for licence income paid to other institutions. Licence income may therefore be double counted when income is reported for more than one institution. A better alternative would be to report "adjusted gross income".

NOTES ON THE METHODOLOGY OF THE OECD SURVEY OF PATENTING AND LICENSING ACTIVITY ON PROS

Methodology

In order to collect original data on the patenting and licensing practices of public research organisation (PROs), the OECD Focus Group developed and administered a questionnaire on the patenting and licensing activities of PROs (Annex 3). It asks PROs about the organisational structure of their TTOs, their intellectual property portfolio and their licensing practices and income. Participating countries included: Belgium, Canada, Denmark, Germany, Italy, Japan, Korea, the Netherlands, Norway, Spain, Switzerland, Russia and the United States.

Definition of PROs

PROs for this project were defined as including: *i)* all research-performing universities, both public and private; *ii)* research laboratories and agencies operated and fully funded by the government; *iii)* other research organisations that receive a significant share of their total funding from public sources.

Pilot test of questionnaire

In October 2001, the Netherlands ran a pilot of the OECD Questionnaire on the Patenting and Licensing Activities of Public Research Organisations. The questionnaire was finalised in November and sent to all members of the TIP Working Party. The Focus Group met an additional two times to discuss the implementation of the questionnaire, participation in case studies and preliminary results.

Administration of the questionnaire

Countries chose different approaches to administering the questionnaire. Not all countries surveyed asked their TTOs to respond to the questionnaire, nor did all countries cover both universities and non-university PROs. Korea, Italy, the Netherlands, Norway, and Spain surveyed all PROs.

Other countries surveyed a subset of PROs, *e.g.* only universities, as in Japan and Spain. Finally, for countries that have recently surveyed the IP activities of all or some of their PROs, a third option was to use available surveys to answer the questions in Part II of the questionnaire, as Australia and United States chose to do. Annex Table 1 presents the total population surveyed, the number of responses received and the number of valid responses.

Lessons from the survey

The experience of conducting the survey provided lessons on ways to improve it. For certain questions, for example, the response rate was very low or the responses were unreliable. These questions could be reformulated or dropped in future surveys. In several cases, experts suggested additional questions that might be included in the survey. If data on R&D expenditures are hard to obtain, for example, a question could be included about the number of full-time equivalents (FTEs) involved in research as a measure of a PRO's research intensity. The questionnaire was unable to normalise TTOs' responses according the size of the PRO as respondents were unable to identify the PRO's total research expenditures. This has complicated cross-country comparisons.

Cross-country comparisons of survey responses are limited for several other reasons. In some countries, experts warned that the PRO populations surveyed were not representative of all the country's PROs. In addition, comparisons would be more meaningful if PROs could be broken down by type – for example, only university-based PROs or only public laboratories. Moreover, it was noted that distinctions among PROs by technological or scientific specialisation probably have an important impact on technology transfer activities and any measures of productivity. Future work could try and draw these distinctions more clearly.

The data from the survey were not corrected to take account of the size or research intensity of the various responding PROs. To draw conclusions about a normal or desirable range of IP productivity, future studies will have to take into account research staff and/or research expenditures.

The survey could be expanded to discuss other forms of technology transfer from the public to the private sector. The questionnaire was very narrowly focused on formal mechanisms of technology transfer – patents, other IP instruments and licences. Other channels of technology transfer, as well as other intangible contributions that PROs make to the economy, are incompletely captured by the questions asked. Similarly, future surveys could attempt to capture better the effects of strategic IP behaviour by PROs on their public research and teaching missions. While this survey explored the safeguards included in licensing agreements that guard against potential problems, it did not try to quantify such impacts.

Most importantly, such surveys should be repeated on a regular basis. The responses here represent one year's data, which gives a static snapshot of IP activity at PROs. More interesting to policy makers is the evolution of patenting and licensing activities over time. Despite these caveats, it is hoped that the project results give member countries a more quantitative sense of the impact that patenting and licensing have on PROs themselves and the impact that their activities may have on the broader economy. The data would be much more useful if collected systematically over time whether by governments, associations of PROs or other institutions.

Annex Table 1. Population surveyed and response rates

	Year	Total population Univ.	Total population PROs[1]	Population surveyed Univ.	Population surveyed PROs[1]	Valid responses Univ.	Valid responses PROs[1]
Australia: National survey of research commercialisation	2000	-	-	39	46	34	36
Medical research institutes			-		25		15
Research divisions in CSIRO			-		21		21
Belgium (Flanders):Ministry of Flanders	2001	-	-	-	-	4	3
Germany: Federal Ministry of Education and Research	2001		96		36		30
Helmholtz Centre			15		14		14
Fraunhofer/Max-Planck Patentstelle			1		1		1
Garching Innovation			1		1		1
Leibniz institutes			79		20		14
BAM & PTB			-		-		2
Italy: CNR/University of Siena	2000-01	-	-	28	5	-	-
PRIs of the Ministry of Education and Research				n.a.[2]	3	-	-
Ministry of Health					1	-	-
Ministry of Industry		-	-		1	-	-
Japan: METI	2000-01	-	-	24		17	
Technology licensing office approved by the competent minister		-	-	23		16	
Independent administrative institute		-	-	1		1	
Korea	2001	-	-	18	46	8	19
Government research institutes			-		19		10
Engineering research centres			-		27		9
National research laboratories			-		305		
Netherlands: MERIT	2000-01	-	-	23	13	21 (19)	12 (9)
Norway: STEP	2001	30	-	16	48	9	25
Major Norwegian universities		4		4		-	
Colleges (formally linked to FORNY)		26		12		-	
Research laboratories			-		16		8
- Fully funded by the government			8		8		-
- Affiliated to public support structure (FORNY)			-		8		-
Institutes (significant public funding and research)			128		32		17
Spain: Ministry of Science and Technology	2000-01	-		-		18	
Switzerland: CEST	2001	19	28	60	28	35	9
Federal institutes of technology		2		2		-	
Cantonal universities		10		10		-	
Universities of applied sciences		7		48		-	
Federal Research laboratories			4		4		-
Federally supported PROs			23		23		-
Federally supported international organisation			1		1		-
United States: AUTM/Dept. of Commerce	FY 2000	-	-	168	10	168	10
Russia: Transtechnology Ltd.	2001	-		60		28	

1. PROs = non-university PROs.
2. The Italian Conference of University Deans indicated that the population was 36.4% of all R&D-intensive institutes.

GLOSSARY OF TERMS

Conflicts of interest

A situation in which a public obligation competes with a private interest. For example, at a PRO, research may compete with financial interests. Some institutions and governments have issued guidelines to prevent or limit an employee's conflicts of interest with his/her involvement in commercial activities, such as collaborative research with or licensing to an industrial partner. Conflicts of interest can exist for an organisation as well as for an individual.

Last year (calendar or fiscal)

The questionnaire asked TTOs to report on quantitative data such as the number of patents, licences, and research expenditures in the "last year". Respondents were asked to chose either the most recent fiscal or calendar year for which they had full records. All responses are then for the chosen definition and year. Most countries chose 2001 or 2000 as the "last year".

Public research organisations (PROs)

PROs include:

- All research-performing universities, both public and private.

- Research laboratories and agencies operated and fully funded by the government.

- Other research organisations that receive a significant share of their total funding from public sources.

Reach-through rights

The claim in a licence that the licensor's intellectual property rights extend to any downstream products or inventions a licensee generates based on the licensed technology.

Requirements to work an invention

Some licences include a requirement that the licensee make good faith efforts to use or exploit ("work") the licensed technology and can include milestones to ascertain whether progress is being made.

Research funding

When PROs are asked to identify the total research expenditures of their institution, they are asked to include in their calculation core or institutional funding provided on a steady annual basis by public sources for research activities; sponsored research in the form of grants or awards from the government (regional, national or supranational) to pursue specific (often ongoing) research projects; and contract research for which one party (either a public or private entity) pays a PRO to undertake a specific task or research activity and the agreement outlining the work to be done takes the form of a contract.

Right of first refusal

The right of first refusal is a clause in a contract which declares that party A has the right to review any inventions that party B generates (within the boundaries delimited by the contract) in order to determine whether it would like to claim ownership of the invention or be granted an exclusive licence. If party A does not exercise its right, party B is free to protect and exploit the invention as it sees fit.

Spin-offs and start-ups

Spin-offs are firms established by staff from a PRO to develop or commercialise an invention. Start-ups are new firms established specifically to develop or commercialise an invention licensed from a public research organisation, but without staff participation from that PRO.

Technically unique inventions

Several questions asked about patent applications and grants for technically unique inventions. This means that multiple applications or grants for the same invention in different jurisdictions should be counted as just one application or grant. For example, five patents for the same invention in five patent jurisdictions would be counted as one technically unique patent.

Technology transfer offices

Technology transfer or technology licensing offices are those organisations or parts of an organisation which help the staff at public research organisations to identify and manage the organisation's intellectual assets, including protecting intellectual property and transferring or licensing rights to other parties to enhance prospects for further development. A PRO may have a single centralised TTO, it may have several TTOs associated with it (*e.g.* for different schools or departments), or it may outsource to an external TTO which has several client organisations.

For the questionnaire, the units engaged in the management of technology transfer are referred to as technology transfer "offices". The groups at a PRO for which the technology transfer office manages intellectual property are referred to collectively as the TTO's "institution".

OECD QUESTIONNAIRE ON THE PATENTING AND LICENSING ACTIVITIES OF PUBLIC RESEARCH ORGANISATIONS

I. GENERAL QUESTIONS

> **NOTE**: *A PRO is a publicly funded research organisation. PROs include: i) all research-performing universities, both public and private; ii) research laboratories and agencies operated and fully funded by the government; iii) other research organisations that receive a significant share of their total funding from public sources (for example, research institutes or teaching hospitals).*

1.   Which of the following best describes your workplace:

A dedicated technology transfer or licensing office within a PRO   ☐

A division of a PRO that is not dedicated to technology transfer as its main mission   ☐

An external firm or organisation that provides technology transfer services to a PRO   ☐

Other (please describe_____)   ☐

A.   In what year was your office established? _____   Don't know ☐

> **NOTE**: *Your workplace is hereafter referred to as your "office".*

2.   Is your office engaged in technology transfer or intellectual property management for any of the following? *Please check all that apply.*

Public university   ☐

Private university   ☐

Research or teaching hospital   ☐

Publicly-funded research institution (government laboratory)   ☐

Research park or incubator affiliated with a university or public research institute   ☐

Other (please describe_____)   ☐

A.   Does your office manage intellectual property for *more than one* university or public research organisation?

No ☐   Yes ☐

> **NOTE**: *Any of the above organisations for which you manage intellectual property are hereafter referred to as your "institution".*

3.   Is your office involved in any of the following activities? *Please check all that apply.*

Assessing the patentability of inventions ☐

Applying for patents (or arranging for an outside expert to apply) ☐

Arranging licences for inventions developed by your institution ☐

Obtaining licences for researchers within your institution (licensing-in) ☐

Negotiating research agreements between your institution and firms ☐

A.   How many employees (full-time equivalents) currently work at your office on any of these activities?

_____

NOTE: *If you checked none of the options in questions 2 and 3, please proceed to the comments on the last page. Otherwise, proceed to question 4.*

---

4.   What percentage of your institution's intellectual property is managed by your office?

☐ 100%   ☐ Over 75% but less than 100%   ☐ 25% to 75%   ☐ Less than 25%

A.   If less than 100%, who else manages your institutions intellectual property?

_____

5.   What is your institution's policy on the ownership of intellectual property rights?

Check all that apply if ownership can vary.

Ownership held by:

Your institution ☐

Researcher or inventor at your institution ☐

Organisation or firm that funded the research ☐

The government ☐

Varies by type of contract with the research funder ☐

No formal policy ☐

Don't know ☐

6.   Do the intellectual property or licences generated by individual researchers influence their recruitment, career advancement, bonuses, or salary? *Please check all that apply.*

	Recruitment	Tenure/career advancement	Salary/bonus	No influence	Don't know
Intellectual property	☐	☐	☐	☐	☐
Licences	☐	☐	☐	☐	☐

7. **Most of the following questions ask about patents, licences and spending in the last year. Please choose either the most recent fiscal or calendar year for which you have full records. Please give all responses for your chosen definition and year.**

Most recent fiscal year ☐ Starting: _____Day _____Month

Most recent calendar year ☐ Which year? _____

Also, please answer the following questions only for intellectual property and licences handled by your office. If you manage intellectual property for both universities or public research organisations AND for private firms, answer all questions ONLY for universities or public research organisations.

---

8. **Has your office used any of the following methods to find licensees for your institution's technology in the last year?**

	Not used	If used, how successful was it for finding licensees?		
		Low	Mid	High
Advertising in magazines, journals or on the Internet	☐	☐	☐	☐
Informal contacts of your researchers or inventors	☐	☐	☐	☐
Informal contacts of your office	☐	☐	☐	☐
Technology brokers or consulting services	☐	☐	☐	☐
Electronic marketplaces and auctions*	☐	☐	☐	☐
Other (_____)	☐	☐	☐	☐

For example, Internet forums where IP and technology from multiple sources can be bought and sold.

9. **In the last year, what were your organisation's total expenditures on research and development (include core and institutional funding, grants and contracts)? On 1 January 2001, EUR 1 = USD 0.94.**

Less than EUR 5 million ☐ EUR 5-50 million ☐
EUR 50-100 million ☐ >EUR 100 million ☐
Don't know ☐

A. **Approximately what percentage of this research and development spending was funded by private firms, for example for contract research?**

_____% **Don't know** ☐

10. **In the last year, approximately how much did your office spend on the following intellectual property (IP) activities for your institution?**

IP management (patent application & renewal fees, etc.)	_____	Don't know ☐
Licensing and other costs to transfer technology from your institution to other organisations or firms	_____	Don't know ☐
Licence fees and other acquisition costs for technology used by your institution (licensing in)	_____	Don't know ☐

II. YOUR INTELLECTUAL PROPERTY PORTFOLIO

> *Several questions ask about **technically unique** patent applications or grants. For example, count five patents for the same invention in five jurisdictions as **one technically unique patent**. In other words, do not count multiple applications or grants for the same invention in different jurisdictions as more than one application or grant.*

11. **What is the total number of currently active, technically unique patents in your institution's patent portfolio?**

_____

A. **How many technically unique patents were granted to your institution in the last year?**

_____

B. **Were any of these patents granted in the following jurisdictions?**

Count patents on the same invention made in different jurisdictions.

Your country	Yes ☐	No ☐
European Patent Office/other European patent office	Yes ☐	No ☐
United States Patent and Trademark Office	Yes ☐	No ☐
Japan Patent Office	Yes ☐	No ☐
Other (which country:_____)	Yes ☐	No ☐

12. **How many technically unique patents did your office apply for in the last year?**

_____

A. **How many of these patent applications were in the following fields?**

Health, pharmaceuticals, medical (including relevant biotechnology)	_____
Food, agro-industry, (including relevant agro-biotechnology)	_____
Information technology, electronics, instruments	_____
Production technology, new materials	_____
Energy, environment, transportation	_____
Other _____	_____
Don't know ☐	

13. **Patents are only one type of intellectual property (IP). In the last year, how many of the following IP actions were undertaken by your office on behalf of your institution?**

	Number	Check if this is only a rough estimate
Invention disclosures	_____	☐
Copyright registration for computer software or databases	_____	☐
Copyright registration for educational materials	_____	☐
Copyright registration for multimedia	_____	☐
Industrial design registration	_____	☐
Plant breeder's rights applications	_____	☐
Execution of non-disclosure or confidentiality agreements	_____	☐
Other _____	_____	☐

14. **How many spin-offs and start-ups were established last year specifically to develop your institution's intellectual property (IP)?**

Spin-offs: a new firm founded by staff from your institution to develop or commercialise an invention.

_____ Don't know ☐

Start-ups: a new firm to develop or commercialise an invention developed by your institution, but *not* founded by staff from your institution

_____ Don't know ☐

III: LICENSING PRACTICES

15. **How many licences were granted last year for the following types of intellectual property owned by your institution? Count *all* licences granted. Enter 0 if necessary.**

		Check if this is only a rough estimate
Total number of licences granted	_____	☐
Patented inventions (patent granted)	_____	☐
Patent-pending inventions (in application phase)	_____	☐
Non-patented inventions (no application planned)	_____	☐
Copyrighted materials	_____	☐
Industrial designs	_____	☐
Plant breeder's rights	_____	☐
Other	_____	☐

_____

16. Did any of your licence agreements last year provide the following types of exclusivity? Please check all that apply.

	No	Yes
Fully exclusive for the lifetime of the patent (single licensee)	☐	☐
Exclusivity limited to a specified number of years	☐	☐
Exclusivity limited to a specific territory	☐	☐
Exclusivity limited to a specific field or market type	☐	☐
Other type of exclusivity	☐	☐
Non-exclusive (your firm may license to other firms or organisations)	☐	☐

17. In the last year, did your institution give a licence to:

	No	Yes	If yes: How many licences were granted?	How many of these licences were *non-exclusive*?
A small firm with fewer than 500 employees	☐	☐	_____	_____
A large firm with more than 500 employees	☐	☐	_____	_____
A university or public research organisation	☐	☐	_____	_____

A. How many licences were given to parties located:

Domestically (includes non-national firms located in [your country])	_____
Abroad (include subsidiaries of domestic firms in other countries)	_____

18. Approximately how many of your institution's active licence agreements include:

	All	Some	None	Don't know
Requirement to work the invention	☐	☐	☐	☐
Requirement to work the invention in [your country]	☐	☐	☐	☐
Right for licensee to delay publication of papers	☐	☐	☐	☐
Reach-through clauses for your institution[1]	☐	☐	☐	☐
Licensor (owner) has right of first refusal for future inventions by the licensee institution	☐	☐	☐	☐

1: Your institution's intellectual property rights extend to products or further inventions based on the licensed invention.

19. **In the last three years, has your institution:**   **No**   **Yes**

	No	Yes
Threatened or brought an infringement suit against an unlicensed user?	☐	☐
Been threatened with an infringement suit?	☐	☐

If yes to the latter, has the number of threatened infringement suits against your institution changed between 1998 and the last year?

Increased by _____%   No notable change ☐   Declined by _____%

IV: LICENCE INCOME

20. **In the last year, how many of your institution's active licences for its intellectual property earned income? (exclude trademarks)**

_____

21. **What was your institution's gross income last year from its intellectual property? (exclude trademarks)**

_____ **(domestic currency)**

> *Do not deduct IPR management costs. Include income from licence fees (licence issue fees, annual payments, termination payments, end-user fees); running royalties from product sales; cashed-in equity, etc.*

A. **How was this gross income distributed among the following:**

Your office (cover costs, etc.)   _____%

The inventor   _____%

The research group or department where the inventor works   _____%

The central administration of your organisation   _____%

Other (please explain): _____   _____%

                                                             100%

22. **In question 11 above you gave the total number of technically unique patents in your current patent portfolio. How many of these have ever been licensed?**

_____

A.   How many of these patents are currently earning licence income?

_____

23.   Most licence income is generated by a small number of "inventions" which can be protected by patents, copyright, know-how, etc. Starting with your most profitable inventions, how many accounted for 20% and 50% of your gross income from intellectual property in the last year?

> NOTE: **Excludes** *trademarks. If the same number of inventions account for both your top 20% and 50% of income, please enter the same number in each line.*

> *Number of inventions responsible*
>
> Top 20% of income   _____
>
> Top 50% of income   _____
>
> Don't know   ☐

V: COMMENTS

Do you have any comments?

_____

_____

_____

_____

_____

_____

_____

_____

REFERENCES

Arundel, A. and C. Bordoy. (2002), "Patenting and Licensing by Dutch Public Research Organisations", final report submitted to the OECD Focus Group on IPRs and Innovation, May.

Australian Research Council (2002), *National Survey of Research Commercialisation Year 2000*, Australian Research Council, Canberra.

AUTM (Association of University Technology Managers) (2002), *Annual Licensing Survey FY 2000*, AUTM, Northbrook, Illinois.

Bekkers, R. and B. Sampat (2003), "Rapporteurs' Summary Report", commissioned by the OECD for the Joint OECD-Netherlands Expert Workshop on the Strategic Use of IPRs by Public Research Organisations. Available at: www.oecd.org/pdf/M00037000/M00037899.pdf

European Commission (EC) (2003), "Study to Evaluate the Efficiency and Coherence of IPR Rules Applicable to Publicly Funded Research", forthcoming, Brussels.

Gering, T., U. Schmoch and O. Werner (2002), "Case Study on Intellectual Asset Management in German PROs and IP in the German Biotechnology Sector", unpublished draft to the OECD Focus Group on Innovation and IPRs, OECD, Paris.

Gu, W. and L. Whewell (1999), *University Research and the Commercialization of Intellectual Property in Canada*, report prepared for the Expert Panel on the Commercialization of University Research of the Advisory Council on Science and Technology, Industry Canada, Ottawa.

Kneller, R. (2001), "Technology Transfer: A Review for Biomedical Researchers", *Clinical Cancer Research*, Vol. 7, pp. 761-774.

Lita, S. (2001), "Debunking the Bayh-Dole Myth: Forgotten Contributors to the Rise of Academic Capitalism", The Elliott School of International Affairs, The George Washington University. 5 December.

Mowery D. and Sampat, B. (2001), University *Patents and Patent Policy Debates in the USA, 1925-1980*, Oxford University Press, London and New York..

Nelsen, L. (1998), "The Rise of Intellectual Property Protection in the American University", *Science*, Vol. 270, No. 5356, pp. 1460-1461.

OECD (2001), "Fostering High Tech Spin-offs: A Public Strategy for Innovation", *STI Review No. 26*, OECD, Paris.

OECD (2002), "Interim Results of the TIP Project on the Strategic Use of IPRs at PROs", internal working document, June.

Pammoli, F. and F. Donadio (2002), "Italian Report on the Implementation of the OECD Survey on Patenting and Licensing Activity", unpublished report to the OECD.

Thursby J., R. Jensen and M. Thursby (2001), "Objectives, Characteristics and Outcomes of University Licensing: A Survey of Major U.S. Universities", *The Journal of Technology Transfer*, Vol. 26 (1-2), pp. 59-72.

Vock, P. et C. Jola (2002), "Patent- und Lizenzaktivitäten 2001. Umfrage bei Hochschulen und anderen öffentlich unterstützten Forschungsorganisationen", Centre for Science and Technology Studies (CEST), Bern.

PART II

CASE STUDIES

Part II contains a series of case studies on various aspects of the protection of intellectual property in a number of member countries.

INTRODUCTION

This section provides a summary of the country case studies and presents the main policy lessons.

Chapter 4

INTRODUCTION AND OVERVIEW

by

Pim den Hertog, Dialogic, Netherlands
Thomas Gering, Ventratec, Germany
Mario Cervantes, OECD Directorate for Science, Technology and Industry

Introduction

The romantic idea of innovation as the result of the creative efforts of an isolated, individual inventor who successfully puts a new product or process on the market is a thing of the past. Innovation is now generally accepted as the result of the work of various actors – public research organisations (PROs), firms, intermediary institutions, etc. – that jointly, and quite often in competition, interact, not only to create new knowledge but also to diffuse this knowledge and translate it into competitive goods, services and processes. In this so-called systemic notion of innovation, industry-science relations (ISRs) and the management of knowledge transfer between them are generally perceived as being at the heart of an innovation system.

Intellectual property rights as a key framework condition for innovation

Further, it is increasingly acknowledged that, aside from policies aimed more directly at encouraging innovation and better links between industry and science, it is essential to provide the appropriate framework conditions. These may include more tangible factors, such as the availability and quality of the financial infrastructure, the communications infrastructure, standards setting and normalisation, as well as intangibles such as an entrepreneurial culture, innovation governance structures or trust in the political-economic system. In this context, intellectual property rights (IPR) play an important role. In most OECD countries, there is a greater awareness and quite often a "rethinking" of IP management issues, by both industry and PROs. As a result, there is a trend towards more active management of intellectual property (IP), or intellectual asset management (IAM), and a greater institutionalisation of such practices. At PROs this is reflected, for example, in the activities of dedicated technology transfer offices (TTOs) and their personnel.

Case studies provide the story behind the figures

Many OECD countries have enacted, or are considering, policy changes regarding the ownership, management and exploitation of IP arising from publicly funded research. Many PROs are actively reformulating their IP strategies. The OECD surveys of IP policy and of TTO personnel have mapped, for the first time and for a number of OECD countries, the state of affairs regarding IP policies and practices in general and publicly financed research performed by PROs in particular.[1]

The 12 case studies from 11 countries included in this volume provide the "policy stories behind the figures". They aim at increasing insight into how PROs shape IPR strategies and how policy makers steer and facilitate this process. The case studies make it possible to understand better the differences in approaches to managing IP at PROs through their discussions of:

- The variety of institutional structures and the related variety of approaches to IP management.

- The policy mixes used, which are partly the result of how IP rights were ensured in the past.

- Specific changes in IP policies and the kinds of trade-offs that took place during the policy process.

- Practical difficulties for implementing new policies: the establishment of new TTO structures, working with new kinds of standard contracts, changing the attitudes of individual researchers.

Some of the case studies delve into more specific topics, such as:

- How PROs deal with IP in pioneering fields such as biotechnology or biomedical technology.

- How IP management is shaped in individual PROs.

- How IP policies are developing in an economy in transition.

- The role spin-off companies based on IP play among the various channels for commercialising public research results.

- How incentive structures for individual researchers are evolving.

This introductory chapter presents, largely on the basis of the case studies included in this volume,[2] salient points and observations regarding PROs' IP strategies and some of the policy lessons learned. It then briefly outlines the contents of this volume before drawing attention to some remaining challenges and unanswered questions. One clear conclusion from the many case studies is the tremendous scope for mutual learning. However, as the case studies also illustrate, institutional structures, the size of research funding, the research culture and history, the extent of ISRs and technological specialisation are all very country-specific. Therefore, importing policy solutions without a critical assessment and adaptation to the national context is most likely to lead to sub-optimal policy outcomes.

Development of IPR strategies in PROs

Technology transfer has been a buzzword for many years, and the question of how to organise it between public and private institutions has greatly interested policy makers, scientists and industrialists over the past two decades.

In recent years, policy makers have become more interested in IP issues and the IP policies of PROs, particularly in light of the increase in US academic patenting that followed the 1980 Bayh-Dole Act in the United States. Universities and other PROs in OECD countries and elsewhere are increasingly under pressure from governments to improve their performance in the area of IP management and exploitation. In addition to many other activities, TTOs or departments are now called upon by heads of universities and public research labs to find ways to generate income and to market academic inventions.

The case studies presented in this volume highlight some of the main issues and lessons regarding the development of IPR strategies at PROs which can be of use to policy makers in science and technology as well as to technology transfer professionals.

Lesson 1: A PRO's institutional background affects its approach to IP management and commercialisation

The technology sector in which a PRO carries out its research activities as well as its focus on applied or basic research affects its opportunities with regard to IP management and licensing.

In some technology sectors, such as biotechnology, applied and basic research can no longer be distinguished as they were in the past. Under certain circumstances, basic research results can be applied directly in the value chain. In such technology sectors, IP and its exploitation can be an excellent technology transfer mechanism, creating significant added value for the industrial application and potentially providing a monetary return to the originating PRO.

The case studies make clear the diversity of the various categories of PROs in terms of their mission, institutional structure and management. Universities, fundamental research organisations, government labs and contract research organisations that are publicly financed in part play different roles in innovation systems, generate different types of knowledge for different clients and therefore require different IP management processes. A contract research organisation may choose to use its background IP to attract new contract research and develop jointly with industry new foreground IP, on a one-to-one basis or in programmes in which various partners participate (*e.g.* IMEC's Industrial Affiliates Programme). Its IP management will differ markedly from that of a basic research organisation, such as Germany's Max Planck Society. A university with research groups in different technological fields and a different type of staff (including students) will need yet another IP management strategy. PROs that mainly undertake applied collaborative research find themselves under particular strain, as their work is very likely to result in joint inventions with contributions provided both by the PRO and the collaborating company or companies. As ownership and user rights to the IPR need to be allocated or shared, opportunities for licensing to third parties can be a complex and difficult exercise.

Therefore, a "one size fits all approach" to IP management in PROs is unlikely to work. Moreover, IP management comes at a cost and cost considerations play a role. For all these reasons, various models of IP management and organisation of TTOs co-exist.

Lesson 2: Intellectual asset management involves more than PRO inventions; it needs to address valuation mechanisms and appropriate exploitation mechanisms

Discussions of a more active approach by PROs to IPR and its commercial exploitation are often driven by an understanding that PROs need to improve the legal protection of their inventions and seek to commercialise it more actively by using this legal protection. However, IAM is an integral process which needs to be implemented institution-wide. It should not focus on inventions alone but on any IP generated by scientists and researchers in the course of their work at the PRO.

Scientist and researchers are often unaware that their results are patentable. However, patent legislation does not view academic inventions in the same way as scientific peer review. A slight improvement over research findings can still make a striking patent.

Such issues need to be addressed across the board in an internal IAM process which focuses not only on patentable inventions but also tries to identify the commercial value in any PRO product. Only after this is done can a decision be taken as to the appropriate exploitation mechanisms. These include straightforward licensing of the IP, use of the IP in collaborative research projects with industry, setting up a spin-off company for the commercial exploitation of the results. Confidential non-patented results (such as software source code) can be an important exploitation route. Moreover, it should be recalled that in addition to patents, other forms of IP such as copyright (for software) can also provide opportunities for licensing and technology transfer in general.

Lesson 3: Collaborative research requires a particular intellectual asset management strategy

A balance has to be found between generating income from collaborative contract research and reserving certain intellectual assets which the PRO may want to license or use as a basis for start-up companies. Most companies require exclusive paid-up access rights to results obtained in the framework of collaborative projects. PROs need to be cautious when deciding whether or not to accept such contractual conditions because these ultimately determine whether or not the PRO is likely or able to license to a third party. For start-up companies, such contractual conditions can be detrimental as investors are generally reticent when IP portfolios are not definitely free from access rights of third parties.

The Belgian case study provides some insight into the experience of a large PRO operating in the field of information and communication technologies (ICT). It indicates that PROs should not avoid collaborative research results and joint IP rights, but that they must allocate applications and designate field-of-use rights early in the process in order to optimise the technology transfer process.

Lesson 4: Creating revenue is not the main motive

The case studies make it abundantly clear that royalty income is everywhere limited when compared with investment in research. Even in very experienced institutions with a significant track record, royalty revenues exceeding 5% of the investment in research are the exception rather than the rule. However, it is significant that this revenue is not associated with specific work commissioned to the PRO, so that the PRO is free to decide about its use. Most PROs use such funds to develop their technology transfer support mechanisms in order to help make them more self-sufficient.

The main objective of PROs in becoming more active in the field of IPR and licensing is the desire to make their findings of use to society. IPR gives industry an incentive to obtain research results which can only benefit society once they reach the market.

The US example clearly demonstrates this, as institutions' royalty income is significant (approaching USD 1 billion in 2001). What is more important is the fact that their IPR and licensing activities are becoming a significant factor in the US economy, with turnover for licensed products of almost USD 100 billion and an estimated 300 000 jobs secured or newly created in industry (AUTM, 2002).

Lesson 5: IAM requires a long-term, broad commitment from PRO management; an IAM programme will require considerable investment and it may be some time before it breaks even

PROs need to understand that IAM requires a change in management practices that will affect the entire institution on all levels as well as a long-term commitment. On average, TTOs active in IAM need more than seven years to break even. Many inventions need to be processed and many patent application prosecuted, but only a percentage will be commercially exploited and only a minor percentage will create very high revenue. In addition to changing their management practices and structures, PROs need to allocate the necessary personnel to cope with the challenges of making the new structures work effectively.

Lesson 6: Some non-patented IP may be commercially useful

To create a technology transfer opportunity, not everything needs to be or even can be patented (for legal reasons). Software is the best example. Most software is not patentable but the confidential source code may create an excellent business opportunity. In most cases, keeping the source code confidential would not create concern in scientific circles because a scientific publication may simply include an example of the benefits obtained from using the finding. However, to market the finding, the PRO's results have to be configured in a way that an end-user will accept as useful. Most PRO results of this type are not so configured because they are created by individual researchers who need to solve specific problems in a laboratory environment; the needs of potential end-users are rarely taken into account. In other words, these unprotected results need to be developed to the point where end-users consider such products over alternative solutions offered on the market.

Lesson 7: A start-up development strategy needs to be rooted in the PRO's IAM model

In recent years, job creation has been a focus of political discussions in many countries. The examples of PROs in English-speaking countries and some institutions in the Benelux countries and Scandinavia have motivated the political level to demand that PROs actively develop business activities and increase the propensity to generate technology-based start-ups.

Policy makers need to understand that the creation of a start-up or spin-off is only one of the exploitation mechanisms at a PRO's disposal for obtaining maximum benefits from its research results. Not all research results are a potential basis for a successful start-up, and spin-offs are not the only way to support entrepreneurship at PROs. In most cases, PROs – for commercial or legal reasons – will have to consider more traditional technology transfer routes, like co-operative research or licensing, to moderate the potential risks. Many technology exploitation projects would be too risky or require too big an investment Start-ups can also create potential conflicts: the Korean case study shows that PRO scientists were too actively engaged in spin-off activities at the expense of their regular duties.

However, industry will sometimes hesitate to take on technological opportunities offered by the PRO owing to the high degree of uncertainty involved in developing an invention. If the process of IAM at the PRO is sufficiently attentive to reserving exclusive rights to IP positions which may be valuable in the context of a start-up, it may be possible to achieve the optimal mix between more traditional exploitation activities and start-ups.

The Dutch case study provides valuable insight into these management issues. The management of a technology transfer programme geared towards exploiting IP through a start-up requires a mature programme which possesses not only sufficient IP and legal know-how but also the other disciplines needed to develop an entrepreneurial concern.

Lesson 8: The need for professionalism in IAM and the consequences for hiring professionals

The political level needs to understand that IAM is a professional activity and that the motives of IAM personnel are not generally those of the scientific community. Because IAM activities are extremely complex and require a mix of qualifications, knowledgeable IAM professionals are extremely sought after and their job description at a PRO is only marginally different from that in industry. Consequently, successful IAM programmes at PROs pay competitive wages and adopt industrial management practices by combining base salary with performance-related salary components.

In some European countries, PROs find it hard to recruit such talent. The civil-servant management systems in some European PROs and their dependence on regional or federal government approval make it extremely difficult to change salary structures to take the realities of labour markets into account. The French study illustrates how the relaxation of rules governing the entrepreunerial activities of public researchers can at least mitigate some of the barriers to greater interaction between scientists and industry.

The Hague workshop strongly identified this as a major drawback to the rapid development of professional IAM programmes at PROs. To develop effective IAM policies and procedures at PROs, it will be essential to allow for sufficient flexibility in the management approaches used.

Lesson 9: The type of TTO models adopted by PROs depends largely on the environment in which they operate but involves trade-offs between economies of scale and proximity

Finding the optimal structure for TTOs is a focus of national discussions in some countries. Should each university or PRO develop an on-campus/on-site operation or does it make sense to stimulate regional TTOs in order to create critical mass, thereby optimising cost-benefit ratios? This discussion is often driven by the fact that successful IAM programmes at PROs, especially in the United States, generally involve only one PRO and that regional co-operation is virtually non-existent in that country. However, most US PROs, including universities, have much bigger research budgets than their European counterparts. The number of disclosures of inventions has to be high enough on an annual basis to justify employing a full technology transfer team, which will generally require at least five full-time equivalents to ensure the mix of qualifications needed.

Advocates for local solutions argue that close co-operation between IAM personnel and scientists is essential for maximising the effectiveness of an IAM programme. The findings of this project suggest that it is too early to favour one solution over the other. However, policy makers grappling with this issue should consider the following insights that have emerged:

- Creating a very large IAM programme at a single university or other PRO will inevitably prolong the time required for the TTO to break even.

- Creating an off-campus or off-site TTO that is too far removed from the main research organisation will suffer from insufficient outreach to researchers who might provide valuable technology input. Indeed, evidence from the OECD survey shows that most IP that has been successfully licensed from PROs involves co-operation and participation by the researchers/inventors.

Lesson 10: The case for limited government support for TTOs at PROs

The findings of the case studies, the surveys and the workshop in The Hague are ambivalent with regard to an increase in government support for IAM programmes. Too much support could lead to sub-optimal performance, thereby creating potential losses rather than revenues and consequently less than optimal return for society at large. However, looking at the overall array of findings obtained in this project, it is clear that significant investment is needed to develop an IAM programme and that it will break even only after a period of seven years or more on average.

Government support will be needed if the budgetary basis of the individual PRO does not provide sufficient flexibility to allow it to allocate the necessary investment.

While IAM has become a mission of some PROs, education and diffusing basic scientific knowledge through scientific publications and people remain core missions of PROs and research universities, especially as concerns new graduates. In this context, governments must balance the commercial exploitation of IP resulting from public research with maintaining openness and access to scientific knowledge more broadly.

Lesson 11: Successful transfer of IP takes time but integrating IAM into the overall knowledge transfer strategy of a PRO can help increase the type and amount of knowledge that is transferred

IP management involves carefully managing and diffusing newly generated knowledge into society. This is often understood simply as patenting and licensing. Most PROs transfer their knowledge in various ways, including supporting spin-offs, taking equity in start-ups, helping out small and medium-sized enterprises (SMEs), providing training courses and distributing written information. In some cases, patents and licensing (as often on non-patented knowledge as on patented knowledge) are the most appropriate way to diffuse and at the same time protect newly generated knowledge. IP management also involves selectivity and knowing when to apply for a patent, when to look for other forms of IP protection, when to facilitate a spin-off and when to rely on other forms of knowledge transfer. As the German case studies show, the more experienced and established TTOs offer the whole array of services. Similarly the older, more established TTOs in Spain offer a much more advanced set of services, ranging from arranging contract research to facilitating spin-offs.

Overall policy lessons

Although the scope of the various case studies is quite different, it is possible to extract some important overall IP policy lessons in addition to those presented above. IP policies in general and the management of IPR at PROs are not completely separate policy activities but two facets of the effort to make innovation systems more dynamic. The list of lessons presented below is far from complete, and a close reading of individual case studies will reveal many additional policy lessons.

Lesson 1: More strategic approaches to creating and exploiting R&D require reconsidering IP policies

In several of the countries studied, changes in the business and public-sector environments for R&D coincide with an increase in attention to the management of IP at PROs. Businesses are changing the way they carry out R&D, partnering among themselves and with universities and other PROs to fund and perform R&D, and/or licensing in and licensing out technologies. For their part, governments are taking a more strategic approach to steering and funding research, owing to fiscal pressures as well as to social demands for science to respond to social, economic and environmental concerns. While governments have long been conscious of the contributions of public research to economic development, over the past two decades they have made the commercialisation of public research results a more explicit goal for universities and other PROs. IPR is one area in which governments have sought to clarify the ownership of inventions and the obligations of institutions performing government-funded research. This has resulted in new legislation, regulatory frameworks and recommendations for dealing with IPR in countries as diverse as Canada, Denmark, France, Germany, Korea and Russia. Not surprisingly, given their different innovation systems and governmental structures, both the actual changes and the way in which these countries derived their new or revamped approach to the treatment of IPR at PROs differ considerably.

Lesson 2: IP policy for PROs can be perceived as contributing to knowledge management in innovation systems as a whole but starts from the availability of an excellent science base

Intellectual asset management should be viewed in the broader context of research and innovation policy. The rationale for facilitating IP management at PROs in the longer term should be to increase the codification and subsequently the diffusion and use of knowledge generated (largely, but not exclusively) by public funds. It should not be motivated by seeking a "quick win" or generating income for PROs in the short term. There may be a danger in focusing too narrowly on IP policy, as this could obscure the relative contributions made by PROs to research and innovation. Establishing IP policies and urging PROs to strengthen their IAM while cutting back research budgets is not the way to implement IP policies and increase the quality of ISRs. Ultimately, the success of IAM depends on an excellent science base able to create a continuous stream of scientifically and commercially valuable results.

Lesson 3: Fostering more explicit IPR practices and policies at PROs does not necessarily mean amending the legal framework; regulations, recommendations and changing IP culture in general are also important

The emulation of Bayh-Dole legislation is generally seen as the way to encourage the commercialisation of PRO research. Changing the law, however, is a lengthy process and does not always ensure as much flexibility as introducing new policies and/or administrative procedures or recommendations and making efforts to change PRO culture with respect to claiming IP. Canada's reform of its IP policy for Crown procurement contracts took not the form of legislation but of guiding principles to be followed by contractors. Similarly, while the institution has owned IP at PROs in France from the outset, the legislation lacked requirements on reporting or publication delays. The charter on IP at French universities clarifies the issues of managing IP in research contacts with industry. The case study on the policy of the US National Institutes of Health (NIH) on sharing research tools also illustrates the power of guidelines if effectively implemented by the parties concerned. One could even think of a funnel of options – as was recently done in Ireland for example – where changing the law is an option that can be considered if other options fail. In practice, policy makers in individual countries have to decide what mix of measures fits best in their respective countries.

Lesson 4: Reform of IP policies at PROs should involve funding agencies, PROs, scientists and industrial partners as well as other actors in the technology transfer value chain

Putting a new IP policy in place is generally seen as a major balancing act. A consultation procedure seems to smooth the way. IP policies cannot be changed and implemented overnight. Because a number of stakeholders can take the opportunity to frustrate the process, it seems to pay off to involve stakeholders early in the process and balance their interests from the start. Several of the case studies highlighted the utility of this. The Korean example stressed the importance of understanding the relationships between firms and PROs as well as anticipating new relationships such as those formed when entrepreneurial professors launch new spin-off companies. The process of policy reform in several countries is characterised by the "governance of the research system". In Canada, a federal country with a decentralised research system, reform emerged at the initiative of the government and involved a broad consultation process with various funding agencies, contractors and representatives of the scientific community. In contrast, in Denmark, the government attempted to reform the professor's privilege concerning inventions developed with public funds by requiring the transfer of the rights to all forms of IP to the institutions. Owing to a lack of consultation – although the government had on earlier occasions held consultations – the government had to scale back the reform to cover only patented inventions and utility models. On a more specific aspect, the US case study on sharing research tools in the biomedical field showed the value of investing in a broad consultation process when reforming IP policies and practices.

Lesson 5: Implementing new approaches to IP and changing behaviour take considerable effort, require capacity building and time

Changing laws, regulations and the rhetoric of IP management at PROs is one thing; making sure the new approaches to dealing with IP matters in PROs are adopted and integrated in wider technology or knowledge transfer strategies of PROs is another. Germany's suppression of the professor's privilege and the transfer of the right of ownership to universities provides an interesting example of the gap between a change in legislation and a change in behaviour. On the one hand, the university sector has not had an incentive to make the protection of IP part of their research missions; on the other, collaborating firms complain about being asked to pay market prices for licensing technology. Meanwhile, some scientists view technology transfer officers as competitors or obstacles to their co-operation with client firms. There is a similar problem in Korea where potential licensees still approach the inventor-scientist rather than the TTO. In general, professional IAM may imply that industry's contract research with PROs may mean market prices and fewer opportunities for inexpensive inroads into interesting bodies of knowledge. The Danish case also illustrated the considerable effort involved in implementing the new law on inventions at public research institutes. In Russia, IP legislation has changed considerably, often resulting in a legal vacuum where only experts can find their way; the lack of clarity seriously hampers international co-operation in science and technology.

Lesson 6: IP policy should provide incentives to scientists as well as institutions

IP policies that do not include incentives for individual researchers to disclose their invention are bound to fail. Although the motives of individual inventors are various, both financial and non-financial, in the end they must have a reason to comply with the PROs' IP management rules. This may be financial compensation or another form of recognition such as additional financing for free research. Most IP policies implemented today include substantial compensation for individual researchers and their group or department, although at the same time, PROs need to have some room to develop their own policy. The Korean and French examples illustrate the need to ensure that incentives exist for scientists as well as for the institutions that have title to IP. In France, reforms to grant researchers a greater share of royalties from licensing revenue coincided with the lifting of restrictions on their ability to start up a company. In Korea, a new IPR framework for PROs was instituted, but there were no particular incentives to encourage scientists to work with the TTOs, with the result that many scientists continued to use personal links to industry to commercialise inventions. In Russia, however, the early adoption of incentive structures for sharing royalties with individuals against the background of an underdeveloped institutional framework had a detrimental effect in that scientists and PROs had conflicting goals.

Lesson 7: Creating professional TTO infrastructures needs long-term investment in terms of budget and policy attention and professional R&D management

In several of the case studies as well as at the workshop in The Hague, attention was called to the need for a professional TTO infrastructure. TTOs are often too small, and it is sometimes hard, especially at universities, to hire professional staff. TTO personnel not only need good market contacts to commercialise knowledge but must also be well linked to R&D staff. It is hard for a TTO to function in a PRO where IP is not included as a part of R&D management. Creating professional TTOs can take years – as the German and Spanish case studies illustrate – and they will not succeed if they are treated as profit centres from the start. They should be valued for their role in knowledge diffusion. The chance of turning a TTO into a real profit centre (*e.g.* through a few "golden eggs"; by selling equity in a successful start-up; by negotiating profitable research contracts) is the exception rather than the rule. To create a top-level TTO requires substantial initial investment as well as including the cost of IP management in regular research contracts and programmes. This is not only a matter for the PROs, and should be facilitated through deliberate IP policy efforts over a number of years.

Lesson 8: The entrepreneurial spirit at PROs – including dealing professionally with IP – should not develop at the expense of PROs' basic task of research and teaching for the benefit of society

IP management is important, but should not be at the expense of PROs' responsibilities in terms of fundamental research and education. Pressures to work on the IP portfolio or to commercialise knowledge and develop an entrepreneurial spirit may lead researchers to concentrate on taking out patents or establishing and managing their own spin-off. The Korean case study points to the need for PRO employees to take their formal teaching and research responsibilities seriously and not to over-emphasise entrepreneurship. In a similar vein, PROs should take out patents or other forms of IP protection selectively, as not all results need to be appropriated or should remain in the public domain. The Danish case study also warns not to think of spin-offs as the only way to increase entrepreneurship at PROs, as spin-offs may develop at the expense (especially in terms of human resources) of the PRO itself. The case studies from Canada, France and the United States also provide examples in which guidelines or administrative regulations have been used to encourage the protection of public access to IP generated with public research funds. Ultimately, IP policy is about balancing support for commercialisation of publicly funded research and entrepreneurship at PROs, on the one hand, and the protection of public access to IP generated with public research funds, on the other.

Lesson 9: IP policy making and IP management would benefit from close monitoring of IP at PROs

When revising IP policies, it is helpful to know the situation prior to any modifications and be able to ascertain after some time in what ways performance has changed. Although performance will be affected by other factors as well (for example the sorts of technologies on which research concentrates, the degree to which IP performance is used for research evaluation), regular surveys of PROs – as practised in the United States and Canada on a regular basis by AUTM – would be helpful not only for measuring performance, but also for benchmarking countries and categories of PROs. The OECD survey of patenting and licensing activities at PROs, reported in parallel to this volume (OECD, 2003), is an important step into this direction.

Lesson 10: Pay attention to the link between IP policies and policy making involving innovation

IP policies should not be treated in isolation. They are a crucial element of the framework conditions for successful innovation systems. They are part of the wider category of knowledge transfer policies that are affecting the heart of many innovation systems, *i.e.* the shaping of ISRs. Many innovation policy makers are working to improve them. IP policies cannot turn mediocre innovation systems into top performers, but attention to IP is one ingredient in managing an innovation system. IP management may, for example, help to create regional growth poles and trigger regional growth (as it does in the life sciences, for example). It may play a role in attracting knowledge-intensive industries and knowledge workers, not least because of its promotional effect. Eventually it will have an impact on competitiveness, not only through requirements to work an invention locally, but also by making knowledge tradable. Differences in IP policies and IP practices between and even within individual countries make co-operation in S&T and innovation sometimes difficult and costly. Ultimately, IP policies and IP management should reduce rather than increase transaction costs and so increase the scope for international co-operation in S&T and innovation.

Having a proper IP framework in place can be seen as having the right incentive structures for motivating PROs, firms and individual inventors to co-operate in S&T and innovation and to put a fair price on knowledge. Providing the wrong incentives increases transaction costs within an innovation system and may reduce its productivity and efficacy. Well-developed IP policies are a necessary, but not sufficient, condition for a well-functioning innovation system. Other conditions also need to be met, such as reasonable research funding and industry that not only is capable of producing knowledge but is capable of linking into knowledge bases as well. There the link between IP policy making and wider innovation policy making comes into play.

Summary of the case studies

The case studies show that the policy and institutional context for commercialising knowledge from PROs as well as the IPR strategies of PROs themselves have already changed or are changing considerably in a large number of countries. In some cases, PROs have initiated the changes; in others, new incentives were introduced to facilitate and steer these changes. The 12 case studies from 11 countries included in this volume provide a wide range of experience with IPR policies and management of IPR at PROs.

Table 1. Lessons drawn from the case studies

Country	Insight gained/lesson learned (selection)
Part II. Government Policies for Managing Intellectual Property at PROs	
Canada Recent changes in IP policies related to Crown procurement contracts	▪ Changing the law is only one option when changing IP policies. Regulation and recommendations (model contracts, etc.) are others ▪ Investing in a broad consultation process may help reach a solution agreeable to most stakeholders ▪ IP matters in publicly funded contracts are wider than R&D contracts between governments and PROs ▪ The process of revising IP policies involves many stakeholders and is a multi-annual effort. ▪ Costs of implementing (changed) IP policies are considerable ▪ For IP policy making, measuring the commercialisation of IP (from PROs) is valuable, although hard to accomplish
Denmark Changing IPR regulations for researchers	▪ Investing in consultation before putting new IP policies for PROs in place helps to get the new regime accepted ▪ IPR affects co-operation in research considerably and sensitivity to the different situations of co-operating partners is essential ▪ Competition law (especially in an EU context) sets limits to IP policies and IP management by PROs ▪ Uncritically copying foreign solutions can be counterproductive ▪ Too eager attempts to increase the number of IP-based spin-offs/start-ups from PROs may damage the functioning of the PROs.
France Legal framework for managing IP at PROs	▪ IP-policies are part of a wider framework of innovation, notably technology transfer policies. ▪ IP management at PROs involves not only various forms of IP and technology transfer, but also incentives for individual researchers ▪ Active IP management by PROs affects co-operation between industry and PROs and the type of contracts used ▪ IP management at PROs cannot be approached only as a legal issue, but has an important cultural element as well (for PRO, researchers and clients)
Russian Federation Legal framework for managing IP at PROs	▪ IP regulations are an important framework condition in any innovation system. ▪ IP regulations and initiatives aimed at furthering innovation should be balanced to provide consistent incentives for the players involved, including PRO. ▪ For an economy in transition the current "legal vacuum" and complicated situation regarding IPR in general leads to a lack of clarity, uncertainty and a widening of the gap between formal regulation and actual practices. ▪ Too easy adoption of IP policies from abroad without proper attention to the specific conditions of the importing country can be counterproductive. • Unclear IP policies in combination with substantially lower level of innovation in industry can seriously hamper international co-operation in S&T and innovation.
Part III. Putting IP Policies into Practice	
Germany IP asset management at PROs	▪ PROs use IP differently from industry. They should not decide too easily to grant (esp. non-exclusive) licences as this can weaken their position in future independent commercialisation efforts. ▪ IP management and IP policies should be part and parcel of wider policies aimed at managing ISRs. PROs with different institutional characteristics and operating in different technology sectors develop different models for managing their IP ▪ Changing the rules (*e.g.* publicly financed contract research) does not change behaviour overnight owing to required changes in administrative procedures and culture
Switzerland University technology transfer in Switzerland:	▪ A complex legal framework for commercialising research from PROs can coincide with a fine track record in commercialising IP from PROs. ▪ In addition to patenting and licensing, TTOs can play an important role in negotiating research agreements with industry and others and so help to attract (contract) research
Spain The evolution of knowledge management strategies in PROs	▪ IPR management has to be organised alongside R&D and knowledge management at PROs ▪ Creation and functioning of TTOs may require government intervention and (initial) financing to acquire critical mass. ▪ TTOs function at different levels ranging from managing contract research to being involved in IP based spin-offs Strategic use of IPR at PROs is not simply the result of a good legal environment and incentives but of having research capabilities and the administrative competencies to protect and exploit research results.

Table 1.Lessons drawn from the case studies (cont'd.)

Country	Insight gained/lesson learned (selection)
	Part IV. Leveraging IP for Biotechnology
Germany IP in the German biotechnology sector	▪ Various models of exploiting IP by PROs can co-exist and are part of wider technology transfer strategies.
Korea Regulatory regime governing IP management at PROs (with a focus on biotechnology)	▪ IP regulatory regimes should pay attention not only to the relation between the state and PROs and PRO-scientists, but also to that between PROs and private firms. ▪ When discussing rights of individual PRO scientists in relation to IP, attention should be paid to scientists' obligations and responsibilities to PROs in the case of an IP-based spin-off. ▪ Government IP policies for PROs should have some built in flexibility to allow for the diversity of PROs ▪ It is important to allocate funds to manage IP when financing research (otherwise the desired extra patents and licence income will not materialise) • IP management policy must be viewed as part of broader innovation policy making, as providing sufficiently large-scale R&D funding to assist basic research can be more important than subsidising the costs of patenting and licensing.
United States Policy to ensure the sharing of unique biomedical research resources (at NIH)	▪ Steering how PROs and other stakeholders deal with the sharing of unique research tools in the biomedical field does not necessarily imply steering by legislation. Consultation and recommendation are other ways ▪ In a delicate matter such as the sharing of research tools it is of utmost importance to balance the interests of the general public and the actors directly involved ▪ Changing rules about the sharing of research tools is one thing, but implementing it and changing a research culture requires lengthy efforts ▪ The Bayh-Dole Act covers far more than granting IP to the executing research organisation.
	Part V. Channels for Transferring IP to Industry
Netherlands IP based spin-offs of PROs in the life sciences and ICT	▪ Spin-offs have advantages over other forms of technology transfer when the technology is radically new ▪ There is no single best model for successful IP based spin-offs ▪ Existing national programmes for new technology-based firms are a useful stimulus but programmes should focus on support in later stages. ▪ PRO and government policy should better focus on spin-offs with a product model, as these have a much larger potential than those with a service model.
Flanders Changing business, R&D practices and IP management in ICT (IMEC)	▪ Changing business and R&D practices (sharing risks, costs and scarce talent) necessitates new forms of IP management ▪ Research efforts of dissimilar actors can be pooled while generating unique IP portfolios for participating organisations ▪ Active IP policies (including spin-offs) may help to anchor a PRO to a region and create regional knowledge spillovers

The case studies that follow this introductory section are organised into four parts. Part II presents case studies that focus mainly, although not exclusively, on the legal and policy framework for managing IP at PROs in Canada, Denmark, France and Russia. These case studies illustrate the variety of approaches used in different national innovation systems, the legal and regulatory solutions initiated over the past few years and the ways in which the institutional diversity of PROs is dealt with. Part III focuses on how IP policies are implemented in the different national and institutional context and highlights the experience of Germany, Spain and Switzerland. In Part IV, three case studies describe IP policy making and IPR management for a single sector, biotechnology. They take different approaches:

- The German case study looks at how technology transfer and IP management are arranged in various types of PROs.

107

- The US case study shows how IP regarding biomedical research tools is dealt with at the NIH, a major player in biomedical research.

- The Korean case study uses the biotechnology sector to illustrate trade-offs in IP policy and IP management.

Part V addresses specific examples of how IP is transferred to industry either through licensing or through the creation of spin-off companies. One case study discusses how IP-based spin-offs from PROs have been formed in the Netherlands and how they are managed, keeping in mind the PRO, the spin-off and the policy perspective. The second provides an example of how IP is dealt with in public/private partnerships at IMEC, an ICT research institution in Flanders.

The individual case studies offer various recipes for bringing about these changes. Such recipes cannot be simply transferred to other countries owing to differences in institutional structures, policy traditions, organisation of research funding, research culture and history, industrial specialisation and the ways in which the interface between science and industry has developed over time. However, these dissimilar approaches offer tremendous scope for mutual learning. Table 1 highlights a few of the intriguing lessons learned from individual case studies.

Remaining challenges and areas for further research

In most OECD countries, the issues of IP policy making and in particular, IP management, at PROs are high on the agenda. Developments in this area are moving rapidly and require in-depth analysis. Some topics for further research that were identified in the course of this OECD project include:

- How to better measure the performance of PROs and countries in terms of their performance on commercialising publicly financed research and managing an IP portfolio. The two OECD surveys provide important information but also show the need for additional information and analysis.

- The relationship between implementing IP policies and IP management, on the one hand, and the level and direction of public and private investments in basic R&D, on the other

- The degree to which industry-specific IP regimes are feasible and desirable, especially as most IP management is limited to a few technology and industry sectors (although this might be different if patents on software and business methods are granted on a large scale).

- Which indicators can best be used to assess and benchmark sensibly the IP performance of PROs.

- How to deal with the fact that a limited amount of IP is responsible for most of the income generated from IP. This distortion needs further analysis as working with averages may result in inappropriate policy advice regarding encouraging IP management at PROs.

- There is a tendency to focus on patents and patented knowledge when IP in general and licensing in particular are discussed. However, many licensing agreements involve non-patented knowledge. Better understanding of the licensing of non-patented IP is needed to be able to advise PROs on best practice licensing strategies.

- From the point of view of science and innovation policy, there is a danger, perhaps a fear, that if PROs pay too much attention to IP management, their research programmes may be influenced more by commercial than scientific considerations. It is important to understand how licensing strategies affect research programming.

- How are specific IPR policies and innovation policies related? Some ideas about how the two are linked are presented, but in practice IPR and innovation policies develop too much in isolation. It would be interesting to know how the two can reinforce each other.

NOTES

1.   The survey results and an analysis of the results are reported separately (OECD, 2003).

2.   It also draws on the results of the workshop on the strategic use of IPR by PROs, held on 17 October 2002 in The Hague, which are summarised by Bekkers and Sampat (2003).

REFERENCES

AUTM (2002), *AUTM Licensing Survey: FY 2000. Survey Summary*, Association of University Technology Managers, Inc., Northbrook, Illinois.

Bekker, R. and B. Sampat (2003), Rapporteurs' summary report commissioned by the OECD for the Joint OECD-Netherlands Expert Workshop on the Strategic Use of IPRs by Public Research Organisations. Available at: www.oecd.org/pdf/M00037000/M00037899.pdf

OECD (2003), *Patenting and Licensing at Public Research Organisations: International Trends and Policies*, OECD, Paris.

GOVERNMENT POLICIES FOR MANAGING INTELLECTUAL PROPERTY AT PUBLIC RESEARCH ORGANISATIONS

This section provides the background behind recent legislative action or policy measures in Canada, Denmark, France and Russia to grant universities and other public research organisations greater control of their intellectual property.

Chapter 5

POLICY ON TITLE TO INTELLECTUAL PROPERTY
UNDER CROWN PROCUREMENT CONTRACTS IN CANADA

by

Jeanne Inch, Director, Marketplace Innovation, Innovation Policy, Industry Canada

with assistance from

**Donovan Vernon, Industry Canada; Elizabeth Blackburn, Natural Resources Canada;
Michel Grenier, Treasury Board Secretariat, Government of Canada**

Introduction

The Government of Canada has recognised for some time the importance of ensuring that Canadians benefit from its investments in research and development (R&D) and that the commercialisation of that R&D generates economic growth and jobs for Canadians. Critical to this objective is the management of intellectual property generated with government funding.

The federal government is a key player in Canada's innovation system, both as funder and performer of science and technology (S&T), including R&D. Federal support for R&D is provided in four ways: direct grants to university researchers; procurement-based support through Crown procurement contracts for goods and services; intramural support through in-house basic and applied research; and industry-based support through contribution agreements.

Government expenditures on S&T are, first and foremost, used by federal departments and agencies to fulfil their missions. For many departments, generation of IP is secondary to the delivery of public goods, *e.g.* an effective regulatory system; safeguarding of public health and safety; protection of the environment; and furtherance of basic science and acquisition of knowledge. Given the importance the government has placed on the commercialisation of R&D results, federal science-based departments and agencies (SBDAs) recognise that the goal of commercialisation is part of their science mandate and that commercialisation should be a priority when the opportunity for commercial exploitation presents itself.

In 2001, the federal government funded about 18% of the R&D conducted in Canada. Of a total of CAD 3.7 billion, almost CAD 2 billion was spent for performing intramural R&D, mostly in government research laboratories. The other CAD 1.7 billion went to universities, business and private non-profit organisations to support extramural R&D activities performed by these groups. Between 1996 and 2001, the proportion of federal R&D funds spent on extramural activities increased from

37% to 48%. In that period, the R&D performed by the federal government put greater emphasis on public health, industrial production and technology, and non-oriented (or basic) research.

This case study focuses on the management of intellectual property arising from Crown procurement contracts[1] between government departments, including SBDAs and the private sector. The government spends approximately CAD 10.5 billion annually for the procurement of goods and services, a substantial portion of which is for R&D.[2] The objective of a Crown procurement contract is to acquire goods and services, not to generate intellectual property (IP). However, much IP is generated as a result of contracts to private-sector contractors (individuals, businesses, universities, non-government organisations, non-profit organisations).

Prior to 1991, IP ownership rested with the federal government. However, since the early 1990s, the Canadian government has taken the view that a private-sector enterprise is more likely and better equipped than the public sector to develop the technology to the point of commercial exploitation. Moreover, while it may be appropriate for an SBDA to do basic research, it is not appropriate for government departments to exploit the inventions or products they develop for commercial purposes. The government's role to facilitate that commercialisation.

IP management is complex, as it links technological, legal and policy issues. However, the government faced the additional challenge of formulating a policy that was sufficiently flexible to be applied across all government departments and agencies, including public research organisations (PROs), precise enough to protect the public good interests of the government and able to serve the economic interests of the private sector.

This chapter reviews the history of the development, revision, implementation and evaluation of a government policy establishing ownership of the IP arising from Crown procurement contracts. The case study spans the period from 1954 (when the government issued a Policy on Allocation of Patent Rights in Research and Development Contracts) to 1991 (when the government introduced the Policy on Title to Intellectual Property Arising under Crown Contracts) and finally to 2000 (when a revised Policy on Title to Intellectual Property Arising under Crown Procurement Contracts was approved).

The revision exercise for the 2000 policy was led by the department of Industry Canada responsible for "commercialisation". All government departments were implicated. Especially active were the SBDAs, those with research laboratories, as well as Public Works and Government Services Canada (PWGSC), which is responsible for administering large procurement contracts on behalf of the Government of Canada.

The policy challenge was to ensure that the policy would be flexible enough so that it could be administered by all Crown procurement contracts covering all types of IP and would balance the needs of the general public, government personnel and the private sector.

With the approval in 2000 of the policy on Intellectual Property Arising under Crown Procurement Contracts, the question of the ownership and licensing of IP created by contractors was resolved. Given the Canadian government's investments in contracting, this policy represents an important source of IP for contractors. This policy and its impact on commercialisation of government-funded IP by contractors will be assessed in 2000-04.

This chapter shows the difficulties involved in providing this balance, the need to involve key stakeholders within and outside government, and the challenges of implementing a policy with a long-term goal – commercialisation of IP – that is difficult to measure in the short term.

History of IP policy 1954-2000

Beginning in 1954, the government's policy was that all design rights and patents created in the course of R&D contracts were owned by the government.[3] That policy allowed the government to license IP for the purpose of commercial exploitation and favoured the use of non-exclusive licences.

Between 1954 and 1991, however, other policies began to promote the use and commercial exploitation of IP created in the course of Crown procurement contracts. A policy adopted in 1978[4] encouraged the contracting out of R&D work to increase the innovation and research capacity of industry; the IP developed in the course of such contracts belonged to the Crown.

In 1986, it was decided that, although all copyright resulting from work done on behalf of the Crown belonged to the Crown,[5] the Crown should, in general, grant permission to use this copyrighted work.[6]

Between the early 1980s and the mid-1990s, there was a sudden worldwide surge of interest in the value of IP and its management. Governments and businesses increasingly came to recognise the potential economic and social benefits of IP and sought ways to protect it for exploitation. The business community began to pressure the government for IP ownership, recognising that the IP had commercial value. At the same time, to protect their investments in R&D, the SBDAs were requesting exceptions to contractor-owned IP.

IP policy adopted in 1991

In 1991, the government decided that it should take steps to promote greater commercial exploitation of IP generated under Crown procurement contracts. At the request of the ministers responsible for S&T and commercialisation (the Minister for Industry, Science and Technology and the Minister of State for Science), the Treasury Board adopted the Policy on Title to Intellectual Property Arising under Crown Contracts.[7] The policy allowed contractors to own the IP they created in the course of their work under Crown procurement contracts involving R&D (and any other procurement contracts), with six exceptions. It is important to emphasise that this was a policy, not a law or regulation.

There was confusion about the implementation of the policy almost immediately after its introduction in October 1991. In December 1991, it became necessary to clarify whether the policy applied just to R&D contracts or to all Crown procurement contracts. The policy, itself, stated: "to encourage commercial exploitation of Intellectual Property (IP) developed in the course of Crown Contracts.... The policy applies as broadly as possible to all goods and services contracts involving R&D activities."[8] The Treasury Board favoured interpreting the policy as encouraging contractor ownership of IP for all contracts issued for the procurement of goods and services in all Crown procurement contracts, subject to six specified exceptions.

There were also concerns about the exemptions, which were open to different interpretations by the contractor and the government officials. One example was that the government would retain ownership of background technology when "the Contractor is simply adding to the technology package by providing a service". There were ambiguities in three other exemptions: "national security", when "the contractor has no intention or capability of pursuing commercialisation in a timely manner in Canada", and "mutual agreement". Other exemptions were more straightforward: when the government had "prior obligations to a third party or parties (such as a research partner or research consortium)" and when "the main purpose of the work is to generate knowledge and regulatory information for public dissemination".

Other difficulties of interpretation related to software development contracts and the rights of the Crown to protect, modify or share the source code. It became clear that the exceptions to contractor ownership, as stated in the policy, were not adequate to protect government's investments. In December 1991, the Treasury Board Secretariat issued letters of clarification stating that the list of exceptions to contractor ownership provided in the policy was not exhaustive. The door was opened for greater use of the exemptions to contractor-owned IP.

There were also problems with the application of the policy across government. Because the exemptions to contractor ownership were open to various interpretations, the policy was applied differently from department to department. In the view of the contractors, the policy was not being applied consistently across government.

In 1992, another major change occurred in how the government managed its IP. The Canadian Patents and Development Limited[9] (CPDL) was dissolved. CPDL's mandate was to manage the IP belonging to the government and universities; its goal was to make available to the public the industrial and intellectual property resulting from publicly funded R&D. Simply put, CPDL acted as a "custodian" of the IP. After its dissolution, departments became responsible for the management of their IP.

Complicating factors

A further complication arose in 1993 when Treasury Board ministers approved a Policy on Retention of Royalties and Fees from the Licensing of Crown-owned Intellectual Property. This policy allowed departments and agencies to receive an annual appropriation equal to all revenues arising from the licensing of Crown-owned IP. It appeared that this policy inadvertently created an incentive for the Crown to own IP in order to obtain revenue from licensing it. At that time, renewed emphasis was put on revenue generation targets for departments and agencies, especially following the 1992 "programme review", when the government made massive cuts in the budgets of many departments. Licensing government-owned IP was seen as potential revenue.

The revenue generation policy also raised a question as to whether there should be a direct return to the government (through royalties or other types of revenue sharing with the private sector) when government funds were used to generate the IP or whether priority should be given to maximising economic growth, that is, leaving the IP with the contractor.

During the 1990s, there was also considerable disagreement among departments and agencies about the appropriateness of the intent of the 1991 policy. It appeared that the 1991 policy did not reflect the fact that government departments and agencies have different mandates. For the most part, they procure the same goods and services, *e.g.* office supplies, studies, photographs, furniture, cars, speeches, temporary help. However, in the case of R&D, their objectives are very different: the Canadarm,[10] a vaccine against a new virus or a database of meteorological data.

In short, it became obvious that the scope of the 1991 policy was unclear; there were difficulties of interpretation and its application across government was inconsistent. Finally, there was a perceived conflict between the 1991 IP policy, which directed contractors to own the IP, and the 1993 policy on Retention of Royalties and Fees from the Licensing of Crown-owned Intellectual Property, which encouraged departments to retain IP in order to obtain fees from licensing it.

Evaluation of the 1991 policy in 1995

In 1995, Industry Canada and the Treasury Board Secretariat jointly commissioned a study to determine the status of the policy. It concluded that information about the policy and its application had not been adequately disseminated to contract officers and other government officers involved in contracting work; that ambiguities in the policy made consistent interpretation and application difficult; and that the 1993 Treasury Board policy on revenue retention created an incentive for the Crown to retain IP ownership in some cases.

The study also noted some concern about the exception to contractor ownership in the policy because of "mutual agreement". Anecdotal evidence suggested that contracting authorities were, in some cases, using the threat of withholding future contracting opportunities to "extract" "mutual agreement" from bidders and single suppliers, in order to permit the Crown to retain the IP.

Because the 1991 policy did not have a monitoring/reporting requirement, the above conclusions were based on anecdotal evidence rather than quantitative data. No adequate government-wide database of statistics captured the extent of the IP developed or the disposition of ownership as a result of specific R&D procurement contracts or more general procurement contracts for goods and services involving R&D. For example, Public Works and Government Services Canada, the department that handles over 60% of all government procurement contracts, estimates that only about 2-4% of total procurement contracts involved IP or the development of IP.

On the basis of these findings, stakeholders from the government and industry indicated that major revisions were needed to take into account two important factors. One was the need for departments and agencies to receive, and be able to use, the deliverables contracted for (not for purposes of generating revenue); the other was the need for consistency with other government policies concerning IP.

Direction from the top

At the highest level of government, there were also calls for revision of the policy and recognition of the importance to economic growth of commercialising IP generated with public funds.

In 1996, a Government Caucus Task Force on Commercialisation of Federal Research[11] was established to examine, among other issues, the range of options available for commercialisation of government research; who should own research performed in government labs and to whom should any resulting profits flow (the government or the company using the research in a commercial application); as well as approaches used by other countries to commercialise government research.

Second, the Liberal Party of Canada's 1997 election campaign policy document[12] included a chapter on commercialising government research. It stated, "We must do a better job of getting the results of federal government research out of our labs and research facilities and into the commercial marketplace... we must also improve the regime for intellectual property ownership to clarify who has the right to commercial exploitation of new scientific developments resulting from federal contracts."

Finally, the October 1999 Speech from the Throne reinforced the government's commitment to commercialise research from universities and government research centres. Throughout this period, commercialisation had been one of the four elements of the government's policy approach to stimulating innovation in Canada.

With a government mandate to review and revise the 1991 Crown procurement policy, Industry Canada, the department responsible for "commercialisation", took the lead in the policy revision process that extended from 1996 to 2000 when the revised policy was approved by Treasury Board.

Objectives of the review process

The main objectives of the review process were to revise the 1991 policy so that it would be responsive to the private sector, which wanted to own and commercialise the IP, while it protected the Crown's interests where necessary. The long-term goal was to maximise the commercialisation of IP and benefit Canada in terms of jobs and economic growth. The short-term, more pragmatic, goal was to ensure that the policy would be easier to administer consistently across government.

An interdepartmental working group was formed, comprised of representatives from Industry Canada, the Treasury Board Secretariat and PWGSC. Between 1996 and 2000, this working group undertook extensive consultations within the government, at both the working and senior management levels. The departments and agencies most engaged were the so-called SBDAs, those with a research mandate (PROs) and a vested interest in the results of the R&D[13] performed in procurement contracts for them. The Department of Justice was involved to ensure that the revised policy was consistent with national and international laws, treaties and regulations governing IP and procurement. Government contracting personnel, at both the working and management levels, also participated through the Treasury Board Advisory Committee on Contracts.

Outside government, Industry Canada consulted 11 industry and academic associations representing the spectrum of the contractor communities; together, they represented the majority of Canadian business, as well as universities, whose faculty can contract with government.[14] These associations were concerned primarily with protecting the contractor's right to ownership of IP and, if that was not possible, with ensuring their ability to license IP owned by the government.

It took over three years to reach an agreement on the policy principles, with compromises by all parties. Once the policy principles were agreed, the need for absolute clarity – without the use of too much legal language – became the next challenge. Towards the end of the policy development process, most of the attention focused on definitions. Lawyers representing the industry associations and the legal counsel for several different government departments spent several months working out precise and clear definitions, using precise and clear wording.

In 2000, after four years of consultations, drafting and redrafting, Treasury Board Ministers approved the policy on Title to Intellectual Property Arising under Crown Procurement Contracts.

The policy challenges

In the course of the policy revision process, the basic principles of the 1991 policy did not change. They are as follows:

- The government's primary objective in entering into Crown procurement contracts is to receive the deliverables contracted for and to be able to use those deliverables and any intellectual property arising by the virtue of such Crown procurement contracts for government activities.

- The government has an overall objective of promoting economic growth and job creation in Canada and has made specific provision for social and economic development objectives to be pursued through procurement.

- The government believes that commercial exploitation of IP contributes to economic growth and job creation.

- The government believes that commercial exploitation of IP is best achieved by the private sector.

Even though it is much simpler than that of some countries, the Canadian legislative and policy framework that affects the transfer or commercialisation of technology is quite complex. Several federal statutes govern intellectual property,[15] other acts have implications for IP[16] and international conventions and agreements exist to which Canada has subscribed.[17] Finally, laws and policies apply to technology transfer "activities" that involve the Crown.[18] Some of these statutes and regulations leave little flexibility for negotiations between government representatives and third parties wishing to commercialise new IP.

Given the above, the question of the allocation of rights to IP developed, in whole or in part, with public funds is complex. Over the period 1991-2000, the government faced several challenges as it worked towards a revision of the 1991 policy.

The need for flexibility

The greatest challenge was the need for flexibility in policy governing ownership of IP arising from procurement contacts. First, the policy had to govern all procurement contracts, from the simple (writing a report for Heritage Canada) to the highly complex (developing a new space technology application for the Canadian Space Agency). In fact, there was considerable discussion as to whether the policy should apply to all Crown procurement contracts or just to R&D contracts. Consideration needed to be given to the fact that intellectual property can arise from all types of work, from the development of a Web site to writing a speech to designing a building.

Second, the policy had to apply to all government departments, with their very different mandates, programmes and services. One can only imagine the different perspectives and requirements of contracting personnel at Human Resources Development Canada and at the Department of National Defence, the largest contracting department.

Third, government research establishments, as part of government departments and agencies, contract primarily for R&D.[19] These research agencies undertake technology and scientific research for a variety of reasons: testing drugs for the market, developing new methods for protecting the environment, developing leading-edge communications technology.

Fourth, the development of this government-wide policy was constrained because it could not be adapted for different sectors or technology fields as requested by the contracting community. The one exception was software, which is covered under the Copyright Act.[20] This issue was raised by the information and communications technology (ICT) companies because of the importance of retaining ownership of source code.

Finally, the policy was to cover all types of IP. As defined in the policy, IP includes: "inventions; computer software and databases; literary, artistic, dramatic or musical works; books, papers; educational materials; industrial design; trademarks; integrated circuit topography; new plant varieties". The policy does not apply to the ownership of, or the right to use, any trade names or trademarks or to personal information (which is protected by the Privacy Act).

Different stakeholders/divergent views

Another challenge was the reluctance of some at working level within government to release control of the IP generated through contracts. This reluctance existed despite the fact that, at the highest levels, the government had clearly stated that efforts were needed to ensure the commercialisation of intellectual property arising from government investments. There was a natural inclination, at working level, to retain ownership, in part to have better control over the future use of the IP. This reluctance existed even though contractors would commercialise the IP owned by the Crown through licensing.

It was argued that the Crown needed to retain ownership to preserve its freedom of action to undertake R&D projects, maintain an integrated portfolio of research results to maximise the potential value of that portfolio and prevent the potential failure of industry to exploit the resulting IP. Regarding the latter, there was concern that the IP might be lost because the contractor might relocate to the United States, be bought out by a foreign company (for the IP), not commercialise the IP or go bankrupt or out of business.

On the other hand, private-sector contractors argued that ownership of the IP was essential if they were to commercialise it. A licence was insufficient for accessing the necessary financing for that commercialisation.

The contractor community was also concerned about the potential constraints placed upon them by the government's intention that IP generated with government funding should be commercialised in Canada for the benefits of Canadians or be commercialised within a specified period of time. While there was no universal policy or directive to promote IP commercialisation in Canada, all federal departments act according to the principle of providing benefits to Canadian citizens.

From the government's perspective, the logic was simple: Canadian taxpayers fund the development of the IP and therefore should benefit. Commercialisation of IP in Canada generates jobs for Canadians; if there are no jobs, there are no economic benefits.

The policy options

Throughout the policy revision exercise, the government had three options. The first was to leave the 1991 policy unchanged but provide intensive training on its implementation. The second was to adopt the US approach (the Bayh-Dole Act) by legislating the presumption of IP ownership by the contractor with very limited exemptions for the Crown. The final option was to revise the 1991 policy to reaffirm its application to all Crown procurement contracts for goods and services, remove ambiguities and deal with complex IP-ownership situations through a mechanism that would identify the rights and obligations of all parties involved.

It should be noted that consideration was given to the option of joint ownership of the IP between the Crown and the contractor. This concept was proposed to mitigate the problems associated with the cross-licensing of contractor and Crown-owned background IP. After much study and consultation with the Department of Justice, the idea was abandoned because of legal and administrative problems concerning Crown liability associated with joint ownership.

The three options, each with pros and cons, are outlined below.

Option 1 was to leave the 1991 policy document as it was but provide intensive training on its implementation and application:

- Training would be the quickest and easiest way to respond to the application issues surrounding the 1991 policy.

- Most government departments would accept this option given that the ambiguities in the 1991 policy provided them with a great deal of freedom as regards retaining ownership of the IP.

- Retaining the existing exemptions to contractor-owned IP would be unacceptable to the private sector, which contended that ambiguities in the 1991 policy regarding exemptions led to the Crown owning the IP. In other words, retaining the existing exemptions would be seen by the contracting community as reverting to the 1954 policy.

- Training alone would not address the major concerns and complaints of the private sector, namely, the ambiguities over exemptions and the lack of a consistent, transparent approach to the implementation of the policy across government.

- In addition, training could not be provided without first explicitly defining how all departments and agencies should address the associated contractual issues when title to IP is vested with the contractor.

- Finally, the expectation of government ministers that the intent of the 1991 policy – to commercialise IP generated under Crown procurement contracts – would not likely be realised.

Option 2 involved adopting a modified US approach (Bayh-Dole Act) by legislating the presumption of IP ownership by the contractor with modifications.[21]

- This option would respond to the government's view that there should be fewer exemptions to contractor ownership of IP and that any necessary exemptions should be clear and precise.

- Industry would be pleased with the virtual elimination of Crown ownership of IP and addressing the issue of ambiguities in the 1991 policy.

- It would be more difficult for the Crown to retain ownership of the IP, even when there were legitimate reasons to do so, such as national security.

- Legislation would ensure contracting approaches would be consistent across government.

- A legislative approach would make it difficult to effect changes (in law) to take into account unique contracting circumstances relating to IP ownership which might arise in future.

Option 3 involved revising the 1991 policy to reaffirm its application to all Crown procurement contracts for goods and services, remove ambiguities and deal with complex IP ownership situations by establishing a mechanism to identify the rights and obligations of all parties involved.

- The 1991 policy presumption of contractor ownership of IP would be maintained and the goals of the government regarding commercialisation of government-supported research would be met.

- The exemptions would be restricted to the minimum required by the Crown and be made clearer and more specific.

- The exemptions would address both straightforward contracts (such as a workshop for Human Resources Canada) and complex, multi-year contracts (such as constructing a frigate for the Department of National Defence).

- A contractual mechanism linked to the policy would allow the Crown to use contractor-owned IP for its own non-commercial purposes, without having to enter into separate licensing agreements.

- The policy would make explicit other provisions (to be incorporated into contracts) that define the rights and obligations of the Crown and contractors with respect to foreground and background IP.

- Explicit provisions could be added to maximise the commercial exploitation of IP by contractors and require them to exploit IP to the benefit of Canada, in terms of jobs and economic growth (the latter where permitted by WTO and NAFTA).

- The right of the Crown would be established to share, under certain circumstances, in the revenue stream from contractors' exploitation of IP.

The 2000 IP policy

The government chose to adopt Option 3 primarily for two reasons. It would provide the flexibility that government departments needed and would respond to the concerns of the contracting industry. This option addressed the weaknesses in the 1991 policy: the ambiguities that made consistent interpretation and application difficult and departments' concerns regarding the application of the policy. It also resolved the problems of obtaining quantitative data and the use of exceptions.

This option met the need for the policy to be consistent with the mandates of departments and agencies to transfer in-house government-owned IP through licences to the private sector for commercial use. It recognised that the government issues procurement contracts for a variety of reasons, including supporting partnerships with third parties, completing technology packages to be licensed to third parties and purchasing goods (*e.g.* furniture, cars, office supplies).

While the intent of the 1991 policy was not changed, the 2000 policy differs from the 1991 policy in six significant ways:

- The 2000 policy clearly applies to all Crown procurement contracts.

  To ensure greater consistency of application and equitable treatment of all contractors, the policy clearly covers all Crown procurement contracts, not only R&D contracts. It covers all IP created by contractors in the course of their work under all Crown procurement contracts, with the exception of trademarks and the constraints set out in Section 12 of the Copyright Act. The policy does not cover grants, contributions or collaborative arrangements. Furthermore, the policy does not affect the background IP already owned by either the contractor or the Crown.

- The exceptions to the policy were clarified to meet the needs of both government and industry. The 2000 policy vests to the contractors the ownership of the IP that they create in the course of their work under Crown procurement contracts, except for five types of exceptions where the ownership of the IP rests with the Crown:

  – National security.

-   Where statutes, regulations or prior obligations of the Crown to a third party or parties preclude contractor ownership of the foreground IP.

-   When the contractor declares, in writing, that he/she is not interested in owning the foreground IP.

-   Where the main purpose of the Crown procurement contract, or of the deliverables contracted for, is:

    -   To generate knowledge and information for public dissemination.

    -   To augment an existing body of Crown background IP as a prerequisite to the planned transfer of the augmented Crown background IP to the private sector, through licensing or assignment of ownership (not necessarily to the original contractor), for the purposes of commercial exploitation.

    -   To deliver a component or sub-system that will be incorporated into a complete system at a later date (not necessarily by the original contractor), as a prerequisite to the planned transfer of the complete system to the private sector (not necessarily to the original contractor), through licensing or assignment of ownership, for the purposes of commercial exploitation.

-   Where the foreground IP consists of material subject to copyright, with the exception of computer software and all documentation pertaining to that software.

- **Government's right to require the contractor to commercialise the IP in Canada and/or within a specified period of time.**

  When the contractor owns the IP, the Crown may require that it be exploited in Canada and/or within a specific time frame, to the extent that the requirement is consistent with Canada's trade agreement obligations [*i.e.* subsidy codes under the World Trade Organisation (WTO) Agreement on Subsidies and Countervailing Measures (SCM)].

  The purpose of this requirement is to help ensure that benefits accrue to Canada and Canadian citizens. If departments choose to use this "benefits to Canada" clause, they would need to specify concrete measures to assess whether or not there is compliance and the consequences of non-compliance. Depending on the nature of the IP or the economic and technological conditions prevailing in Canada, demands for commercial exploitation in Canada may not be practical.

- **Licensing provisions enable the contractor to license Crown-owned IP and the Crown to license contractor-owned IP.**

  Licensing provisions ensure that the Crown will have the ability to use the IP for legitimate purposes associated with the deliverables under the contract, even when the contractor owns it. They also facilitate commercial exploitation of the IP by the contractor when the Crown owns it.

- **Personal information was explicitly stated to be outside the policy.**

  In order to meet the Crown's obligations under the Privacy Act, personal information[22] was explicitly stated to be outside the policy. The policy also does not apply to foreground IP in any compilation or database containing personal information or Crown-supplied information, which cannot be exploited without using that personal information or Crown-supplied information.

- A mechanism was created for collecting data and reporting on application of the policy and the use of exceptions by all government departments.

The 2000 policy includes a section on monitoring which states that each and every department should maintain a record of all Crown procurement contracts valued over the threshold for solicitation of bids as set out in the Government Contracts Regulations.[23] This record should specify the contracts that provide for contractor-owned foreground IP, the contracts that provide for Crown-owned foreground IP and the exception(s) invoked. The reporting requirement of the 2000 policy ensures transparency, facilitates monitoring and does not place undue burden on departments. Each year, all departments submit the data to Public Works and Government Services Canada, which, in turn, compiles the data for the *Annual Report to Treasury Board on Contracting Activity*, which is published annually by Treasury Board and made public through its Web site.[24]

In addition, Industry Canada addressed the implementation, application and interpretation problems encountered with the 1991 policy. Extensive consultation with government and industry helped ensure their agreement and support for the revised policy. Industry Canada also led the development, through an interdepartmental working group, of an implementation guide, which was widely disseminated to departments and posted, along with the policy, on the Treasury Board Secretariat Web site. Industry Canada also held information sessions for key departmental contracting personnel across the country so that they, in turn, could develop appropriate training for their own staff.

Finally, an integral part of the policy is the requirement that Industry Canada and the Treasury Board Secretariat monitor the application of the policy and oversee an interdepartmental evaluation of the policy in 2003-04. This evaluation will examine, among other issues, the factors that affected the process of implementation and management of the policy and the impacts, both intended and unintended, upon the contractors and the Crown.

Conclusion

For the Canadian government, intellectual property and the commercialisation of IP generated with public funds remains a priority. In February 2002, the government released an Innovation Strategy which identifies knowledge performance (encompassing both research and commercialisation of that research) as one of four challenges facing Canada.[25] There is a focus on key themes related to commercialisation, including the need for clear IP policies that support the commercialisation of university research.

With the approval of the 2000 policy on Intellectual Property Arising under Crown Procurement Contracts, the question of the ownership and licensing of intellectual property created by contractors was resolved. Given the investments in contracting made by the Canadian government, this policy represents an important source of IP for contractors.

The process of revising the 1991 policy was extremely difficult at times, given the complexity of the issue, the need for flexibility as well as clarity and the diverging views of the players involved. In many respects, the revision process was also a communications exercise.

Many policy lessons were learned. The first was the need for each stakeholder to understand and accept the objectives and constraints of the other stakeholders. Government personnel needed to accept the importance of vesting the IP with contractors for the long-term economic benefits of

Canada. They needed to accept the risk of IP going offshore, given the global marketplace and the competition among industries.

On the other hand, it was vital for the contracting community to accept the government's right to retain ownership in specific cases, especially in cases of national security, but also for large, multi-contractor projects involving several different elements of IP.

They also needed to understand the restrictions placed on the policy by other regulations and legislation (*e.g.* the Privacy Act, international agreements). Regarding the "benefits to Canada" clause, contractors needed to accept the government's ultimate goal, which is to commercialise government-funded IP in Canada, or within a specified period of time.

A key lesson was the need to involve all parties in the discussions, consultations, drafting, redrafting and review of drafts. Hundreds of hours were spent defining the issues and discussing different perspectives with procurement specialists, contracting personnel, legal staff, IP experts and R&D managers in key departments and agencies. Especially active were the science-based departments and agencies, those with research laboratories and PWGSC, which is responsible for administering large procurement contracts on behalf of the Canadian government.

Industry Canada and its partners in the revision exercise had two objectives during these consultations. One was to listen to the perspectives of those who would implement the policy. The other was to promote the more strategic and long-term goal of commercialisation for the economic benefit of Canada and Canadians. In some cases, this was not an "easy sell".

Perhaps the greatest policy lesson was the need for flexibility in a policy to be administered by all government departments for all Crown procurement contracts covering all types of IP. Extensive discussions focused on the many different situations faced by contract managers, all in aid of finding a compromise that was true to the government's objective – contractor-owned IP, with a few precise and clear exceptions.

The importance of balancing the needs of the Canadian public and government personnel with those of the private sector was another lesson learned. While the principle of the policy was accepted by the contracting community, there was scepticism about how it would be interpreted and implemented. To address these concerns, the policy included a requirement for all departments and agencies to report on the IP and on which exemptions they were invoking. To help ensure that contracting personnel understood the policy and how to apply it, Industry Canada developed and disseminated an implementation guide and provided training to contract personnel in all departments.

The hardest lesson was that it was not possible to respond to all the requests of the contracting community. The contractors wanted the government to establish an ombudsman to review complaints by contractors, or potential contractors, regarding misinterpretation of the policy. It was the government's view that recourse processes are already available in the procurement process and that such concerns could be raised with the responsible department's senior management or minister.

The contracting community also expressed concern over the requirement that the IP be commercialised in Canada and/or within a specific period of time. Again, the government would not budge on this issue, given its stated goal of increasing benefits to Canada from its investments.

The question of how to enforce such a policy remains. The Canadian government's administration is not centralised but is shared by all departments and agencies. It is almost impossible to ensure that government departments and agencies are consistent in claiming "exceptions" to retain

Crown ownership. There is still room for interpretation, even though the revised policy identifies specific instances where Crown ownership of IP is justified and requires that the Crown specify in all cases in solicitation documents or the Crown procurement contract whether the Crown intends to keep the ownership of such IP.

Particularly difficult to enforce is the requirement for contractors to commercially exploit the IP in Canada and/or within a specific period of time. The commercialisation of IP is subject to the ever-changing global marketplace, intense competition among firms and the resources available to contractors.

Assessment of the application of this policy and its impact on commercialisation of government-funded IP by contractors will be undertaken in 2003-04, when Industry Canada will undertake a formal evaluation and report back to Treasury Board ministers. Some of the questions to be raised include how the 2000 IP policy is affecting public/private co-operation and whether PROs are more actively managing their IP in Canada. Certainly, one objective will be to determine if contractors, who now have ownership of the IP, are in fact commercialising it, and commercialising it in Canada.

It is important to point out that, two years after approval of the 2000 policy, there have been no complaints from the private sector, either formally or informally.

NOTES

1. Crown procurement contracts do not include contributions by the private sector to the government, grants and collaborative arrangements, *i.e.* those arrangements or activities in which all parties have shared or compatible objectives, contribute resources and share in the benefits of collaboration, *i.e.* the ownership of IP.

2. The largest procuring departments are the Department of National Defence, which has a separate research agency (Defence Research and Development Canada); Public Works and Government Services Canada (PWGSC); and the Canadian Space Agency.

3. Allocation of Patent Rights in Research and Development Contracts, Treasury Board Minute 468904, 18 August 1954.

4. Chapter 314m of the *Administrative Policy Manual (Science and Technology – Contracting Out)* December 1987.

5. Section 12 of the Copyright Act.

6. Treasury Board Circular 1986-25 (TB 801628).

7. TB 817067, 19 September 1991.

8. Treasury Board Memorandum, December 1991.

9. Canadian Patents and Development Limited was a Crown corporation the aim of which was to assist in making more available to the public, through industry, the licensable products of publicly financed and publicly or institutionally performed research.

10. Canadarm is perhaps one of the best known Canadian accomplishments in space. Designed and built by the Canadian firm Spar Aerospace Ltd., the Canadarm was a gift from Canada to NASA's space shuttle programme. The first Canadarm, technically called the SRMS (space shuttle remote manipulator system), flew on the shuttle Columbia in 1981. NASA then bought Canadarms to equip the rest of the shuttle fleet. The Canadarm has consistently and successfully been used to release satellites into orbit, retrieve them if they malfunction and aid in their repair.

11. December 1996 – Lastewka Committee.

12. *Securing our Future Together: Preparing Canada for the 21st Century.*

13. Agriculture and Agri-food Canada, Atomic Energy of Canada Limited, Canadian Food Inspection Agency, Canadian Institutes of Health Research, Canadian Space Agency, Communications Research Centre, Environment Canada, Fisheries and Oceans, Health Canada, Industry Canada, National Defence, National Research Council Canada, Natural Resources Canada, Natural Sciences and Engineering Research Council, Royal Canadian Mounted Police and Transport Canada.

14. Information Technology Association of Canada, Canadian Advanced Technology Association, Alliance of Manufacturers and Exporters, Canadian Chamber of Commerce, Aerospace Industries

Association of Canada, Canadian Federation of Independent Business, Canadian Defence Industry Association, Shipbuilding Association of Canada, Ottawa-Carleton Economic Development Corporation, Association of Universities and Colleges of Canada, Canadian Association of University Research Administrators.

15. The Patent Act, Trade-marks Act, Industrial Design Act, Copyright Act, Integrated Circuits Topography Act, and Plant Breeders' Rights Act.

16. Competition Act, the Corporations and Labour Unions Return Act, the Income Tax Act and the Excise Tax Act.

17. Paris Convention for the Protection of Industrial Property, NAFTA and the WTO.

18. Public Servants Inventions Act and the Financial Administration Act; the Treasury Board Policies: Contracting Policy, the Award Plan for Inventors and Innovators Policy, IP Policy in Procurement Contracts.

19. National Research Council, Defence Research and Development Canada, Communications Research Centre, Drug Inspection Agency, Canadian Space Agency, the Canadian Food Inspection Agency, as well as laboratories in other departments such as Agriculture, Environment, Fisheries and Oceans, Natural Resources.

20. Under the Copyright Act, the ownership of IP rests with the government, including software.

21. Under this Act, exemption to contractor IP ownership is only in cases of national security or upon application to a designated minister, and rights and obligations of contractors and Crown to foreground and background IP are defined.

22. As defined under the Privacy Act (R.S.C.) c. P-21.

23. http://laws.justice.gc.ca/en/F-11/SOR-87-402/index.html

24. www.tbs-sct.gc.ca/pubs_pol/dcgpubs/Contracting/siglist_e.html

25. The other challenges identified were skills, the innovation environment and community-based innovation. See www.innovationstrategy.gc.ca

Chapter 6

CHANGING IPR REGULATIONS FOR RESEARCHERS IN DENMARK

by

Sven Milthers[1]
Patenting and Licensing Officer, Patenting and Licensing Unit, University of Copenhagen

Introduction

Since 1957 Denmark had exempted university researchers from the standard rule that inventions done by an employee shall be disclosed to the employer, who has the right to take title to the invention within a (short) period following disclosure and with "proper" compensation to the inventor. Only full-time university researchers were exempted, not researchers at other PROs, including hospitals; however, researchers at university-related hospitals in particular considered themselves as covered by the exemption.

From the beginning of the 1970s, reports from various committees, from research councils to government committees on co-operation between industry and research, suggested changes to the system, but until 1998 no significant changes were made. The reasons included protests from the researchers' trades unions (who considered the proposals to be equivalent to nationalisation of commercial rights), universities' resistance to the rather bureaucratic and distant body proposed to handle the researchers' IPR, and lack of political will to get the necessary legislation through parliament. In public, industry representatives were very anxious to have the regulations changed "in order to have one institutional counterpart instead of up to ten individual inventors". In private, a number often admitted that they did not want any major changes to the system, as it was often much easier to get a good deal with an individual once-in-a-lifetime inventor than it might be with a system of professional licensing offices in the larger government research institutions.

Before the new law, only one of the twelve Danish universities had an office that truly dealt with technology transfer. This was the technically oriented University of Aalborg, which had been very active since the late 1980s in a primarily regional technology transfer operation supported by the European Communities as part of the EC regional policy for "peripheral districts" in member countries. In the late 1980s, the other universities and a few hospitals had established embryonic industrial/external liaison offices which dealt mainly with advising on applications for external funding of research projects. A few other PROs – some of the government laboratories – had had functioning TTO operations since the late 1950s. In the mid-1990s, a few hospitals developed their external liaison offices in the direction of a TTO, but this was not a general trend in Danish hospitals at the time.

Innovation policy in Denmark has for many years focused on improving conditions for innovative entrepreneurs. This has included establishing better funding possibilities, public financial support for professional advice on management, recruitment, marketing, patenting, etc. The only programme formally combining higher education with innovation was for many years the special "industrial PhD programme" whereby a company could be refunded about half of the costs (including salary) for a PhD student preparing his/her thesis in the company lab with guidance from a university professor. The new law is a first step in recognising that PROs' higher education responsibilities include participation in innovation in close co-operation with industry as well as training scientists who can be employed in industry after graduation (and then trained in innovation).

This case study first presents the situation prior to the new law on inventions at public research institutions, which entered into force in June 1999 and discusses the main features of the new law and how it was implemented, including the handling of disclosures at PROs. Next, the ways in which the new law seem to affect technology transfer operations are examined. A more analytical section then looks at lessons learned about dealing with IPR at PROs: the effects on co-operation, the dangers of uncritical adoption of approaches used abroad, the possible negative effect on the PRO of too enthusiastic commercialisation of the results of public research. Finally, Denmark's experience and the lessons learned are summarised.

The situation prior to the new law on inventions at public research institutions

In August 1998, the Ministry for Research and Technology made available to all universities and governmental research institutions (national laboratories) a preliminary proposal for a new law on "intangible rights". The main feature of the proposed law was to give universities and research institutions the right to take over all IPR of research employees, establish a secrecy period of up to 12 months and sanction researchers who did not comply with the new rules on disclosures. The response was unanimous protests from universities, professional associations within academia, professors of law in the area of intangible rights and from all kind of agents in branches of society affected by the proposed changes to the general IPR regulations.

In response to the heavy criticism, the ministry lowered its ambitions and in November 1998 presented to parliament a proposal for a new law on inventions at governmentally controlled research institutions. The main changes were that the proposal was now restricted to inventions that were either patentable or could be protected as utility models, that the institution had four months to decide whether to take title and rights to commercialise the invention, that it now included all employees, that the sanctions had been removed and that hospitals were not included, as they are owned by the regional authorities (counties).

After lengthy discussions in the parliamentary committee, which included a closed session with IPR specialists and representatives of a few relevant interest groups, the proposal was changed on two major points:

- The period for the institutional decision was shortened from four to two months (in order to respond to employee criticism).

- The law was to include all PROs, i.e. hospitals were added (upon request from the hospital authorities, who wanted a share in the implementation grant).

The law was passed in parliament almost unanimously on 27 May and signed by the Queen on 2 June 1999.[2]

Features of the new law

In order to get a correct picture of the relation of this law to the general discussion of technology transfer or dissemination of knowledge to society by PROs, a brief description of the main features of the law is useful:

- The law only concerns inventions that can be protected under the international rules of patents or utility models but not know-how in general or other IPR-protectable knowledge. In this connection, it must be remembered that, according to other acts of parliament, researchers at universities and other PROs had an obligation to publish their research results and to take part in international scientific development "without (unreasonable) delay".

- The law regulates all inventions at PROs, not only those by researchers. Thus, whereas the law can be considered to diminish the previous rights of university researchers, it improves those of other university employees as well as all kinds of employees at other public research institutions (primarily hospitals and national laboratories).

- Disclosure of any invention ("possible invention") to the institution is obligatory and must be done without delay. If the invention takes place within the framework of an agreement on co-operation that was legally entered into before 1 July 1999, the institution must respect the provisions of the agreement even though it does not comply with the new law. However, the invention must still be disclosed to the institution which will have to decide whether these conditions are fulfilled in the individual case.

- The institution must within two months tell the inventor(s) whether it wants to take title to the invention. If the institution does not claim title within this time, the inventor(s) can exploit the invention without further delay. If the institution takes title to the invention, the law stipulates that it will have to give a fair share of the eventual net income from the exploitation of the invention to the inventor(s) and that the ministry has to approve the guidelines for this split of income for each PRO. In general, the universities and hospitals decided to split the net income in three equal shares to be given to the inventor(s), the department and the institution. If the inventor(s) has/have the right to exploit the invention then (s)he/they can keep two-thirds of the net income, the other third to be shared by the institution and the relevant department.

- Only the head of the institution can authorise the institution to sign an agreement with external partners on rights to future IPR, and this must normally be part of an agreement on research co-operation. Individual researchers are not allowed to enter into such an agreement and thereby risk limiting the institution's freedom to decide in which direction research should be developed and with which partners.

- Each institution must decide upon its own local rules on how to share eventual net revenue (as mentioned above); these rules must be (and have been) approved by the ministry.

- Normally, the institution receives a down payment and royalties based on income from sales when it licenses IPR to a company. The new law makes it possible for the institution to accept equity in the company as full or partial compensation, instead of the traditional types of remuneration, if the company makes such an offer. However, universities and national laboratories are still not allowed to establish a company to develop the invention in order to exploit it and only invite investors to take part in developing the company when the invention has somewhat matured. Hospitals in the counties, however, can enter into the establishment of a company if they meet a number of conditions.

- When approving the law, the parliament set aside a (small) special grant of about EUR 2 million a year to make implementation more attractive to the institutions in the first four full years (2000-03).

Putting the new law into practice

The law was approved by Parliament in late May 1999, with 1 January 2000 set as the date for full implementation of the new regulations. Since a few national laboratories had been working actively under the former general IPR regulations, the universities and university hospitals suggested establishing a working group with experienced IPR administrators from those PROs along with representatives from the larger universities and university hospitals to discuss and eventually agree on practical guidelines for the implementation of the law and to further the mobility of researchers among institutions and lower potential barriers to inter-institutional research co-operation. Both the Ministry of Research and Ministry of Industry participated in the group as observers. The working group was established late in June, began work in August and presented its results at a workshop for the future administrators of the law at institutional level at the beginning of November.

The working group developed a proposal for a standard declaration of disclosure to be used by all institutions upon their individual decisions. This was done both to remove obstacles to the disclosure procedure in cases where researchers from different institutions had made a joint invention and to ensure that all institutions received the information necessary to evaluate the properties of the invention. Some of the topics to be dealt with in the declaration were considered to be compulsory for all institutions, but it was also recognised that the missions and working conditions of different categories of institutions could necessitate different information on the invention before the head of the institution could take a decision.

The working group also developed a set of proposals for standard documents and procedures to be used by the institutions. The material included documents concerning the participation of master's and candidate students in projects with external (commercial) partners and their adherence to the new regulations, as well as letters covering the administrative work, primarily internal, to be carried out to document the different stages of each case.

The working group had a long discussion on the possibilities of drafting "standard" agreements on licensing and on research co-operation with industrial partners. It decided not to draft such standard documents but drew up a rather long list of elements to be considered during the process of drafting individual agreements. It also reached an agreement with the ministry on the limits to the institutional guidelines on the splitting of income, leaving room for minor differences.

In terms of handling disclosures internally at PROs, the working group recommended that all PROs adopt a system as similar as possible to the one used for a number of years at the Risoe national laboratory. There, the disclosure is first discussed with the head of department who makes a first judgement of whether the potential invention is ready for disclosure to the institution, *i.e.* sufficiently documented and presented. The head of department forwards the disclosure to the patent administrator, who makes a preliminary study of whether the disclosure contains the information necessary to start the decision-making process. The patent administrator then convenes a meeting of the patent committee, which has a variable membership since it consists of the deputy director and the head of the department that forwarded the disclosure. The inventor and eventual advisers/experts take part in this meeting, at which the committee decides what the institution wants to do with the invention. If the decision is positive, it will include a budget for eventual external assistance to evaluate the patentability of the invention and costs for the eventual filing of an application as well as a preliminary strategy for its commercialisation. The conclusions of the patent committee are approved by the head of the PRO.

Individual procedures at PROs differ both in terms of the composition of the decision-making body and the division of labour between the administration and the committee. These differences are mainly due to differences in institutions' structure and culture.

Effects of the new law on operations of TTOs at PROs

With the coming of the new law, handling of inventions became a duty of all PROs. To stimulate the implementation of the law, the parliament decided to grant a total of about EUR 8 million to the institutions in 2000-03. This implementation grant could only be used to cover the "external costs" of patenting and marketing inventions, with a limit of EUR 20 000 per invention for expenses. Thus, it could not be used to cover salaries and other internal costs for establishing a technology transfer operation, for instance. The institutions could only get access to the funds upon application, specifying the expected number of disclosures. For the first two years only universities and university hospitals could apply but in the last two-year period, applications from all PROs have been accepted.

So far most of the intellectual property and technology transfer activities have been carried out in campus units, but some geographically close institutions have established joint offices or very close "virtual" co-operation. It has from time to time been suggested to establish a few technology-specific TTOs, but so far the proximity of the TTO to researchers has seemed more important when setting institutional priorities and deciding on the development of technology transfer.

At first, all universities (apart from Aalborg) were somewhat uncertain as to the precise content of the new obligations and the resources needed and thus hesitant to establish true TTOs with a broader mission. This was apparent in the responses to the OECD questionnaire of spring 2002. In the beginning, a number of small PROs assigned the job to a current administrative employee as a very small fraction of his/her duties. Only some of the major institutions established new full-time positions for these activities.

During 2002, however, there was a notable expansion of institutional manpower for this activity which continues in 2003. The basis for the expansion is the rapidly increasing number of inventions disclosed to the institutions since January 2000 and the realisation that an invention or a patent application does not market itself. There are no precise statistics showing the annual increase in disclosures since the implementation of the new law, but it is the impression of all TTO staff at universities and university hospitals that disclosures doubled between 2000 and 2001 and continued to increase in 2002. It takes hard work to get an invention presented to potential and relevant industrial partners and to negotiate an agreement to achieve a result that is acceptable to all parties. It also reflects the increasing understanding of the need for reasonably precise agreements on how to handle and share potential IPR when a co-operative research project is started (or even planned), especially when the project has both university and industry participants. Expansion has been largely funded internally by the institutions, but some have received support from government, local government and/or private sources.

Overall, inventions in biotechnology/molecular biology are most numerous at Danish PROs, but this varies according to the field of specialisation of individual institutions. Other important fields include IT, engineering, physics and chemistry in general. Table 1 shows the distribution among types of institutions and fields of inventions of disclosures handled at universities and university hospitals that receive funding from ministerial grants. Since the national laboratories did not take part in the grant scheme in 2000-01, comparable figures are not available for them at present.

Table 1. Distribution of disclosures at universities and university hospitals, 2000-01

	Universities	University hospitals
Biotechnology/medico-technical	53	45
Biotechnology/agro	9	
IT and electronics	31	
Production and materials	16	
Energy and environment	13	
Total	122	45

Some lessons learned about dealing with IPR at PROs

It is probably too early to evaluate the effects and effectiveness of the new law. However, a few lessons can be shared. The following sections address the handling of co-operation between PROs, both nationally and internationally; the handling of co-operation between industry and PROs; the trade-off between benefiting from foreign experience and maintaining national traditions and regulations; and the danger of over-emphasising the benefits of research-based inventions as a basis for entrepreneurship of PRO staff.

Handling co-operation between PROs both nationally and internationally

Researchers from different institutions often co-operate on research projects, and they do so to get the best results based on the combination of their special qualifications. Such research projects can lead to inventions and these should be secured for later exploitation.

It is essential to reduce as much as possible the administrative burden of commercial exploitation, and it is also essential to ensure that the interests of those involved are taken into account.

Quite a few of the typical "consortium agreements", sometimes between domestic and foreign PROs and often including industrial partners, have rather burdensome centralised means of handling potential inventions. One way to deal with this is to avoid centralised procedures and instead have a combination of rules with the following content:

- A definition of the field/scope of co-operation that is as precise and narrow as possible and a description of the interests and "qualifications" of each individual partner in the specific project/field.

- An invention belongs to the partner(s) that made it or where it has been made, according to national legislation.

- Disclosure must be made at the institutions involved according to the rules of each PRO.

- The partners involved must decide on how to handle the invention on a case-by-case basis, preferably nominating one institution as responsible for administering the chosen strategy and determining who must involve the other partners at certain defined milestones (typically in due time before the major steps in the patenting process). It is important that these "invention consortia" can act decisively in the commercialisation process and not be stopped by a slow and burdensome decision-making process in every discussion with a potential industrial partner.

- The costs and the potential benefits are shared by the eligible partners willing to participate according to national regulations. The cost sharing can be done either at milestones or at regular intervals.

These recommendations can become even more important with the constantly changing and differing rules on IPR in the European and/or OECD countries and should be applicable to situations both with and without industrial partners.

Handling co-operation between industry and institutions

It is essential that both parties respect the very different backgrounds and conditions of the other partners interested in participating in the project in question.

It has often been said that universities cannot – and will not – protect the commercial secrets of industrial partners. This can be true to a large extent, not because of lack of respect for companies' need to keep certain vital information about their products secret, but because universities are educational institutions that teach students up to the highest academic levels. Universities may therefore prefer not to have such secrets and leave any eventual co-operation on sensitive items to individual consultancy by the professor at premises outside the university, primarily in the company. This type of co-operation between university and industry is more highly developed in the United States and the United Kingdom than in Denmark. It should be further developed in Denmark and there should be openness about this kind of contract so as to avoid obvious conflicts of interest, especially for university employees.

An obligation not to publish results in international scientific journals for a period longer than one to three months is unacceptable to universities, especially in the case of co-operation projects at the frontier of international research, where it is essential to be first to publish on the subject in the highest ranking international scientific journals. In the United States, the standard condition is one month to evaluate a draft publication followed by an obligation of secrecy for another two months if the company wants to file a patent application. This has been (and still is) difficult to understand and accept for a number of industrial partners, at least in Denmark.

A last example of the barriers adduced is that universities demand excessive prices from industry both for co-operative projects and for development projects for which the university does the development that would have been done in the industrial company if it had the necessary qualified staff or equipment. It is argued that the government covers the universities' basic costs. However, universities are state institutions that must respect the regulations of the Ministry of Finance, the national auditing agency and European Union rules on competition. The regulations of all these agencies have placed a number of restrictions on how to define the true costs to be borne by the external partner and how to define when a research project can be considered "co-operative". If the university does not follow these rules quite strictly, they can be heavily criticised and even "punished" by the authorities. Universities are not allowed to do development work for industry unless they charge "market price" and they are not allowed to give (too) favourable treatment to external partners because this might give them a government-financed competitive advantage.

The trade-off between benefiting from foreign experience and maintaining national traditions and regulations

The issue of the use of research results in industry has been under constant discussion for several decades. Typically, when a delegation of high-ranking decision makers and/or civil servants has gone abroad to find inspiration for new legislation, they have found very interesting means of handling certain aspects of this issue and have tried to import or copy them more or less unchanged at home. The problem is that they often do this by establishing a new institution or organisation without realising that almost all the surrounding conditions will differ, *e.g.* the national taxation system, social security, funding of housing, funding of entrepreneurial activities, etc. This practice of "policy learning" is not restricted to Denmark.

From the point of view of the PROs, it would be better to clarify that the responsibility for making the best social use of the results of their participation in the innovation process should lie with the PRO, on the condition that they can act on reasonable market conditions when they participate in technology transfer.

The danger of over-emphasising the benefits of research-based inventions as a basis for entrepreneurship by PRO staff

In current discussions about increasing the use of research-based inventions in future industrial production, there has been a strong tendency to make the contribution of universities equivalent to the number of new university start-ups or spin-offs in one year compared to the previous year. This is a very narrow policy view and may even be harmful to the universities if followed to the extreme.

The point is that a large number of researcher-inventors have absolutely no intention of becoming entrepreneurs with their own start-up company, rightfully so for many of them. They primarily want to have their inventions used to benefit society, to get extra funding for their research activities in case of successful commercialisation and to continue their university research and teaching. They might be persuaded to take up a part-time position as research director in a company if needed to get the transfer of the invention and the surrounding technology well in place and put the further development process along the appropriate road, but the sooner they return to their research laboratory and new research projects the better.

It could be rather disastrous for universities if all creative researcher-inventors left them permanently to join new companies. Research would most likely become less innovative, and the researchers remaining at the universities would likely be much less aware of the potential commercial possibilities of their research. The teaching of students and thus future researchers would suffer from the lack of good role models of inventors in the teaching staff, and this might weaken the innovative approach of universities in the years to come.

Conclusions

With the adoption of the new law on inventions at public research institutions, the Danish government took a considerable step towards giving university PROs in particular the additional responsibility of participating with industry in innovation. The new law allows PROs to own patents and utility models based on the work of PRO personnel. The conditions are strict. Disclosure of an invention to the PRO is obligatory, and the PRO must indicate to the inventor(s) within two months whether it wishes to take title to the invention. If it does, the inventor(s) receive(s) a fair share of the eventual net income. The participation of PROs in IP-based spin-offs is strictly regulated. In practice, it is only feasible as (part of the) remuneration for IPR developed in co-operation with industry.

Changing the law was a first step. Implementing it was a second step that required considerable effort. Insofar as possible, this was prepared jointly with the PROs, using standard documents and procedures but leaving the individual PRO some freedom. In addition, the procedure for handling disclosures of inventions at PROs was standardised using the system developed at the Risoe national laboratory as a point of departure. However, procedures at individual PROs may differ to reflect differences in their organisational structure and institutional culture.

In conclusion, to establish a working technology transfer system, it is necessary to:

- Break down external and internal walls and barriers to communication and understanding between industry and academia.

- Create much better conditions for mobility between industry and universities, in both directions. This could include making it easy for university researchers to take part-time and/or temporary positions in industry and vice versa.

- Give universities and other PROs full responsibility for their participation in society's innovation process.

- Ensure that top management in both industry and at PROs takes responsibility for innovation and sees the development of innovation as their most important strategic responsibility.

More general lessons learned on the broader topic of commercialising research results of PROs include the need to:

- Reduce as much as possible the administration burden involved in national and international co-operation for the exploitation of the results of co-operative research, while respecting the interests of the various partners.

- Respect the different backgrounds and situations of partners in co-operative research between PROs and industry, regarding for example openness in contract research carried out by university professors, publication delays and using "fair" market prices when universities engage in development projects for industry.

- Take care not to adopt foreign experience uncritically.

- Make the best social use of the results when PROs participate in the innovation process.

- Avoid presenting the number of PRO spin-offs and start-ups as the optimal way to commercialise the results of public research. This is not the only way to commercialise these results and taken to the extreme can be harmful to the operation of PROs.

If all of this is kept in mind when commercialising the research results of PROs, it will provide a sound basis for the development of a "knowledge-based economy".

NOTES

1. The observations in this study are those of the author, who is solely responsible for the conclusions.

2. An English version of the Act on Inventions at Public Research Institutions is available on the Web site of the Danish Ministry for Science, Technology and Innovation (www.videnskabsministeriet.dk/temaer/opfindelser i offentlig forskning)

Chapter 7

FRENCH TECHNOLOGY TRANSFER AND IP POLICIES

by

Alain Gallochat
Advisor, French Ministry of Research and New Technologies
Associate Professor, University of Panthéon Assas – Paris 2

Introduction

Over the past few years, the French authorities have given innovation and its protection greater priority. Other countries, such as the United States and some European countries, had acknowledged their importance even earlier.

French public research is composed of several categories of public research organisations (PROs):

- EPST (établissements publics à caractère scientifique et technique), such as the CNRS (Centre national de la recherche scientifique – www.cnrs.fr), INSERM (Institut national de la santé et de la recherche médicale – www.inserm.fr), INRA (Institut national de la recherche agronomique – www.inra.fr), INRIA (Institut national de la recherche en informatique et automatique – www.inria.fr).

- EPIC (établissements publics à caractère industriel et commercial), such as the CEA (Commissariat à l'énergie atomique – www.cea.fr).

- EPSCP (*établissements publics à caractère scientifique, culturel et professionnel*), including universities and public engineering schools that undertake research (France has more than 90 universities).

Table 1 gives the number of priority patent applications filed in France during recent years by some EPST and EPIC.

Table 1. Priority patent applications filed in France, 1997-2000

	1997	1998	1999	2000
CNRS	106	102	168	161
INRA	16	21	31	27
INSERM	61	64	67	79
CEA	197	208	217	210

Source: OST, 2001.

Although the overall situation improved, the figures in Table 1 do not give an exact picture of innovation carried out in these organisations. In particular, it was difficult to get figures for universities, whose laboratories are increasingly joint laboratories, *i.e.* controlled by both an EPST and the university. In most cases, for inventions obtained in joint laboratories, patent applications, if any, were filed under the name of the EPST alone, so that universities' results in terms of innovation were not recognised. Over the same period, royalty income of these organisations increased substantially, by 20% for INSERM and 100% for CNRS, for instance. Despite the improvements, French public research faced major problems:

- A lack of relationships with industry.

- Inadequate financial return for the PROs (as pointed out in a report from the French *Cour des Comptes*).

- An extremely low number of patent applications filed by the PROs.

The problem was both cultural and legal. The legal issue involved the status of researchers, which precluded them from undertaking the commercial development of their inventions outside their laboratories. In this respect, the 1999 law on innovation and research greatly improved the situation (see the following section).

As far as the cultural problem is concerned, it will take time to change researchers' behaviour. To encourage such changes, the French authorities developed in 2001 recommendations or guidelines (discussed below).

Basic or specialised training in the area of intellectual property is a key issue which must eventually be discussed by the relevant ministries. This will undoubtedly require much time and effort, as such training should not be limited to scientific disciplines.

The law on innovation and research

In order to deal with the weak relationships between public research and industry and to facilitate the use of the results of public research in industrial products or services, the French authorities presented a new law which was adopted by Parliament.[1] The law was mainly intended to promote the creation of innovative technology companies and the transfer of research funded by the public sector to industry. In their presentation of this law, the French authorities summarised the existing unsatisfactory situation:

> "France has considerable resources in terms of science and technology but combining research discoveries with industrial applications is achieved less easily than in other industrialised countries. The shortfall in this collaboration can be

seen in the structures, in the difficulty of setting up effective partnerships between research establishments and companies and in the low level of contacts between research workers and the economic world.

"Thus, while experience shows that the economic utilisation of the results of research is an important factor underpinning the dynamism of the economy, the number of companies created every year using the results of research funded by the public sector remains too low. It is, however, precisely these companies that have the strongest growth potential.

"The purpose of the law on innovation and research is to reverse this trend and provide a legal context that fosters the creation of innovative technology companies, notably by young people, whether they be researchers, students or employees."

This law made a significant change in the innovation and research landscape by improving researchers' mobility. Previously, if they worked outside their laboratory setting, they would lose their civil servant status. The law also introduced provisions to foster co-operation between public research and industry. Other provisions were directed towards improving the fiscal and legal framework for innovative companies.

Researchers' mobility

The law allowed researchers to create a company to develop and exploit their research results while maintaining their civil servant status. Researchers, teacher-researchers, engineers, young holders of doctorates, technical and administrative staff can now be involved in creating a company to exploit their research. They can participate as partners or managers of the new company for a period of time (a maximum of six years), at the end of which they can choose between returning to the public sector or staying with the company.

Under the law, the researcher's organisation can pay the researcher's salary during the start-up phase, so that those involved in starting up companies are not penalised in terms of their research careers. A contract defines the link between the company and the research establishment whose work is being exploited.

Until 1999, a researcher was allowed to spend a limited amount of time providing scientific support (consulting activity) to industrial companies. The new law broadened this option to allow research staff to provide scientific support to a company developing their research work while remaining in the public sector. A researcher can now spend up to 20% of his/her time in this consulting activity.

However, to form a company, offer consulting activity to the company or manage or act as a director of the company, researchers must receive approval from the relevant PRO, following advice from a national committee (*Comité national de déontologie*) in charge of examining the requests presented in accordance with Article 25.1 (creating), 25.2 (consulting) or 25.3 (managing) of the 1999 law. By the end of 2001, 168 requests had been approved and as of 30 June 2002 the number had risen to 236. Most refusals have been due to the fact that researchers' requests came after the company had been set up, although the law stipulates that approval must be obtained prior to the company's creation.

In addition, the law provides that a research employee can contribute to the capital of a company that is developing his/her research. She/he can hold up to 15% of the company's capital. The employee agrees, in return, not to take part in any negotiations between his/her organisation and the company.

Co-operation between public sector research establishments and companies

In 1999, the French authorities were of the opinion that researchers' mobility was necessary but not sufficient to foster co-operation between public research and industry and therefore included in the 1999 law two important provisions concerning incubators and SAICs (*services d'activités industrielles et commerciales*).

Creating company incubators

It appeared that there were many valuable projects that might lead to the establishment of new companies as either spin-offs or start-ups and to the creation of new high-technology jobs. However, most of these projects failed to do so because they lacked legal, technical and financial advice. Therefore, the 1999 law allowed higher education and research establishments to set up incubators to provide premises, equipment and material for young companies and for those hoping to create companies. This measure encourages in particular the creation of high-technology companies by research staff and students.

As of 1 January 2002, 31 incubators in various parts of France had been officially recognised;[2] since 1999, 239 innovative companies have been created after passing through these incubators.

In addition, the 1999 law also established a national competition to promote the formation of innovative companies, whether or not coming from an incubator. Winners receive a financial award. Since the creation of the competition, around 500 companies have been set up and created some 2 800 jobs (www.recherche.gouv.fr/technologie/concours).

Creating SAICs

Before 1999, most EPST and EPIC had their own technology transfer office (TTO), either as an internal service or as a subsidiary. Universities, however, almost never had a TTO or similar service. When preparing the 1999 law, the French authorities considered it very important for universities to have such a service. This meant finding qualified personnel outside the universities, as they were not available within them. The problem was to offer an attractive salary, which was not possible if those hired had civil servant status. Therefore, it was necessary to create a structure for hiring qualified people at a salary corresponding more or less to what they might obtain in the private sector.

Furthermore, in order to take rapid decisions, the structure had to be flexible and reactive, and rules for public accounting were difficult to apply to such a structure. The 1999 law therefore provided for SAICs to cope with these difficulties. According to the law, universities and research institutes could create SAICs to manage their research contracts with companies or with other public-sector bodies. These services could also cover activities such as patent management, service provisions and editorial activities. More flexible budgetary and accounting regulations were implemented to make it possible to carry out these activities on a business footing and to recruit staff.

However, it took some time to set up the SAICs, because it was necessary to define which industrial and commercial activities were involved and therefore subject to taxation. This is not an easy task, and the problem has yet to be fully resolved.

Some PROs preferred having a subsidiary rather than a SAIC. From 1 January 2003, all the industrial and commercial activities of these subsidiaries will be subject to taxation under the rules applied to the income of industrial companies. For the SAICs, only those activities deemed profitable will be subject to taxation. For example, financial compensation arising from an R&D agreement will not be considered as profitable if the IP results are owned or at least co-owned by the PROs, but will be deemed profitable if the industrial partner owns the results (in this case, the R&D agreement is considered a service agreement that falls within the scope of profitable and taxable operations).

Implementing decrees were published in 2002 concerning the functioning of the SAICs. During an experimental phase which started in early 2002, five universities were selected (Le Havre, Paris 13, Rennes 1, Lille 1, Saint-Etienne) and eight more were selected by the end of April 2002 (Nancy 1, Paris 11, Paris 6, Caen, ENS Lyon, INP Toulouse, INSA Toulouse, Rennes 2). This experimental phase terminates in early 2003. The experimental SAICs are publicly funded, with a total allocation of EUR 1.6 million in 2002.

As noted above, the 1999 law also included new fiscal and legal provisions, which are summarised below.

The fiscal framework for innovative companies

Liberalising the BSPCE scheme

The law liberalises the company founder's share warrants scheme (BSPCE – *bons de souscription de parts de créateur d'entreprise*) to cover all new and expanding companies. The scheme, which allows purchase of shares in a company at a price fixed in advance, is restricted to companies created less than 15 years ago. The law reduces from 75% to 25% the share of the company capital that must be held by physical persons when the warrants are issued. The law also extends the benefits of BSPCE to companies registered on the New Market.

Liberalising the FCPI scheme

The innovation investment funds (FCPI – *fonds communs de placement dans l'innovation*) has been improved to enable them to invest in all innovative companies. These funds, which attract personal savings into new innovative companies by means of tax incentives, can now invest in any company approved by ANVAR (*Agence française de l'innovation*), provided that the company is not more than 50% owned by an existing company.

Making research tax credits more valuable

Finally, the provisions of the 1999 law with regard to research tax credits (CIR – *crédit d'impôt recherche*) should promote the recruitment of research staff. The operating costs rate, set according to staff costs, has been increased to 100% for companies employing a young doctorate holder. This provision enables companies to co-operate with a highly qualified person capable of providing them with the latest advances in a specific field. This complements the adaptation of the CIR in the 1999 budgetary law in order to promote innovative companies (notably through immediate reimbursement of the tax credit). The CIR is not limited to small entities, although MSE (medium-sized entities) with less than EUR 40 million in revenue take particular advantage of this measure. In 2000, the CIR amounted to EUR 529 million and concerned 6 344 companies which declared total research expenses of EUR 10.25 billion.

The legal framework for innovative companies

Extending the scope of the simplified joint stock company scheme

The current status of limited liability companies is not very well suited to the needs of young risk companies with high growth potential. The simplified joint stock company scheme (SAS – *société par actions simplifiée*) has been extended so that all innovative companies can benefit from it. The scheme offers great flexibility:

- Greater contractual freedom suited to the rapid expansion of these companies enabling rapid modification of the capital structure and relationships among shareholders.

- The possibility of issuing preference voting shares enabling the founders to maintain control over the company without limiting access to new capital.

- Paperwork reduction for companies with limited administrative resources and called on to make quick decisions.

- The possibility of forming a company with a single partner.

Recommendations for the adoption of an intellectual property charter

Immediately after the implementation of the 1999 law, it appeared to the French authorities that it was necessary to focus the attention of PROs, particularly universities, on the protection and exploitation of the results of their research. Mainly owing to their culture, researchers were not familiar with IP issues and left some of their results unprotected, which made their development and exploitation by an industrial partner highly unlikely. The authorities also found it necessary to point out the importance of being professional when negotiating with an industrial partner.

Therefore, the Ministry of Research prepared recommendations or guidelines concerning the protection of the results and the partnership with industrial companies. The recommendations were prepared jointly by representatives of the ministry, PROs and industry.

Since March 2002, the recommendations have been presented in more than 20 French administrative areas, and will be presented in the remaining areas in the first half of 2003. It is felt important to explain why such recommendations have been prepared and to receive comments and criticisms from users. Among criticisms, the lack of human or financial resources is often cited.

In June 2001, the recommendations were sent to all heads of PROs. The aim was not to impose a policy but to draw attention to the issue of adopting a policy based on the guidelines contained in the recommendations. More and more universities, EPST and EPIC are in fact adopting a charter based on the recommendations, which address six issues concerning the in-house situation but also external partnerships, including with industry (www.recherche.gouv.fr/technologie).

The charter is part of a policy to maximise the social and economic impact of the results obtained by PROs in order to create employment, facilitate the creation of new companies and respond to social needs. Therefore, the minister of research sent, along with the recommendations, a cover letter pointing out that results must be exploited in partnership with companies in a professional and trustworthy climate. Visibility of the results should be ensured, along with recognition of the role of the participating teams. New research agreements should be reached and follow-up of inventions should be guaranteed in the interest of both companies and institutions. The institutions should be remunerated and the research teams motivated through incentive measures. Finally, it should be considered that these efforts increase the attractiveness of France in a competitive world.

These recommendations point out different possibilities for protecting and exploiting PROs' results either alone or in collaboration with private or public partners, including industrial ones. According to the nature of the results, the different means available are as follows:

- Industrial property can be protected by the filing of an application or by secrecy. Depending on the field, the application concerns the patent system, the plant variety certificate system or the semiconductor products protection. Know-how should be protected through a confidentiality agreement.

- Protection of literary and artistic property concerns in particular software and databases. Specific reference is made to the exploitation of software through a GPL (general public licence); the institution decides on the method of protection and exploitation.

- The collection of biological samples falls within the scope of protection of databases mentioned above.

- Living matter constitutes a peculiar field owing to rapid international evolution in the relevant regulation (including European Directive 98/44). The revision of the French laws on bioethics will deal with this issue.

Having called attention to the principles enabling PROs to obtain the best possible protection for their research, the recommendations then deal with ownership of results when these are obtained in one PRO, involve several PROs or a joint laboratory and when the partnership includes an industrial company.

Principles related to the ownership of the results

The recommendations clearly insist on the fact that the preferred solution is for the PRO to own its results or at least own them jointly (the French legal situation concerning the ownership of results is discussed below).

According to the recommendations, ownership or joint ownership of results will: facilitate the follow-up and the visibility of inventions; allow the institution either to retrieve exploitation rights, should the industrial partner fail to exploit the results, or to engage in partnerships with others in different industry fields; make it possible to better negotiate their exploitation, should the industrial partner modify its shareholding or its strategy; promote the creation of new companies in accordance with the law on innovation and research.

Application of these principles in a partnership

To promote better links between PROs and industry, some recommendations and words of advice are given to alert PROs to the importance of this issue.

Recommendations

Ownership, or at least joint ownership, is strongly recommended. A joint ownership agreement must be signed by both parties.

It is possible to make a distinction between the ownership and the commercial exploitation of the invention. The industrial partner can take full ownership, if the invention only concerns the partner's very specific domain. However, in this case, financial compensation in addition to payment for the cost of the research should be negotiated.

In applying the principles, account should be taken of: what is contributed by each party; the most appropriate way to exploit the results; the wide variety of situations faced by different institutions; the need to conclude an agreement within a reasonable period of time (making a clear distinction between high-value commercial exploitation and more ordinary inventions for which the negotiating period should be reduced).

In cases of joint ownership agreements involving several institutions, only one institution should be in contact with the industrial partner and in charge of administering the agreement. Industry is likely to find this difficult to accept, probably because of industry's cultural environment, but also because of the lack of professionalism of some PROs. Through their recommendations, the authorities seek to modify this cultural environment and to improve the professionalism of PROs.

In the case of consultant agreements and contract research for which ownership is determined by the partner ordering the research or consultancy, *i.e.* when no inventive work is involved in making such agreements, specific treatment is envisaged.

Words of advice

In the case of a partnership with industry, PROs should take special care in the following areas:

- Ownership of the results, bearing in mind that in cases of joint ownership, an agreement on ownership must be concluded when the R&D agreement is made, taking into consideration:

  - Scientific and/or legal situation (patents, etc.) prior to the R&D agreement.

  - Field/domain of the collaboration.

  - Full cost of the programme.

  - Development plan specifying which party bears the cost of protecting the invention, including abroad, and which is responsible for initiating infringement suits and for bearing the cost.

- Licensing, and more particularly the granting of exclusive licences. In the latter case, particular care should be taken when defining the domain, when setting minimum annual royalties and addressing the possibility of transforming exclusivity into non-exclusivity, if the invention is not exploited properly within a given period of time.

Among the various possible relationships between PROs and industry, specific attention is paid to spin-off or start-up companies. For these, the principles must be adapted to take into consideration the high importance of ownership of research results and such companies' lack of funds. Two situations should be distinguished:

- The results were obtained by the institution before the creation of the spin-off or of the start-up. In this case, the institution should, in principle, have the ownership of the results and grant an exclusive licence to the start-up. It should be recalled that some investors are reluctant to allocate funds to a spin-off or a start-up that only has an exclusive licence; they want the company to have full ownership.

- The results are obtained after the creation of the spin-off or start-up. A collaboration agreement should be concluded between the spin-off or start-up and the institution, possibly with joint ownership.

In both cases, assigning the rights to the start-up can be envisaged, if this is the most appropriate way to commercialise the results; in this case, the institution should receive shares in the start-up.

In addition to ownership of results and partnerships, the recommendations address the organisation of intellectual property in order to promote better professionalism in the PROs, while also satisfying the aim of public research, *i.e.* to increase general knowledge.

Organisation of intellectual property

It is important to reconcile respect of intellectual property and the need to inform the public, particularly in the case of inventions in sensitive fields, such as biotechnology. Therefore, some measures have been presented and attention will be drawn to them in the near future.

Care to be taken to protect results adequately

Researchers, broadly defined, need to become more aware of intellectual property issues so that they do not disclose their results inappropriately. They must also be aware that they are not the owners of their results, which are owned by their institution, although they have the right to have their name mentioned on patents. The head of the institution is responsible for filing a patent application, applying for a plant variety certificate, a utility model or an application concerning software. As a result, the researcher is to be informed that he/she is not entitled to: decide whether to file patent applications for his/her inventions; allow an industrial partner to file the patent applications; preclude the filing of a patent or a plant variety certificate application by his/her institution through unreasonable disclosure.

The use of laboratory books is to be developed and be mandatory.

The filing of a patent application is not a goal in itself, but a preliminary step before the commercialisation of the results. It is justified only if there is a market, possibly in the medium term. Therefore, patents should be abandoned if they are not exploited within a reasonable period of time.

It will be some time, however, before this part of the recommendations is fully enforced.

Organisation of commercialisation services

A key issue is the creation of such services in public institutions. The law on innovation and research should facilitate the creation of such services, possibly through the formation of a SAIC, whose staff must have an appropriate profile and be trained in preparation of agreements. Practical experience, a good knowledge of intellectual property issues and experience in litigation are desirable.

Agreements and licences should be negotiated in close collaboration with lawyers, experts in intellectual property and in the technical field and specialists that are well acquainted with industry.

Institutions with a limited patent portfolio may be most interested in obtaining partners at local level.

Specific mechanisms are needed to facilitate linkages between the services and laboratories. Liaison personnel should be named.

In conclusion, the minister of research who signed the cover letter of June 2001 to the recommendations insisted on the importance of improving the professionalism of the staff assigned to the commercialisation of research findings in public institutions.

Other legal issues

Ownership of inventions involving salaried inventors, particularly in the public sector

Right to title

The right to title is clearly established by the French CPI (*Code de la propriété intellectuelle*). Article L.611-6 provides that:

> "The right to the industrial property title referred to in Article L.611-1 shall belong to the inventor or his successor in title."

Specific treatment is given to salaried inventors who have an employer. Article L.611-7 of the French CPI (www.legifrance.gouv.fr) makes a distinction among the various situations that are summarised in Table 2 and apply to inventors from both the private and the public sectors.

Table 2. Sources of inventions and rights to title

Inventions realised by an individual	Right to title
a) In the performance of a work contract to carry out research corresponding to the person's effective functions or to studies explicitly entrusted to him/her.	**Employer** has full right to title
b) Although the conditions of a) are not fulfilled, the invention falls within the employer's field of activity or uses the employer's knowledge or means.	**Employee** has right to title, but the employer is entitled to have the ownership assigned to him
c) All other cases	**Employee**

In all cases, the employee must inform the employer of the invention. The employer gives the classification of the invention proposed by the inventor as a), b) or c). In case of disagreement, a national committee (CNIS – *Commission nationale des inventions de salariés*) arbitrates.

However, a problems arises for the PROs in which inventors may be researchers but also trainees, students or post-docs. When the students, trainees or post-docs receive financial compensation (a salary or something similar), they are considered as salaried persons so that their inventions, if realised according to case a), are owned by the PRO employing them. The situation is much more complex when such persons are not salaried. In that case, Article L.611-7 of the French CPI does not apply and only Article L.611-6 of the French CPI applies. This means that the patent application will be filed under the sole name of the trainee, student, or post-doc when he/she has done the work alone, or jointly with any researchers from the PRO involved. Such a situation could develop in future, and ways to cope with this problem are being studied. Furthermore, Article L.611-9 indicates that:

> "The inventor, whether salaried or not, shall be named as such in the patent; he may also oppose such identification."

Co-ownership (joint ownership)

More and more often, an invention is made by several inventors from different PROs (or a combination of PROs and industry). In this case, when applying Article L.611-6, the patent application is filed under the names of the different employers, resulting in a jointly owned title. The French CPI provides for such joint ownership of patents; Article 613-29 stipulates the rights and obligations of the joint owners.

However, the provisions of this article are very strict (for some acts, unanimity of all joint owners and/or a court decision). For this reason, many still oppose joint ownership. However, it is always possible for future joint owners to avoid falling under Article L.613-29 and Articles L.613-30 and L.613-31 (relinquishment of his share by a joint owner), by concluding a freely negotiated joint ownership agreement, defining the rights and obligations contractually accepted by the joint owners. This departure is possible under Article L.613-32.

The recommendations described above clearly favour this method, provided that the joint-ownership agreement is signed as early as possible, at the same time as the R&D agreement for instance. Such an agreement would include, among other clauses, provisions related to the decision to file a patent application or any other IP title, to extend the priority filing in foreign countries, to license the title, along with a clear statement of who bears the cost of these different actions.

While some industrial partners are still reluctant to engage in joint ownership, others have already signed a general agreement with CNRS that includes this possibility.

Financial incentives for inventors in the public sector

According to Article L.611-7 of the French CPI, additional remuneration is to be provided to inventors entitled to benefit under case a) (see Table 2). This provision applies only to those inventors in the private sector whose additional remuneration is often quite limited. In case of conflict, cases can be brought before the CNIS.

Article L.611-7, paragraph 5, provided that the situation of public-sector inventors would be envisaged at a later date. This was only done in 1996, through two decrees dated 2 October 1996 (Nos. 96-857 and 96-858, which were modified by Decrees Nos. 2001-40 and 2001-41).[3]

Decree No. 2001-40 is directed at the additional remuneration for inventors referred to in Article L.611-6; this additional remuneration represents 50% of the net revenues received by the establishment employing the inventors, up to a fixed amount (around EUR 60 000 a year) and 25% of revenues above this. According to Decree No. 2001-41, similar remuneration, in terms of percentages and fixed amounts, is available for persons having participated in the creation of software, plant varieties and know-how. The categories of persons entitled to receive this additional remuneration are listed in the decrees.

Nevertheless, these decrees are not fully satisfactory for the following reasons:

- The inventors who are researchers in PROs but not specifically mentioned in the decrees are not entitled to receive any additional remuneration.

- As mentioned, inventors who are not salaried are not entitled to receive additional remuneration, but they must be considered as joint owners, which creates a rather complex situation.

- The treatment is different for inventors who are PRO researchers entitled to the additional remuneration, for inventors who work in PROs but who are not entitled to such remuneration and for private-sector inventors who often receive very limited, often token, additional remuneration.

Care must be exercised in such complex situations, since, in the same scientific R&D programme, future inventors of different types work together but later receive substantially different additional remuneration.

Conclusion

The 1999 law on innovation and research, followed by the 2001 recommendations, sent a strong message to PROs to improve the protection and the exploitation of results derived from public research. Of course, PROs must be assisted in a task which is completely new for some of them. The French authorities are conscious that much effort is needed to reach the goal fixed by these texts. However, these efforts concern not only the PROs but also industry. Thus, on 11 December 2002, Nicole Fontaine, in charge of industry, and Claudie Haigneré, in charge of research and new technologies, announced jointly new measures in favour of innovation,[4] and a new law on innovation may be prepared early in 2003. Among these measures are:

- New legal status for business angels.

- Under certain conditions, recent innovative companies obtain a tax reduction.

- Investments in R&D may lead to a tax reduction; the CIR is to be revised.

- Further measures to foster co-operation between researchers and industry, to acknowledge researchers' efforts devoted to innovation and to give researchers an incentive to file more patent applications.

- Measures to attract more students to science and innovation.

NOTES

1. Law No. 99-587 of 12 July 1999, published in the *Journal Officiel* of 13 July 1999. The text is available at www.legifrance.gouv.fr

2. See http://France.incubation.free.fr or www.recherche.gouv.fr/technologie/mesur/incub for further information.

3. Decree Nos. 96-857, 96-858, 2001-40 and 2001-41 are available on www.legifrance.gouv.fr

4. See www.recherche.gouv.fr/plan-innovation or www.industrie.gouv.fr/plan-innovation for the full text. Interested persons can comment on the measures.

Chapter 8

LEGAL REGULATION OF PROTECTION AND COMMERCIALISATION OF INTELLECTUAL PROPERTY CREATED BY RUSSIAN PUBLIC RESEARCH ORGANISATIONS

by

Dr. Natalia Zolotykh
Deputy Director General, Legal Office, Transtechnology, Moscow

Purpose

This case study focuses on the Russian Federation's experience in shaping state policy on intellectual property (IP) created by research organisations (scientific institutes, research institutes, Russian Academy of Sciences, universities) as a result of research and development (R&D) financed from public resources. Special attention is paid to the legal framework for innovation activity in the Soviet era and to the Russian Federation's attempt to provide a balance between the interests of all participants in the innovation process, including the state. Attention is also given to the measures to be taken by the Russian government to create a coherent and effective system of legal protection of intellectual property and the commercialisation of technologies created by public research organisations (PROs).

The case study also addresses civil and legal problems for the co-operation of research organisations with different entities, including the Russian Federation, scientists and private companies, including foreign ones, on matters of creation, protection, transfer and use of intellectual property rights (IPR) created with support from the federal budget.

Methodology

This study analyses legislation and other legal documents in the field of financing, creation, protection and use of intellectual property. It draws on interviews with participants in the innovation process, in particular representatives of the state scientific research centres and universities, the Ministry of Industry, Science and Technologies of the Russian Federation, the Russian Agency for Patents and Trademarks, the Ministry of Economic Development and the Ministry of Education.

The case study is also based on statistical data of the State Committee for Statistics of the Russian Federation, official materials of the Russian Agency for Patents and Trademarks, materials of plenary hearings at the State Duma and reports of government bodies.

Legal framework for the protection and use of intellectual property in the USSR

General characteristics of the innovation system of the USSR

The innovation system of the Soviet Union was typical of a planned socialist economy. It was based on a system of command management of economic activity involving research institutes and industrial enterprises. The cornerstone of this system was a state monopoly on the ownership, use and disposal of the economic rights, information and results of the scientific and technological activity and IPR of these entities. Strict, centralised state management of the creation and transfer of R&D results, as well as IP, excluded development of market relations by innovation enterprises, drastically reduced their interest in competitive research and its industrial use and worked against the development of international scientific and technological co-operation.

It is true that the Soviet Union had many excellent scientific achievements which opened the way to new areas of technological development. However, it is common knowledge that the speed of a fleet is determined by that of the slowest ship. For this reason, the individual scientific and technological achievements of soviet research organisations failed to raise the general technological level of industry and reduce the gap between research and industry.

As a result, the commercial value of a substantial part of the scientific potential of the country was lost, and the technical level of the country's industrial complex generally lagged well behind that of industrially developed countries. To a considerable extent, this unfavourable situation existed not only in the innovation sphere but also in the economy as a whole.

Legal framework for patent and licensing by PROs in the USSR

The patent and licensing activity of PROs in the USSR reflected the soviet view of an innovation system. There was no legal framework in the usual sense of the term. No single legislative act regulated patenting and licensing activity, only regulations and special guidelines published by state bodies entrusted with executive power.

Soviet research organisations and scientists did not own rights to the results of their intellectual efforts and therefore could not seek their commercial exploitation either in the country or abroad.

The results of scientific research, including protectable results, could only be transferred, free of charge, in the country and in the framework of the Council for Mutual Economic Assistance (CMEA).[1] A commercial form of transfer was used only in relations with industrially developed countries that were not members of CMEA. However, research organisations and scientists had no intellectual property rights and could not license their scientific and technological results. These functions were carried out by a state organisation (Licensintorg), which was established to protect the interests of the Soviet Union in matters of licensing. Licensintorg had monopoly rights, conferred to it by the state, to make licence agreements for transferring the right to use soviet inventions and know-how to foreign companies. Although organisations and authors of inventions did not participate in the licensing process, they sometimes participated in negotiations with potential licensees, but only in a technical capacity. Their opinions concerning the commercial conditions of a licence agreement were not taken into account. When Licensintorg concluded a licence agreement, the organisation that developed the licensed technology could receive a payment, which did not exceed 30% of the price of the licence. This payment could only be used in a way determined by the state. Out of this sum, the enterprise was obliged to remunerate authors of inventions and persons who helped in its creation and realisation (for example, employees who participated in the preparation of patent applications, persons who prepared the technical documentation, interpreters, etc.). The amount of such remuneration was small and strictly limited in terms of the maximum allowed.

A similar scheme of legal protection of scientific and technological results was created by soviet organisations outside the country. Upon a state order, the Chamber of Commerce and Industry gave a monopolistic right for patenting soviet inventions abroad to its section, called "Soyuzpatent". A decision on the foreign patenting of soviet scientific and technological results was taken by state bodies with executive power with funding from the state budget. It took into account the scientific value of an invention, its technical importance and protection of the state's scientific prestige. Economic criteria, in particular the commercial potential of the invention, did not essentially affect decisions on foreign patenting.

In spite of strict centralisation and the monopoly on patenting and licensing of soviet inventions abroad, the soviet government paid considerable attention to the organisation of inventive, patent and licensing work at state research organisations. For example, a survey of patenting and licensing activity of PROs, carried out by the working group on innovation and technology policy, showed that most patent divisions (similar to technology transfer offices) were created between 1971 and 1980.

This was due to the fact that the state took special measures concerning the creation and state financing of divisions responsible for patenting and licensing work in soviet research organisations. Additional stimulus for the creation of patent divisions during this period was the adoption of state and branch standards, which stipulated conducting patent investigations at different stages of the innovation cycle, revealing potential sources of IPR, filing patent applications within the country, etc., with strict state control with respect to their observation.

Legal regulation of intellectual property in the transition period

The restructuring of the social and economic sphere, which began in the mid-1980s, was accompanied by the rapid development of market relations. This required substantial changes in the legislation of the USSR, including that related to IPR.

At the end of the 1980s and beginning of the 1990s, the Soviet Union adopted legislation and special regulations in the areas of intellectual property, taxation, investment policy, restriction of monopolistic activity, stimulation of competition and foreign economic relations, which differed markedly from the previous soviet legislation.

The USSR Law on Inventions of 1991 was truly revolutionary. After almost 70 years, the state abolished the authorship certificate and its monopolistic right to all inventions created by state organisations in favour of a form of patent protection of intellectual activity which gave authors of inventions exclusive rights to ownership, use and disposal. There were no restrictions on the transfer of patent rights to third persons, including foreigners.

There were also no serious restrictions on the rights of authors of inventions (employees) for "employee's inventions" created in the course of employment duties or based on work assigned by the employer. The only exception would be an employee's voluntary refusal of his right to a patent by concluding an agreement with his employer defining the rights and obligations of the parties, including those relating to the transfer of rights for the use of an invention to third persons. Official data show that this rarely occurred. Thus, employer organisations, essentially PROs, only had the right to use an "employee's invention", created and patented with state budget resources, in its own manufacturing. As the overwhelming majority of PROs do not have manufacturing capacity, this was hardly an option. They therefore could not get commercial return from intellectual property created by their employees with the use of state money and in course of their employment duties.

Obviously, essentially automatic granting of exclusive rights for "employee's intellectual property" to authors, *i.e.* PROs employees, did not stimulate organisations' innovation activity. It interfered with the initiation of international scientific and technological co-operation, considerably increased the risk of uncontrolled leakage of technologies, including military ones, from Russia, and caused enterprises to refuse patent protection of the results of scientific and technological activity.

During this period of time, there was a drastic decline in PROs' patent activity, which was accompanied by the dismantling of the patent divisions of public organisations. The transition to new methods of managing the economy, which coincided with a sharp reduction in the state financing of R&D, aggravated the situation. In spite of an apparent increase in the number of international licence agreements, payments for licences plunged. Thus, the transition to a market economy in the scientific and technological sphere, which was made more difficult by the absence of adequate legal and economic mechanisms, was quite difficult for soviet enterprises and for the Soviet Union as a whole.

This period was difficult for soviet scientists and inventors as well. Lacking the necessary knowledge, experience and financial and legal support, including from the organisations in which they worked, most were unable to make use of their legal right to their intellectual property. Moreover, their attempts to enter the world technological market by themselves (owing to a lack of demand backed by funds at home) were viewed negatively by foreign companies, which were unwilling to spend time and money to acquire IP obviously burdened with the rights of third persons (notably the Soviet Union itself[2]). They were also viewed negatively by their own organisations, which felt that individuals attempting to find an application for their inventions were selling at dumping prices scientific capital created by a large team over a long period of time and disclosing confidential information with high commercial value.

A paradoxical situation arose, in which IP with high potential value created by soviet research enterprises drew no commercial interest and was not sought after by industry at home and abroad because of a lack of clarity in the legislation regarding its ownership and disposal.

At the beginning of the 1990s, it became obvious that IPR policy required modification aimed at strengthening the role of organisations in terms of the ownership and use of intellectual property and eliminating many inconsistencies in previously adopted legislation. The disintegration of the Soviet Union in December 1991 hastened this process.

Legal regulation of intellectual property resulting from research by PROs

Advantages and disadvantages of the legal system of the Russian Federation as regards innovation

At the end of 1992, a set of laws regarding intellectual property was adopted by the Russian Federation.[3] The provisions of these laws were adapted to fit the standards defined in TRIPS and were co-ordinated with the norms of most international agreements and conventions. These laws lay the foundation for Russia's legal system in the area of protection and use of the results of scientific and technological activity.

In particular, the Patent Law established that an author, or any physical or legal entity indicated by the author, can act as patentee (irrespective of the source of financing), and, in the case of an employee's invention, an employer, if not otherwise specified in the agreement between the employer and the employee.

The participation of the Russian Federation and its entities in relations regulated by the patent legislation is not envisaged directly. Therefore, the Russian Federation can at present only implement its rights to patents obtained with the use of federal budget resources on the basis of a special federal law, Decree of the President or a Resolution of the Government of the Russian Federation.

Official patent statistics show that the articles of the Patent Law on the developing organisation's rights to results of "employee's" scientific and technological activity stimulated patent activity by such organisations. However, the survey of patent and licensing activities of PROs showed that the lack of clarity in matters of ownership and use of intellectual property created with the use of federal budget resources considerably complicated this process.

These issues were not clarified in the laws on intellectual property rights or in other legislative acts relating to the results of R&D obtained by PROs.[4] At the same time, according to the opinion of many experts, they were indirectly reflected in the Civil Code,[5] and the law "On Information, Informatisation and Protection of Information".

For example, the Civil Code gives state clients[6] preference for obtaining rights to protectable results created in the course of scientific research, experimental design and technological work. However, this mechanism is used only when the participants do not define ownership rights and use of inventions in an agreement. Although this aspect of the Civil Code does not directly relate to R&D results obtained with the use of federal budget resources, many lawyers think that it can be used by analogy to obtain rights to intellectual property obtained during the execution of scientific research and experimental design funded by the federal budget.

A different approach to ownership of rights is recorded in the law "On Information, Informatisation and Protection of Information", which establishes that the Russian Federation and its entities are the owners of information resources, created, acquired and accumulated with the use of resources from the federal budget and these entities' budgets.

Analysis of the legal framework governing intellectual property shows that Russian legislation takes sometimes quite opposing approaches to recording the rights to intellectual property of different actors (*i.e.* the Russian Federation, PROs, scientists) as well as for different forms of scientific and technological results, *e.g.* those submitted in the form of patented inventions, information or know-how. This makes it quite difficult for research organisations to select the most effective form of protection when commercialising technology under conditions of independent economic activity, in order to preserve their rights to created research.

In the mid-1990s, the legal vacuum in respect of the ownership and disposal of intellectual property created with the use of federal budget resources could be partly filled through the provisions of a state contract for the performance of scientific research and experimental design. However, this form of civil commitment between state bodies and performing organisations was obligatory only for a certain category of state clients and was not widely used in the civil scientific and technological sphere. Therefore, organisations that were not administratively subordinated to a state client considered themselves free from any obligation to transfer to it any rights to intellectual property obtained during the performance of work.

This period of time was characterised by active privatisation of state enterprises and a lack of control of the use and transfer of R&D results. There was as a result a redistribution of rights to the results of scientific and technological activity, an outflow from the country of the most valuable inventions from a commercial point of view and of highly qualified scientific personnel as well as a loss of industrial production. The legal vacuum in respect of ownership and disposal of intellectual property created with federal funding led to many disputable relations, from a legal viewpoint, between participants in the financing, creation and use of intellectual property. This was one of the basic reasons for the undermining of the international community's trust in the effectiveness of technological co-operation with Russia.

The resulting situation led the government to address the need to develop explicit intellectual protection policies. This involved a comprehensive analysis and a combination of organisational and legal mechanisms that would help shape an effective system of protection, defence, transfer and use of intellectual property obtained with financing from the federal budget. At the same time, the government sought to encourage the modernisation of industry and the commercialisation of scientific and technological results through relevant measures.

Legal acts regulating ownership and disposal of intellectual property created with federal budget resources

Explicit policy in respect of the ownership and use of intellectual property, obtained as a result of scientific research and experimental design financed fully and/or in part with public resources, is an important factor in activating the innovation process. It is especially important for countries where the majority of scientific research, experimental design and technological work is funded from the state budget. The Russian Federation is one such country.

In the Russian Federation, the first attempts to formulate the key provisions of state policy in this respect were only made at the end of the 1990s. A first step was the Decree of the President of the Russian Federation "On state policy for the introduction of the results of scientific and technological activity and objects of intellectual property in the sphere of science and technologies into an economic turnover" (22 July 1998, N 863). In execution of this Decree, the government adopted the Resolution "On the use of the results of scientific and technological activity" (2 September 1999, N 982).

At approximately the same time, legal acts were adopted regulating the activity of entities engaged in innovation, including PROs, when commercialising the results of scientific research, experimental design and technological work of military, special and dual use. They include the Decree of the President of the Russian Federation "On legal protection of the results of scientific research, experimental design and technological work of military, special and dual use" of 14 May 1998 (N 556) and the Resolution of the Government of the Russian Federation "On paramount measures for legal protection of the interests of the state in the process of economic and civil legal turnover of the results of scientific research, experimental design and technological work of military, special and dual use" of 29 September 1998 (N 1132) adopted in execution of this decree.

The above decrees and resolutions, which set the framework for state policy in respect of IPR and innovation strategy, were used as a foundation for this case study. The main provisions of these legal acts confirmed the tendency, already apparent in legislative acts adopted in the mid-1990s, to establish the rights of the Russian Federation to the results of scientific and technological activity obtained with funds from the budget of the RSFSR and the federal budget and to determine a strategy for their disposal and use.

According to the state policy, state clients generally dispose of such rights on behalf of the Russian Federation, but for rights to the results of intellectual activity of military, special and dual use, state clients co-ordinate with the Ministry of Justice, represented by the Federal Agency for Legal Protection of the Results of Intellectual Activity of Military, Special and Dual Use.

All performers of scientific research, experimental design and technological work funded from the federal budget to meet state needs, which involves technologies of military, special and dual use, can preserve the right to obtain a patent or other protection document (envisaged by the legislation of the Russian Federation) for themselves, as well as the right to use the results obtained, only with the consent of the Ministry of Justice and the state client. As a rule, civil intellectual property is used to meet state needs[7] on the basis of a free, non-exclusive licence granted at the discretion of a state client. For purposes not associated with federal state needs, rights to scientific and technological intellectual property obtained with the use of federal budget resources can be transferred to third persons under licence agreements.

Theoretically, the provisions of the state policy in respect of intellectual property rights and innovation were aimed at creating the conditions for preserving the country's intellectual potential and its effective use, by securing the rights and legitimate interests of all legal entities, including the state, in the areas of creation, legal protection and use of the results of scientific and technological activity and IPR.

However, the policy did not take into account international experience and the background of scientific research in the Soviet Union. Serious drawbacks in these legal acts, which aimed at obtaining rapid implementation of the results of domestic investigations and developments in the world market, more than at shaping an effective system of commercialising inventions and creating competitive high-technology enterprises, have not helped to establish a favourable environment for innovation.

It is remarkable that the concept of protection and use of intellectual property obtained with the use of federal budget resources in a commercial context, contained in the above legal acts, was not accompanied by corresponding legal, organisational and economic mechanisms. This was exceptionally slow because of heated debates on this subject in government, scientific and industrial circles, with the result that such mechanisms were not available to state clients and performing organisations.

In particular, the key and most disputed provision pertained to the recording with the Russian Federation of all rights to the results of scientific and technological activity obtained with the use of federal budget resources. As a result, not a single patent application was filed with the Patent Office of the Russian Federation (and not a single patent was issued) for intellectual property obtained with the use of federal budget resources, the rights to which, according to the state contract, belong to federal bodies entrusted with executive power.

The survey of patenting and licensing activity of PROs, which carry out the overwhelming majority of R&D funded from the federal budget, shows vividly that the adoption of the above-mentioned legal acts has not stimulated them to protect and commercialise their IP. The survey also indicates that, under present legal conditions, public organisations do not wish to disclose to the state client information on protectable objects of intellectual property, although they are obliged to do so in accordance with the conditions of the overwhelming majority of state contracts. Considerable results of R&D protected as know-how and some successful efforts at commercialisation are an indirect confirmation of this.

Specific aspects of financial support to PROs

The adoption of these legal acts presented PROs with another extremely difficult problem relating to co-financing of scientific research, experimental design and technological work from federal budget sources. Co-financing of scientific research from several sources is a widespread practice worldwide. Russia is no exception. Such financing is widely used, for example, to link the budget resources of several state clients, budget and private resources, as well as budget resources of a state client and foreign investor, budget resources and grants, etc.

Financing from different foundations of state ministries and establishments, which receive money from federal budget sources for target financing of R&D (in accordance with targets and purposes determined in the charters of these foundations), is also widely used in Russia to support scientific R&D.

Although the legal acts discussed here do not specifically include provisions pertaining to different types of financing, analysis of these documents in combination with other legislative acts[8] offers a basis for affirming that they can be applied to such financing. Moreover, the provisions of these legal acts should be taken into account even when the research work is fully financed from non-budget sources (for example, private firms). Even in such cases, it is highly likely that in performing R&D, research organisations will use some background IP they have created using state budget resources, which they will then transfer to the financing party, despite the fact that, according to the above legal acts, this IP is with some exceptions[9] the property of the Russian Federation.

Characteristic features and specific peculiarities of contractual relations

Under the present legal framework, an important role is played by state contracts. They may introduce some clarity into relations between a state client and the performer (PRO) in terms of ownership and disposal of intellectual property as well as its transfer to third persons. At the present time, there is no established model for state contracts, which are obligatory for all state clients. Therefore, each state client, in the framework of its competence and the legal system, can determine the rights and obligations of the performing body with respect to intellectual property obtained in the framework of a state contract.

In practice, therefore, individual state clients take their own approach to defining relations with performers regarding ownership and disposal of rights to IP and record them in state contracts. There are substantial differences among state contracts concluded by different federal bodies entrusted with executive power. Moreover, many state clients are still guided by the provisions of the "Typical state contract for the performance of scientific research, experimental design and technological work".[10] This contract was approved before the adoption of the above-mentioned legal acts and places less stringent conditions on the performer's ownership and disposal of the rights to intellectual property. In particular, it allows for the possibility of joint ownership of rights to intellectual property and it stipulates the right of the performer to use the results of work, including those capable of legal protection, for their own needs. During the performance of scientific research, experimental design and technological work, a performer has the right, with the consent of a client, to attract third persons, including foreign organisations. Here, the rules on general contractors and sub-contractors apply. Responsibility to the client for the consequences of non-performance or improper performance of obligations by a sub-contractor is borne by the general contractor. This also relates to the performer's obligation to transfer the right to intellectual property to a state client. Therefore, when conducting work under a state contract, a general contractor has to include relevant conditions of the state contract into agreements with sub-contractors and to verify that they are complied with.

The overwhelming majority of state contracts lack provisions obliging the performer to use, and moreover to commercialise, its scientific and technological results. This would appear to be due to the lack of clarity regarding the legal disposal of intellectual property obtained with the use of federal budget resources and to the practical impossibility for most state organisations to implement such a condition of a contract owing to a lack of qualified specialists and financial support for the protection and commercialisation of intellectual property.

As practice shows, state clients, especially those represented by federal bodies of executive power, do not take on such obligations, which are beyond the scope of their competence and are not supported by sufficient financial, human and information resources.

Analysis of the activity of state clients with respect to the economic use of the results of R&D attributed to them, based on official statistical data, sources of patent information, as well as interviews with official representatives, clearly shows that they do not manage to provide for the protection and effective management of intellectual property obtained with the use of federal budget resources, for a number of objective and subjective reasons.

Thus, although the government's plan of measures in the field of social policy and modernisation of the economy for 2000-01 (section "Innovation Economy") included among its priority tasks the development of the commercial use of the results of scientific R&D created with the use of the state budget resources, mechanisms for the ownership and use of the results of R&D and the Russian government's means of managing this process still remain unclear.

Legal regulation of relations between an employee and employer at PROs

Relations between the author of an invention (employee) and the organisation in which he works (employer) play an essential role in the activation of the innovation process to the extent that they optimise mechanisms to reveal, protect and commercialise intellectual property. The legal basis of such relations is found in the Constitution of the Russian Federation, the Labour Code, the Civil Code, laws in the field of intellectual property, in particular the Patent Law, the laws On Copyrights and Allied Rights, On Legal Protection of Computer Programmes and Data Bases, On Achievements in Breeding (Selection), etc.

Study of the legal system and interviews with authorities of PROs show that the greatest difficulties for organisations are the conditions for maintaining confidential information secret,[11] the access to such information given to a scientific worker for implementing his employment duties and the prevention of unfair competition between employee and employer.

Although Russia's present legal system contains provisions that allow an organisation to regulate its relations with an employee with respect to the secrecy of confidential information, the present Labour Code, which took effect from 1 February 2002, gave employers the specific possibility of incorporating conditions on non-disclosure of a secret protected by the law into a labour contract.

It is obvious that scientific and technological activity has certain peculiarities, in terms of keeping information confidential. Practice shows that maintaining the confidentiality of an employer's information cannot be ensured by the terms of a labour contract. Yet employees cannot be exempted from the obligation to keep such information secret. It seems expedient, to avoid causing economic damage to an organisation, to include in a labour contract a provision that the employee will keep information confidential upon cessation of labour relations with this employer, as long as the employer determines that the information remains confidential. Based on this provision, after termination of the labour contract, the parties can conclude a non-disclosure agreement, as used in civil legal relations.

A related situation arises when an employer, after the expiration of a labour contract, needs to attract a former employee for a certain activity (in particular, for preparation of patent applications and responses to examination offices) relating to the results of R&D containing confidential information, created with the participation of the employee when employed by that organisation.[12] Taking this into account, it is expedient to record in a labour contract the right of an employer to attract (under conditions agreed by the parties) an employee upon the expiration of the term of the labour contract for work in which the employee participated during his employment in order to avoid possible violation of the latter's copyright and economic damage to an organisation.

After the cessation of a labour contract, its arrangements should find their extension in the above-mentioned civil legal agreement between the parties. Although mechanisms for the legal regulation of relations between employee and employer are widely developed in world practice, they are at present poorly adapted to the Russian labour system. Its expressed social character presupposes the unconditional superiority of the rights of an employee over those of an organisation. As a result, the economic interests of organisations are often affected by unfair actions by an employee who refuses to accept his obligations with respect to the non-disclosure of a commercial secret or to be engaged in civil legal relations with an employer after the termination of his employment obligations. Another acute problem which requires an immediate solution is the existence of Russia's secondary labour market which presupposes that employees have more than one job, including with a competing organisation.

It is obvious that such problems could partly be prevented through legislation on competition. The founding legislative act of the Russian Federation in this field is the law "On Competition and Restriction of Monopolistic Activity in Commodity Markets". However, although this law creates a legal basis for regulating competitive relations, it does not provide for effective regulation of such relations regarding intellectual property, owing to the lack of standards suited to the peculiarities of relations in the spheres of science, technology and innovation.

The competition law extends only to relations affecting competition in commodity markets in the Russian Federation and cannot be applied to relations between physical persons not registered as entrepreneurs or between an employee and employer.

IP legislation also does not sufficiently cover the innovation sphere, as it does not contain provisions regulating competitive relations with respect to IPR, leaving employees with vast opportunities for engaging in unfair competition with respect to an employer or investor, and owing to the lack of economic use of their monopoly on intellectual property by owners, there is no effective resistance.

The above drawbacks of Russian legislation make investments in scientific, technological and innovation activity riskier and lead to a decrease in activity and the scale of innovation and modernisation of industry. To encourage innovation activity by public organisations, it is necessary, above all, to improve legislation concerning the regulation of competitive relations to stimulate scientific, technological and innovative activity.

Conclusions and proposals for the shaping of a legal framework for the creation and commercialisation of intellectual property created with the use of federal budget resources

General conclusions

The Russian Federation has undoubtedly made considerable efforts to develop its national innovation system, the most important component of which is the state policy on matters of ownership, use and disposal of intellectual property. At the same time, the low level of innovation by Russian PROs, revealed in particular in the persistent decrease of protectable scientific and technological results created and commercialised by them, is vivid testimony to its inefficiency.

The investigation of the four basic legal acts of the Russian Federation that are the foundation of the state policy for using intellectual property for economic return has demonstrated that these mechanisms of regulation and stimulation of innovation activity are less than optimal and that there is a lack of legal, organisational and economic measures that would encourage this process.

Thus, some mechanisms to regulate and stimulate innovation activity, relating, for example, to granting an employee considerable rights to the results of intellectual activity created in the performance of his employment obligations, were borrowed from practices of other countries without considering the appropriateness of their application to Russia. Other general mechanisms for granting organisations greater rights to intellectual property created by them, along with measures for putting an end to unfair competition in the scientific and technological sphere, have not yet been implemented. This increases the technological lag of Russian industry and to a great extent deprives the scientific and technological sphere of further guides to potential development. This negatively affects the topicality of research for industry and possibilities for further commercialisation of R&D. The substantially lower level of innovation in Russian organisations, compared to analogous enterprises of the countries of the European Union, the United States and Japan, is a serious obstacle in the way of international co-operation in innovation.

Basic recommendations

Further modification of the national innovation system is one of the most important tasks of the Russian Federation.[13] The achievement of this goal is impossible without the creation of an effective system of financing, creation, protection and use of intellectual property, including that created with the use of federal budget resources, aimed at activating the modernisation of industry and the commercialisation of scientific and technological results. It also requires the development of related measures for the implementation of this system.

The creation of this system will require Russia to eliminate uncertainty in matters of ownership, use and disposal of intellectual property created with the use of federal budget resources and to adopt the necessary legal, organisational and economic measures to encourage the use of intellectual property for economic return. There is an evident need for a clear determination of rights and obligations of all participants in legal relations in the field of financing, creation, protection and use of the results of intellectual activity, including the Russian Federation.

It is obvious that no matter how good the legislation and legal standards, the exercise of intellectual property rights will not be effective if the state's system for controlling the observation of rights granted by law is weak and there are no measures to enforce these rights. For this reason, a special place should be given in the state policy to the improvement of enforcement. Piracy in the field of audio and video products, computer programmes and databases, which raises risks of international sanctions against Russia, has unfortunately put the matters of protection of rights of owners of intellectual property into the background. At the same time, this problem will become more acute unless adequate measures are adopted by the state.

Along with the paramount measures indicated above, Russia's innovation system requires infrastructure transformations. Technology transfer offices should become one of its components. These structures, with highly qualified consultants, are called upon to help scientific research organisations protect and commercialise technologies developed with public financing, as well as to help attract investments in technological projects, the creation of links between research organisations and industry and the development of international co-operation.

NOTES

1. Subjects using inventions protected in the form of an authorship certificate in the territory of the Soviet Union were obliged to pay authorship remuneration to inventors (the total amount for all authors of the invention could not exceed RUB 20 000, approximately the equivalent of USD 35 000). The state and the enterprise that created an invention could not claim payment for its use within the country.

2. One should bear in mind that most scientific and technological discovers are not created *ex nihilo*, but are based on previous knowledge, information and rights, which may belong to third persons.

3. It included the following legislative acts: the Patent Law, On Legal Protection of Computer Programmes and Databases, On Legal Protection of Integrated Micro-circuits Topologies, On Legal Protection of Achievements in Breeding, On Copyrights and Allied Rights, On Trademarks, Service Marks and Appellations of the Places of Origin of Goods.

4. For example, the law On Science and the State Scientific and Technological Policy establishes that the legislation of the Russian Federation determined the order in which are used the results of scientific investigations of the Russian Academy of Sciences and the branch academies of sciences (including patented inventions), made from the federal budget resources. However, no legislative acts of this period contained provisions relating to R&D results obtained fully or in part by state research organisations with the use of federal budget resources.

5. The first part of the Civil Code of the Russian Federation was adopted on 21 October 1994.

6. A state client is a state body with the necessary investment resources (federal bodies with executive power) or an organisation entrusted by a state authority to dispose of such resources (including a federal state enterprise, a state establishment).

7. State needs (including federal state needs) are the needs of the Russian Federation for goods (works, services) to solve tasks involving the country's life support, defence and security and to implement federal target programmes and international target programmes in which the Russian Federation participates. Such needs may be met using state budget resources and non-budget sources of financing.

8. In particular, articles 244-255, 257-258, 769-778 of the Civil Code of the Russian Federation.

9. According to the Resolution of the Government "On the use of the results of scientific and technological activity", rights to results obtained from the resources of the budget of the RSFSR, in the part of the USSR state budget which constituted a union budget, and the resources of the federal budget, had to be recorded with the Russian Federation, if:

    – Rights for such results are not included in the privatised property in the established order.

    – These results are not objects of exclusive rights of legal or physical persons.

    – No applications were filed to obtain exclusive rights to these results in the established order.

10.   The "Typical state contract for the execution of scientific-research, experimental design and technological work" is an annex to the "Typical regulation on the order of placing orders for the execution of scientific research, experimental design and technological work of applied character for state needs by way of conducting auctions (competition) and other methods of purchasing and on the order of concluding state contracts" approved by the Ministry of the Economy (Order N 130 of 17 October 1997), Ministry of Finance (Order 74 п. of 17 October 1997) and the Ministry of Science and Technologies of the Russian Federation (Order N 94 of 17 October 1997).

11.   In the Russian Federation "employment or commercial secret" means information with an actual or potential commercial value because it is unknown to third persons, on the condition that there is no free access to it on a legitimate basis and that the owner of the information takes measures to protect its confidentiality (article 139 of the Civil Code). This definition of commercial secret is almost equivalent to the notion of "secrets of production (know-how)", given in the Fundamentals of the Civil Legislation of the Union of SSR of 31 May 1991, which is applicable in the territory of the Russian Federation where it is not in contradiction to the Civil Code. The confirmation of this is the essential coincidence of the criteria of the protection of a "commercial secret" and of "secret of production".

12.   The need to attract such an employee is explained not only by the need to do this work but also stems indirectly from legislation on IPR, for example, the Patent Law, the law on copyrights and allied rights, which require recording with the author (creator) of copyrights which are inalienable.

13.   From the end of 2001, Russia considerably increased its efforts to develop policy in the field of IPR, including IP created with the use of federal budget resources. In particular, on 30 November 2001, by the Order of the Government the "Main trends of implementation of the state policy for drawing the results of scientific and technological activity into economic return" were approved, according to which authorised federal performing bodies, including those to which the functions of state clients for scientific and technological products were entrusted by the decision of the government, should provide for recording with the state the rights to intellectual property and other results of scientific and technological activity created with the use of federal budget resources, which are directly related to securing the country's defence and security, as well as those to be brought to industrial application by the state. These federal bodies have to effectively exercise the rights recorded with the state within their competence with the aim of industrial application and realisation of the relevant products, attracting development organisations when necessary. According to the logic of this document, in all other cases, the rights to the results of scientific and technological activity are transferred to a development organisation, to an investor or to another economic entity.

At the end of last year, the State Duma of the Federal Assembly of the Russian Federation adopted three resolutions related to this question. These resolutions established the need to introduce, following a corresponding decision of the State Duma, changes and amendments into the Patent Law, into the laws On Legal Protection of Integrated Micro-circuit Topologies and On Legal Protection of Computer Programmes and Databases, relating, in particular, to the rights to receive protection documents for intellectual property obtained with the use of the federal budget resources, as well as state stimulation of the creation and use of scientific and technological results.

PUTTING IP POLICIES INTO PRACTICE

This section explores how Germany, Switzerland and Spain have implemented new policies to foster greater patenting activity and the commercialisation of research results.

Chapter 9

MANAGEMENT OF INTELLECTUAL ASSETS BY GERMAN PUBLIC RESEARCH ORGANISATIONS[1]

by

Thomas Gering, Ventratec GmbH, Munich, Co-ordinator

and

Ulrich Schmoch, Fraunhofer Institute for Systems and Innovation Research (ISI), Karlsruhe

Introduction

During the 1990s, the commercial exploitation of government-funded research performed by public research organisations (PROs) became a focal point of discussions about technological innovation. Beginning in 1996 and following a trend in industry, as well as the successful implementation by universities in the United States of a broad-based intellectual property (IP) exploitation system, the German federal government developed a series of measures geared towards more consistent protection of knowledge created by universities and other PROs in the course of government-funded research. They include:

- Publication of an international comparative report on patenting and licensing by universities in Germany, France, Switzerland, the United Kingdom and the United States.[2]

- In 1997, addition of prosecution costs regarding intellectual property to the list of costs reimbursable under government-funded research grants and contracts.

- From 1998, sponsorship of external lectures at universities providing teaching in the field of intellectual property protection.

- In 1999, implementation of new federal regulations governing the commercial exploitation of results obtained in the context of research grants and contracts granted by the Federal Ministry of Education and Research (BMBF) (the German version of the US Bayh-Dole Act).

- Reform of a section of German employer-employee law[3] (*Arbeitnehmererfindungsgesetz*) dealing with inventions by teaching faculty at universities (the so-called professor's privilege). After 7 February 2002, professors at German universities are required to report any inventions to the university. The university can take title to the invention, thereby acquiring the obligation actively to prosecute such intellectual property.

- In early 2002, implementation of a federal sponsorship programme for universities and other PROs, enabling them to hire outside services in the field of IP prosecution and licensing.

Under this scheme, the federal government suggested that PROs co-operate in clusters so that external service organisations could establish critical mass.

- Beginning in 2002, it is planned to network external service organisations so that nationwide professional development and training measures, as well as the exchange of best practices, can be established.

Most of these measures deal specifically with the university sector. In terms of assessing the results of these changes, a good deal of time will be needed before an evaluation yields valuable data.

As shown in the section on statistical information below, before the implementation of the new system most intellectual property was owned by individual members of German universities or by industrial sponsors. Therefore, relatively reliable statistical data relating to the filing of IP applications by university staff can be obtained, but for various reasons – some of which are described below – it is impossible to obtain data on financial revenue received by individual inventors.

In other PROs, however, since 1957 and the inception of employer-employee law, the legal structure relating to ownership of inventions has been identical to that of the corporate world. It obliges inventors to disclose inventions to the employer (PRO) and gives the employer the option to take title. As a result, the large number of non-university PROs in Germany has generated significant data on IP prosecution and licensing, as will be seen in the statistical section of this chapter.

These initiatives in the field of intellectual property rights and their management and exploitation, known as intellectual asset management (IAM), reflect certain changes in general innovation policy during the second half of the 1990s. Until the early 1990s, innovation policy was mainly concerned with following technological trends with a view to safeguarding the nation's position in the global scientific community while stimulating interaction with industry. This interaction was to steer publicly funded research by using the perceived knowledge of industrial concerns about market trends.

The recent focus on IAM has followed from a perception that Germany is still a leader in the international scientific community but seems to trail other nations in capitalising on the results through the development of commercial applications.

Against this background, this case study examines:

- The management of intellectual assets by PROs in general. Given that PROs generally cannot use their IP to manufacture and sell products, how can they use their IP in the framework of collaborative research, licensing and/or the creation of start-up companies?

- Some of the major non-university PROs in Germany and their objectives. How do their objectives influence the development of IP and IAM strategies?

- Statistical data on IP prosecution and licensing by German PROs. For the reason given above, these data do not include data on licensing by German universities.

- The new regulation on IP resulting from government-funded research performed by PROs. Since March 1999, PROs receiving research grants from federal ministries can elect to take title to any IP generated in the course of the research. However, if they do so, they are obligated to protect the IP and to market it actively to industry so that the private sector can exploit it commercially. In fact, PROs have to file an exploitation plan when filing grant applications. This discussion includes results of telephone interviews with PROs receiving research grants under the new regulations, as well as institutions administering such grants for the federal government and supervising their commercial exploitation. Have IAM practices changed at German PROs as a consequence of the new administrative regulations?

Generally, this case study aims to provide deeper insight into IAM practices and procedures at various German PROs.

Statistical data on IP prosecution and licensing by German PROs

General situation

The following analysis of patents and licences of PROs in Germany refers to the most important public research organisations; it does not include all PROs. Specifically, the following institutions are considered: universities, the Helmholtz Association, the Max Planck Society and the Fraunhofer Society.

For the interpretation of the data on patents and licensing, it is important to be aware of the different volumes of R&D carried out by these institutions. Universities are by far the largest segment, with EUR 7.9 billion of R&D in 1999. The R&D spending of the Helmholtz Association was EUR 2.3 billion, that of the Max Planck Society EUR 1.0 billion and that of the Fraunhofer Society EUR 0.7 billion. The ratio among these institutions is thus 100:29:13:9. Although the share of non-university PROs in Germany is relevant, universities are the most important public actor in the German innovation system.

Universities

In principle, it is not possible to provide reliable statistics on university patents and licences in Germany, since until recently the university professors privately owned their inventions. Therefore, only in rare cases, such as Karlsruhe and Dresden, did the universities establish patent and licence offices. Consequently, the professors appeared as patent assignees or sold their inventions to interested companies so that the companies (and not the professors) appear as assignees on the patent applications. Nevertheless, it is possible to provide quite reliable statistics on inventions made by professors because in Germany the title "professor" is exclusively used for university professors, and they generally use it in official documents. In a special database, the title "professor" is searchable in the inventor category so that statistics can be compiled from 1970.[4] In the data on patent statistics presented here, patent families, *i.e.* inventions for which at least one patent is filed, are used. There is therefore no double counting if follow-up applications are filed in other countries.

Furthermore, only patent applications published 18 months after the priority application date are counted, *i.e.* the publication is not equivalent to a grant. Applications withdrawn before publication are not included.

Given their volume of R&D, it is not surprising that universities apply[5] for more patents than the other PROs considered (Figure 1). Since 1970 the number of university patents has steadily increased. This is only due in part to an increase in the research activities. The emphasis by universities on the technological exploitation of their research results has also gained importance.

However, it is not possible to compute licence income of universities, as this information is generally not centralised or collected in a systematic way. It can also be assumed that a survey of all German professors would not lead to reliable information, as they might not be willing to disclose sensitive personal data.

Figure 1. Patent applications of German PROs

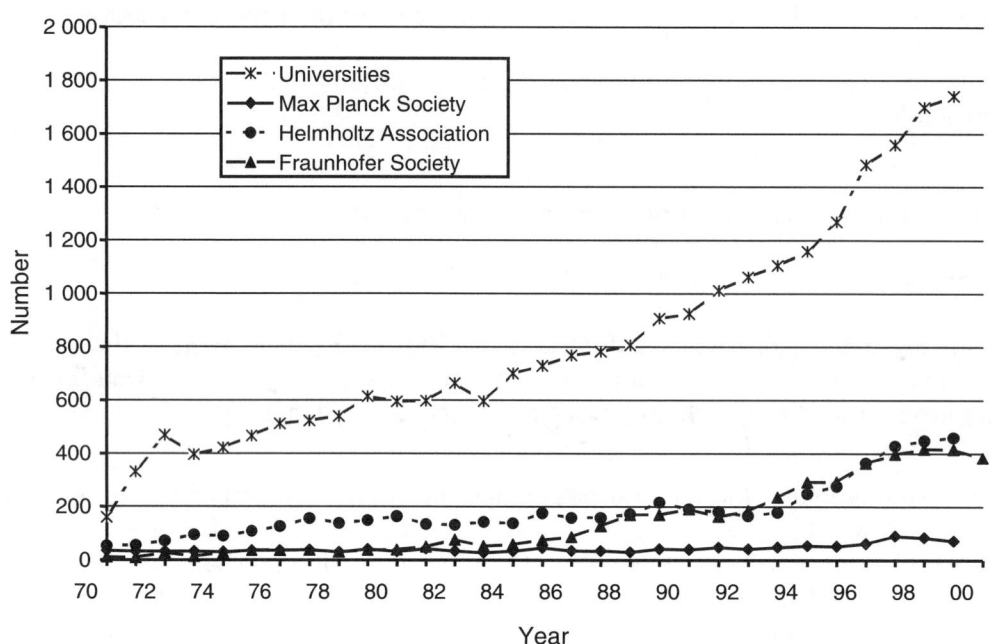

Source: PATDPA (STN), WPINDEX (STN); *Fraunhofer Patentstelle: Jahresbericht 2000/2001.*

Helmholtz Association

Helmholtz centres have always actively patented, and their patenting has increased since the beginning of the 1990s (Figure 1). Like universities, they have changed their orientation towards technological exploitation. In parallel with increases in patent filing, licensing income has increased as well (Figure 2). However, licence income has grown faster than the number of patent applications, an indication of more systematic licensing activities by the centres.

Max Planck Society

The Max Planck Society focuses on basic research. The number of patent applications is therefore low in relation to its research volume. Nevertheless, there is a general upward trend in the filing of patent applications over the last decade. While the number of patent applications is moderate, income from licences is considerable (Figure 2). For the reasons, see the section on IAM practices at German PROs.

Fraunhofer Society

Although the Fraunhofer Society's research volume is modest, it contributes significantly to patent applications of PROs. Its share increased during the 1990s. At present, the number of Fraunhofer patent applications is comparable to that of the Helmholtz Association. This is linked to the institution's focus on applied research and technology transfer. With regard to income from licences, it should be noted that about 40% of Fraunhofer patents are not taken with the intention of licensing; rather, they are used to support the acquisition of research contracts. Licence income grew considerably in the last years owing to the patent department's stronger focus on licensing activities.

All in all, patent activities by PROs increased markedly in the 1990s. In non-university research organisations, the generation of licences has become more important.

Figure 2. Licence income of German PROs

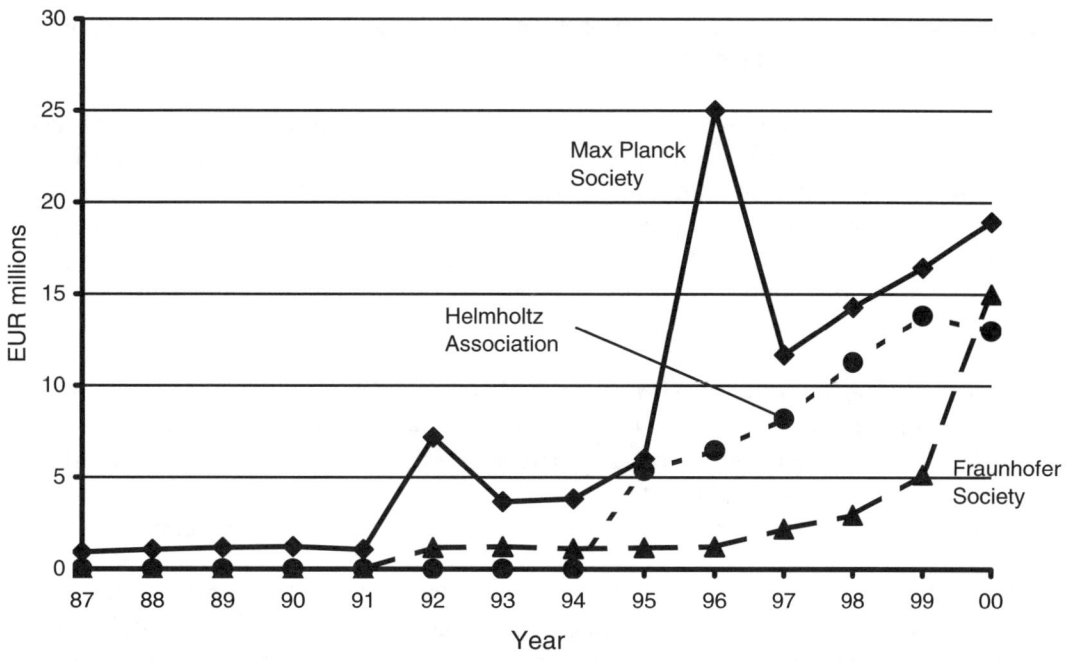

Source: Max-Planck-Gesellschaft, *Jahrbuch*, different years; BMBF; *Fraunhofer Patentstelle: Jahresbericht 2000/2001.*[6]

Intellectual asset management at PROs

There is a major difference in how PROs address the protection and commercial exploitation of intellectual property created in the course of their research when compared with the approach developed and used by industry. Industry traditionally uses intellectual property rights (IPR) mainly to protect their products and processes from being copied by competitors. Licensing to and from third parties, using IP in the course of collaborative research or to spin off companies, is at most a secondary objective of corporations. Recent trends indicate that these industry objectives are under review.[7]

However, PROs are generally prohibited from actively participating in the market through the manufacture and sale of products and processes, in most cases because of their public not-for-profit status. Instead, they use intellectual property rights in the following ways:

- Attracting third-party investment for the commercial development of scientific research results.

- Actively developing broad IP coverage for their research portfolio with a view to attracting industrial partners for collaborative research projects (see the discussion of Fraunhofer Gesellschaft below).

- Licensing intellectual property to interested industrial companies.

- Developing spin-off companies, which either obtain licences to PRO intellectual property or benefit from assignment of the intellectual property.

- Marketing and promoting public relations for the institution, particularly in the area of trademarks.

- Setting up incentive programmes to provide an opportunity for additional remuneration for innovative scientists and researchers.

As a consequence, PROs involved in collaborative research with industrial partners have to be cautious in developing their licensing policies. If they do not reserve certain areas of their IP portfolio from the granting of non-exclusive rights to industrial partners, then they may well find that third parties will not wish to use their IP for licensing or for forming spin-off companies because they cannot grant them exclusive rights to the IP. PROs can only overcome this dilemma by strategically planning their research programmes, and this can create serious challenges given the orientation towards discovery that is central to most PROs.

However, knowledge about the value of individual IPRs in different industry sectors is important for PROs. For example, it is generally in the life sciences (rather than the physical sciences, including engineering), that IP from PRO laboratories generates high value. This is partly because of the regulatory approvals often needed before life-science products can be brought to market and the sheer size of the investment required to push these products through the development chain.

In contrast, IPRs generally have limited value in engineering and information technology (IT) because these industries tend to develop technology in incremental steps and generate huge IPR portfolios around that technology to maximise protection against competitors trying to circumvent their IPR. This means that to generate income from PRO licensing in such technological sectors, PROs generally must have a longer-term commitment to a certain product area, on the basis of which they build a strategic IPR portfolio.

In many PROs, such activities are difficult to manage, especially in universities, which are principally designed to create human resources that leave the institution after a relatively short period of time.

In summary, the management of intellectual assets depends on an array of preconditions that may differ among PROs. The following sections describe different German PROs and analyse how they have dealt with these managerial challenges.

Differing approaches to IAM by German PROs

This section looks at how PROs have dealt with IAM, especially in the light of some of the constraints mentioned above. Attention focuses on the Helmholtz Gemeinschaft, a grouping of the former so-called "large public research centres", the Max Planck Gesellschaft, and the Fraunhofer Gesellschaft. This part of the case study draws heavily on previously published results [8] as well as the results of the OECD questionnaire.[9]

Beyond these institutions, only a limited percentage of PROs actively pursue existing IAM opportunities. So far, most have taken a networking approach, with an external service institution working for several PROs located in the same region. This approach is underlined by the federal government's so-called *Verwertungs-Offensive* (Exploitation Offensive) of 2002, which has so far resulted in almost 20 patent exploitation agencies working primarily for universities but also for smaller non-university PROs. Given that most of these activities only started in 2001 or early 2002, data are either not available or not representative and are not included in the section on statistical data below. As the questionnaire results obtained by the Federal Ministry of Education and Research clearly show, the regional university licensing agencies have so far only gained prominence in federal states where they were founded early on and where the number of co-operating PROs as well as their individual sizes are significant, as in the state of Bade-Württemberg. This agency, which now employs more than 15 full-time equivalents, was started in 1987, and since 1995 has been responsible for the licensing of results from all higher education institutions in this state, which has more than 15 universities and polytechnic institutes. Annual invention disclosures now exceed 200 and a significant number of new patent applications and licences are granted every year. The other regional university licensing agencies are much younger and smaller in size.

In addition to the institutions discussed in this section, an overview of the entire PRO landscape in Germany would have to include the 79 Leibniz institutes as well as the institutes directly linked to individual federal ministries or regional governments. These include, for example, the federal institute for materials research (*Bundesanstalt für Materialforschung*, BAM) and the federal physico-technical institute (*Physikalisch-technische Bundesanstalt*, PTB). Most of these institutes have little or no IP activity, and some are now linked to external service institutions; BAM and PTB are linked to the Fraunhofer Patent Centre. The questionnaire results revealed offices of one-half to about three full-time equivalents working in IAM at these institutions. Their individual patent and licence portfolios generally remain at a level of fewer than 50 active patents and fewer than ten new licenses annually. Income from these operations is generally insignificant.

Furthermore, a complete overview would also have to look into the *Fachhochschulen* (polytechnic universities or universities of applied sciences, as some have recently called themselves). Because they started out as pure teaching institutions and have only been formally allowed to perform research following on legal changes in the second half of the 1990s, most have yet to achieve any real significance in the field of IAM. However, there is a tendency by regional governments to incorporate the Fachhochschulen in efforts to develop regional service institutions in the field of IP and licensing.

Helmholtz Gemeinschaft

Within the German federal research system, the 15 large public research centres occupy a special position. They were founded by the Federal Republic in the mid-1950s and formed a major part of the national R&D capacity. In 1970, an association between the large research centres was established; in 1995 it became the Helmholtz Association. At that time, the institutions were legally independent organisations. Most institutions operated within the legal framework of a foundation, others like a company. In 2001, the members of the Helmholtz Association decided to bring all the institutions into the association so that they would in future operate under the same umbrella. With that reorganisation came a restructuring of the financing system. The former way of financing research institutions by budgeting the institutions themselves was abolished. The new financing system allocates funds by research topic. This fits with the Helmholtz Association's new aim of bringing together organisationally what belongs together thematically. The R&D budgets are now distributed on the basis of long-term research programmes.

The base funding of the Helmholtz Association accounts for approximately 75% of the overall budget; 90% of the base funding is provided by the federal government and 10% by the state in which the individual centre is located. There are currently 15 Helmholtz centres engaged in a wide variety of research. About 25% of the overall budget is earned in the context of research grants and contracts and or co-operation projects with industry.

The fundamental objective of the Helmholtz Association historically has been to perform basic research with large instruments and devices. Despite the fact that this should have been of interest to industry, there was little relationship between the large public research centres and industry except in the field of nuclear research. Since the late 1970s, efforts have been made to improve industry's co-operation with, and exploitation of, the Helmholtz R&D capacity.

Until the mid-1990s, co-operation of Helmholtz centres with industry could be described as follows:

- Co-operative research programmes and development projects.

- Manufacturing and development contracts to industry.

- Research contracts from industry.

- Patent, know-how or distribution licences to industry concerning Helmholtz results.

- Use of laboratories and equipment by industry.

- Mutual exchange of employees as well as continuing education and training measures.

In line with the reorganisation of the Helmholtz Association, treatment of patent applications and IAM in general has changed during the last decade. During the 1970s and 1980s, Helmholtz IPRs were mostly related to nuclear technology, a field in which the Helmholtz centres had strong co-operation with industry. But since their reorientation, especially that of the big former nuclear research institutes in Karlsruhe and Jülich, the centres have entered many new research areas, such as environmental technology, biotechnology and materials research. In the 1990s Helmholtz institutes have therefore started to become an IPR player in a variety of disciplines.

In these new areas, the Helmholtz centres initially focused on basic research, so that there was little contact with potential industrial partners. Many new inventions had, and often still have, spin-off possibilities; the Helmholtz Association wanted to commercialise results protected by IPRs that emerged from basic research but found it difficult to identify industrial partners. Some of the Helmholtz centres established special offices or departments for the commercial exploitation of patents and licences. The stage of development and the size of these offices vary widely; some employ less than one full-time equivalent, while others have about ten employees who deal with IPRs, licensing and IAM in general.[10] It is not yet clear how IAM strategies will change following the reorganisation of the Helmholtz Association in 2001, but the present organisation for IPRs and licensing is likely to undergo further development. One example is the newly established IAM company, Ascenion GmbH, which is meant to become responsible for the commercial exploitation of IPRs generated in the four Helmholtz centres that focus on biotechnological research.[11]

In summary, IAM in the Helmholtz Association mainly started in two centres focused on applied nuclear research and then diversified into other research and basic science disciplines in the 1990s. It therefore had to adjust its IAM approach to these different industry sectors and also to different transfer mechanisms (straightforward licensing to formerly non-related industrial parties, creation of start-up businesses, etc.).

Fraunhofer Gesellschaft

The Fraunhofer Society is the leading organisation for applied science and research in Germany. It was founded in 1949 and currently consists of 55 institutes. It is a private non-profit organisation (*eingetragener Verein*) for which the Federal Republic and the *Länder* (federal states) provide the basic budget.

The Fraunhofer Society performs research for industry, in the framework of both publicly co-funded collaborative projects or under direct commission. In recent years, up to 40% of Fraunhofer's budget was obtained from industrial customers, up to 30% came from public institutions (including the European Union) as research grants and contracts and approximately 35% is allocated as base funding.

The so-called "Fraunhofer model" is based on financing basic needs while giving the institutes incentives to collaborate with and secure research contracts from industry. To that end, the volume of basic financing is linked to success in obtaining research contracts and public research projects and rises as a result of that success. In practice, the Fraunhofer financing model has three elements:

- Financing the institutes to conduct basic research may in future form the basis of industry-oriented knowledge transfer.

- Research projects commissioned by public agencies allow long-term development of technology that improves core competencies and is oriented to industrial needs.

- Research contracts with industry allow direct use of those competencies by industry.

This financing model has been very successful over the last three decades: the turnover now is ten times what it was in the 1960s. This success is based on the balance of the different areas of knowledge creation and its transfer. Direct research contracts with industry are the prime method of technology transfer. Without the focus on basic research, the pool of knowledge, and subsequently applied science, would dry up. This model of a mix of applied, basic and contract research is also found in other European countries, *e.g.* the Netherlands (TNO), Finland (VTT) and Norway (SINTEF) and even the United States (Batelle or SRI).

Another important task of the Fraunhofer Society is performance of strategic basic research commissioned by federal agencies. This focus on applied and basic research results in a remarkable output of patent applications – as can be seen in the statistical section below – which equals the volume of the much larger Helmholtz Association. Among German PROs, the Fraunhofer Society has the highest ratio of patent activities to number of research scientists employed.

The Fraunhofer Society established a special institute, the Fraunhofer Patent Centre (*Fraunhofer Patentstelle*), which does not perform any basic or applied research but only deals with IPRs and their management. Founded in 1955 to undertake technology and knowledge transfer, it is one of the most traditional institutes of the Fraunhofer Society and the oldest institution of its kind in Germany. It transforms inventions into patents and licences and acts like a service organisation not only for the Fraunhofer institutes, but also universities and individual inventors. The original intention of the founders of the Fraunhofer Patent Centre was to provide everyone with the opportunity to get expert assistance when needed and in return to make society more prosperous. All clients of the Centre have access to all its services, such as the acquisition and the evaluation of IPRs, inventions and technologies, the filing of intellectual property applications, technological consulting, strategic planning, negotiation and issuance of licences, collecting of royalties and much more. It is by far the biggest IAM institution in Germany working almost exclusively for PROs; it currently employs more than 70 full-time equivalents, has annual royalty income of more than EUR 20 million and receives more than 2 000 invention disclosures annually, most of them from outside the Fraunhofer organisation.

Until recently, the most common path towards commercial exploitation was to collect licence fees and royalties from industry. However, in some cases, the creation of a start-up company can be an alternative for the effective commercialisation of an IPR.

The Fraunhofer Patent Centre has experimented with a number of mechanisms aiming at increasing the likelihood that a licence to its IPR will become commercially successful. Some of these mechanisms are:

- The development of prototypes showing the technical feasibility of patented inventions.

- Sponsoring IPR applications of company founders based on agreements that provide for sharing benefits if the start-up enters the market.

- Supporting start-up entrepreneurs through consultancy, including the provision of services under the federal innovation programme INSTI.[12]

- In 2000, it launched support schemes for start-up entrepreneurs by forming its own start-up company, Ventratec GmbH. When Ventratec takes on a project, it also acquires an equity stake in the start-up.

In parallel, the Fraunhofer Board of Management established a Venture Group under the supervision of the central legal department. The Venture Group is specifically responsible for consulting employees at Fraunhofer institutes who may plan to become self-employed. The Board, together with the Venture Group, has been instrumental in setting up a new venture capital fund that is intended to become operational by the end of 2002.[13]

Generally speaking, the multitude of technology transfer activities at Fraunhofer have led to a substantial presence in IAM in the German PRO landscape, as indicated by the findings of the OECD questionnaire.

However, a closer look at Fraunhofer's IAM practices reveals internal inconsistencies that so far seem to limit its effectiveness. Almost none of the institutes plans IAM in a strategic way. The Fraunhofer financing model has led to strong dependency on domestic collaborative grants and direct contracts,[14] and both the institutes and the central administration regularly provide industry with cheap access rights to Fraunhofer results and IPRs. One of the consequences of this practice can be seen when IPR prosecution costs are compared with royalty income. Here Fraunhofer ends up with a minor surplus. In fact, only one of the 54 research institutes generates substantial royalty income;[15] virtually all others lose money with their patents and claim that these are necessary if they are to remain attractive to co-operation partners in industry.[16] This practice not only has a detrimental effect on royalty income, it is also a systematic problem for start-ups, as exclusive rights to intellectual assets are almost always needed to secure third-party investment.

Clearly, the Fraunhofer Patent Centre is the major player in IAM involving PROs in Germany, but because of the inconsistencies mentioned, this know-how does not so far seem to be used systematically by Fraunhofer research institutes.

Max-Planck Gesellschaft

The Max Planck Society, with its 81 institutes and other research institutions, is part of the system of institutionally financed PROs. Its role is to perform world-class basic research. It also concentrates on scientific areas requiring large specialised equipment.

The Max Planck Society is also linked to industry by the inclusion of industrial partners as members of the *Hauptversammlung* (general meeting), which elects the members of the Senate and helps to determine the general direction of the Society. The Senate determines the main areas of scientific research.

The institutes are associated with the Max Planck Society in two different ways: their directors are scientific members of the *Hauptversammlung* and with other institutional members they build the scientific council of 270 members. This council is divided into different scientific areas and gives advice to the Senate. This structure is very important to knowledge transfer efforts, because it means that the central committee only partly guides individual institutes, which are generally free to determine their own research topics.

About 85% of the budget of the Max Planck Society is provided as institutional funding by government sources, a minor percentage is own income, and 10-15% is received as research project funding, mainly from public sources.

The research activities of the Max Planck Society are very heterogeneous. These activities include technical and natural sciences as well as the humanities. The individual institutes concentrate on technology and the natural sciences, areas where inventions and knowledge suitable for patent protection are created. While not every invention is patentable, some institutes have built up strong links with industry because of their historical development (the metal industry) or because of their increasing start-up activities (biotechnology). In terms of its patent activities, the Max Planck Society is one of the smallest of the PROs mentioned here because it is not primarily focused on development and applied science. The patent activities are concentrated mainly on areas such as biotechnology, pharmaceuticals, organic chemistry, food and measurement-testing technology.

Responsibility for the commercial exploitation of Max Planck patents does not lie with individual institutes;[17] it was given to a subsidiary, Garching Innovation GmbH, founded in 1970. During the past decade, the number of patent applications filed by Garching has remained at an almost constant level, although there has been an increase in licence income and start-up activity, as can be seen in the section on statistical data.[18]

Garching Innovation's IAM practices are very similar to some of the activities of American universities. The PRO delivering the research results (Max Planck) aspires to scientific excellence and direct contracts with industry are limited, especially with regard to collaborative research; therefore, the institution had to develop sophisticated management practices very early in order effectively to deal with spin-off-type inventions which need to be actively marketed worldwide to customers with whom it does not necessarily have a business relationship when the first contact is made.

In terms of numbers, the results are impressive, as the questionnaire results show. Although the institution only receives about 120 invention disclosures annually, it runs a portfolio of over 650 active patents, concludes about 100 licence agreements every year, and in 2001 had royalty income of about EUR 40 million.

The same holds true with regard to the stimulation of start-ups based on IP generated by the PRO. Garching Innovation was the first German institution to experiment with equity deals, and it currently has the largest portfolio.[19] Present conditions in financial markets strain the development of this business sector and may lead to changes in the Max Planck Society's overall approach to IAM.[20] In summary, in addition to the Fraunhofer Patent Centre, Garching Innovation serves as a second role model in Germany, but the circumstances with regard to their "mother" PRO are quite different.

Rules and regulations governing the exploitation of results of federally funded research at PROs

Germany has had a tradition since the late 1950s of direct contract-based research funding by the federal government. The initial policy regarding results and their exploitation was that what had been paid for by taxpayers should be available to all. Although German PROs were generally entitled to claim ownership to IP generated in the course of federally funded research, they rarely did so because they were required to license non-exclusively and also to share the proceeds with the government.[21]

Since the early 1980s, discussions have continued to circle around the question of whether or not this policy effectively promoted or hindered technology transfer. Not only were very few patent applications filed as a consequence of federally funded contract research by PROs, but evidence seemed to accumulate that, in most cases, mandatory, non-exclusive granting of rights for commercial exploitation prevents industry from adopting these results for development.

As a consequence of these discussions (which lasted more than a decade), the federal government implemented new policies and procedures in 1998.[22] The cornerstones of the new administrative regulation, can be summarised as follows:

- As early as applying for a grant, PROs have to file a so-called exploitation plan, in which they must assess the likelihood of results that could be commercialised. They also must describe the management process they will implement to achieve commercial exploitation. The grant application can project the costs associated with likely patent applications, and this figure may be included in the grant application.

- PROs receiving government research grants and contracts can elect to take title to IP generated as the result of those research projects.

- If they do not take title (according to German employer–employee law, taking title means that they have to prosecute IPR applications actively), they must notify the granting body in due time so that the government can take appropriate action to obtain patent coverage for the results if it so desires.

- PROs have to share the proceeds of commercial exploitation with their inventors.

- The government no longer participates in revenue sharing.

- There are no particular restrictions on the licensing of rights to research results; European industry, however, is favoured. PROs have to obtain government approval if they intend to license to companies outside the European Union.

The first project grants under the new regulations were administered in 1999, and some are now approaching the end of the period of federal funding, as most grants are for a period of up to three years.

The changes in administrative regulations concerned not only publicly funded research institutions. At the same time, the federal government changed the administrative regulations regarding publicly funded research projects performed by industry. In fact, one of the main aims of the new set of regulations was to improve industry's ability to innovate. This motive lay behind the introduction of the so-called exploitation plans, particularly where collaborative projects between industry and PROs have to be managed. Clearly, this leads to restrictions with regard to the design of individual administrative regulations for the PRO sector.

Also, it has been only three years since the new administrative regulations were implemented, so any evidence on experience has to be treated with caution, as institutions confronted with the new regulations generally need a period of transition.[23]

Nevertheless, experience with the new regulations in Germany are of interest, as it may allow for a comparison of the effects of similar changes in other countries and could provide other nations with valuable insight as they implement similar policies and procedures. This study did not aim to provide a comprehensive description of the German scene regarding these issues, as this would require a labour-intensive series of interviews with a large number of institutions managing grants on behalf of the federal government (the so-called *Projektträger* institutions) and with a variety of PROs. Instead, representatives from two German universities, a German non-university PRO and two *Projektträger* institutions were interviewed. The institutions were selected at random, and their feedback is not representative of the entire German PRO landscape. The institutions interviewed were: the Humboldt University at Berlin, the Technical University of Stuttgart, the *Forschungszentrum Karlsruhe*, the *Deutsches Zentrum für Luft- und Raumfahrt* (DLR) in its function as a *Projektträger* and the *Projektträger Produktion und Fertigungstechnologien* (PFT) (Production and Manufacturing Technologies).

In particular, an effort was made to obtain evidence on the following issues:

- Do the *Projektträger* have exploitation plans on file for all funded projects?

- Do these plans generally envisage patent protection for the research results?

- Did the number of patents and patent applications obtained from grants significantly rise over the level obtained under the previous regulations?

- What is the procedure in collaborative grants? Do the *Projektträger* enforce a consistent transfer policy in co-operation projects with industrial and PRO participation?

- What is the opinion of PROs on the new regulations? Do they generally appreciate the new opportunities in technology transfer provided to them by virtue of the new regulations?

- Did the PROs specifically react to the new regulations, *e.g.* by reorganising their internal processes regarding technology transfer?

The new regulations and technology transfer processes within PROs

When the new regulations were enacted, the PROs had to change their internal management procedures to benefit from the opportunities presented. Especially in universities, the management of federally funded contract research had been decentralised substantially over the previous ten years. In some universities, the central administration was not at all involved in the management of research grants – the departments and institutes applied for the grants. The only central administrative responsibility in this process was to check the budget forms and sign off on them. In most cases, the central administration did not even have copies of the work proposed on file.

The situation was slightly different for non-university PROs because they always maintained a more stringent policy regarding technology transfer and enforcing employer-employee law,[24] and some at least tried to develop an active patent policy to protect their results and use IPRs as a mechanism for technology transfer.

In all PROs, however, the new regulations created the need for a new management approach by central administration in that researchers needed to be consulted on the new regulations, the new mechanism of the exploitation plan had to be implemented, and some forecasting had to be developed regarding patentable results that were likely to be obtained. As a relatively big share of such federal grants and contracts involves industrial collaboration in the research projects, one of the most important elements of early-stage consulting is the negotiation of co-operation contracts with the relevant partners, which can be a labour-intensive process.

Universities

In the universities interviewed, the new regulations have not so far created any major changes in the management approach. The substantial additional manpower needed to reap the possible benefits of the new regulations in the medium to long term has generally not been made available by senior university management. This means that the personnel responsible for grant applications at the level of the central administration have generally tried to provide enough additional information to their scientists to allow them to adopt new strategies in their dealings both with the *Projektträger* institutions and potential industrial partners. A more active approach regarding the building up of patent portfolios has apparently not emerged. In fact, central university administrations often mentioned that the procedures required in the grant applications with regard to possible patent protection and the reimbursement of associated costs are far too complicated and leave much of the risk with the university, which is one reason why senior management is reluctant to take a more active approach.[25] In essence, the universities appreciate the new regulations and occasionally experiment with using them, but they have so far neither shifted management practices nor substantially increased the number of university IPR applications resulting from work under government grants and contracts. One university also mentioned that they did not feel a particular diligence at *Projektträger* institutions with regard to exploitation plans and that the university administration was doubtful whether such plans existed in all cases for projects that were funded.

These findings are in line with the approach taken by both universities and the federal and regional governments with regard to IPRs as a mechanism for technology transfer in general. As mentioned earlier, the old professor's privilege was abolished. The aim was not to develop IP and licensing programmes individually at universities, but to develop a networking approach among universities and possibly other PROs in a region, through external service firms that are generally organised as limited liability companies. On the one hand, this shows that successful licensing programmes require critical mass. On the other hand, regional IP and licensing institutions need to be able to root their activities in local university administrations, which use the opportunities for creation of invention disclosures, enforcement of employer-employee law, a consistent approach to collaborative research agreements, maintenance of ownership to IP and insurance of uncompromised rights to such IP.

In the period after the implementation of the new administrative regulations and before the reform of the professor's privilege under employer-employee law, senior university management generally took the position that most inventions were not under the direction of the university and that therefore no changes were needed in the management approach. It is too early to tell whether this position has changed following the reform of employer-employee law in early 2002; however, the interviews seem to indicate that senior university management now expects external service and licensing offices to do the job without the need for any internal changes to the management approach to publicly funded research projects, inventions and IP in general. Clearly, the resources of these external licensing operations will not be sufficient to achieve such a major change in culture and administrative practices in the many universities with which they generally collaborate.

Non-university PROs

As mentioned above, the situation for non-university PROs was initially different from that of the universities, because most had a tradition of working with the employer-employee law and the active prosecution of their own patent portfolios.[26]

One interview of a non-university PRO indicated that the new administrative regulations were an opportunity, whose benefits were still to be realised. It became clear that the requirement of filing an exploitation plan with the grant application may put the PRO in a weak negotiating position with industrial partners. Potential industrial partners also benefit from new administrative regulations regarding their participation in publicly funded research projects,[27] which gives them the opportunity to retain exclusive ownership to the results they achieve in the project. Knowing that a co-operation agreement and the exploitation plan are generally prerequisites for approval of a collaborative grant involving PROs, bigger industrial entities especially tend to enforce contractual regulations that generally do not give PROs more freedom of action with regard to the future commercial exploitation of their results. Because PROs often cannot wait until contract negotiations with industrial collaboration partners go in their favour, they tend to accept unfavourable conditions to speed up the grant process.[28]

This also influences PRO behaviour with regard to the active prosecution of IPRs that could result from their federally funded R&D projects. If a PRO knows at the beginning of a federally funded research project that any IPRs generated are unlikely to be licensable because of user rights already given to project partners, they will be conservative in their prosecution decisions, especially with regard to expensive international IPR applications.

Projektträger **institutions**

Two *Projektträger* institutions were interviewed in the context of this case study. Their answers were similar in the sense that both saw the new regulations and their implementation as being in their infancy. Although they said that they enforce the filing of exploitation plans with grant applications, they stressed the wide variation of the content of such plans. The DLR (German Aerospace Centre) which manages a huge variety of research programmes for different federal ministries, has implemented an internal focus group studying current practice with regard to exploitation plans because it was found that there may be different good practice models associated with different fields of research or technological areas. However, results of this working group were not yet available.

The *Projektträger* were sensitive with regard to collaborative research and the exploitation plans and concrete steps towards commercial implementation taken by PROs. Some enforce guidelines regarding possible clauses in collaborative research programmes, and some even provide model agreements. However, at the federal level, the position has always been that there should be no interference with direct negotiations between future project partners, and this was generally the approach taken by the *Projektträger*.

The PROs view this approach from a different perspective. One PRO specifically mentioned the large variation in positions taken by individual *Projektträger* institutions. Some strongly reinforce the PRO's position with regard to IP and user rights to foreground[29] research results, while others are not at all interested in this issue and gladly accept an outright paid-up transfer of foreground results to industrial project partners.

Bearing in mind that, in statistical terms, these interviews are not sufficient to determine practices at the *Projektträger* institutions, it would seem appropriate to study these issues in more detail, as they clearly have a substantial effect on the ability of PROs to benefit from the new administrative regulations on IP and licensing.

The *Projektträger* found PROs generally somewhat uncertain about the demands and opportunities given to them by virtue of the new administrative regulations. Although they mentioned the professional level of exploitation activities at the Max-Planck Gesellschaft, the Fraunhofer Gesellschaft and the Helmholtz Association, they also said that at universities (including *Fachhochschulen*) and smaller non-university PROs, individual researchers are often overwhelmed by the number of administrative requirements and the legal demands of industrial project partners, so that they struggle through the grant application process in hopes of obtaining grant funding but not interested in their own future potential exploitation activities. The *Projektträger* did not see fundamental changes in how PROs approached government-funded research programmes, *i.e.* the new administrative regulations did not motivate the PROs to try to capitalise on new opportunities through new IAM strategies.

Also, neither *Projektträger* institution saw a trend towards more patent applications as a consequence of the new administrative regulations. One working in the life sciences mentioned that the tendency of some PROs to become involved with start-up companies created additional managerial demands for *Projektträger* institutions that were not necessarily foreseen when the requirement of exploitation plans was enacted.

Conclusions

Analysis of the new administrative regulations implemented in Germany since 1998 concerning government research grants and contracts brings out a number of important findings, especially in the light of increasing experimentation in many countries with new policies to stimulate innovation and technology transfer. These findings can be summarised as follows:

- The entire process chain[30] needs to be taken into account when developing such policies.

- All players in the process chain need to operate under appropriate incentive systems.

- Break-ups at interfaces between partners in the process chain need to be avoided.

Universities have so far not been motivated to make these issues a high priority. The intermediaries (*Projektträger*) were apparently insufficiently integrated into the implementation of the new regulations by the PROs with a view to stimulating a shift in PRO IAM practices.

The small number of institutions interviewed is insufficient to provide statistically meaningful data. But they indicate a trend that warrants further investigation.

In addition to the conclusions regarding the new administrative regulations, the present case study leads to the following conclusions:

- German PROs increasingly focus on the development of IAM procedures.

- IPR applications are on the rise across the variety of the country's research organisations.

- Licensing income from these operations is modest, and only a very small number of technology transfer institutions at German PROs have been able to establish a significant track record.

- Most PROs struggle with defining good practice for their institution, particularly in view of institutional peculiarities and existing technology transfer links with industry.

- German PROs generally take decisions about the granting of user rights in IP, the eventual assignment of PRO IP to third parties, user rights to foreground IP in collaborative research projects, and whether or not PRO IP is used in company start-ups or spin-offs on an *ad hoc* basis.

- In most PROs, these decisions are heavily influenced by internal politics, specifically with regard to whether legal issues dominate or whether the focus is on the active development of a business activity.

- It was not possible to identify a benchmarking system that would allow PROs to decide more systematically the best route to commercialisation (spin-off, licence, R&D collaboration).

- Universities, which are in the early stages of developing IAM practices, are torn between maintaining old management practices and taking up the challenges of a new system, particularly in view of shortages of qualified technology transfer personnel.

- Several interest groups and their lobbyists are gearing up to undermine change. Industry wants easy access to researchers and, if possible, to qualified technology transfer personnel, but it does not accept true market prices for the research being performed and for the granting of user rights to PRO IP. Investors complain because they have lost their direct access to researchers (under the former professor's privilege) and the opportunity to purchase IP and know-how at rather low prices because the university now asks questions about valuation. Not least, researchers complain because they feel that only the scientific inventor can really evaluate and do the deal and that university administrators stand in their way, blocking technology transfer.

NOTES

1. This case study was made possible by a grant from the German Federal Ministry of Education and Research (BMBF).

2. G. Becher, T. Gering, O. Lang and U. Schmoch (1996), "Patentwesen an Hochschulen. Eine Studie zum Stellenwert gewerblicher Schutzrechte im Technologietransfer Hochschule-Wirtschaft", BMBF, Bonn.

3. In Böhringer (2002), "Die Novellierung des Hochschullehrerprivilegs (§ 42 ArbnErfG)", *Neue Juristische Wochenschrift*, 952.

4. For the detailed methodology, see G. Becher *et al.* (note 2).

5. As explained above, university applications in this context are those developed in universities and in particular by the teaching staff. Most of these patent applications are not owned by the universities, but by the individual inventor(s) or their industrial partners.

6. Because the *Fraunhofer Patentstelle* (Fraunhofer Patent Centre) is also licensing out IP owned by third parties, including university researchers, their total actual licensing income is higher than the figures reported in Figure 2; in 2000, it was almost EUR 20 million.

7. K. Rivette and D. Kline (1999), *Rembrandts in the Attiic: Unlocking the Hidden Value of Patents*, Harvard Business School Press, Boston, Massachusetts.

8. U. Schmoch, G. Licht and M. Reinhard (2000), *Wissens- und Technologietransfer in Deutschland*, Fraunhofer IRB Verlag, Stuttgart.

9. J. Velling, *Bundesministerium für Bildung und Forschung* (BMBF) (2002), Results of German PROs drawn from the OECD survey on IPRs and their management by publicly funded research organisations, unpublished, Bonn, July.

10. Accordingly, the results in terms of valid patents and active licences as well as annual royalty income vary greatly. Some apply for less than five new patents annually, while others, like the Research Centre Karlsruhe, run impressive portfolios that yield respectable royalty income, in this case EUR 2 million in 2001.

11. See Chapter 12 in this volume.

12. INSTI – *Innovationsstimulierung in der deutschen Wirtschaft* (Stimulation of Innovation in the German Economy), a support programme launched by the federal government in 1995, which administers a big array of stimulation measures, particularly in the field of IPR.

13. www.venturecommunity.fraunhofer.de/news.php3?sessionid=54425e4cb3378afdfe2a7913c3ae57d0.

14. With project partners in industry.

15.   In an area where the institute deliberately reserved the IP without granting rights to collaborative project partners while building an impressive IPR portfolio over a period of almost ten years.

16.   However, they do not use some form of benchmarking to support this theory.

17.   With one notable exception, the *Max-Planck Institut für Kohleforschung* (Institute for Carbon Research); see also H. Martin (2002), *Polymere und Patente*, Wiley-VCH Verlag GmbH, Weinheim.

18.   See also Chapter 12 in this volume.

19.   See Chapter 12 in this volume.

20.   A more proactive approach to the acquisition of seed and start-up funds may become necessary as a consequence of the substantial drying up of private seed funding.

21.   Or transfer them entirely to the government.

22.   *Bekanntmachung über die Nebenbestimmungen für Zuwendungen des Bundesministeriums für Bildung, Wissenschaft, Forschung und Technologie vom 9. Oktober 1998* (BAnz Nr. 199 vom 23.10.1998).

23.   Also, in some of the research programmes, new and old administrative regulations co-existed for a certain period of time.

24.   In universities, this involved the professor's privilege which was only abandoned in February 2002; see the introductory section.

25.   For example, see E. Büring (2002), "Neue Zuwendungsbestimmungen des BMBF, was machen die Universitäten daraus", in Th. Gering (ed.), *Gewerbliche Schutzrechte aus deutschen Hochschulen und deren Verwertung*, BMBF, Berlin.

26.   See the section above on the PROs and their approach to IAM. The difference from universities also results from the so-called professor's privilege which was only abolished in February 2002. Because this privilege did not exist in non-university PROs, a consistent mechanism regarding invention disclosures (which are legally required from employees in Germany) had to be developed early on. In most universities, such a mechanism did not exist before the end of the 1990s.

27.   *Nebenbestimmungen für Zuwendungen auf Kostenbasis an Unternehmen der gewerblichen Wirtschaft für Forschungs- und Entwicklungsvorhaben* (NKBF 98).

28.   This may be even truer for universities.

29.   The term "foreground" research results is generally used in collaborative research agreements for the results to be achieved in the research project governed by the particular agreement.

30.   Consisting of the institutional background, the individuals involved and their particular set of objectives, the research funding allocated and the results envisaged and obtained as well as the technology transfer mechanisms used.

Chapter 10

UNIVERSITY TECHNOLOGY TRANSFER IN SWITZERLAND ORGANISATION, LEGAL FRAMEWORK, POLICY AND PERFORMANCE

by

Patrick Vock[1]
Centre for Science and Technology Studies (CEST)

Introduction

At present, technology transfer activities in Swiss higher education institutions are bottom-up and based on decentralised decision making. This leads to different institutional solutions for technology transfer as well as a legal framework that lacks simplicity and clarity. Nevertheless, in international comparisons, Swiss technology transfer performs quite well. Is this a contradiction, as one would assume at first sight? Recent studies[2] shed more light on the conditions, mechanisms and extent of technology transfer in Switzerland. This chapter examines these insights and tries to address the apparent contradiction. It first describes the context and organisation of technology transfer and then analyses the legal framework. After discussing the policy relevance, the most recent empirical evidence on technology transfer is summarised. Some conclusions follow.

Context for and organisation of technology transfer at universities

To better understand the discussion of technology transfer and related policies, the following paragraphs give some background concerning the institutional settings in which technology transfer operates.

Heterogeneous institutional context

Commercialisation of the results of publicly supported R&D in Switzerland involves many actors, visions, mechanisms, etc. A vital precondition of technology transfer is the performance of research. In 2000, R&D worth around CHF 10 billion was carried out in Switzerland, around three-quarters of which was performed by the enterprise sector (CHF 7 890 million), almost one-fifth by the higher education establishments (CHF 2 025 million) and only a little more than 1% by the federal state (CHF 140 million) (BfS, 2002). Publicly funded research is performed by a variety of organisations that differ in terms of their profile and subordination (see Box 1).

Organisation and management

Technology transfer is an issue in all Swiss universities, although its priority varies. The institutionalisation of the technology transfer however differs considerably according to size, strategy and subordination of the university (see Box 2). Normally, a person or an internal or external office is in charge of technology transfer for the whole institution. These activities are often supplemented by those of subunits such as departments or schools or even by the scientists themselves. Most technology transfer offices (TTOs) are less than ten years old. They generally only deal with intellectual property (IP) management for their home institution. For the cantonal universities, some TTOs manage IP for several institutions. TTOs are involved in a broad range of technology transfer activities of which negotiating research agreements is most common and licensing-in the least common. The negotiation of research agreements is a support activity for university staff and is hardly ever initiated by the TTO.

In late 1999, the Swiss Network for Innovation (SNI) was established on the initiative of the State Secretary for Science and Research. The goal of the foundation is to support tertiary education organisations in their technology transfer activities. All cantonal universities, the federal institutes of technology, the universities of applied sciences, other research institutes as well as private companies are members of the network.

Incentives to commercialise

Different factors influence researcher's propensity to commercialise their results. There is a potential tension between the academic and business cultures owing to the different goals of "first to publish" and "first to apply". The patenting and licensing survey (Vock et Jola, 2002) showed that IP and licences rarely influence recruitment, career advancement or the researcher's income. However, there must be other incentives to commercialise since the survey showed that especially in higher education institutions, in addition to the official TTOs, institutes and individual researchers are involved in IP activities. Naturally, the ownership rules that apply to intellectual property are important. These are analysed in the next section of this chapter.

Legal framework for commercialisation

The legal situation governing the commercialisation of university research results is quite complex. No comprehensive overview is readily available. The patent and licensing survey conducted in 2002 included a question on IPR rules which shows that the intellectual property resulting from research often belongs to the organisation. Furthermore, ownership depends on the type of contract or is attributed to the organisation or firm that financed the research. A special analysis[3] was needed to capture the details of the legal regime for commercialisation. The ownership rights for IP in the Swiss higher education sector are summarised below. Following a short description of the principles for IP ownership involving students, a more in-depth analysis of ownership rules for employees is undertaken.

Ownership rules under Swiss IP laws and their modification through organisation-specific rules

As in other countries, intellectual property is regulated in special national laws. Separate laws exist for different categories of IP, such as patents, designs, plant varieties, trademarks, copyright and topographies of semiconductor products. These laws specify the ownership of IP at the time when it is created. Depending upon the category, different owners are defined. These rights can be transferred. The ownership rules for intellectual property specified in the IP laws can be modified through other regulations in the higher education sector, especially with respect to registration or employment at higher education institutions.

Ownership rules for students

Rules determining the ownership of IP arising from activities of registered persons such as students theoretically may be found at various levels in different regulations (university laws, regulations of institutes, etc). In reality, almost no rules are laid down at the highest possible level of a given institution (but they may exist at a lower level). When no general or specific rules concerning IP ownership exist, the IP belongs to the creator of the IP, thus the student. If the student is employed in some manner by the institution, different rules apply, depending on whether the IP was created as part of the student's studies or employment.

Ownership rules for employees

Frequently, the rules concerning employment contracts determine the ownership of IP. There is no common rule for the different IP categories or for private and public organisations. Although the focus here is on PROs, the rules for the private sector are explained to show the differences. Table 1 gives a synopsis of the ownership schemes that apply.

Table 1. Ownership rules and owners in the case of an employment relationship

	Employment relationship based on private law	Employment relationship based on public law
Inventions	Ownership rule according to employment contract Subordinate: OR 332 (owner: employer)	Ownership rule according to public regulations Subordinate: patent law (owner: inventor, *i.e.* employee)
Designs	Ownership rule according to employment contract Subordinate: OR 332 (owner: employer)	Ownership rule according to public regulations Subordinate: design law (owner: designer, *i.e.* employee)
Plant varieties	Ownership rule according to employment contract Subordinate: OR 332 (owner: employer)	Ownership rule according to public regulations Subordinate: Law on the Protection of New Plant Varieties (owner: plant breeder, *i.e.* employee)
Works (copyright)	Ownership rule according to employment contract (transfer of rights according to purpose of contract) Subordinate: copyright law (owner: employee)	Ownership rule according to public regulations (transfer of rights according to purpose of contract) Subordinate: copyright law (owner: employee)
Software	According to copyright law transfer of rights to use to the employer For this transfer of rights no special rule is needed in the employment contract	According to copyright law transfer of rights to use to the employer (this is controversial) For this transfer of rights no special rule in the employment contract is needed (this is controversial; thus with the absence of a public rule a legal uncertainty occurs)
Trademarks	The applicant is owner The employer must make sure that the application is in his name.	The applicant is owner The employer must make sure that the application is in his name.
Topographies of semiconductors	The producer, *i.e.* the employer, is the owner	The producer, *i.e.* the employer, is the owner

Note: OR = Swiss Code of Obligations (*Obligationenrecht*); Public regulations means: 1. General rule, such as a law, 2. individual agreement, such as a public employment contract.

In the case of inventions, designs, plant varieties and copyright-protected work, similar reasoning applies. The rules specified for the employer-employee relationship under scrutiny are decisive for ownership. If there are no such rules, "fall back", or subordinate, regulations apply.

In substance, for employment contracts under private law which apply to firms, the IP rules of these contracts apply. If no rules are specified, the Swiss Code of Obligations (which regulates contract law) stipulates that ownership of inventions, designs and plant varieties belongs to the employer. In the case of works, ownership is attributed to the creator of IP, *i.e.* the employee, under the copyright law.

In the case of employment contracts under public law (applicable for most higher education institutions), IP ownership is determined by public rules, if they exist. These public rules can either be general in character, *e.g.* laws or other regulations, or they may relate to the specific public employee contract. If there are no specifications for IP ownership, then the rules of the relevant IP laws apply and ownership belongs to the inventor, designer, plant breeder or creator of the work, *i.e.* the employee.

Software is protected under copyright law but with some particularities. By law, the employer is explicitly given the right to use the software. This is certainly true for private firms, but in the author's view it also applies to higher education institutions as employers (but this is somewhat controversial). Trademarks and topographies of semiconductors belong to the employer.

IP ownership rules for employees at different higher education institutions

As indicated in Table 1, IP rules in higher education institutions are very much dependent on what is found in the relevant public law (such as university laws or cantonal public employment laws). Analysis of institution-specific rules as well as the subordinate rules of the specific IP laws yields the relevant ownership rules for individual universities.

Almost all higher education institutions follow some public rules that determine ownership at least for one IP category. Decrees that cover all IP categories are not very common.

Most higher education institutions have rules for inventions, and most often they retain ownership for the institution. On some occasions, the rights are attributed to the cantons or the inventors. One-third of all higher education institutions have rules for the ownership of designs, copyright-protected works or software. Ownership sometimes varies with employment status (professor, assistant, technical personnel, etc.).

Ownership rules for external funding

University research often involves external funding. The inclusion of a third external party may modify IP ownership rules. Therefore, some higher education institutions have issued rules concerning external project funding. Generally, these principles leave room for adaptation in the contract negotiated with the organisation sponsoring the research. The most important public funding agencies have created standard rules concerning intellectual property rights (IPRs), which can, however, be modified by rules in individual contracts. The Swiss National Science Foundation, which sponsors pure and oriented basic research, as well as the Commission for Technology and Innovation, which co-finances joint academia-industry-projects, waive their rights. The funding for policy-oriented research by the government does not follow any standardised rules.

A national rule exists but is not binding

The previous discussion of ownership rules shows quite clearly that in Switzerland, no standardised and unified ownership rule exists, either for all higher education institutions or for all categories of intellectual property. This is because the institution-specific rules usually do not cover all IP categories and because the regulatory competence in the higher education sector is split between the state and the cantons.

Nevertheless, an attempt has been made to standardise ownership rules. The national research law specifies that the granting of federal funds can be tied to the condition that IP rights must be transferred to the employer. However, this rule is not binding.

Policy relevance of technology transfer and the legal framework

In the Swiss political arena, knowledge and technology transfer activities involving higher education institutions are seen as beneficial, but this is not a widely debated issue. In 2002, two reports taking stock of the various arguments and the present status of economic growth and innovation in Switzerland were issued. In the growth report (Seco, 2002), issued by the office in charge of economic policy, innovation is singled out as one important driver of growth. Protection of IP is mentioned very generally as an important precondition for innovation. But technology transfer by higher education institutions and the legal framework are not discussed or analysed in detail. In addition, when discussing the barriers to innovation, the rules for intellectual property are not mentioned.

In a more specific report on innovation in Switzerland (BBT, forthcoming), issued by the office in charge of innovation policy, special emphasis is placed on the application of knowledge and the strengthening of the interface between industry and academia. It is explicitly mentioned that owing to the different characters and goals of the various higher education institutions it would be inappropriate to commit them to a uniform transfer policy. It should be left to the institutions themselves to find optimal solutions. Nonetheless, the report urges the need to study the question and recommend measures to facilitate and reduce costs of the protection of intellectual property.

Thus, it is not surprising that the national innovation policy emphasises the importance of knowledge and technology transfer but not via a uniform technology transfer policy. For the period 2000-03, the Swiss government[4] set five strategic goals for tertiary education, research and technology, one of which is the valorisation of knowledge (Bundesrat, 1998). Three measures affecting technology transfer were proposed: first, the introduction of standardised rules for IPRs applicable to federal funds in the research law (described above); second, amendment of the law for the universities of applied sciences with IPR rules, not to determine who owns IP but so that the partners specify this in a contract; and third, the establishment of the Swiss Network for Innovation (also mentioned above).

Then, in November 2002, the government sets three strategic goals for 2004-07, which included the strengthening of research and the promotion of innovation (Bundesrat, 2002a). The improvement of knowledge and technology transfer as well as of the interface between science and industry has taken on greater importance, with many more references than in the earlier policy document. The previous changes (legal changes in the research law and the establishment of the SNI) are judged successful. The new policy thrust is the substantial augmentation of funds for basic as well as applied research, financed by the Swiss National Science Foundation and the Commission on Technology and Innovation. A minor change in the research law establishes the competence for federal expenditures to valorise knowledge (the financing of the SNI as well as a technology information platform).

To summarise, change to the legal rules for intellectual property arising from higher education institutions is currently not a priority of federal policies. This assessment is in line with the recommendations of the advisory body to the Swiss government, the Swiss Science and Technology Council. In its most recent policy document, the council singles out nine policy priorities including the improvement of knowledge transfer but does not mention intellectual property rights (SWTR, 2002). In 2001, federal and cantonal authorities established the Swiss University Conference to co-ordinate the activities of the cantonal universities and the federal institutes of technology. The conference can take binding decisions on guidelines for the valorisation of university knowledge. This competence has not been used so far.

Besides the formulation and implementation of an overall tertiary education, research and innovation policy, the federal administration has to formulate the framework for specific higher education institutions, *e.g.* the two federal institutes of technologies. The relevant law is currently under revision. Among the changes are: to include the request to exploit research results as an objective of the institution, to give the institution the possibility to invest in firms for the purpose of knowledge transfer, and to reformulate the rules for intellectual property. The document presenting the proposal to parliament (Bundesrat, 2002b) argues that the assignment of property rights in the current situation is not clear enough and therefore puts forward rules for all categories of IP applicable to the federal institutes of technologies. In September 2002, the Council of States discussed the proposed changes as did the first chamber of the parliament. The changes mentioned above were adopted without discussion. Only the speaker of the committee in charge of previewing the proposals mentioned the lively discussion in the committee about the pros and cons of investing in private firms and the change in the rules for intellectual property rights.

Performance of university technology transfer

Following the previous presentation of the institutional and legal setting as well as some policy initiatives, the following paragraphs discuss the actual technology transfer activities.

Empirical evidence on the technology transfer process

The recent survey on patenting and licensing activities of PROs provides aggregated data on Swiss technology transfer, the first of its kind. In general, the numbers show quite substantial technology transfer activities. However there are some difficulties in providing and interpreting the data. The available evidence is presented below in a format consistent with the technology transfer sequence (see Figure 1). Research and technology transfer are intertwined activities and parallel each other in certain phases.

Figure 1. Some Indicators for research and technology transfer

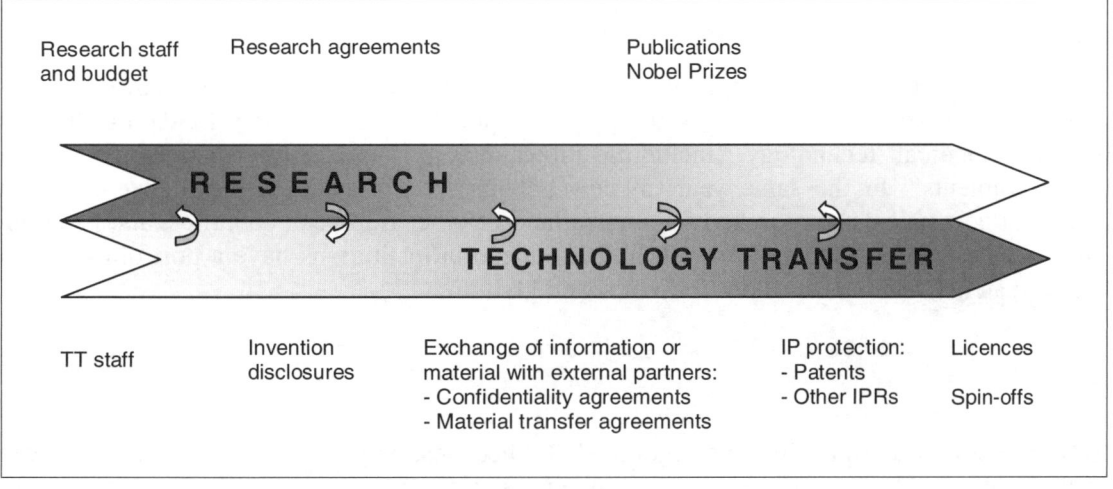

Research resources, research agreements, publications, etc.

Research is a precondition for technology transfer, and thus the volume of research is an indication of the potential for technology transfer.[5] With around 13 000 person-years engaged in R&D in higher education institutions and a budget of CHF 2 billion, Switzerland invests quite substantially in research. Unfortunately, no overall information on research agreements is available, but experts observe vigorous activity. The performance of Swiss academic research in international perspective is quite impressive given its modest size. This is well documented for example in the number of Nobel Prize winners as well as in bibliometric indicators.[6]

Technology transfer staff

A highly skilled and motivated expert staff combining various skills and competencies is necessary for successful technology transfer. Around 20 full-time equivalents are engaged in technology transfer for the Swiss universities, whose staff ranges from virtually zero to four full-time equivalents. This is a well-networked expert community.

Invention disclosures

When the first results of research appear and scientists begin considering commercialisation, a first step might be to contact the TTO of the home institution. A document which often accompanies this step is the invention disclosure. TTOs of the Swiss higher education institutions received 241 of these in 2001.

Confidentiality agreements and material transfer agreements

During research, it is often necessary to exchange information and materials with external partners such as universities or firms. These exchanges are formalised through contracts so as not to jeopardise the commercialisation of possible results. In 2001, the TTOs issued 157 non-disclosure or confidentiality agreements and 60 material transfer agreements. These figures, especially the former, most likely underestimate the situation as such contracts do not have to be concluded by the TTOs and equivalent rules are contained in many research agreements.

Patents

In 2001, TTOs filed 132 patent applications. In a single organisation, the maximum number of patent applications a year is over 40. Most patent applications are in the fields of "Health, pharmaceuticals, medical technology (including biotechnology)" and "Information technology, electronics, instruments". In the same year, 59 new patents were granted to the higher education institutions. Most new patents were issued for Switzerland or other European countries, and patenting in the United States is also common. Overall, higher education institutions have a portfolio of more than 900 active patents, and one has a portfolio of several hundred.

Licensing

In 2001, higher education institutions negotiated 200 licences, only a small portion of which were linked to active patents. Many are based on copyrighted materials (81), patent-pending inventions (33) or non-patented inventions (27).

The patent and licensing survey provided data on the patent portfolio of PROs, the licences based on the patents of the portfolio, and the licences of the portfolio that generate income. To compare these figures the data should refer to the same population.[7] Table 2 shows that one out of two patents in the portfolio is licensed. Of the licensed patents. around half earn income.

Table 2. Patents, licences, and income

	Higher education institution	Research organisation	Total
Patent portfolio	308	237	545
Patents of the portfolio which were licensed	156	96	252
Patents of the portfolio which were licensed and earn income	71	38	109

PROs reported more than CHF 8 million in licence earnings. However, income figures were poorly reported. On average, 50% of gross income goes to the research group or department where the inventor works. The remaining 50% goes to the TTO, the inventor and the central administration of the organisation.

Exclusivity is a major issue as regards exploitation and diffusion of knowledge. Two-thirds of the survey respondents have non-exclusive licence agreements, about half reported licence agreements that are exclusive for the lifetime of the patent or agreements with exclusivity limited to a specific field or market type. Less common is exclusivity limited to a specific number of years or to a specific territory. Most licence agreements provide that the licence must be worked, but not necessarily domestically. Reach-through clauses as well as rights to delay publications or of first refusal occur but are not the rule. To find licensees, TTOs and researchers most often rely on informal contacts. Licensing-in is not very common.

Spin-offs and start-ups

The creation of new firms out of the activities of public higher education and research organisations is widespread in Switzerland and has become more frequent in recent years. In almost all organisations, more or less active promotion of establishing new firms can be seen, despite some occasional impediments. Empirical evidence is scattered, but a recent study has tried to compile data for all of Switzerland (Vock, forthcoming). Given to the lack of a clear definition of spin-off, ten criteria were used to characterise the relationship between the newly founded firm and the higher education institution. Preliminary analysis shows that spin-offs most often include employees as founders or that the new firms result from the R&D of the higher education institution. This shows that spin-offs are indeed a valuable mechanism for IP transfer. New firms that licensed technologies or received equity investments from higher education institutions were less frequent. Almost 400 spin-offs were identified, most of them still active. The two federal institutes of technology play a major role contributing two thirds of all spin-offs, while cantonal universities are responsible for 20%. The rate of formation gradually increased between 1994 and 2000, and now stands at around 50 new firms a year. These figures are roughly in line with the results of the patent survey of 2001 which reports 46 spin-offs (firm founded by staff) and 22 start-ups (firm to commercialise an invention but not including staff).

Productivity

Discussions about technology transfer, especially in a political context, often lead to a demand for assessing the productivity and efficiency of the technology transfer process and for comparisons between organisations or countries. It is very difficult to describe the technology transfer process adequately and to monitor it with simple indicators. Furthermore, there is no single model of successful technology transfer. Nevertheless, indicators interpreted in context can lead to an informed discussion aimed at improving knowledge and technology transfer. The following should be seen in this perspective.

Productivity is the relation between output and input. The first difficulty is to select output and input indicators that are meaningful for assessing the technology transfer process. For this, the intended objectives[8] of the technology transfer process are crucial, and they have to be measurable with indicators. Unfortunately, these issues have not been fully resolved, leaving room for future work. Table 3 offers a pragmatic approach, which uses available indicators.

Table 3. Comparison of some indicators between the United States and Switzerland

Input	Research expenditures	USD 29.5 bn	21	CHF 2 bn	R&D expenditures (only HEI)
Output	Invention disclosures	13 032	47	280	Invention disclosures (HEI and RO)
	US patent applications	6 375	36	175	Patent applications (HEI and RO)
	US patents granted	3 764	34	112	Patent grants

Note: HEI = higher education institution; RO = research organisation. The central column shows the relation between the US and the Swiss figures.
Source: AUTM (2002); BfS (2001); Vock and Jola (2002). The AUTM survey includes 190 US and Canadian organisations (universities and research organisations).

At first sight, the significantly lower relation of input than of output may support the hypothesis that technology transfer is more active in the United States than in Switzerland. However, this needs to be qualified. As noted above, the figure for invention disclosures in Switzerland is strongly underestimated; the interpretation of the number of patent applications as an output indicator is difficult owing to the different application strategies of TTOs (some select before application, others after); the lower number of patent grants is not surprising considering the age of the TTOs and their young patent portfolios.

Table 4. Comparison of some indicators between the Netherlands and Switzerland

Per thousand full-time equivalents

	Netherlands	Switzerland
Patent portfolio/R&D personal	41.4	98.3
Confidentiality agreements/R&D personnel	40.9	16.9
Patent applications/R&D personnel	11.0	14.2
Patent grants/R&D personnel	6.3	6.4

Note: In analogy to the Dutch study, data for higher education institutions were used for Switzerland. The number of R&D personnel in the disciplines "natural sciences, medicine, technical sciences" is taken as denominator (9 300 person years).
Source: MERIT (2002); Vock et Jola (2002).

The comparison between the Netherlands and Switzerland confirms the hypothesis that the patent portfolio of Swiss higher education institutions is quite large, when the comparable age structure of the TTOs is taken into account. Swiss and Dutch universities show a similar propensity to patent.

Conclusion

This chapter has described technology transfer in Swiss universities as operating in a heterogeneous legal and institutional environment and yielding good results. What superficially appears as a contradiction is merely proof that technology transfer can work without the need for a centralised and uniform system. The Swiss experience shows that there are different approaches to successful technology transfer and that technology transfer managers can deal easily and pragmatically with historically developed structures. If not a uniform, straightforward ownership regulation, what is it then, that might explain the relative success of Swiss university technology transfer? The discussions with experts point to some soft factors such as the high motivation of the transfer personnel, close ties to academia as well as the lack of unnecessary and detrimental political interference.

Furthermore, the analysis has shown that technology transfer and the relevant legal environment lack policy priority both in higher education institutions and the federal state. For universities, technology transfer is a supporting activity and not a prime objective. The legal framework governing technology transfer is deemed to be acceptable, since changes are not on the political agenda for innovation policy.

If technology transfer moves up the political agenda, two observations should be kept in mind. First, the establishment of successful technology transfer takes time; it cannot take place overnight by changing ownership rules or investing huge amounts of money. Second, the most effective leverage for enhancing technology transfer is within the higher education institutions themselves. Internal structures, procedures, priorities and the university culture have to be adapted to internalise a real commitment to technology transfer. Appropriate incentive structures, regulations and adequate resources are supportive, but not of prime importance. In the same spirit, there is some room for improvement. Besides fostering a commitment to technology transfer within individual institutions, resources spent on technology transfer should be increased and better pooled to exploit economies of scale owing to the need for a certain critical mass for successful operation. Ownership rules for IP could gain in clarity with improved regulation, as is now proposed for the federal institutes of technology. Further, appropriate regulation of investment in firms for the purpose of technology transfer as well as rules for conflict of interests might also help.

As a last observation, this chapter has shown the difficulty of assessing the performance of technology transfer. Up to the present, there is no consensus on how to describe productivity. To compound matters, there is no single role model for technology transfer.

NOTES

1.   The author gratefully acknowledges comments and assistance of the editors of this volume as well as H. Reutimann, U. Hinrichs, C. Jola and M. Streit.

2.   In 2002, CEST participated in the OECD exercise to survey the patent and licensing activities of PROs (Vock et Jola, 2002) and also analysed ownership rules for intellectual property arising from publicly funded research (publication forthcoming).

3.   The analysis was performed by CEST and can be accessed at www.cest.ch. A written publication is forthcoming.

4.   The goals and proposed measures (legal changes, credit requests, etc.) of the Swiss government concerning tertiary education, research and technology (ERT) are described in a message to parliament covering a period of four years. For the period 2000-03, the document (Bundesrat, 1998) was issued in 1998 and discussed in parliament in 1999. The ERT-message covering 2004-07 (Bundesrat, 2002b) was issued in November 2002 and will be discussed in 2003 in parliament.

5.   Of course, the link between research and commercialisation is influenced by many factors such as the disciplinary orientation of the research or the type of research (basic, oriented, applied research as well as development).

6.   The bibliometric analysis by CEST includes the creation of a Champions League, a set of around 1 000 top-performing research organisations in the world. The Swiss higher education institutions show up disproportionately in this Champions League.

7.   Thus, the table only includes organisations that provided data for all the three questions.

8.   TTOs describe the objectives of technology transfer differently, but the following are frequently mentioned: *i)* facilitate the commercialisation of university discoveries for the public good; ii) reward, retain and recruit faculty and students; *iii)* forge closer ties to industry; *iv)* promote economic growth; and *v)* generate income. The objectives of the TTO of the University of Pennsylvania have been taken as an example. See: www.finance.upenn.edu/ctt/

REFERENCES

AUTM (2002), *AUTM Licensing Survey: FY 2000. Survey Summary*, Association of University Technology Managers, Inc., Northbrook, Illinois.

BBT (forthcoming), *Die Schweiz im weltweiten Innovationswettbewerb*, Bundesamt für Berufsbildung und Technologie (BBT), Bern.

BfS (2001), *Personelle und finanzielle Ressourcen der Hochschulen 2000*, Bundesamt für Statistik, Neuenburg.

BfS (2002), *F+E in der Schweiz, Finanzen und Personal*, Bundesamt für Statistik, Neuenburg.

Bundesrat (1998), *Botschaft über die Förderung von Bildung, Forschung und Technologie in den Jahren 2000 – 2003* (98.070), Schweizerischer Bundesrat, Bern.

Bundesrat (2002a), *Botschaft zu einer Teilrevision des Bundesgesetzes über die Eidgenössischen Technischen Hochschulen* (ETH-Gesetz) (02.022), Schweizerischer Bundesrat, Bern.

Bundesrat (2002b), *Botschaft über die Förderung von Bildung, Forschung und Technologie in den Jahren 2004 – 2007* (02.089), Schweizerischer Bundesrat, Bern.

MERIT (2002), *Patenting and Licensing by Dutch Public Research Organisations*, Final report, May 2002 (Arundel, Bordoy), Netherlands.

Seco (2002), *Der Wachstumsbericht. Determinanten des Schweizer Wirtschaftswachstums und Ansatzpunkte für eine wachstumsorientierte Wirtschaftspolitik*, Staatssekretariat für Wirtschaft (Seco), Bern.

SWTR (2002), *Ein Neun-Punkte-Programm zur Förderung von Wissenschaft und Technologie in der Schweiz*, Schweizerischer Wissenschafts- und Technologierat, Bern.

Vock, P. (2002), "Swiss Science and Technology Policies. Recent Developments (late 1999 to 2001)", Centre for Science and Technology Studies (CEST), Bern.

Vock, P. (forthcoming), "Unternehmensneugründungen aus dem Hochschulsystem", Centre for Science and Technology Studies (CEST): Bern.

Vock, P. et C. Jola (2002), "Patent- und Lizenzaktivitäten 2001. Umfrage bei Hochschulen und anderen öffentlich unterstützten Forschungsorganisationen", Centre for Science and Technology Studies (CEST), Bern.

Chapter 11

THE EVOLUTION OF KNOWLEDGE MANAGEMENT STRATEGIES IN PROS: THE ROLE OF S&T POLICY IN SPAIN[1]

by

Clara Eugenia García
Department of Business Administration, Universidad Carlos III de Madrid

and

Luis Sanz-Menéndez
CSIC Unit on Comparative Policy, Consejo Superior de Investigaciones Científicas

Introduction

Current social and economic trends, dominated by market globalisation, technological innovation and the economics of information and knowledge, have renewed interest of both policy makers and social researchers in intellectual property rights (IPR) regimes (Maskus, 2000). In the specific field of scientific and technological research, IPR concerns are the protection of knowledge produced through international co-operation (EC, 2002a), the role of S&T policies (EC, 1999) and the management of IPR in the context of publicly funded research (EC, 2002b). The management of IPR in public research organisations (PROs) has been addressed mainly through legal protection and commercialisation of their scientific and technological research activities (OECD, 2002a; 2002b).

Discussion of IPR and knowledge management in public research organisations (PROs)[2] might be framed as part of a broader debate including: *i)* patterns of interaction and co-operation between academic research and business organisations; *ii)* alternative funding sources of R&D activities conducted by PROs; *iii)* the impact of strategic science and technology (S&T) policies; and *iv)* the legal framework for IPR protection. Figure 1 represents the three axes along which the management of IPR within Spanish PROs evolved. This chapter argues that the increasing relevance of strategic use of IPR in PROs is the combined effect over the last 15 years of three processes. First, the growth of the public research system (Muñoz *et al.*, 1999). Second, the increasing relevance of "external funding", either from public competitive sources such as the national R&D plan and the EU RTD framework programmes or business funding (Sanz-Menéndez and Cruz, 2003). Third, the emergence and consolidation in these institutions of technology transfer offices (TTOs) aimed at fostering technology transfer and creating economic value from scientific research. Consequently, IPR management in Spanish PROs is related to the increase in the relevance of contract-based research which lead to the growth of patent applications, licensing agreements and exploitation of IPR by these institutions. Thus, protection of research outcomes and effective management of IPR in PROs are likely to be strongly associated with an increase in targeted research, funded with a view to competitive advantage, and more specifically with a tightening of the relationships between PROs and business firms. These trends cannot be isolated from the development of research management capabilities within PROs, commonly in their TTOs.

Figure 1. The management of IPR within PROs

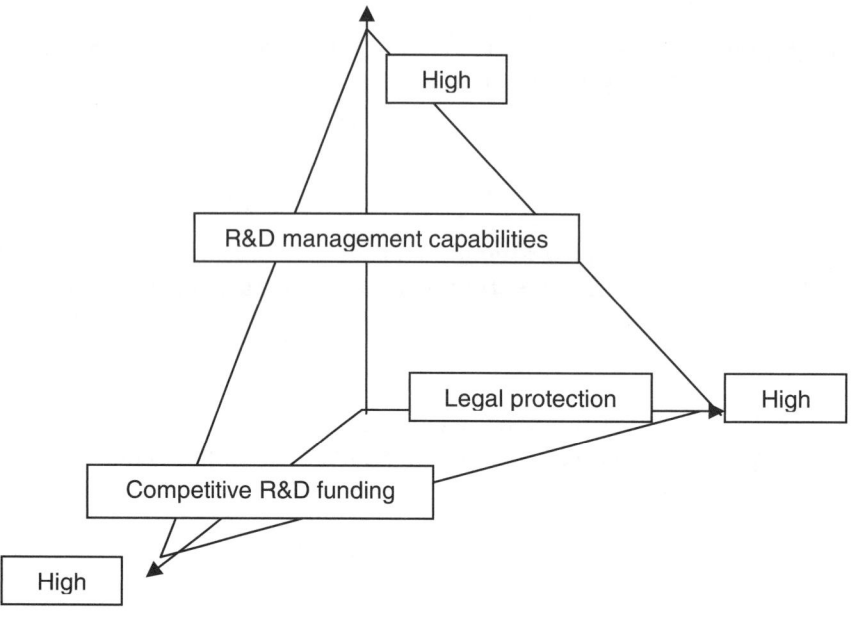

Source: Garcia and Sanz-Menéndez (2002).

This chapter examines the factors and explanatory variables that account for the performance and trends[3] in Spanish PROs' contract-based research with business, technology transfer and IPR management (Figure 2). It is an important issue, as the Spanish national system of innovation lags that of other European countries (EC, 2002c).

Figure 2. Government and higher education R&D expenditures financed by business and abroad

Percentages, three-year averages

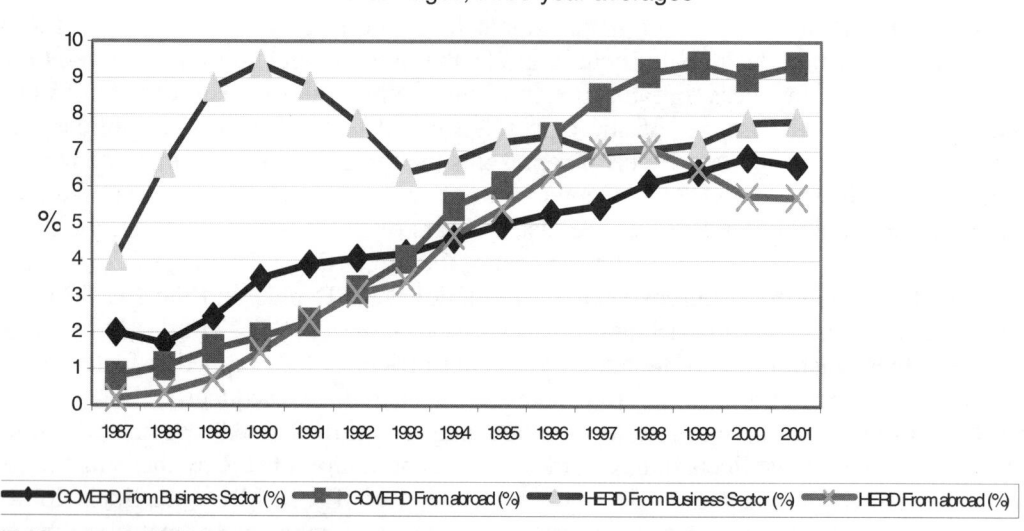

Source: INE (*Spanish Statistics*), various years.

Public S&T policies have driven the acquisition of organisational and managerial capabilities by PROs and, more specifically, support the creation and consolidation of TTOs. TTOs were designed to promote ISRs, technology transfer and the management of contract-based research and to protect, license and exploit IPR in their home institutions. In the pursuit of such goals, Spanish TTOs have helped to extend R&D management from funding to commercialisation and are today prominent actors in the context of research and IPR.

This chapter first focuses on the basic characteristics of Spanish S&T policies to provide a general framework for the analysis. Second, the creation and evolution of TTOs are presented in the context of Spanish public policy initiatives. Third, the management of research in PROs and the role played by TTOs in the evolution of contract-based research are discussed. Fourth, IPR is situated within the Spanish legal framework, along with PROs' use of patenting to protect IPR resulting from in-house research. Fifth, PROs' commercialisation, licensing and spin-off practices are examined as strategies to deal with IPR opportunities and barriers. Finally, some conclusions about present and future challenges are drawn, and some actions for increasing the organisational effectiveness of IPR management within PROs are noted.

S&T in Spain: the policy context

Only in the early 1980s did the underdevelopment of the Spanish R&D system emerge as a critical policy issue. The Socialist Party (PSOE) designed a set of dramatic reforms affecting science and research organisations. First, the University Reform Act (LRU – *Ley de Reforma Universitaria*) of 1983 redefined the framework for the organisation and governance of higher education institutions (HEIs) and favoured the diffusion of a research culture by means of specific incentive mechanisms which have significantly contributed to expanded ISRs.[4]

The Science Law established the regulatory framework for Spanish PROs.[5] Together with the principles of Spanish S&T policy, based on competitive government funding, the law introduced a set of organisational reforms affecting PROs (Alonso *et al.*, 2001).

Since 1988, the implementation of S&T policy is mainly assured through the National R&D Plan, monitored by CICYT (Inter-ministerial Commission for S&T), on the basis of the national R&D programmes[6] and various ministry-based R&D programmes. While the national programmes correspond to the so-called strategic R&D, the latter aim at funding mission-oriented research or non-targeted academic research.[7] Therefore, since the late 1980s, competitive public research funding has been directed towards "priority areas" and, fostering "free speculative research" (Sanz-Menéndez, 1995; Sanz-Menéndez and Muñoz, 1994).

Over the years, the effects of targeted public funding have been: *i)* an increased emphasis on research applications and the transfer of results; and *ii)* a strong awareness of IPR in PROs. This awareness is closely related to technology transfer and targeted research, since transfer implies co-ordination of R&D activities through contractual mechanisms and co-operation agreements between public and private organisations. Paradoxically, the national R&D programmes, throughout the period analysed, have been criticised for their academic bias (Sanz-Menéndez *et al.*, 1993). However, this bias may be the unintended outcome of weak institutional policy faced with increasing academic interests and lobbyist practices (Sanz-Menéndez, 1997).

Finally, the framing of the S&T problem, together with the rhetoric of S&T policy, led to an attempt to address simultaneously the country's widely acknowledged endemic problems: *i)* significant scientific underdevelopment; and *ii)* a substantial technological gap.[8] Together with individual and organisational incentives to foster research within PROs, the promotion of ISRs has been based on a set of very simple principles. First, technology transfer and commercialisation of research was attached to specific units created within PROs that were also supported by public funds. Second, "research management capabilities" would evolve as research in PROs reached a threshold level.

A public policy initiative: the creation of TTOs in PROs

R&D management is not a simple task, and its complexity increases in organisations such as universities and some PRCs, where R&D strategies are often shaped by the interests of individual researchers, and where a heterogeneous knowledge base, involving different S&T fields, coexists. R&D management becomes critical for the success or failure of PROs in a context of competitive public funding, targeted research and technology transfer and exploitation. It requires making and managing contractual relationships, seeking external funding opportunities, matching internal research capabilities and industry demands, as well as the necessary legal advice and the monitoring and control of IPR when both public and private actors are involved.

As a direct consequence of the S&T policies described above, public research laboratories and universities were confronted, at the end of the 1980s, with a new set of rules for their research activities, but they lacked in-house expertise and managerial capabilities to pursue the new S&T policy goals. With the exception of the National Research Centre (CSIC)[9] and a few universities such the Polytechnic University of Catalonia (UPC), the management of ISRs involving contract research was mainly conducted by external entities, university-firm foundations (*Fundaciones Universidad-Empresa* – FUE), acting as intermediaries between university professors and business firms. Today, however, almost all Spanish HEIs and public research centres (PRCs) have a specialised in-house unit or TTO that manages relationships between the institution and economic actors. These units have recently expanded their activities from the early establishment of mechanisms to foster research and co-operation to strategic management of research activities, including IPR, and the support of university-based industries.

TTOs emerged under the first National R&D Plan (1988-91). The successful adoption of the new rules and the promotion of targeted research were strongly dependent on the development of an appropriate environment for industry and science co-operation. The links between PROs and business firms required to achieve targeted research goals[10] led at the end of 1988, to the promotion of offices for the transfer of research results (OTRI) (CICYT, 1990; 1991).

The rationale for policy intervention was to "mobilise R&D potential from the business sector" and contribute to "the articulation of the science-technology-industry system". ISRs were crucial to: *i)* ensure economic returns to research supported by public funds, based on the idea that technological progress occurs through co-operation between public institutions and business firms; and *ii)* encourage firms to apply research results of PROs.

This rationale was translated into the creation of "interface units" to enhance and promote ISRs. Previous international experience, including the French ANVAR and the British Technology Group (BTG), and two Spanish in-house units (CSIC's *Oficina de Valoración y Transferencia de Tecnología*, created in 1985; the *Centro de Transferencia de Tecnología* (CTT) of the Polytechnic University of Catalonia, created in 1987) served as organisational archetypes.[11] The functions to be developed by such units were, among others: *i)* the promotion of PROs' research activities;[12] *ii)* the identification of transferable research results generated by research groups and their dissemination in the business environment; *iii)* the design of technology transfer mechanisms from PROs to business firms, including professional advice to help firms to adopt foreign leading-edge technologies; and *iv)* the provision of internal administrative and professional support to research groups for writing research contracts and managing research outcomes, including patenting and licensing agreements (CICYT, 1990).

This public policy initiative led to the allocation of a three-year grant to universities and PRCs to create these interface units or strengthen existing ones.[13] The total annual amount devoted to this was ESP 5.6 million for personnel and operating costs (about EUR 52 000 in 2002 prices). Ever since the first three-year programme, subsidies to TTOs have become institutionalised, although, on average, the need for public funds has decreased, as illustrated by the TTOs' total expenditure budgets.[14] However, in the 1990s, government support to TTOs[15] was crucial to the development and survival of such units and to R&D management activities in PROs that lacked internal resources and capabilities. Moreover, average figures hide increasing heterogeneity within TTOs.[16]

The impact of government subsidies on the creation of TTOs in PROs has been unquestionable. Since the beginning of the programme, the number of TTOs has grown in universities, PRCs and new organisations such as private technological centres and industry associations. Before 1989, there were seven TTOs in PROs, five offices in universities (Ramon Lull, Barcelona, Navarra, Autónoma de Barcelona and Polytechnic University of Catalonia) and two in PRCs (CSIC and IRTA, the agricultural research centre). At the end of the First National R&D Plan (1988-1991), 32 of the 39 existing universities had a TTO unit. However, it took about eight years for these administrative units to be institutionalised in the Official Registry (Orden 02/16/1996, BOE 02/23/1996).

At present according to National Registry data, there are 164 TTOs. They are the interface units between business firms and PRCs and public and private universities and between these and a heterogeneous set of profit and non-profit organisations, namely FUE, science and technology parks and technological centres. In 2002, university TTOs represented 32% of the total units registered, PRCs 10% and TTOs at technological centres 43% (Figure 3).

Figure 3. Evolution of the stock of TTOs by type of home institution, 1990-2000

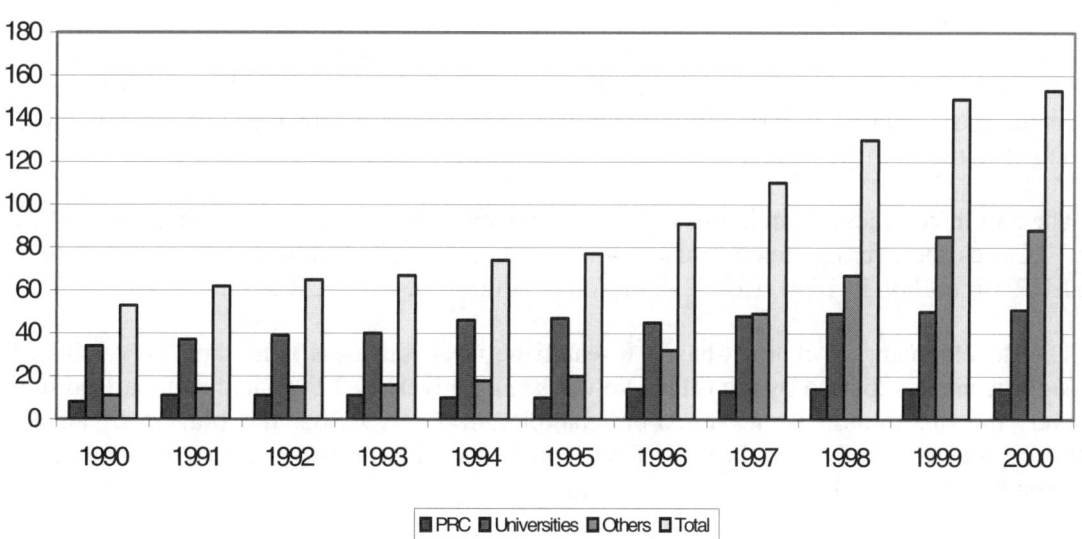

Source: CICYT (1991-2002).

In 1994, TTOs carried out their activities with very few experts; the average was two technicians and two administrative staff. Consequently, their activities mostly involved managing research in PROs (two-thirds of their work load) (Fernández and Conesa, 1996). Although they have grown, Spanish TTOs still have an inward focus (SRI International, 2000).

The units are particularly active in the management of contracts under the EU R&D Framework Programme, competitive public funding and the search for external funding. Because PROs want external funding, TTOs have to engage in various forms of research management.

In spite of their common origin and the adoption of organisational archetypes, TTOs now differ according to the size and sources of their budgets, their activities and organisation.[17] For example, most university TTOs have become responsible for the management of European R&D Framework Programme research contracts, while only 50% manage competitive national research funding (Red OTRI Universidad, 2002).

Hence, Spanish TTOs have tried to create their own "identity" within their institutions.[18] Data for December 2001 (Red OTRI Universidad, 2002) indicates 435 employees (FTE) in 48 university TTOs, of which 195 technicians, 210 staff and support personnel and 30 grant holders. About a quarter of the TTOs had more than 20 employees. Universities' TTOs have, on average one technician for 165 university researchers, and each technician has about 85 research contracts a year and manages an average of EUR 2.5 million a year in research contracts.

The TTOs have gained external visibility over the last decade, but in many PROs, they still lack internal legitimacy. The research constituencies are reluctant to accept these units as legitimate actors in the S&T system. Therefore, their ability to influence the organisation of the knowledge structure has often been marginal, especially as others powers may dominate the university culture.

R&D management within PROs and the role of TTOs

As noted above, external and competitive funding has been a key driver in the evolution of the Spanish public research system. Contract research increases with external sources of funding and is managed by the TTOs. In fact, about 60% of external research funding received by Spanish universities is contract research managed by TTOs. In 2000, contract-based activities of PROs represented more than EUR 500 million overall,[19] with about 70% for R&D or technological support contracts (Figure 4).

The rise in contract research also reflects the increase in the management efficiency of PROs and their TTOs, as the average amount of contract funding per TTO indicates. This figure has evolved from EUR 1.6 million in 1990 (EUR 2.4 million at 2000 prices) to EUR 3.3 million in 2000.

The development of contract-based research between business firms and universities has also been significant, as reported by the OTRI Network (i.e. university TTOs) and summarised in Figure 5. However, the distribution is uneven. For example, in 2001, CSIC, the biggest Spanish research institution, received EUR 35 million in R&D contracts with business firms, or about 25% of the institution's total external funding.[20]

Figure 4. Contract research funds managed by Spanish TTOs, 1990-2000

EUR millions

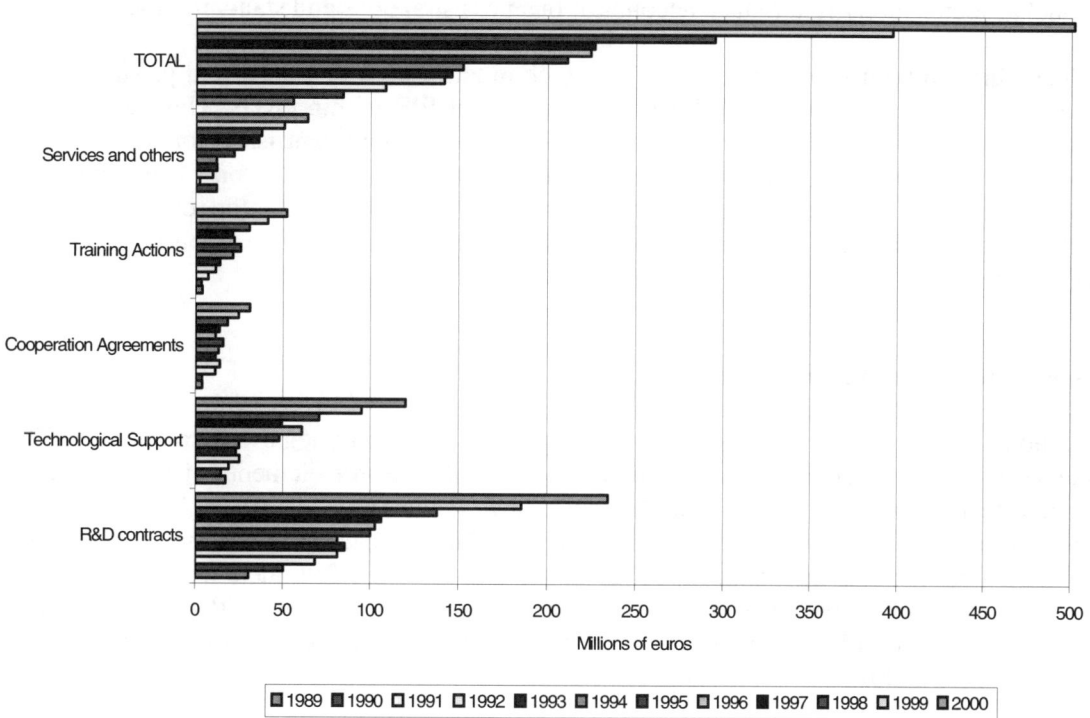

Millions of euros

| 1989 | 1990 | 1991 | 1992 | 1993 | 1994 | 1995 | 1996 | 1997 | 1998 | 1999 | 2000 |

Source: CICYT (1991-2002).

Figure 5. R&D contracts managed by university TTOs

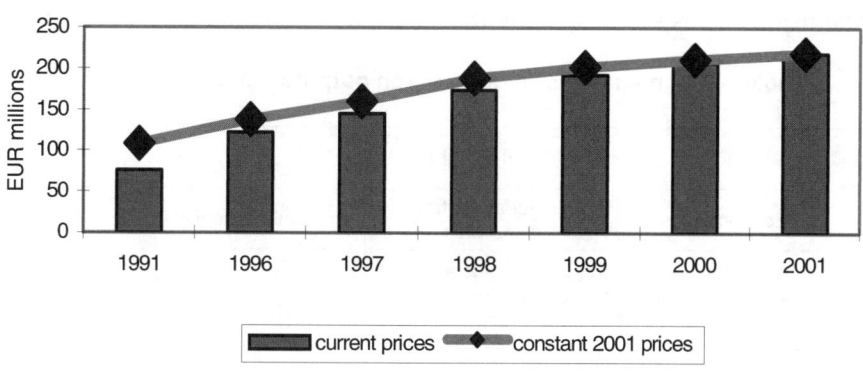

current prices ◆ constant 2001 prices

Source: Red OTRI Universidades (2002).

More generally, about 25% of the TTOs received more than two-thirds of the total amount of contract research carried out by universities. The distribution is linearly correlated not with the size of the institutions but with the size and managerial efficiency of their TTOs. Contract-based research and external research funding are linked to the quality and culture of the university's research base and its managerial and administrative capabilities.

The spread of patenting, licensing and other mechanisms is the combined effect of contract-based research and the development of TTOs' dynamic managerial capabilities. This learning process is triggered by the rise in various types of ISRs, which involves acknowledging that IPR goes beyond traditional academic copyright to take account of business strategies and standard practices.

Thus, through their management of research contracts with both public and private actors, TTOs are crucial to the introduction and diffusion of a culture of IPR within PROs. This has been a process of learning by doing in which their IPR has become a very significant issue for business partners.[21] However, this learning is neither evenly distributed nor linear. On the one hand, the volume of contract-based research affects the dynamic capabilities of TTOs. On the other, the nature and characteristics of firms and their technological fields also affect TTOs' responses in terms of IPR management.

The legal context and research management[22]

Although there have been significant developments in Spain's legal environment for IPR since the late 1980s, patent regulations have been relatively stable. Some elements of the legal context for IPR that affect research in PROs include: *i)* the new Patent Law of 1986; *ii)* the adaptation and adoption of new regulations imposed by the European Patent Office (EPO) which the Spanish Patent Office joined in 1986 as associate member and since 1989 as full member; *iii)* new regulations concerning semiconductors (1988) and software protection (1991); *iv)* the TRIPS Agreement (1994); *v)* the EU directives on biotechnological research; and *vi)* the commercialisation (1998) and protection of plant varieties (2000).

The basic regulatory framework for PRO patents is the Patent Law (1986). Articles 15-20 assign ownership to the employer (universities and PRCs) but grant the inventor the right to "fair compensation". Hence, PROs and HEIs have a significant degree of freedom in terms of managing IPR between the institution and its faculty members or between the former and its business counterpart if the invention is the result of contract research funded by the firm. In other words, IPR is subject to bilateral contractual mechanisms and shaped by the bargaining power of each participant.

Table 1. IPR management of research outputs: an overall view

Source of funding	IPR rights			Role of TTO in IPR management
	Economic rents	Residual control/ ownership	Transfer decision	
Public R&D funding	Sharing by PRO and researchers	PRO (but if decision not to file, then researchers)	PRO	Yes
Public R&D funding in the context of joint collaborative projects	Sharing by PRO (researchers) and firm regulated by previous agreement	Firm	Firm	Bilateral contract provisions if applicable
Private research funding (contract R&D)	Joint sharing optional	Joint sharing optional but usually firm	Usually firm	Bilateral contract provisions

Source: Authors, based on the contribution to EC (2002b) by Martinez et Armesto.

Table 1 shows the basic characteristics of IPR management for research outputs of Spanish PROs. The information is organised according to the basic elements of IPR: *i)* the rights granted to the patent holder and the legal assignment of those rights to either individual or institutional actors; and *ii)* the main source of the funding of the research. Ownership of the IPR for research outputs of PROs varies, depending on the source of R&D funding and bilateral agreements between the parties involved: individual researchers and PROs; or individual researchers, PROs and business firms. Ownership of patentable research supported by either "institutional funding" or "public R&D project funding" is granted to PROs, which is then the patent assignee. For "public S&T competitive funding" and for joint research projects, the usual case is "joint ownership" and is normally subject to negotiation by project participants; IPR protection is managed according to the provisions of the research contract.

The remainder of this section explains how the IPR process is managed in PROs, where decisions on IPR protection are made through "internal procedures". Usually, individual researchers inform PROs about results that might be successfully exploited commercially. TTOs must analyse and advise, within a period of three months, under which legal forms the results might be protected. If the evaluation is positive,[23] the patent documents are drafted by TTO experts together with the inventors; advice from external experts is requested only in specific cases. The first filings normally follow procedures for patent rights granted in Spain.[24] The patent applications are normally extended under licence agreements and the licensee, who chooses the relevant countries, supports both examination and maintenance fees. However, IPR protection, extension and litigation involving Spanish PROs are subject to some restrictions. First, universities are exempted from paying fees for patent applications fees and utility models at national level, while other PROs cover the full cost. Second, international extension costs are usually not covered by PROs' regular budgets. Third, for joint inventions (PRO/business) patent rights and IPR management are commonly allocated to the company.

The sharing of profits (fair compensation) is standard practice. In universities, shares are distributed according to the statutory regulations of each university. The participation of inventors (including students) in benefits derived from commercial exploitation of research results is also based on each university's statutory regulations (and varies between a half and a third). In PRCs, profits are shared equally among the institution, inventors and the Board, which distributes its third according to variable criteria (RD 55/2002, 18 January). In both universities and PRCs, in cases of joint ownership, these provisions also apply.

The licensing of PRO patents is managed through bilateral agreements between the institution and the licensee, except in the case of joint ownership where it is subject to previous contractual agreements. The common practice for joint inventions (PROs/business) resulting from contract research or a publicly funded joint research project is to allocate the patent rights and IPR management to the company.

The management of IPR in PROs

From research to patents

The long-term evolution of IPR in PROs is reflected in the number of patents filed by their TTOs, and the trend is similar to that for research funding. However, IPR protection, measured by the total number of patents filed, has also increased as universities have become aware of its importance for research.[25] University-based patents represent more than two-thirds of the total number of patents filed by PROs (Figure 6). The new IPR management practices have emerged owing to the exemption of fees for universities filing national patents, the work of their TTOs and the learning and adoption of practices and values aimed at protecting and commercialising research outputs.

Figure 6. Total number of patents filed by PROs

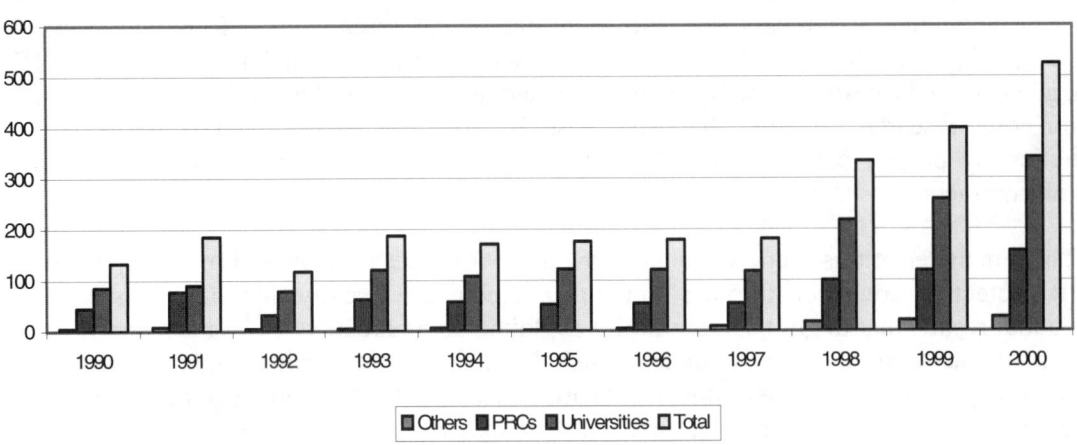

Source: CICYT (1991-2002).

PROs, and especially universities, generally protect IPR at national level;[26] about 20% of patent applications are filed directly at international level, mostly via the EPO or the Patent Convention Treaty (PCT). Moreover, PRCs (*i.e.* CSIC) patent at international level more than universities. In 2000, CSIC filled 96 patent applications in Spain with extension to other countries in 2001 and had 528 patents, of which 367 registered in other countries. In contrast, TTOs in Spanish universities (Red OTRI Universidades, 2002) reported a total of 224 new applications for 2001, 40 of them extended internationally (Figure 7). In terms of the stock of university patents at the end of 2000, only 110 out of 1 045 were international.

Figure 7. Total patents filed by university TTOs

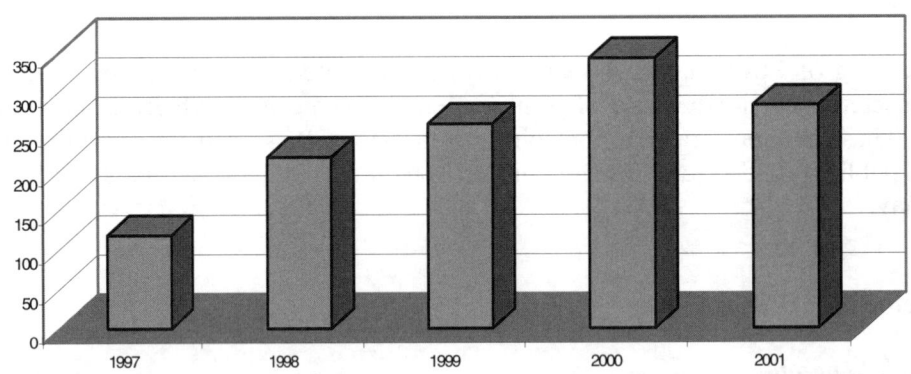

Source: Red OTRI Universidad (2002).

Differences between CSIC and universities in the evolution of patent applications and the relative strength of CSIC in technology transfer and IPR management are directly related to CSIC's earlier development of its TTO.

Table 2. Distribution of the stock of patents technological classes and type of PROs, 1978-97

Percentages

	1978-97 Universities	1978-97 PRCs	1978-87 All PROs	1988-97 All PROs
I Electrical engineering	9.7	6.6	5.1	9.6
1 Electrical machinery and apparatus, electrical energy	3.0	1.0	0.3	2.8
2 Audio-visual technology	0.7	1.0	1.1	0.8
3 Telecommunications	1.5	1.4	0.5	2.0
4 Information technology	2.2	2.1	2.2	2.2
5 Semiconductors	2.2	1.0	1.1	1.8
II Instruments	28.6	12.7	12.7	23.3
6 Optics	3.2	0.9	0.8	2.5
7 Analysis, measurement, control technology	19.4	9.2	8.9	16.2
8 Medical technology	5.2	0.5	1.1	3.3
9 Nuclear engineering	0.7	2.1	1.9	1.3
III Chemistry, pharmaceuticals	38.1	53.9	58.2	40.7
10 Organic fine chemistry	13.2	28.1	38.5	11.8
11 Macromolecular chemistry, polymers	2.2	3.7	5.4	1.7
12 Pharmaceuticals, cosmetics	3.5	0.9	0.5	2.8
13 Biotechnology	12.7	8.7	5.7	13.2
14 Agriculture, food chemistry	2.0	6.5	3.2	5.5
15 Chemical and petrol industry, basic materials chemistry	4.5	6.1	4.9	5.8
IV Process engineering, special equipment	19.4	23.9	22.9	21.5
16 Chemical engineering	3.5	4.7	4.3	4.1
17 Surface technology, coating	2.7	1.7	1.6	2.5
18 Materials, metallurgy	5.7	9.8	11.1	6.3
19 Materials processing, textiles, paper	1.0	4.2	3.5	2.5
20 Handling, printing	0.7	0.0	0.0	0.5
21 Agricultural and food processing, machinery and apparatus	2.7	2.1	1.9	2.6
22 Environmental technology	3.0	1.4	0.5	3.0
V Mechanical engineering, machinery	4.2	2.8	1.1	4.8
23 Machine tools	0.5	0.2	0.0	0.5
24 Engines, pumps, turbines	0.2	0.2	0.0	0.3
25 Thermal processes and apparatus	0.2	0.9	0.8	0.5
26 Mechanical elements	0.2	0.0	0.0	0.2
27 Transport	1.7	0.2	0.3	1.2
28 Space technology, weapons	0.0	0.0	0.0	0.0
29 Consumer goods and equipment	0.2	0.5	0.0	0.7
30 Civil engineering, building, mining	1.0	0.9	0.0	1.5

Source: Authors, based on a sample of 975 patents in the OEPM, with first application by a university or PRC, using OST-FhG-ISI conversion table from IPC.

At universities, the distribution of IPR is very skewed; as for contract-based research, a few universities make most of the patent applications. Hence, 20% of public HEIs hold 80% of the stock of patents granted to Spanish universities. Again, IPR management in Spanish PROs follows an evolving but not linear trajectory from research management to contract research and IPR management. This non-linearity is associated with both learning and the diffusion of best practices among research management communities, mainly TTOs.

This situation has to be analysed in the context of the scientific specialisation of Spanish PROs. Patterns of patent specialisation are quite different for universities and for PRCs. These differences are evident in a sample of 975 patent applications by PROs. Table 2 summarises these results, pointing out the technological competencies of Spanish PROs according to the fields in which they held patents.

The patent applications filed by PRCs are dominated by chemical technologies owing to CSIC's strong research potential in organic and inorganic chemistry and its multiple applications in emerging areas. In contrast, applications filed by universities clusters around control and measurement technologies. Nevertheless, there is an increasing trend in PROs to patent research outputs in leading S&T areas such as biotechnology and related fields as shown by a comparison of patents filed from 1978 to 1987 and from 1986 to 1997.

It is worth emphasising that differences in the protection of research outputs by the means of available IPR instruments cannot be fully understood outside of the institutional and S&T policy framework in which research and technology management has evolved. Moreover, since technology transfer was institutionalised in PROs' TTOs, their functions and concerns have evolved from basic research management support to more complex activities ranging from publicly funded research projects to the management of contractual agreements with business actors and direct involvement in IPR management. In fact, through their TTOs, PROs are becoming active in the management of IPR by exploring the entrepreneurial possibilities of their research base.

Licensing, commercialisation and direct exploitation of IPR by PROs

In contrast with patent applications, PROs rarely commercialise their research output through licensing agreements. In 1994, the 56 licences managed by TTOs generated a revenue of ESP 30 million (approximately EUR 170 000) (Fernández and Conesa, 1996); six years later, university TTOs reported 114 technology licences under exploitation (stock) and EUR 1.2 million in revenue. In 2001, there were four new licences with net income of EUR 400 000.

As for patents, CSIC is the most active and prominent actor in the management of IPR through licensing agreements. In 2000, 74 of its national patents and more that 200 of its non-Spanish patents were licensed, with total revenue of over EUR 2 million, exclusively generated, however, by a very small number of the patents. For example, only two patents held by CSIC, one for sequencing technologies, exploited by a subsidiary of Pharmacia, and one on petroleum, exploited by a multinational, account for 30% of the royalty income. The same is true for universities; two patents, one for diabetes control and one for dietary supplements, generate most royalties at the University of Barcelona.

Factors inhibiting the use of licensing are: *i)* the small number of research patents with economic value on the global technological market; *ii)* the lack of leading-edge and innovative SMEs; and *iii)* the barriers to be overcome to be able to license out or, alternatively, to exploit their own research base. The insider view of such barriers is not only the lack of financial resources to engage in international licensing agreements but also economic and managerial inefficiencies for pursuing such licensing agreements, taking into account the limited number of patents that might be of commercial interest worldwide. PROs cannot support these activities in the absence of economies of scale. To avoid inefficiencies, they have sometimes been forced to sell the patent to a third party as a way to minimise the transaction costs associated with licensing. Another route, not yet used, is to delegate of the exploitation of IPR from the Spanish patent holder to a third party, such as the British Technology Group (BTG).

Owing to such barriers to the commercialisation of research through licensing, PROs and their TTOs have taken an active role in the promotion of research-based firms, often but not necessarily at university science parks. However, research-based firms have been a second-best alternative to a market for PRO research results. Moreover, public S&T policies at regional level are crucial for encouraging the creation of research-based firms. Regional governments provide subsidies and soft loans to innovators (academic research groups) as well as entrepreneurial advice for setting up market-oriented activities. Regional agencies such as CIDEM in Catalonia and SPRI in the Basque country have been especially successful. CIDEM gives direct subsidies to research groups (up to EUR 100 000), monitors the financial needs of the new research-based firm and aids in the search for venture capital. CDTI, the central government agency for industrial technology development, also has a programme called NEOTEC. However, the long-term success of these policy measures is limited by a narrow product range and the low potential for product diversification.

The adoption of alternative strategies to cope with licensing barriers is more difficult for PRCs that for universities. Universities enjoy greater managerial and financial autonomy, which allows them to participate in venture capital projects. Table 3 shows recent trends in the direct commercial exploitation of IPR by Spanish universities.

Table 3. TTOs and university research-based firms

	Stock of firms created to December 2000	Firms created in 2001
Total firms created	99	77
Of which spin-offs and start ups	15	36

Source: Red OTRI Universidades (2002).

In the field of IPR management and commercial exploitation of their knowledge base, universities have recently followed three different strategies. First, they have created joint research-based firms.[27] Second, they have used their own risk capital to support and participate in research-based firms. The pioneering initiative of the University of Santiago de Compostela (Galicia) illustrates this point. Its capital risk fund, UNIRISCO, promoted and controlled by the university and with capital of EUR 5 million, provides financial aid to 20 start-ups. Third, in PRCs with higher administrative barriers,[28] researchers may develop new research-based firms directly[29] and obtain a licensing agreement from their home institution. This alternative has been successfully adopted by the National Centre for Biotechnology-CSIC, where Bionostra commercialises genetics-based diagnostic tools that apply to a wide set of crops and genetically modified organisms (GMOs).

Universities' current activities to promote research-based firms are illustrated by the fact that by 2001, 20 had established programmes dealing with spin-offs, and four reported an active role in promoting venture and risk capital initiatives, such as the entrepreneurship programme IDEA from the Polytechnic University of Valencia or the risk capital fund, UNIRISCO at the University of Santiago de Compostela. As pointed out above, public universities have been involved in the development of science and technology parks over the past decade, and they play a leading role in at least 20. Science parks and research-based firms are often complementary, and many universities have developed related services, such as the innovation centre Las Cúpulas, University of Barcelona, or UNINOVA, the incubator for spin-offs created by the University of Santiago de Compostela.

The learning process and development of dynamic capabilities in the field of technology transfer described in this chapter have accelerated in the last five years. However, differences among TTOs are increasingly relevant, as they are likely to increase as the focus shifts from IPR management through patents to strategic IPR management via licensing and commercial exploitation. Licensing activities and the creation of new research-based firms have emerged in the early 2000s. The strategic management of IPR for PROs requires more than a good legal environment and researcher incentives, it also requires strong and dynamic managerial capabilities in their TTOs. However, as the most recent experience shows, it is a long way from the development of organisational and managerial capabilities to the creation of the alternative resources and instruments needed to exploit, either through licences or directly, the output of research activities.

Conclusion

It is argued here that IPR management, and knowledge management, in Spanish PROs is an outcome of S&T policy efforts of the late 1980s and early 1990s. These policy initiatives planted a seed that, in some PROs, has grown into organisational structures for technology transfer and IPR management. The trajectory of these units shows how they have enlarged their field of action from administrative tasks to technology transfer, to the promotion of ISRs and to IPR management. They have been crucial actors in the creation and consolidation in their home institutions of a research culture including technology transfer and IPR protection. Knowledge management capabilities and competencies have evolved, in many TTOs, from simple contract research activities to more complex functions linked to protection, commercialisation and exploitation of IPR.

First comes the culture of "protection", which is similar to the culture of "publication of research results in papers", and later the idea of commercialisation and strategic use of the PRO's stock of knowledge. Advances in the functions of TTOs range from managing contract research to being involved in IPR-based spin-offs. Fewer than a dozen PROs, however, have fully developed their competencies in the area of strategic use of IPR. They play a very active role in protecting (and extending to other countries) the knowledge produced in-house and have started to license IPR to firms or to develop companies that exploit the stock of knowledge in the PROs.

The research management capabilities of PROs are increasingly heterogeneous in terms of protection of research through IPR. Some already organise their resources in terms of: *i)* the management of research in the area of public competitive funding area; and *ii)* business contract research. Additionally, they strongly encourage the provision of specialised services for patenting and protecting IPR. TTOs have generally found strong complementarities between contract research management and IPR management. However, they suffer from their small size in relation to their real needs for knowledge management and, therefore, from the lack of economies of scale in the pursuit of their goals.

PROs have unexploited technological capabilities but severe constraints on the licensing out of their patents. More efficient commercialisation of their IPR would require a concentration of resources and administrative capabilities in a collective organisation, or a network of organisations, acting as pool of resources and providing commercialisation services for the PROs.

Spanish PROs are more actively involved in spin-offs and start-ups than in commercialising IPR themselves. Public policy intervention in the form of subsidies to and accompaniment of new technology-based firms is helping to transform researchers into entrepreneurs, thereby dealing with the problems of exploiting IPR through the creation of a company.

The strategic management of IPR is not the simple result of the right incentives and legal framework, it requires organisational capabilities and the administrative competencies to protect and exploit the research results. The study of the strategic use of IPR by PROs has drawn attention to the crucial role of organisational capability, usually in TTOs, to deal with contract research, technology transfer and the protection and commercialisation of knowledge outcomes obtained from publicly funded research. A conclusion is that IPR management in PROs has to be integrated with appropriate R&D and knowledge management.

The Spanish case study shows that there is room for government intervention aimed at addressing PROs' needs for commercialising R&D outcomes. Government intervention must solve the "collective action problem" by providing the basis for the creation of collective infrastructure: a single, centralised unit that co-ordinates and assesses PROs and their TTOs with respect to IPR management.

NOTES

1.   Thanks to Pim den Hertog and Thomas Gering for their comments and suggestions on an early draft and to Rogelio Conde-Pumpido and Xavier Testar for their insights. The usual disclaimers apply.

2.   PROs include universities, public research centres (PRCs) owned by government and non-profit institutions strongly dependent on public funding sources. This chapter focuses on the management of IPR within Spanish universities and PRCs.

3.   These trends are the significant increase of R&D financed by industry and conducted by PRCs and universities; the movement towards the use of all forms of IPR; and the trend to license and commercialise the knowledge pool accumulated in PROs.

4.   LRU (art. 11) granted university professors, all with civil servant status, the opportunity to conduct research together with the business sector on a contract basis. This translated into a direct economic incentive through a significant increase in personal income. The further application of this disposition allowed university researchers to increase their regular wage base by 350%. This provision of the law has been used effectively by engineering departments in polytechnic universities owing to the applied nature of their research activities and technological development consultancy work.

5.   The Law for Promotion and General Co-ordination of Scientific and Technical Research (*Ley de Promoción y Coordinación General de la Investigación Científica y Técnica*) was passed in 1986 (*Ley 13/86*).

6.   The national R&D programmes define some of Spain's research priorities, *e.g.* biotechnology, information and communication technologies, new materials, etc.

7.   Some examples are "general promotion of knowledge (PGC)", aimed at funding academic non-targeted research and the "Health Research Fund" (FIS), exclusively focused on funding health and biomedical research based on health priorities.

8.   Traditional indicators used to define Spanish S&T were the low level of resources – expenditures as percentage of national GDP – allocated to R&D and the deficit in the technological balance of payments.

9.   The TTO of the National Research Centre (CSIC) was created in 1985.

10.   Some policy initiatives promoting the relationship between PROs and business firms were already in place, including the so-called concerted projects (*Proyectos Concertados*) funded by CICYT, and technological development projects (*Proyectos de Desarrollo Tecnológico*) under the auspices of CDTI, the Spanish Agency for Industrial and Technology Development.

11.   In addition, a central co-ordinating office (*Oficina de Transferencia de Tecnología*) was established within CICYT to provide support and co-ordinate the actions of individual interface units.

12.   Promotion was strongly associated with the building of knowledge databases and research infrastructures available in the public research system, *i.e.* technological offer or R&D supply inventory.

13. These actions were complemented by other new policy instruments such as the Programme for Technology Transfer (PETRI) sponsored by CICYT in which the public funding of technology and research projects is linked both to business funding and private-public partnerships.

14. Conesa (1997) reports that the average budget of a TTO in 1991 was ESP 22 million a year, which suggests that direct government subsidies represented about 25% of the total.

15. Government support in shaping technology transfer and ISRs in Spain continues with the implementation of a specific funding instrument, the Programme for Basic Action (PAB), devoted to the creation and consolidation of the new interface units. PAB supports personnel costs, current expenditures and IT infrastructure associated with the main functions of the TTOs. Public funding is granted for at least a three-year period, and in practice it is still the main source of funding for a large number of small interface units located in young universities (CICYT, 2002).

16. In 1994, with an average budget of ESP 27 million (approximately EUR 170 000), 30% of the operating TTOs were dependent on direct government subsidies.

17. Despite the diversity of PROs' IPR management services (in-house administrative unit *versus* a more "autonomous unit", possibly with independent legal status), one of the main tasks of most TTOs is to manage patent applications. There are exceptions; for example, one of the biggest research universities, the University of Barcelona, has an independent non-profit foundation (*Fundación Bosch i Gimpera*) as its TTO and the Patent Centre is an in-house unit.

18. A clear attempt in this direction was the creation, in 1997, of the network of university TTOs under the Conference of the Spanish Rectors (CRUE) which today includes the 54 HEI TTOs.

19. In 2000, the Ministry of Science and Technology provided slightly less than EUR 200 million of funding for competitive research projects (Sanz-Menéndez *et al.*, 2002).

20. The overall R&D expenditure budget of CSIC was over EUR 400 million, of which almost EUR 150 million was "external funding" obtained as competitive research grants or contract research.

21. According to data from 2000, R&D contracts between universities and firms usually allocate ownership to firms. Martín and Bravo (1999) report that 11.2% of the research contracts of the last 20 years have led to patents, in contrast with 6.6% between 1978 and 1989, and that 18% of research contracts were the source of new patent applications in the period 1990-97.

22. Thanks to Domingo Represa and Juan Martinez of CSIC's TTO for their valuable comments.

23. In case of a "negative evaluation", the PRO decides not to protect the output of research activities, and inventors can apply for a patent under present legal conditions (but the PRO will hold the right to a non-exclusive licence to use the invention and even 10% the benefits of exploitation).

24. The administrative procedures of the Spanish Patent Office (OEPM) are crucial for determining IPR strategies. In spite of the use of a simple set of rules based on "priority rights", there are significant delays as the OEPM's search report for the test of novelty takes on average 15-18 months after processing the application. This length of time is crucial in a context of rapid technological change and affects the appropriation of the economic rent by the patent holder.

25. Copyright for computer programmes and software is also important, with eight applications by Spanish universities in 2001 and a stock of 42 in December 2000. Universities also manage and apply for IPR for plant varieties, for which they have a stock of 12 and two new ones in 2001.

26. The request for protection usually starts with filing for a national patent, and only when there is clearly either a significant potential for exploitation or a world market do PROs start the process of IPR protection with a European, US or PCT (Patent Convention Treaty) application.

27. The implementation of this strategy is subject to strict controls and legal limitations that prevent universities from engaging in business activities. Often, the rigidities are overcome through the transfer (donation) of a symbolic share in new research-based firms from the research group to the institution signing the licensing agreement.

28. This is the case of PRCs that must have the permission of the Ministry of Public Finance for such entrepreneurial activities.

29. Up to 10% of the social capital of the new firm according to regulations for civil servants. Mobility from PRCs to research-based firm is fostered by the possibility of a four-year leave without resigning one's research position in the home institution.

REFERENCES

Alonso, S., J. R. Fernández and L. Sanz-Menéndez (2001), "Spanish Public Research Centres' responses to changes: diversification of funding resources", pp. 128-154, in D. Cox, Ph. Gummett and K. Barker, eds. (2001), *Government Laboratories: Transition and Transformation*, IOS Press, Amsterdam.

CICYT (1990-96), *Memoria sobre el desarrollo del Plan Nacional de I+D*, Secretaría general del Plan Nacional de I+D, Madrid.

CICYT (1997), *Memoria de actividades del Plan Nacional de I+D en 1997*, Oficina de Ciencia y Tecnología, Madrid.

CICYT (1998-2000) *Memoria de actividades de I+D+I*. Ministerio de Ciencia y Tecnología, Madrid.

Conesa, F. (1997), "Las Oficinas de Transferencia de Resultados de Investigación en el Sistema Español de Innovación", Universidad Politécnica de Valencia, PhD thesis, mimeo.

EC (1999), "Strategic Dimensions of Intellectual Property Rights in the Context of Science and Technology Policy", ETAN Expert Working Group for the European Commission (John N. Adams, chair)., June, DG XII, mimeo, Brussels.

EC (2002a), *Role and Strategic Use of IPR (Intellectual Property Rights) in International Research Collaborations*, Expert Group Report for the European Commission (John N. Adams, chair), April, DG Research, EUR 20230, Brussels.

EC (2002b), "Expert Working Group to Evaluate the Efficiency and Coherence of IPR Rules Applicable to Publicly Funded Research", DG Research, Draft Report, November, Brussels.

EC (2002c), *Science, Technology and Innovation. Key Figures 2002*, European Commission, Brussels.

Fernández de Lucio, I. and F. Conesa, eds. (1996), *Estructuras de interfaz en el sistema español de innovación. Su papel en la difusión de tecnología*, 2 vols., UPV, Valencia.

García, C. E. and L. Sanz-Menéndez (2002), "From Research to Patents within Spanish Public Research Organisations", CSIC-UPC working paper.

Martín, M. and A. Bravo (1999), *Resultados de 2000 contratos universdad-empresa*. Fundación Universidad-Empresa, Madrid.

Maskus, K.E. (2000), *Intellectual Property Rights in the Global Economy*, Institute for International Economics, Washington, DC.

Muñoz, E, M.J. Santesmases and J. Espinosa (1999), *Changing Structure, Organisation and Nature of Public Research Systems. Their Dynamics in the Cases of Spain and Portugal*, CSIC, Madrid.

OECD (2002a), "Interim Results of the TIP Project on the Strategic Use of IPR at PROs", internal working document, OECD, Paris.

OECD (2002b), Draft Final Report on the Strategic Use of Intellectual Property by Public Research Organisations in OECD countries", internal working document, OECD, Paris.

Red OTRI Universidades (2002), "Informe de la Encuesta Red OTRI Universidades 2001", mimeo.

Sanz-Menéndez, L. (1995), "Policy Choices, Institutional Constraints and Policy Learning: The Spanish Science and Technology Policy in the Eighties", *International Journal of Technology Management*, Vol. 10, Nos. 4/5/6, Special Issue on the Evaluation of R&D, pp. 255-274.

Sanz-Menéndez, L. (1997), *Estado, ciencia y tecnología en España (1939-1997)*, Alianza Editorial, Madrid..

Sanz-Menéndez, L. and E. Muñoz (1994), "Technology Policy in Spain: Issues, Concerns and Problems", in G. Aichholzer and G. Schienstock, eds., *Technology Policy: Towards an Integration of Social and Ecological Concerns*, pp. 349-374, De Gruyter, Berlin-New York.

Sanz-Menéndez, L. and L. Cruz-Castro (2003), "Coping with Environmental Pressures: Public Research Organizations Responses to Funding Crisis", *Research Policy*, available at www.sciencedirect.com

Sanz-Menéndez, L., E. Muñoz and C. E. Garcia (1993), "The Vicissitudes of Spanish Science and Technology Policy", *Science and Public Policy*, Vol. 20, No. 6, December, pp. 370-380.

Sanz-Menéndez, L., R. Meza and P. Barrios (2002), "Identificación de los centros de I+D con mayores capacidades científico-técnicas en las Comunidades Autónomas",: Ministerio de Ciencia y Tecnología, Madrid, mimeo, available at www.mcyt.es

SRI International (2000), "Evaluation of Current R&D Activities in Spain and Their Transfer to the Private Sector", mimeo.

LEVERAGING IP FOR BIOTECHNOLOGY

These case studies deal with the regulatory and policy choices faced by public research organisations in Germany, Korea and the United States for patenting and licensing biotechnology inventions.

Chapter 12

INTELLECTUAL PROPERTY IN THE GERMAN BIOTECHNOLOGY SECTOR

by

Oliver Werner[1]
Patent and Licensing Agency (PLA) for the German Human Genome Project
Fraunhofer Patent Centre, Munich

Introduction

In Germany, the patenting of research results in biotechnology increased drastically during the last decade, partly stimulated by fierce international competition, particularly from the United States and the United Kingdom. Discussions in German technology transfer circles have focused on the development by public research organisations (PROs) of biotechnology spin-off and licensing programmes. This case study:

- Describes changes in the legislative, economic and political background for the biotechnology industry during the 1990s.

- Highlights the Federal Ministry of Education and Research's (BMBF) 1995 BioRegio competition as a way to "kick start" German biotechnology.

- Provides statistical data on the trends in patenting in biotechnology in general and by PROs in particular.

- Gives examples of institutions that focus on support for start-up companies of PROs (BioM AG and Biotechnology Centre Heidelberg).

- Introduces three BMBF-funded life science initiatives with three different technology transfer models at the Fraunhofer Patent Centre, with a bias towards licensing of patent-protected inventions (DHGP, NGFN, ICCR).

- Describes the integrated approach taken by an established and a newly founded IP asset management company for two major non-university PROs (Garching Innovation GmbH for the Max Planck Society; Ascenion GmbH for the Helmholtz Life Science Centres).

- Discusses unique features of IP management in the biotechnology field and their impact on technology transfer strategies.

Socio-economic, legal and political background of German biotechnology in the 1990s

General situation

In the United States and the United Kingdom, the commercialisation of biotechnology developed earlier than in Germany. In the United States, the first biotechnology clusters were founded in the Bay Area in 1976 and in Boston in 1978, and the first in the United Kingdom was in Cambridge in 1988. In Germany in the late 1980s and early 1990s, however, the public took a sceptical attitude towards technology in general. This was the result of failures in certain technical disciplines (*e.g.* the accident at the Chernobyl atomic power station 1986 and the resulting fallout that affected Europe) which were also reflected in the strict legislation of the Genetic Engineering Act of 1990. As a consequence, the German pharmaceutical industry relocated biotechnological research and production activities abroad, particularly to the United States. This is probably one of the reasons why employment in the German pharmaceutical and chemical industry decreased steadily until the late 1990s from a peak in 1992; it also contributed to a significantly worse employment situation for biology and chemistry graduates.

At the same time, German researchers successfully competed in many biotechnology-related fields with their American and British colleagues. The Max Planck institutes and the so-called "gene centres" (a result of a joint federal government and industry initiative in the early 1980s) were centres of excellence, which both produced and attracted high-level scientists.

As a result of a better policy on the part of scientists and industry to make available information on biotechnology issues, the attitude of politicians and the public regarding the medical use of biotechnology improved significantly. This led in 1993 to the amendment of the Genetic Engineering Act and the lifting of restrictions on genetic engineering. In parallel, from 1989 to 2000, annual spending by the federal government for biotechnology R&D almost doubled, while the overall R&D budget increased by only 18%. One activity financed by the federal government, the BioRegio competition of 1995, triggered rapid growth in the German biotechnology industry, which is now the European leader in terms of number of companies (332 in 2000[2]).

Because protection of intellectual property is a pivotal issue, especially in the capital-intensive biotechnology start-up field, the 1998 Directive 98/44/EC of the European Parliament and the Council on the legal protection of biotechnological inventions is very important. Even though not all member states (including Germany) have enacted laws and regulations to comply with the directive, it has provided an important legal framework for the protection of biotechnological inventions in Europe.

BioRegio Competition[3]

In 1995, the BMBF initiated the BioRegio competition. Its main purpose was to encourage local biotechnology communities to interact more closely and to promote commercial applications. The competition led to high-level activities in 17 BioRegions throughout Germany, bringing together scientists, industry, venture capital companies and politicians. In 1996, three model regions – Munich, Rhine-Neckar Triangle and Rhineland – were awarded special funding of EUR 25 million each over five years. A fourth region, Jena, was awarded a special prize of EUR 15 million. Since its inception, the BioRegio competition has acted as a catalyst for commercial biotechnology throughout Germany. National and local networks have been generated, facilitating the exchange of knowledge and leading to a striking increase in new start-ups. The number of core biotechnology companies (ELISCOs) increased from 75 in 1995 to 279 in 1999, an increase of 270%.[4]

The success of the BioRegio competition has prompted the BMBF to launch additional initiatives to encourage growth of the German biotechnology industry. The programme BioChance is aimed at high-risk entrepreneurial R&D projects implemented by young biotechnology SMEs and has provided total funding of more than EUR 50 million from 1999 to 2002 for 52 start-up companies.

BioProfile, another BMBF competition in which three regions were selected in 2001, demonstrated the potential of these regions to establish promising commercial biotechnology applications, especially in non-biomedical fields (*e.g.* plant biotechnology). A total of EUR 50 million is provided for five years.

Biotechnology patents: international comparisons and the role of German PROs

From 1985 to 1999, the number of biotechnology patent applications increased by more than 400%, largely owing to an enormous increase in Patent Co-operation Treaty (PCT) applications. However, the number of applications in this field filed directly at the European Patent Office (EPO) has decreased. Interestingly, the relative contribution of the major countries has remained more or less constant over the years. While US applicants filed some 50% of the applications, Germany (10%), France (5%) and the United Kingdom (8%) maintained a constant share. The Japanese share fell from about 15% in the late 1980s to some 10% in the late 1990s. Smaller countries increased their share from about 15% to 20%, indicating that many smaller countries are making efforts to establish a biotechnology industry (Figure 1).

Figure 1. WO and EP biotechnology patent applications 1985-99

Sum of WO+EP patent applications

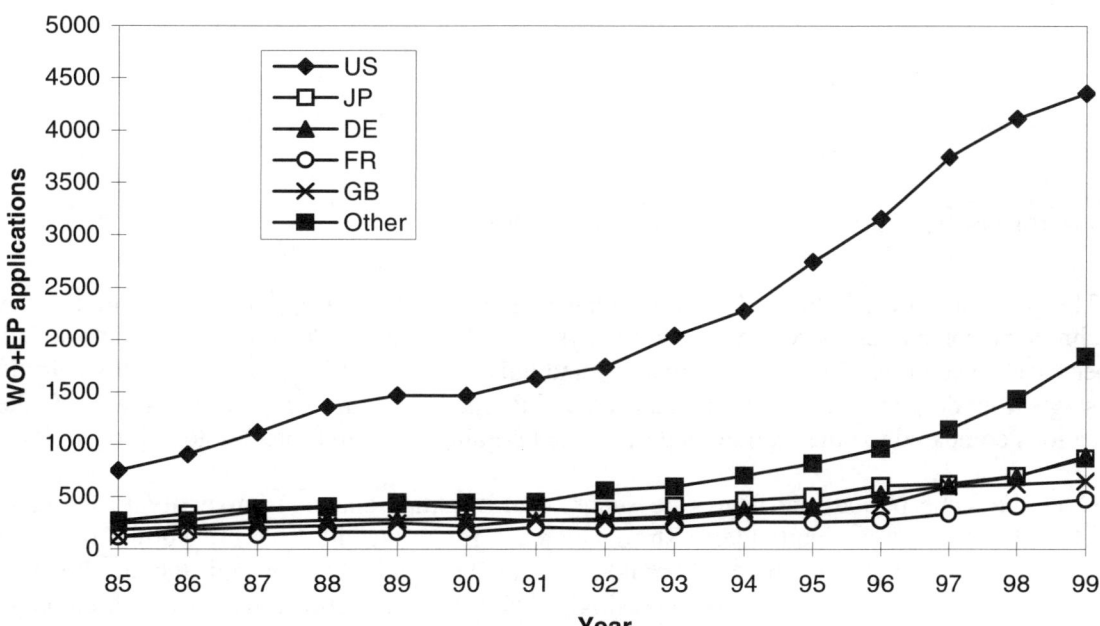

EP = European patent.
WO = PCT patent.
Source: EPAT (STN); WOPAT (STN); Ulrich Schmoch FhG-ISI.

To assess the contribution to German biotechnology patenting of different applicant groups, a search for German patent applications was conducted using the methodology described in Chapter 9 of this volume. From 1991 to 1999, overall biotechnology patenting activity by German applicants increased by more than 170%, paralleling the development of EPO and PCT applications (Table 1).

Table 1. German biotechnology patent applications at the German Patent and Trademark Office 1991-99

	1991				1995				1999			
Applicant	n	nP	%	%P	n	nP	%	%P	n	nP	%	%P
Pharmaceutical industry	144		41		170		31		175		18	
Universities	86		24		145		27		307		32	
University		2		2		10		7		42		14
Professor		24		28		48		33		97		31
Dr. / Dipl.		60		70		87		60		168		55
Non-university PROs	54		15		78		14		164		17	
Helmholtz Association		24		44		28		36		82		50
Max Planck Society		9		17		13		17		20		12
Fraunhofer Society		6		11		11		14		16		10
Others		15		28		26		33		46		28
Biotechnology companies	25		7		81		15		218		22	
Individuals (no academic grade)	21		6		37		7		69		7	
Others	25		7		33		6		35		4	
Total	355	140	100		544	223	100		968	471	100	
PRO share			39				41				49	

n = number of German patent applications.
nP = number of German patent applications by PROs.
% = share of total.
%P = share of the respective PRO group (universities vs. non-university).
Source: PATDPA (STN); Ulrich Schmoch, FhG-ISI; Oliver Werner, PLA.

The pharmaceutical industry lost more than half of its share, dropping to 18% in 1999, while biotechnology companies more than tripled theirs, to 22%. After 1999, the pharmaceutical industry has been well behind biotechnology companies and universities, and likely also non-university PROs. The stagnation of pharmaceutical industry patenting may explain the constant share of German applications compared to other countries despite the booming German biotechnology industry.

Over the same period, the aggregate share of universities and non-university PROs increased from 39% to 49%, with a particularly strong increase for universities. A breakdown of university applications shows that the share of professors stayed relatively constant (about 30%), while universities themselves (14% in 1999) increasingly took title to inventions made by their employees at the pre-doctorate and post-doctorate level. This development is likely to continue given the changes in the German employer-employee law (*Arbeitnehmererfindungsgesetz*) and universities' efforts to establish professional patenting and licensing structures (see Chapter 9 in this volume). Nevertheless, the pre-doctorates and post-doctorates still constitute the strongest applicant group both within universities (55% in 1999) and within the PRO sector as a whole.

Among non-university PROs, institutes of the Helmholtz Association are the most active applicants in biotechnology. The establishment of a professional technology transfer unit for the Helmholtz life science institutes (described below) is expected to further strengthen their position.

BioRegio co-ordinating institutions with a focus on start-up company support

BioM AG Munich

For the Munich BioRegio, BioM AG was established in 1997. Besides its role in supporting and evaluating research proposals concerning the BioRegio funds, BioM very early also started to acquire additional private and public funds and began to provide seed financing for biotechnology start-up companies. Together with a variety of start-up coaching and consulting activities, this soon led BioM to evolve from a co-ordinating institution to a venture capital company. In 2002, its investment portfolio included 29 companies.

Biotechnology Centre Heidelberg

The services provided by BioM to a company are also offered by a triad of functionally connected institutions collectively termed Biotechnology Centre Heidelberg. Also founded as a consequence of success in the BioRegio competition, the non-profit association BioRegion Rhine-Neckar Triangle was established in 1996 to promote pre-commercial applied biotechnology and life sciences. In the Munich area, an unmet need prompted the founding of both Heidelberg Innovation GmbH (HI) and the venture capital fund Heidelberg Innovation GmbH & Co BioScience Venture KG (BSV) in 1997. HI is active in all aspects of start-up coaching and manages the BSV fund, which is also available for seed financing. The BSV fund has a clear biotechnology focus, with investments in 23 biotechnology companies (2002), among them Lion Bioscience, a publicly traded German biotechnology company.

BMBF-funded life science initiatives and associated technology transfer models with a bias towards licensing of patent-protected inventions

The German Human Genome Project (DHGP)

In 1995, the BMBF embarked upon promotion of co-ordinated genome research with the announcement of the funding of the German Human Genome Project. From 1996 to 2003, the BMBF will spend about EUR 100 million on more than 120 scientific projects dealing with genome and cDNA sequencing, functional analysis and animal model systems.

In 1997, the BMBF, the German life science industry and participating academic institutions agreed to establish a new platform to facilitate science-industry collaboration. The Patent and Licensing Agency for the German Human Genome Project (PLA) was founded at the Fraunhofer Patent Centre for German Research (PST). Its objective is the successful detection, protection and commercial exploitation of intellectual property (IP) from the DHGP. Financed by the Association for the Promotion of Human Genome Research (*Foerderverein*), an industry platform with members from large German pharmaceutical and mid-size biotechnology companies, the PLA serves as the central IP management institution for all DHGP scientists. The *Foerderverein* enjoys a three-month privilege on exclusive first-hand information and data from the DHGP, and a right of first refusal for a further three months.

The BMBF obliges scientists to send all publications to the PLA to screen for patentable subject matter in order to minimise novelty-destroying publication. In the course of this screening over the period 1997-2001, more than 500 documents were processed and led to 33 patent applications covering more than 300 genes and bioinformatic and technical solutions.

Commercial exploitation of DHGP inventions is driven by licensing and sale of patented inventions. It is carried out by PST, GI, DKFZ technology transfer or Ascenion (for more on some of these institutions, see below), depending on which institution the patent application is assigned to. In a few cases, patents were also used to create DHGP start-up companies.

The DHGP was, and still is, the first German publicly funded research project that incorporates a distinct and specialised technology transfer model and institution. Although its commercial success has so far been limited, the PLA plays a central role as a university-industry interface and source of IP information for scientists in the biotechnology field. However, certain regulations concerning *Foerderverein* privileges have proven difficult to apply during licensing negotiations. Experience with the PLA has strongly influenced subsequent technology transfer models for publicly funded biotechnology research in Germany, such as the National Genome Network.

The National Genome Network (NGFN)

In 2000, the BMBF provided about EUR 180 million to finance the National Genome Network for 2001-04. The NGFN partially overlaps with the DHGP but focuses more on disease-relevant applications of genome research. The scientific work is organised in a network structure consisting of large core research centres, disease-oriented research networks, mainly with universities and university hospitals, and technology platforms with a specific technological focus (bioinformatics, proteomics). The DHGP and the NGFN are likely to merge in 2004.

The technology transfer unit for the NGFN (TT-NGFN) was founded in early 2002 at the Fraunhofer Patent Centre. Learning the lesson from difficulties with PLA regulations, the NGFN regulations grant no industry privileges. Consequently, TT-NGFN is funded jointly by the BMBF and the core area, which consists of the four big Helmholtz life science institutes (GBF, GSF, MDC, DKFZ) and the Max Planck Institute for Molecular Genetics (MPIMG). TT-NGFN serves as the central entry point for all NGFN IP-related questions, the publication screen and patenting actions. Reflecting the strong involvement of the Helmholtz and Max Planck Society institutes in the NGFN, their technology transfer institutions (GI and Ascenion) are solely responsible for the commercial exploitation of inventions made in their respective institutions after initial patenting in co-operation with TT-NGFN.

In the course of the planned fusion of DHGP and NGFN, there is also a debate among the institutions involved about a merger of the two technology transfer units (PLA and TT-NGFN). It remains to be seen whether two technology transfer models with quite different regulatory policies can be merged and maintain aspects of both, or whether only one will finally survive.

The interdisciplinary centres for clinical research

Following a BMBF scientific competition in 1995, eight medical centres were awarded annual combined start-up funding of EUR 50 million. The *Länder* governments agreed to take over gradually the financing of the centres. In 2002, there was a total of nine interdisciplinary centres for clinical research (ICCRs), which focus on topics as diverse as biomaterials, chronic disease and molecular medicine.

As for other BMBF-funded projects, the medical centres were obliged to engage actively in marketing their research results and IP generated from these results. ICCRs started to fulfil this requirement by holding technology transfer meetings (TTMs) and only recently embarked upon an Internet-based project and technology market to attract industry interest for ICCR technologies and for ICCR-industry co-operation. As a second exploitation channel, a technology transfer unit was set up in early 2002 at the Fraunhofer Patent Centre. It is fully funded by the BMBF for a start-up phase of at least two years.

This combination of exploitation tools aims at integrating the potential of science-industry co-operation projects and a more traditional patenting/licensing approach. This appears similar to a strategy adopted by the Fraunhofer Society and is an interesting and unusual approach in the biomedical field.

Biotechnology transfer companies in PROs active in commercial exploitation of IP

Garching Innovation GmbH

The Max Planck Society traditionally has a strong focus on basic biomedical research. Of the 79 Max Planck institutes (in 2002), 62 are patent-relevant in the chemical-physical-technical (CPT: 29 institutes) and the biomedical (BM: 33 institutes) fields. The ratio between CPT and BM institutes has remained quite constant over the last decade at 50-55% BM institutes.

Since 1970, Garching Innovation GmbH (GI), the technology transfer unit of the Max Planck Society, a wholly owned subsidiary, has been responsible for patenting and licensing inventions from the institutes. Patent applications were fairly constant until the early 1990s when they started to increase. In the late 1990s, they peaked at about a 100% increase over the level of the 1970s and 1980s, largely owing to a massive increase in biotechnology patent applications, which rose from about one-third to two-thirds of applications during the 1990s.

This strong development in biotechnology is even more pronounced in terms of start-up activity. In 1990 GI for the first time supported a company "spin-off" from a Max Planck institute. Since then 50 companies were founded with the participation of Max Planck institutes, of which 37 are in the biomedical field and constitute an impressive 74% of biotechnology companies in the GI portfolio (Table 2). GI actively coached 35 "spin-off" companies.

In summary, during the 1990s GI matured into an integrated IP asset management agency with exploitation activities in both licensing and start-up coaching and has become a major player in German biotechnology. This development was largely driven by the biomedical section of the Max Planck Society, one of the main forces behind Germany's biotechnology boom in the 1990s.

Table 2. Max Planck Society start-up companies 1990-2001

Year	Life sciences	New materials, IT, others	Total
1990	0	1	1
1991	1	2	3
1992	3	0	3
1993	1	1	2
1994	1	0	1
1995	0	1	1
1996	2	0	2
1997	6	2	8
1998	6	0	6
1999	4	1	5
2000	8	4	12
2001	5	1	6
Total	37	13	50
Venture capital financing	28	5	33

Source: Garching Innovation GmbH.

Ascenion GmbH

In contrast to GI and other technology transfer units of public research organisations, Ascenion GmbH specialises in biotechnology inventions. Founded in 2001 by the non-profit Life Science Foundation for the Promotion of Science and Research of four Helmholtz research centres (German Research Centre for Biotechnology, National Research Centre for Environment and Health, Max Delbrück Centre for Molecular Medicine, German Cancer Research Centre), Ascenion provides IP asset management for these centres. Its services include acquisition, evaluation and commercial exploitation of scientific results by both traditional means of technology transfer (patenting, licensing) and start-up support. Ascenion's ambitious goal is to become a prime supplier for biotechnology IP in Germany.

The approach taken by Ascenion involves quite high up-front investments, which have to be justified by future return – a difficult task in the notoriously fickle technology transfer business, particularly in the biomedical field.

Unique features of IP management in the biotechnology field

General remarks

The ultimate goal of IP asset management involving PROs is to generate revenues from their research activities, *e.g.* by sale, exclusive or non-exclusive licensing, collection of royalties, or acquiring an equity stake in spin-off companies. The value of a biotechnology product is subject to a variety of factors that are unique to the biotechnology and pharmaceutical industry and clearly have a strong impact on PROs' technology transfer structures and strategies. Examples of factors influencing the economic value of "IP products" and the resulting requirements for PROs' technology transfer units in the biotechnology field are discussed below.

Technology types

Technologies in the biomedical field may be divided into "platform" and "(pharmaceutical) product".[5] While platform technologies are regarded as auxiliary applications with limited revenue potential, biotechnology research can provide both targets and therapeutics for the pharmaceutical industry with high earnings potential.

Therefore, a major goal of PROs' technology transfer units must be the identification and broad patenting of medically relevant inventions, especially for indications with large markets. This involves a significant allocation of resources to technology scouting and technology assessment, which can be provided only by well-staffed technology transfer institutions. Owing to funding constraints, this requirement is certainly not met by a variety of publicly funded technology transfer units.

The pharmaceutical value chain

Product development in the pharmaceutical field is extremely time-consuming and expensive. It is estimated that from target identification to market a drug takes about 15 years at an estimated cost of about USD 800 million, about 75% of which is attributable to failures along the way.[6] Because of the high costs involved, pharmaceutical companies prefer to license a potential product when it has proven its potential (particularly clinical phase 2) in order to minimise risk.[7] A second consequence of this risk-avoidance strategy is a relative reluctance to license revolutionary products in early stages of development.

All of this has major implications for the biotechnology transfer practice of PROs. Because early licensing is considered difficult and PROs usually do not have the capability to carry a therapeutic product through the developmental stages to the clinical phases, technology transfer institutions must maintain active start-up company support for their researchers to attract investors to new technologies. This includes the ability to acquire equity stakes for IP rights. This is especially a problem for German universities and has to be circumvented by more or less complicated legal constructs. Regardless of whether IP rights are licensed directly or brought into a spin-off company, the long time scale of product development involves high costs for international patent applications and late revenues or royalties. Biotechnology transfer agencies in particular therefore need high-level, long-term funding, which is not provided for some technology transfer initiatives.

The strong German focus on basic research[8] creates both opportunities and dangers for PROs' technology transfer. On the one hand, technology platforms resulting from basic research are often closer to the market and can be used to generate revenues earlier. On the other, possible revolutionary products from basic research are, as mentioned above, harder to license because they are allegedly prone to failure (they may be used by companies to block competitors instead).

Technology transfer strategies

In order to deal with these difficulties and to increase the probability of long-term economic success, a PRO biotechnology transfer institution has to reach a certain size in terms of staff, patenting funds and possibly access to seed or venture capital. This integrated approach exists at present only at Garching Innovation GmbH, discussed above.

One possible compensation for limited size and funds is intense co-operation and networking between technology transfer units. This has already started in the course of the National Genome

Network, discussed above, and is desirable for all three BMBF-funded life science initiatives at the Fraunhofer Patent Centre. Co-operation is still hampered by complicated contract negotiations between the participants, differences in funding structures and obstructive regulations of the so-called *Projektträger* institutions (see Chapter 9 in this volume).

Co-operative science-industry research and development (which is intensely used, for example, by the Fraunhofer Society) has been limited to some DHGP projects and the ICCRs (see above) although the model would appear to be attractive for the cost-intensive biotechnology field. As for the networking approach, difficulties arise with the often complicated co-operation contracts, particularly on IP issues. An essential prerequisite for this type of partnership is early and broad patenting of the PRO's research results prior to co-operation in order to define the groundwork clearly and to attract partners to an exclusive and promising technology.

Conclusion

Commercial exploitation of biotechnology research started late in Germany. Excellent public research institutions and substantial government funding sparked a German biotechnology boom in both universities and industry. This development was accompanied by a massive increase in patenting by PROs and newly founded biotechnology companies. In order to promote patenting, licensing and formation of "spin-off" companies by PROs, a variety of technology transfer institutions with varying approaches, ranging from venture capital to classical patenting/licensing, were established. The peculiarities of the biomedical value chain require highly professional intellectual asset management, which must be able to make long-term investments in promising technologies. Patenting by German PROs in the biotechnology field is likely to increase, given measures taken by the federal government and efforts of PROs themselves to establish professional technology transfer structures.

NOTES

1. With contributions by Thomas Gering, Ventratec GmbH, Munich (co-ordinator) and Ulrich Schmoch, Fraunhofer Institute for Systems and Innovations Research (ISI), Karlsruhe (Statistical Data). This case study was made possible by a grant from the German Federal Ministry of Education and Research (BMBF).

2. Ernst & Young, Pressemitteilung 26.4.2001; www.ey.com/GLOBAL/gcr.nsf/Germany/26_04_01_. Europaeische_Biotech_Industrie_boomt_weiter. Ernst & Young, Integration, Eighth Annual European Life Sciences Report 2001, Cambridge.

3. BMBF (2000), *Funding of Growth, Initiatives in Biotechnology*, Bonn.

4. Ernst & Young (2000), *Gründerzeit, Zweiter Deutscher Biotechnologie-Report 2000*, Stuttgart.

5. See, for example, The Boston Consulting Group (2001), "Positionierung Deutscher Biotechnologie-Cluster im internationalen Vergleich", BCG Germany.

6. The Boston Consulting Group (2001), "A Revolution in R&D", BCG Germany.

7. K. Arnold *et al.* (2002), "Value Drivers in Licensing Deals", *Nature Biotechnology*, Vol. 20, pp. 1085-1089.

8. The Boston Consulting Group (2001) "Wettbewerbsfähigkeit Deutschlands als Standort für Arzneimittelforschung und –entwicklung", BCG Munich.

Chapter 13

REGULATORY REGIME GOVERNING MANAGEMENT OF INTELLECTUAL PROPERTY OF KOREAN PUBLIC RESEARCH ORGANISATIONS: FOCUS ON THE BIOTECHNOLOGY SECTOR

by

Mikyung Yun
Korea Institute for International Economic Policy

Introduction

Transfer to the private sector of basic research undertaken in the public sector for commercialisation is important for technology diffusion and effective use of public sector research. Many OECD countries have recognised that this transfer does not occur automatically and have endeavoured to facilitate transfer of public-sector research results to industry. One solution to this problem was to establish an appropriate IP-management policy, such as the Bayh-Dole Act in the United States.

Korea has recently recognised that much research in universities and public research organisations (PROs) is not being channelled to industry in a timely manner. A major barrier was the lack of financial incentives for PROs as well as individual PRO scientists, and the lack of appropriate institutions to take responsibility and absorb the cost of IP management at PROs. Recent regulatory reforms have therefore focused on this issue. However, subsidisation or managerial assistance for patenting and licensing at PROs is not the only aspect of public-private technology transfer. Regulatory reforms to encourage greater public-private R&D co-operation[1] and to encourage the formation of venture firms have accompanied reforms more directly related to IP management.

This chapter looks at these changes and describes Korea's experience. Throughout, it draws on examples from the biotechnology sector to assess the appropriateness of the direction that the reforms have taken and to draw further policy implications. The biotechnology sector is a major focus of Korea's current science and technology policy and would benefit more from policy lessons than other sectors. Because the biotechnology sector is science-based and related industries rely heavily on basic research for product development, the public-private technology transfer interface has added significance.

It should be noted at the outset, however, that the regulatory reforms are still evolving, and it would be difficult to make a definite evaluation of the effects of regulatory changes. The primary objective of the chapter is therefore to present the Korean experience rather than to make a full assessment of the changes.

To set the scene, the nature of the problem of technology transfer from the public sector to the private sector is explained. The following section examines recent regulatory changes. The discussion then turns to the impact of the changes in general and then to licensing and R&D in the biotechnology sector in particular. The final section comments on the likely success of the changes, identifying some problems, and draws implications for future policy making.

Patenting and licensing activities of PROs: problems of technology transfer

In the late 1990s, there was growing concern in academic and policy-making circles regarding the lack of transfer of technology by PROs, and especially public universities. Despite increasing R&D investment and the rise in patent applications, PROs' share of patent applications was very small, especially considering their share in R&D. Table 1 shows that while the public sector accounted for about 27% of investment in R&D in the late 1990s, it accounted for less than 5% of patent applications, or around 6% of total patent applications by Korean nationals, in both 1998 and 1999. In particular, patenting activities by universities were minimal, representing 0.4% and 0.12% of total patent applications in 1998 and 1999, respectively. Owing to a lack of systematic data, it is difficult to discern trends in PROs' licensing activities. However, according to a 1997 survey by the Korea Intellectual Property Office, only 31% of total patents awarded were licensed. The rate of licensing for state-owned patents was even lower at 19%.

Table 1. R&D and patent applications by PROs, 1998-2000

		1998	1999	2000
R&D[1]	National total	8 104	10 023	12 249
	Public sector (government and PROs)	(27)	(27)	(25)
Patent[2]	National total	75 188	80 642	101 782
	Korean nationals	50 596 (67.3)	55 970 (69.4)	72 831 (71.4)
	PROs total	3 249 (4.32)	3 604 (4.79)	2 972 (3.95)
	University	354 (0.47)	482 (0.12)	629 (0.62)
	Public research institutes	2 895 (3.85)	3 122 (4.15)	2 343 (3.12)

Note: Figures in brackets are the share, in percentages, of patents of applying entities in total number of patents applied.
Source: Ministry of Science and Technology (2001), p. 14; Lee (2001), p. 7; Korea Patent Office (2001), *Intellectual Property Statistics* .

The biotechnology sector was no exception to this trend. Possibly because the level of domestic research lagged the international leaders, successful technology transfer seems to have been much less frequent in this sector when compared to other technological fields. Ahn *et al.* (1998) report that although the number of patents filed and articles published by PROs increased rapidly from 1990 to 1996, technology transfer was very low in general and in particular in the life sciences (Table 2). Over this period, there were only three cases of technology transfer of basic research in the life sciences.[2]

Table 2. Technology transfers from PROs by scientific field, 1990-96

Field	Type (no.) of centres[1]	R&D USD millions	No. of projects	Articles published	Technology transferred	Commercialised products	Domestic patents
Mathematical and physical sciences	SRC (11)	39.3	1 037	3 130	27	9	11
Life sciences	SRC (6)	28.7	872	1 050	3	2	55
	ERC (4)	17.8	918	454	45	29	14
Engineering	ERC (17)	75.0	4 449	3 781	324	168	154
Total	38	160.8	7 296	8 415	399	208	234

1. The figures concern the Centre of Excellence Programme. The Korea Scientific and Engineering Foundation (KOSEF) launched the programme in 1990 to promote excellence in university research and to encourage collaborative and multidisciplinary research among PROs and universities. The programme is divided into SRCs (science research centres) which focus on basic research and ERCs (engineering research centres) which focus on engineering research.
Source: Ahn *et al.* (1998), p. 49.

The consequences are even more unfortunate when considering the fact that most R&D personnel are in universities. As of 1995, almost 35% of all R&D personnel, and more than 77% of PhDs, were in universities. This situation was more pronounced for the biotechnology sector, with more than 38% of all R&D personnel, and more than 78% of PhDs, in universities (Ahn and Chung, 1998).

This situation led many scholars and policy makers to argue that the regulatory regime should be reformed to facilitate the patenting and licensing activities of PROs, to allow them to better benefit from their research efforts and to feed government investment back to the private sector. Lack of financial incentives and specialised institutional mechanisms for technology transfer, especially at public universities, was identified as a major barrier, and overcoming this barrier became a focus of regulatory reform. Thus, the debate in Korea has centred on introducing a regime of the Bayh-Dole type to provide greater flexibility in public IP management and to involve the private sector to a greater extent, rather than on how to mitigate the potential adverse effects of a decentralised IP management regime. Nevertheless, supporting programmes to encourage greater public-private R&D co-operation[3] and spin-offs with greater direct participation by PRO staff, the creation of technology markets and patent fee discount schemes were also initiated.

Regulatory regime governing intellectual property management by PROs

Until recently, Korea had a dual system of IP management by PROs. One system applied to public research institutes and private universities (Table 3). They could own intellectual property (IP) arising from publicly financed research after paying a share to the government and providing appropriate compensation for individual scientists when there is a return to the IP. Although rules regarding disbursement of returns from intellectual property rights (IPRs) allowed as much as 70% to be given to individual scientists in special public research projects, few institutions had specific regulations concerning such distribution rules and in most cases compensation was minimal.

A second system applied to public universities, which under the Patent Law could not own intellectual property arising from public research projects. The IP became state property, and compensation for individual scientists followed rules and regulations concerning inventions by state employees. This allocates a small fixed sum (KRW 500 000 or approximately USD 400[4]) and 10-30% of net licence income to the inventor, depending on the amount of the income. Again, in most cases, the compensation was minimal. According to a 1999 survey by the Korea Institute of Industry and Technology (KINITI), more than half of PROs did not provide any compensation or compensated PRO scientists at less than 10% of returns.[5]

Table 3. IP management regimes by types of PROs

Type of PRO	Pre-reform		Post-reform	
	Ownership	Compensation	Ownership	Compensation
PRO	PRO No TTOs and no institutional funding for IP management	Own rules (rules regarding publicly financed research allowed as much as 70% for special projects)	PRO (TTO) (Facilitation Law)	Minimum 50% (Facilitation Law)
Private university	Same as PRO	Same as PRO	PRO (TTO) (Facilitation Law)	25% (Omnibus Law on publicly financed research)
Public university	State No legal status to operate independent budget to manage licence income	Lump sum per patent plus 10-30% of licence income (rules regarding compensation for state employees)	TTO (Facilitation Law and Patent Law amendment)	Minimum 50% (Facilitation Law)

TTO = technology transfer organisation.

Moreover, neither type of PRO had specialised technology transfer offices (TTOs). They did not provide their scientists assistance with the transfer process, nor was there any funding for the direct costs of patenting and licensing (Joo, 2001). This meant that individual scientists had to finance their own patenting and licensing, although they were likely to receive minimal compensation. There was thus very little incentive for PROs and PRO scientists to patent and license public research results. In PROs and private universities, the incentive problem existed for the individual scientist, and in public universities, both PROs and PRO scientists lacked incentive.

According to a PRO scientist, the innovator should receive 20-30% of the total return from the innovation, plus separate funds for IP management. Otherwise, scientists who have to forego opportunities for academic publication risk too much from patenting their work (Byun, 2002). Consequently, there has been very little patenting activity by public universities, and little university support for IP management by individual researchers. In reality, individual researchers file for protection of research results of public universities and become private beneficiaries of these activities.[6] Despite the apparent breaking of the law, with the result that individuals are appropriating all returns from public resources, the law has not been strictly enforced, in recognition of the above-mentioned incentive problems.

Enactment of the Technology Transfer Facilitation Law

The decentralisation of PROs' IP management began with the enactment in 2000 of the Technology Transfer Facilitation Law. The most important effect of this law is to unify the IP management system of all types of PROs. It simplifies the regulations, and restores balance in incentives for different types of PROs. Under the law, PROs are required to establish TTOs,[7] to which PRO staff disclose their inventions. The TTOs then provide IP management services, ranging from patent assessment and application to licensing. Under the new law, TTOs can benefit from total or partial funding by the government or the PRO itself.

The law allows, but specifies and limits, use by the PRO of income generated by the PRO's intellectual property. At first, it provides that, at a minimum, 15% of net licence income is to be distributed to the PRO scientist-inventor. However, amendment of the implementation regulation in July 2002 raised this to at least 50%. Although exact sharing rules are set by each PRO, this provides a strong financial incentive to patent PRO intellectual property. The rest can be used to meet IP management expenses (including expenses incurred for patenting and licensing, as well as for the operation of the TTO) and further investment in R&D.[8]

Under the amended Technology Transfer Facilitation Law, the PRO must license the technology to parties that want to use it, unless the PRO uses the technology directly or if there is some limitation under other laws. Although equal opportunities should be provided to all potential licensees, priority is given for a specified period of time to firms that contributed to funding of the research.

Another focus of the law is the creation of a technology market. The Korea Technology Trade Center (KTTC) was established under this law to network with TTOs of PROs and other institutions concerned with technology trade. It is thus supposed to act as the central clearinghouse for PRO technology. KTTC also provides analysis of market or technical information as well as technology valuation services.

Amendment of the Patent Law

The Patent Law was also amended in 2001 to bring its regulations in alignment with the changes in the above law. These amendments also eliminate the disadvantage that public universities suffered from by making TTOs in public universities corporations or legal persons. Whereas PROs and private universities are incorporated and can claim private property and operate an independent budget and accounting, Korean jurisprudence holds that public universities are not legal persons that can operate a separate budget and accounting independent of the ministries in charge of them.[9]

This meant that even when allowed to own intellectual property, public universities were unable to appropriate financial gains from licence income. The number of patents held by different types of PROs (see Table 1) amply demonstrates the effects of this imbalance in incentives. Furthermore, patents held by public universities are mostly owned by individual scientists rather than by the university, as noted above. This shows that there was a close relationship between financial incentives and the incidence of patent applications. By redefining the legal status of the TTOs, and allowing them to channel income generated by the IP to the public universities, the recent amendment bypasses this problem.

Other reforms

The changes discussed above were accompanied by changes in other areas of science and technology policy that affect the transfer and commercialisation of PRO technology. In 1999, the Korea Intellectual Property Office started the temporary patent fee discount programme (for application, review and maintenance for the first three years). Initially valid until 2001, the programme has been extended to 2005. Under the programme, a 70% discount is provided for individuals and small firms and a 50% discount for medium-sized firms and PROs.

To encourage transfer of PRO technology to venture firms, the Special Measures on Venture Firms was amended in 1998 to allow PRO scientists to own equity and participate directly in venture businesses. With the PRO's permission, PRO scientists can hold joint positions in venture businesses or take temporary leave. Further, under the SME Start-up Support Act, some 50 PROs are designated as venture incubation centres, providing technical and managerial assistance and low-cost R&D labs and other facilities for small start-ups; many of these start-ups are PRO spin-offs. In most cases, the start-ups agree to donate royalties or equities upon successful commercialisation.

New legislation currently being considered by the National Assembly would allow universities to own equity in venture business by setting up "public-private co-operation centres". These centres will be specialised units that represent universities in all R&D- or IP-related transactions, including joint R&D contracts, patenting and licensing, spin-offs and negotiating for royalties and equities. To encourage participation by PRO scientists, the new legislation also provides for their participation to be taken into account when making performance or promotion evaluations. It is suggested that such centres be subsidised by the government until they can finance themselves using income from successful licensing and venture businesses they have supported.[10]

In addition, a unified regulation regarding the management of publicly funded research was established in 2001. The law unifies rules regulating all publicly funded research, which was formerly regulated by each funding ministry or other public organisation, using different rules. The law imposes unified criteria for project selection and evaluation. It also clearly sets forth rules regarding ownership of intellectual property generated by publicly funded research and how the income generated should be used. However, it leaves room for each PRO to decide how the income should be divided among interested parties. The law therefore removes a lot of the uncertainties that arose from research funded by different ministries using different criteria and rules. Some important aspects of the new law are:[11]

- It allows multi-year contracts for research grants.

- It gives the main research institute ownership of IP and facilities generated from the research. When the main research organisation is a private entity, the participating public organisation is entitled to the IP and facilities to the extent of the government's contribution to funding of the research.

- It gives the participating private firm priority to the right to license the new technology. The PRO must seek its consent before licensing the technology to a third party. However, the licensee must work the patent.

- It specifies that, out of the net licence income, 30% of the government contribution (50% when the main research organisation is a for-profit organisation) should be given to the PRO involved. This portion must be reinvested in R&D or other projects to stimulate R&D or be absorbed by public funds.

- The rest of the net licence income must be distributed as follows: 50% to the inventor or the research team (*i.e.* 25% of total net licence income), 30% (*i.e.* 15% of total net licence income) or more to R&D investment, and 10% (*i.e.* 5% of total net licence income) to operation of the PRO. Remaining portions can be used to meet IP management expenses. Licence income that exceeds the government's contribution can be used for the above purposes, according to distribution rules set by each PRO.

The impact of the reforms

The above changes in the regulatory regime had a rapid and large impact. During the last two years, 20 TTOs have been set up at private universities. The government had provided around KRW 45-60 million (approximately USD 36 500-48 700) per university to finance their operation. These TTOs together registered around 2 500 transferable technologies in their databases and recorded 98 cases of technology transfer to small and medium-sized firms from mid-2001 to mid-2002. Patent-related cases were the major type of intellectual property transferred (41 in all). The majority of technologies transferred (26) were in chemistry, environment and bio-related technologies. Of these 26, ten were biotechnology-related. The Pohang University of Science and Technology (POSTECH) was the most active licensor, representing more than 28% of the total technology transferred. Among private universities, POSTECH also most frequently transferred bio-related technology, licensing five technologies during the period. The impact on public universities cannot be assessed yet, since the relevant amendment dates from late 2001 and became effective only in July 2002. Several public universities are currently in the process of preparing to set up a TTO.

There is some concern that these TTOs are floundering because of the lack of economies of scale and inadequate operating income from licences. For example, as will be shown below, it is difficult to maintain a full-time TTO at each PRO because of an insufficient number of technology transfer cases. Further, income per licence is not adequate for self-financing and given the early stage of most of the licensed projects, the TTOs are expected to depend on government subsidies for the foreseeable future. However, government funding for patenting and licensing costs do not seem to be adequate.

The impact of regulatory changes on PRO participation in venture start-ups is more dramatic. A survey in 2000 by Technobusiness, a consulting firm of 500 scientists in the Daeduk Science Park, revealed that 69% of the scientists were interested in setting up or otherwise participating in venture business. The high level of demonstrated enthusiasm is apparent in the number of start-ups established. Figure 1 shows that while PRO spin-offs had been on the rise since 1997, the number of university spin-offs increased sharply after 1998. By mid-1999, more than 24% of the 4 008 venture firms surveyed by the Office of Small and Medium Enterprises were spin-offs using PRO technology. In 1999, there were 50 PRO start-ups per 10 000 researchers, a high level comparable to other OECD countries such as Germany, Norway and the United States, where PRO start-ups are frequent (20-50 start-ups per 10 000 researchers). In addition, more than 50% of PRO start-ups used venture-incubation centres established in universities (Yoon and Kwon, 2001).

Figure 1. Trends in PRO spin-offs

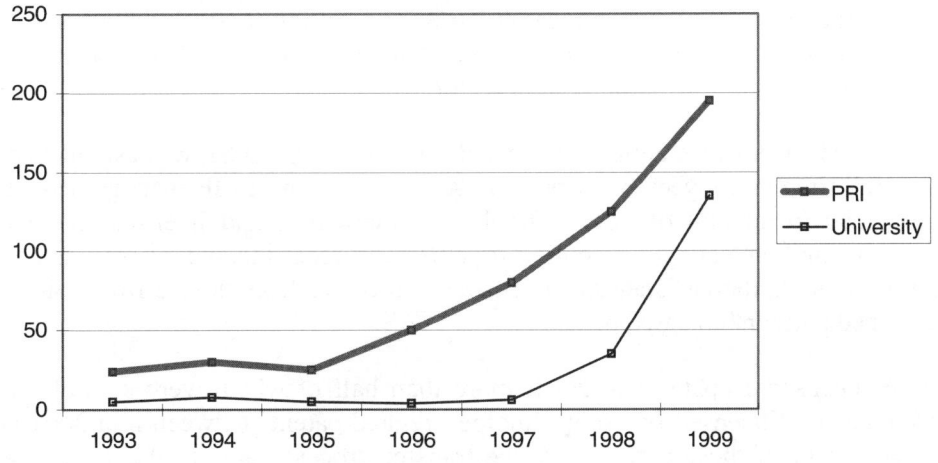

Source: Yoon and Kwon (2001), p. 60.

Machinery, electronics and IT represented major shares of the venture firms surveyed (approximately 23%, 20%, and 26%, respectively). The distribution of technological fields is similar for PRO start-ups alone. However, there is a notable jump in the ratios for IT and biotechnology. While biotechnology constituted a meagre 1.9% of all venture firms, its share increases to 8% when only PRO spin-offs are considered. For the IT sector, the share jumps by more than ten percentage points. These figures show the high dependence of these technological fields on public research (Yoon and Kwon, 2001).

These developments have also created new problems. The exodus of PRO scientists had become serious enough by 2001 that universities began to introduce regulations to limit time spent away from official university work to prevent possible deficiencies in the area of educational responsibilities. Some universities have set maximum ceilings on time allowed for venture businesses, while others have started to require professors to buy university time to compensate for time spent away from university duties. While this seems to be a rational response on the part of each university, it is at odds with government programmes to encourage overall PRO participation in venture firms.

This section has examined changes in the regulatory regime and their impact in general. These changes mostly concern the relationship between the state and the PRO, or between the PRO and the individual PRO scientist. Structuring the relationship between the PRO and the private licensee are left to the contractors. The next section considers licensing policies of PROs in order to understand in more detail how the legal reforms operate at the institutional level and to examine the terms and conditions of technology transfer from the PRO to the private firm. The biotechnology sector is used to gain an understanding of some industry-specific issues.

Licensing and R&D in the biotechnology sector

Licensing policies at PROs: two examples

Pohang University of Science and Technology is a private university established in 1986. It covers a wide spectrum of basic sciences and engineering fields. Among PROs, it is one of the most active patentees in biotechnology. As of 2001, it held a total of 253 patents, 63 of which (26.5%) were in bio-related fields (Table 4). The university regards itself as a non-profit organisation and until recently was not keen to manage strategically its intellectual property rights (IPRs). Although income from licensing in the last year brought a meagre KRW 363 million (USD 295 000), the university now regards intellectual property as an important source of income and feels that licensing is an important means of transferring technology to the private sector.

The POSTECH Licensing Centre, a dedicated TTO for POSTECH, was established in 1999. The TTO has four full-time employees, who provide services relating to IP management. Its main tasks include commercial evaluation of new technologies, marketing and licensing patents, negotiating licence agreements and collecting/distributing royalties and other income, as well as networking with outside organisations. At the last stages of licensing, it receives legal advice from four law firms with which it has signed partnership agreements.

POSTECH licensed 14 patents in 2001, more than half of which were spin-offs by POSTECH staff. As noted above, it licensed five biotechnology-related patents between mid-2001 and mid-2002. At least for the earlier of these agreements, the transfer process came to the TTO at a very mature stage, where the terms of the agreement had already been more or less set.

In general, the terms of licensing agreements are most clearly seen by reading through the model contract of the TTO. The model contract requires the licensed patents to be worked. The effective licensing period is usually to the expiration of the patent. The agreement is renewed annually during this period, and the parties can change the terms of the licence by mutual agreement. However, where the patent is not worked within one year or if it otherwise seems clear that the licensee has no intention of working the patent, the university has the right to cancel the agreement.

Table 4. General characteristics and licensing policies of some bio-PROs

General characteristics

PRO	Nature of IP management office	IPR management	Technically unique patents (field)	Other types of IPR	Licences (patented inventions)
KRIBB (publicly funded research institute)	Division; not dedicated TTO (2 full-time employees)	General IP management (all stages; all patents)	463 technically unique patents (all BT-related)	Invention disclosures (121)	140 (46)
POSTECH (private university)	Dedicated TTO (5 full time employees)	General IP management (all stages; all patents)	253 (63 BT-related)	Invention disclosures (approx. 100; 12 copyright software or database; 2 industrial design)	15 (14)

Licensing policy

Institution	Nature of licence	Type of licensee (locality)	IPR ownership policy	Exclusivity	Licensee requirements	PRO rights	IPR income (2001) (distribution)
KRIBB	17 spin-offs 1 start-up	136 SMEs 4 LEs (all domestic)	Mainly institution, can vary by contract with research funder	Exclusivity, sometimes non-exclusive	Work the invention, domestic requirement, right to delay publication for some agreements	Reach-through clause, right of first refusal for some agreements	KRW 700 million TTO division: 50% to cover costs, etc.; inventor: 50%
POSTECH	8 spin-offs 7 start-ups	14 SMEs 1 LE	Mainly institution, can vary by contract with research funder	Exclusivity	Work the invention for all agreements (no domestic requirement); right to delay publication for some agreements	Reach-through clause, right of first refusal for all agreements	KRW 363 million TTO, none; inventor 40%; department 10%; central administration 50%

BT = Biotechnology.
SME = Small and medium-sized enterprise.
LE = Large enterprise.
Source: OECD Survey on Patenting and Licensing Activities of Public Research Organisations, 2002.

Further, the university reserves for itself reach-through rights and the university's right of first refusal for all licensing agreements. Follow-on research results, expansion and incremental innovation around the original technology undertaken by the licensee are subject to the original licensing agreement. However, if the firm contributed to the research and/or its financing, joint ownership of the resulting patents is allowed. In such cases, patents will be applied for under the names of both the licensee and the university, but the former must bear all the expenses of the process. The university makes no guarantees with respect to the commercial success of the technology.

At the same time, the rights of the licensee are also strongly represented, as POSTECH does not seem to issue non-exclusive licences. In agreement with the university, the licensee can, however, transfer the technology to a third party. The licensing fee, as is typical, consists of two parts: an up-front down payment and royalties as some percentage of sales. Within the university, licence income is divided equally between the inventor and the university, but 10% of the inventor's income is allocated to his department. The TTO is entirely financed by the central administration and receives no special funds from the licence income.

The TTO has not yet established a standard format for technology valuation but is currently working on guidelines. Setting the amount and the rate is the most difficult part of a licence agreement with a private firm. It is particularly difficult in the biotechnology sector because the sector's rapid development makes valuation of the technology extremely difficult. A closer look at the biotechnology sector below suggests that because of reasons such as high capital requirements and a long gestation period between patenting and commercialisation, this sector may require a different approach to IP management than other sectors. At POSTECH, there is a difference among sectors as regards licensing structure and policy (Song, 2002).

The TTO has also established a model agreement for contract research with private firms. A confidentiality clause is an important part of the agreement, but the model agreement allows for academic use of the research results without prior consultation. Research expenses are provided at appropriate stages of the research. The intellectual property emerging from the contracted research is jointly owned, and the firm is expected to pay all expenses related to patenting. The firm reserves priority rights to license the technology and the technology cannot be transferred to a third party without written agreement from the other party. That is, both sides have a right of refusal. Disputes are arbitrated by the law governing private contracts.

The model contracts described above were developed in reaction to the tendency of private firms to claim full ownership of research results and the follow-on research which they fund. In such cases, PROs whose facilities and other amenities were used and PRO employees who took time from their duties as employees had no say in how their inventions were used. The government's promotion of greater co-operation between PROs and private firms seems to indicate a recognition of this problem. The university would like to think of the funding as a grant, which allows it freedom in how the research is conducted. Private firms view research projects as contracted work, the results of which should be delivered to and fully owned by the funder. This is particularly the case when the firm finds it difficult to find responsible counterparts at the PRO when problems arise and is not certain of continued assistance or delivery of know-how regarding the transferred technology.

To provide some perspective, Table 4 compares POSTECH's policy to that of the Korea Institute of Bioscience and Biotechnology (KRIBB). KRIBB is a public research institute that specialises in biotechnology. It is more active in licensing activities and generates greater income from its IPRs, although it does not have a dedicated TTO. KRIBB also has a greater incidence of spin-offs, although these constitute only 12% of all licences. Most licences go to independent small firms. POSTECH has only eight spin-offs, but these represent more than half of its licences and again the rest go mostly to small firms.

Between the two, POSTECH has stricter requirements, in that it requires the licensed patents to be worked, has a reach-through clause and reserves the university's right of first refusal for all licensing agreements. However, unlike KRIBB, it does not prevent the technology from being licensed abroad. KRIBB only requires working of licensed patents in some cases. It also only includes a reach-through clause and the institute's right of first refusal in some licensing agreements.

However, while KRIBB has in some cases issued licences on a non-exclusive basis, POSTECH seems only to have issued exclusive licences. It is difficult to know on what basis KRIBB decides whether to impose certain requirements. Both institutions use field and territory exclusivity clauses, although these are not specified in the model contract of POSTECH. KRIBB's rule regarding how income from the licensed patent is distributed is simpler: the inventor and the institution share the income equally (not discounting IP management expenses). The technology transfer unit or division does not receive any portion of the licence income and is entirely funded by the institute.

IP policies and R&D in the biotechnology sector

This section assesses the impact of decentralised IP policies and increased private participation in public research projects in the biotechnology sector. A particular difficulty in patenting and licensing in this sector is the long gap between the two stages. During the interval, follow-up research and additional patenting are needed to generate sufficient interest by a private firm in licensing the technology. This may require much more work than required for the original patent. Private firms do not license PRO technology when it is still commercially uncertain, especially in biotechnology where risks are exceptionally high. The commercial value of biotechnology mostly derives from new medicines, and much capital and time are required for clinical trials, the results of which are very uncertain.

Despite increased investment in the biotechnology sector as a whole, the funding for government-funded research projects in Korean PROs is extremely small given the risks and the required level of capital. Further, the research topics are very narrowly defined and the time allowed for projects is too short (usually one year) to undertake meaningful research. This contrasts with the US system, for example, under which very general grants are provided (*e.g.* small business grants, research grants) for periods of four to five years or more. This means that scientists can pursue more general basic research, parts of which can be patented and licensed towards the end of the research.

The Korean situation is often driven by bureaucratic ambition to achieve quick and visible returns to government funding. However, a basic research project in biotechnology has very little chance to reach commercialisation, *i.e.* to last from patenting to successful licensing to a major company. Government officials managing funding of research projects would not usually take the necessary risk. There is therefore a tendency to scale down the scope and scale of research to achieve results that can easily be commercialised rather than support the basic research that is crucial for biotechnology. Moreover, government grants do not include separate funds for IP management or licensing expenses, adding the further burden of financing patenting and licensing activities for scientists and PROs.

Boosting the scale of funding is thus crucial for biotechnology research in Korea, and there have been efforts to involve participation of private firms from the beginning of research. The government has promoted co-operative research with private firms and licensing-in of the latter for PRO innovations. Thus, most big research projects are now usually undertaken with the participation of private investment, a trend also evident in other OECD countries.

Since there is no public funding for IP management services, and very little incentive for public research institutions to apply for patents and carry through to licensing, individual scientists are forced to solicit private firms for funding from the first stages of their research, not just near its development or commercialisation. Private firms, however, are not interested in funding technology at this highly uncertain stage. Therefore, what funding they do provide tends to be small. This has an important negative side effect. The lack of commercial interest at this stage forces the PRO-private firm connections to be built on personal ties, rather than on merit or the potential commercial value of the technology.

Consequently, the increased participation of private firms does not entirely solve funding problems. This is also because Korean firms are often not large enough by international standards to commercialise successfully a biotechnology discovery, which generally involves developing new medicines. The largest biotechnology firms in Korea are usually the size of biotechnology venture firms in the United States. Therefore, they can only provide funding for the initial development phase of a project. For clinical trials and final marketing, the technology needs to be turned over to a large pharmaceutical firm. Successful commercialisation would need firms with annual sales of at least

USD 10 billion. This requires targeting large multinationals, but the lack of adequate basic research essentially prevents the development of technology able to attract drug firms of international stature. Korean PROs and companies must concentrate on and specialise in certain stages of R&D and then network with global biotechnology players. Unfortunately, this prevents Korean firms from fully appropriating the fruits of their inventions, where the margins are highest. Most biotechnology venture firms in Korea are currently at a stage where they make health foods, which are relatively easy to commercialise, to generate operating income before embarking upon medical research.

Conclusion

The preceding discussion shows that a host of regulatory reforms to encourage technology transfer from PROs to the private sector have taken place, primarily by providing financial incentives and setting up supporting institutions for IP management. Though only a short time has passed since the changes, and more reforms are in the pipeline, some assessment can be made. The general direction of the changes seems to be appropriate, and there have been some positive results. However, there are signs that some shift in the focus of IP policy, and science and technology policy in general, is necessary. Further, the solutions have created new problems requiring fine-tuning through follow-on reform.

The most important criticism may be that while IP management policy is important, Korea needs to concentrate on the innovation and development stages that would result in high value added upon commercialisation. Although this chapter has argued that public subsidisation or at least financing of IP-management at the institutional level should stimulate greater patenting and licensing activities by PROs, this is probably less important than encouraging more R&D activities in order to generate greater income from intellectual property. The biotechnology sector's high capital requirements for R&D, the procurement of private finance through informal channels, and the long gestation period between initial patenting and commercialisation all attest to this. Providing sufficiently large-scale R&D funding for general basic research is thus probably more important than subsidising the direct costs of patenting and licensing. Clearly, IP management policy must be viewed as part of a broader innovation policy.

Another concern is the lack of economies of scale for TTOs owing to an insufficient number of cases of transfer at any one time and inadequate licence income for self-financing of TTOs. This probably limits TTOs' ability to provide specialised services for each technological field. Yoon and Kwon (2001) suggest that a cluster approach to providing TTO services may be more appropriate. Efforts to overcome this limitation are already beginning to bear fruit. Recently, nine PROs and four public universities in Daeduk Science Park formed a consortium to establish a single TTO.[12] Other universities should follow this example when preparing to set up TTOs. It is difficult to know how TTOs will be complemented or replaced under the new law in the pipeline, which would establish public-private co-operation centres. It may be a good idea for the two types of institutions to merge.

Third, the ownership of intellectual property by public universities is now possible and individual PRO scientists now have strong financial incentives, but individual scientists seem to be little affected by this. Each PRO deals with incentives for PRO scientists, and individual inventors and their research teams now obtain a higher share of licence income, but they still prefer to apply for patents under their own names. This is because no separate funds are allocated for IPR management, and individual scientists still have to finance patenting and licensing activities personally. In the biotechnology sector, this is partly because it is probably easier to secure research funds from the private sector on a personal basis. Also, potential licensees still approach the inventor-scientist first, rather than the TTO, so that licensing cases reach the TTO at a stage where terms and conditions are basically decided, as in the POSTECH example.

Neither POSTECH nor KRIBB directly channel some licence income to fund IP management expenses. The income is channelled to the university, which in turn funds the TTO or technology transfer division. If licence income was managed by the TTO, there might be greater funding for IP management, since TTOs are better informed about market conditions. Incidentally, government programmes to encourage patenting, such as the discount scheme, would benefit from greater targeting. Some have suggested that the patent application fee is extremely low, while the number of patent applications is abnormally high given the amount of R&D performed. On the other hand, a relatively small proportion of these applications goes through the review process and on to actual registration (Sung, 2001). Even very minor inventions with high potential of infringement are being patented, or some are simply using patenting as a way to block other potential patentees. Thus, it may be more desirable not to discount or exempt the patent application fee, while at the same time, allowing for a greater discount on fees for reviews, registration or maintenance.

There has been little experience with guidelines or negotiations for deciding returns for individual PRO scientists for cases of licensing or spin-offs. The sharing rule included in the legislation only sets a maximum cut-off point and therefore only provides very rough guidelines. At the same time, relatively little attention seems to have been paid to the responsibilities and obligations of PRO scientists. There seems to have been little discussion of the governance of invention disclosure rules and the obligations of PRO scientists. Moreover, university management has responded negatively to the enthusiasm for PRO start-ups, although this is at odds with government attempts to stimulate technology transfer by promoting PRO spin-offs. Greater clarification of responsibilities and obligations of PRO scientists is therefore in order.

The changes in the regulatory regime mostly concern the relation between the state and the PRO or between the PRO and PRO scientists. To understand the terms and conditions of technology transfer from the public sector to private firms, the practices of two PROs have been described. The examples of POSTECH and KRIBB show that there are fairly well-established guidelines governing licence contracts. Both institutions require minimum safeguard measures (such as reach-through rights, right of first refusal) to protect public interests, with the university apparently more restrictive. The POSTECH example shows some tension between PROs and private firms regarding how the two perceive contracted research. This may explain POSTECH's greater tendency to prefer spin-offs to direct licensing, as these may give the university more control, especially if it provides incubation centres. The tension would obviously be eased, if there were larger-scale government funding of basic research.

NOTES

1. Various public-private R&D co-operation programmes existed before the changes discussed in this chapter, which only focuses on the recent regulatory changes.

2. Ahn *et al.* (1998, pp. 51-55) further note that out of 638 successful innovations in the biotechnology sector between 1982 and 1997, only three were transferred from government research institutes and one from a university, with Korean firms preferring to license from foreign partners.

3. A variety of programmes (*e.g.* the Centre of Excellence Programme) exist to encourage public sector-industry collaboration. The focus here is on some changes made in the late 1990s.

4. At the exchange rate of 4 October 2002 (KRW 1 230.5 = USD 1).

5. This figure includes both public and private universities as well as PROs. For private universities, the figure would indicate the share for government-funded research. However, universities and PRIs should be looked at separately, for the ratio of universities providing none or less than 10% of returns amounts to 57.5% for universities, while it was 33.3% for PROs (KINITI survey data cited in INEWS 2002. 7. 24. <INEWS.com>).

6. As of 2001, the Seoul National University owned 48 patents (five patents are state-owned), while from 1997 to 1999 professors at this university owned 513 patents (Kim, 2001, p. 8). It is difficult to believe that all of this work was independent of official university work.

7. This is optional for private universities, but if they do so under the law, they can benefit from some funding for TTOs. Currently, 20 private universities have established TTOs under this law and receive some funding from the Office of Small and Medium Enterprises.

8. This rule applies to PROs directly funded by the government.

9. Supreme Court Decision 96 825 in 1997. Patent Court Decision 98 2757 in 1998.

10. Report to the Cabinet Meeting, February 2002, "Comprehensive Plan for Promoting Industry-PRO Cooperation".

11. Regulation on Management of Publicly Funded Research, 2001.

12. *Financial News*, 24 June 2002.

REFERENCES

Ahn, D. and K. Chung (1998), "Suggestions to Promote Technological Transfer by Universities", *Trends in Biotechnology*, 6(1), Korea Institute of Bioscience and Biotechnology (KRIBB), Seoul.

Ahn, D., K. Chung and S. Han (1998), *Building a Scientific Knowledge Base in Biotechnology and Transferring it to Industry: Trends and Issues in the Korean Case,* Policy Research 98-08, Science and Policy Institute (STEPI), Seoul.

Byun, Y.R. (interview of 19 May 2002), Professor, Department of Materials Science and Engineering, Kwangju Institute of Science and Technology (K-JIST)

Joo, N.C. (2001), "Management of Patents at Public Universities: Issues and Directions for Reform", presented at a seminar, Seoul National University (in Korean).

Kim, S.J. (2001), "Legal and Institutional Regime to Promote University Inventions and their Commercialisation", presented at a seminar, Seoul National University.

Lee, S.W. (2001), "Issues and Reforms for the Protection of Intellectual Property Rights in Universities and Research Institutes", presented at a seminar, Seoul National University.

Ministry of Science and Technology (2001), press release, "Regulation on Management of National Research and Development Projects".

Song, K.Y. (interview of 5 June 2002), Licensing Centre, Pohang University of Science and Technology.

Sung, K.C. (2001), "A Study on Directions for Patent Fee Reform", *Intellectual Property 21,* Korea Intellectual Property Office, Seoul.

Yoon, S.M. and Y.S. Kwon (2001), *The University-Industry Linkage System and Spin-offs,* Policy Research 2001-03, STEPI, Seoul.

Chapter 14

DEVELOPMENT OF A POLICY TO ENSURE THE SHARING OF UNIQUE BIOMEDICAL RESEARCH RESOURCES IN THE RESEARCH COMMUNITY

by

Theodore J. Roumel
Assistant Director, Office of Technology Transfer
National Institutes of Health, United States

Introduction and background

The mission of the NIH

It is the mission of the National Institutes of Health (NIH) to uncover new knowledge that will lead to improved public health. This mission is pursued through: *i)* the conduct of research by federal government employees in federal laboratories; *ii)* the support of research through the provisions of funds through grants and contracts to academic institutions, non-profit organisations and for-profit entities; *iii)* the provision of policy guidance to NIH scientists and recipients of NIH funding; and *iv)* support of the global research enterprise.

The NIH has been able to maintain the confidence and support of the American public as displayed by the bipartisan efforts of the US Congress to provide the NIH with funding for its activities. Efforts have been in place to double the NIH budget of fiscal year 1998 within five years. With the passage of an appropriation for the NIH in fiscal year 2003, the NIH budget will be at an unprecedented level of USD 27.3 billion.

It is in the pursuit of the mission of the NIH that the agency became involved in the development of a policy to ensure the sharing of unique biomedical resources.

Issues in sharing of resources

Investigators in the field of biomedical research frequently develop unique research resources in the course of their research and rely on the availability of such resources to carry out basic scientific research. These "research tools" can be exemplified as follows: cell lines, monoclonal antibodies, animal models, growth factors, combinatorial chemistry libraries, cloning tools (such as PRC-polymerase chain reaction), molecular modelling computer software, hybridoma cells, certain types of animals, such as transgenic mice, etc.

Since the onset of molecular biology, biomedical scientists have generated and continue to generate large numbers of research tools that have revolutionised the way research is pursued. With their importance to the furthering of knowledge, research tools must be broadly available to basic scientists in the academic and for-profit sectors.

As early as 1984, concern over the sharing of these tools was a matter of concern, as expressed in the US Public Health Service Grants Policy Statement: "It is the policy of the PHS to make available to the public the results and accomplishments of the activities that it funds. Restricted availability of unique research resources upon which further studies are dependent can impede the advancement of research and the delivery of medical care. Therefore, when these resources are developed with PHS funds, it is incumbent upon investigators to make them readily available for research purposes to the scientific community and to publish the associated research findings."

In 1992, scientists raised serious concerns regarding the cost and restrictive terms under which mice were being made available by companies. In March 1993, the National Research Council held a workshop in Washington, DC, to discuss this issue and potential solutions. However, no significant change occurred. In the early 1990s, many cases in which encumbrances had arisen in the transfer of materials between scientists came to light. Protracted negotiation and the inability to reach agreement for terms and conditions had become a great source of frustration to both academia and industry. NIH was approached by scientists to assist in untangling the web that had been produced.

Creation of special task group

The director of NIH created a special task group from the Advisory Committee to the Director at NIH to work on this task. Support was provided by staff from the Office of Technology Transfer (OTT) at NIH. The charge given to the work group was to:

- Inquire into problems encountered by NIH-funded investigators in obtaining access to patented research tools, including refusals to license, onerous royalty obligations, restrictions on the ability to collaborate with commercial firms, and advance commitments regarding intellectual property rights in future discoveries.

- Identify and assess possible NIH responses in light of the competing interests of intellectual property owners and research users and the role of NIH as a public institution and research sponsor.

- Prepare a report and frame the issues for discussion at the next meeting of the Advisory Committee to the Director.

The work group reported that the problem had many facets, most of them not subject to control by the NIH. Issues arise from complex interactions of many forces including patent law, Congressional action, public and private funding of biomedical research and shifting goals in both the public and private sectors. The work group determined that their focus would be on terms of access to research tools in transactions involving NIH grantees.

Findings

Task group activities

The group developed a protocol, visited several NIH recipient institutions and met with officials from companies to discuss the issues. They gathered information on problems in the dissemination and use of proprietary research tools and on the competing interests underlying the problems for the perspectives of bench scientists, university technology transfer professionals and private firms. Information was gathered through deliberate inquires to persons, through casual and anecdotal information and from reports and accounts submitted to the group from the scientific and trade press.

University and non-profit technology managers provided sample information on licence and material transfer agreements that were found to be objectionable and of concern. Co-operation was received from the Council on Governmental Relations (COGR) and the Association of University Technology Managers (AUTM) which canvassed their memberships. The Biotechnology Industry Organization (BIO) attempted to obtain comments from their membership through a survey instrument; the return rate was quite low but provided some consensus on certain issues and significant differences on others. Individuals at firms were also interviewed. Information from scientists was obtained through comments received in response to advertising in the scientific press and through interviews with scientists at various institutions. The work group believed that the sample might not be broadly representative of the scientific community funded by the NIH.

The work group found that the problem of access looked different from each group's perspective. For example, one person's research tool may be another's valuable end product for sale. There were also differences within groups. For example, a scientist's perception may change when he/she is an importer or an exporter of a tool, as a tool's value is usually seen as greater by an exporter than by an importer. Additionally, some exporters place unrealistic valuations on the tools, and this complicates the ability of the institutions to reach an agreement on the transfer or licensing of the material. Some exporters were found to wish secretly to maintain an edge in scientific competition and thus used clauses to delay or even block distribution. As importers, most scientists did not read the documents and had little patience in dealing with the institutional bureaucracies used to import the materials. Technology transfer professionals were viewed as impediments to research.

Technology transfer professionals are often involved in both importing and exporting tools. However, in some instances, actions are taken by scientists. They often sign documents without review by the institution and compromise their own research as a result. Technology transfer professionals also expressed concern over the growing use of licence agreements and material transfer agreements to acquire and use tools. The increases in volume varied among institutions, with one reporting an increase in one year of 115% in the volume of documents for transfers.

Some common problems were delays and restrictions on publication and rights to future intellectual property, often called "reach-through" clauses, according to which the provider of the tool receives rights, an automatic licence or even ownership to any discovery made through the use of the tool. Signing of such agreements often placed the institution at odds with other agreements it had entered into for support of the project. Additionally, some of the agreements placed the institution in violation of the Bayh-Dole Act and the terms of their federal government awards.

There were concerns over the use of different forms that required analysis and would take staff away from higher priority projects or would delay reviews until other priorities were addressed. The differences involved definitions of tools, restrictions on use for commercial versus research uses, use in research sponsored by commercial entities, and even the sending of materials to other researchers without the permission of the exporting institution.

Private firms varied widely with respect to access to research tools, depending on the nature of the tool, the relationship of the tool to the firm's business strategy and the importance to the firm of university-based research. Some biotechnology firms develop and sell products to end users, and their positions are like those of pharmaceutical firms. Others see their tool as a means to gain royalty income on future products that their tool may facilitate.

Private firms have a fiduciary responsibility to maximise value for their shareholders. However, the work group found that most firms transfer materials and research tools to universities without requiring payment of an up-front fee. They attach value to the intangible good will in working with basic researchers. The work group also found that virtually every firm they spoke with believed that restricted access to research tools was impeding the rapid advance of research and that the problem was worsening.

The work group also reviewed options which the NIH had authority to take to improve access to research tools. They stated that the exercise of some authority would be welcomed by NIH-funded organisations but at the same time it could be viewed as extreme and might create unpredictable consequences.

Recommendations

In their report of June 1998, the members of the group concluded that the best course for the NIH to follow at that time was to use its influence and authority to guide other institutions involved in biomedical research as they respond to the shifting currents. This was viewed as educational efforts and appeals to enlightened self interest, and use of NIH's considerable powers under existing law.

They recommended that:

- NIH should promote the free dissemination of research tools without legal agreements whenever possible, especially when the prospect of commercial gain is remote.

- NIH should promote use of the Uniform Biological Materials Transfer Agreement (UBMTA) and the development of other standard agreements to reduce the need for case-by-case review and negotiations.

- NIH should develop and disseminate guidelines for recipients of NIH funds as to what terms are reasonable in licences and material transfer agreements, addressing both importing of research tools owned by other institutions and exporting of research tools created with NIH funds.

- NIH should review its policies with regard to dissemination of research tools generated under its intramural and extramural funding, and revise and strengthen those policies consistent with the recommendations in the report.

- NIH should promote the establishment of a research tools forum for the biomedical research and development community.

Development of principles and guidelines

Drafting the documents

The implementation of the recommendations was assigned to the Office of Technology Transfer at NIH. OTT staff developed two documents that implemented the report recommendations.[1] A set of principles and guidelines was developed. The principles are:

- Ensure academic freedom and publication.

- Ensure appropriate implementation of the Bayh-Dole Act.

- Minimise administrative impediments to academic research.

- Ensure dissemination of research resources developed with NIH funds.

In addition, the NIH developed guidelines which include specific information, strategies, and model language for patent and licence professionals and sponsored research administrators at recipients' institutions to assist in implementing the Principles on Obtaining and Disseminating Biomedical Resources. Recipients were encouraged to use the strategies, other strategies developed at their own institutions or any other appropriate means of respecting the principles. The main headings in the guidelines for dissemination cover: definition of tools; use of a new simple letter of agreement; ensuring consistent obligations; limiting exclusive licences to appropriate fields of use. For acquiring research resources they cover: ensuring prompt publication; definition of materials; ensuring consistent obligations; and grantbacks and option rights.

Comments from the global research community

Because of the importance of public involvement in the development of policy and the desire to receive comments not only from NIH recipients but also other entities involved in the research enterprise, the original document was published in draft form for public comment on 25 March 1999 (64 Federal Register 28205).

The NIH received 45 letters, each of which contained one or more comments. Comments were received from academic institutions, scientific foundations, pharmaceutical companies, biotechnology companies (including providers of research instruments, biological reagents and genomic data), an industry trade association, professional societies, individual researchers and other individuals.

While there were some comments on minor items in the document, support for the document was overwhelmingly positive. Some believed that the NIH would need to issue a regulation and believed that the document would not be enforceable by law. The NIH did not believe that a regulation was required at that time to facilitate sharing and access to research tools for its recipients. Although the final policy would be issued as grants policy, the NIH has not precluded the possibility of engaging in the regulatory process if widespread problems of access by NIH recipients to NIH-funded research tools continue.

The comments expressing most concern came from small and medium sized companies, seven in all, that are in the business of developing and selling research tools. There was concern that the new document would in effect put the companies out of business when trying to sell to NIH recipients. The document is not intended to place restrictions on the use of companies for the dissemination of research tools and encourages the use of such companies to ensure that tools are available to the general research community. The Pharmaceutical Research & Manufacturers of America (PhRMA) and six other companies supported the new principles and guidelines.

The not-for-profit institutions were supportive of the document as were the associations. Again, there were some minor comments but general support. In one case, the organisation welcomed the NIH action but remarked that other institutions need to adopt the guidelines. Two private foundations wrote to express their opinions. One was concerned that the guidelines might stop companies from doing work or selling tools. The other applauded the document and stated it would adopt the document for its own research funding.

One comment of interest came from a foreign organisation, the *Deutsche Forschungsgemeinschaft*. The director-general wrote to inform the NIH that they had circulated the document among the major public research organisations in Germany. Their response was supportive of the document and they believed it to be a step in the right direction.

After a review of comments and minor adjustments to the document, it was issued as final in December 1999 (see 64 Federal Register 72090).

Early stages of implementation

Upon the issuance of the document on 23 December 1999, the director of NIH asked for a report of activities in support of the new document after one year in effect.

The OTT began a rigorous campaign to inform the research community about the issuance of the new document and the fact that it was a part of the NIH Grants Policy Statement and a term and condition of grant awards. The document is also cited in the terms of NIH research and development contracts.

The initiative started internally with programmes to educate NIH programme staff and grants management and contracts management staff. Several seminars were conducted with the staff and OTT personnel were made members of the key groups at NIH advising on grant and contract operations and policy. OTT staff regularly attend meetings of the Extramural Program Management Committee, Grants Management Advisory Committee, Acquisitions Management Committee to advise on intellectual property and technology transfer issues.

OTT staff also began meeting with recipient groups at the NIH regional meetings held from time to time around the nation and at professional societies such as the Association of University Technology Managers, the Council on Government Relations, the Society of Research Administrators International (SRA) and the National Council of University Research Administrators (NCURA). The focus of the first year's activities was to provide information and education on the new requirements.

On 7 September 2000, OTT issued a request for comments in the Federal Register (65FR54293). It stated that the NIH was seeking comments from NIH recipients, academic, non-profit, government and private-sector entities in biomedical research and development on their experience in implementing and utilising the principles and guidelines document. It was the intent of the NIH to use the comments and anecdotal information received from recipients as the basis for the report to the Advisory Council to the Director of NIH.

The comments indicated that most institutions were still in a learning mode and trying to educate their staff about the new policies and how to implement them within the context of the institutions' own policies and procedures. Some institutions stated that they had altered their policies to be commensurate with the new NIH document. There were comments indicating that there were still significant problems in obtaining research tools arising from NIH-funded projects and the terms were not in compliance with the NIH research tools document for professionals and sponsored research administrators. Clearly, things were in transition and a great deal more education was needed. This served as the basis for the first's year's report to the NIH Advisory Council.

However, just before the report to the Advisory Council was issued, a new player entered the scene. The US Senate was working on review and modification of a bill to make general changes to the way in which federal laboratories operate when commercialising technology. The Senate wished to assist the NIH in moving forward the research tools document and sought technical assistance for developing wording that would provide substantive support. In the end, the Senate offered wording, which was accepted by the Congress and enacted in the Federal Technology Transfer Commercialization Act of 1999, which added wording to the Bayh Dole Act to provide support for the enforcement of the NIH's research tools document. That wording is:

"To ensure that inventions made by non-profit organisations and small business firms are used in a manner to promote free competition and enterprise *without unduly encumbering future research and discovery* [emphasis added]."

This wording provided a clear link to legislative authority for the NIH research tools document. There was no doubt that the NIH had the authority to develop and enforce the research tools document and to issue regulations to implement the document with the full force and effect of law.

As the NIH moved into the second year of the existence of the research tools document, the it issued the new NIH Grants Policy Statement which included the document as a term and condition of each grant award. The Acquisition Management Committee at the NIH had also incorporated the document in each R&D contract. However, the NIH and OTT needed to provide further education to staff at educational institutions. The OTT printed booklets on the principles and guidelines and distributed them internally at the NIH and at all meetings they attended to make it know that the policy is in effect.

Current implementation

At the close of the third year, the NIH continues to rely on recipient institutions voluntarily abiding by the rules. Education is still needed since recipient administrators have a heavy turnover rate and new staff lack knowledge about the policy. Additionally, the OTT is working with scientific organisations to gain access to the scientists themselves to present the policy and what is expected from researchers and institutions. OTT is participating in reviews of NIH grantee institutions to see if the institutions are implementing the policy. It is now working with companies to determine if they will voluntarily change their licensing practices to conform to the NIH policy. While companies are not subject to the policy, their licences often contain terms which NIH recipient institutions cannot accept under the terms of NIH grants and contracts. To reduce friction between institutions and companies and advise companies as to the problems they will encounter in trying to impose terms that many institutions cannot accept, with adverse effects on their sales, efforts are being made to find reasonable terms for all parties. The basic thrust at the NIH is to continue educating the relevant groups and to ensure that NIH-funded tools are being shared with other NIH-funded projects.

The NIH is making presentations to other US federal agencies to attempt to have them adopt the tools document as their policy in order to formulate a government-wide policy. Since the NIH is the primary funder of biomedical research in the US federal government and the issue appears primarily in the life sciences/biomedical research at this time, its efforts have resulted in inclusion in few other federal agency policies. Should the NIH determine that regulations may be necessary, the regulations may be written to encompass any federally funded biomedical and life sciences activities.

As part of the NIH's effort to assist in maintaining a robust global research enterprise, the OTT has been working with staff from governments around the world to make them aware of the research tools document and encourage its adoption in other countries.

As the NIH enters into the fourth year of the implementation of the policy, it anticipates greater adherence to the policy and increased interest in other parties adding the policy to their terms and conditions of funding awards.

NOTE

1. The documents cited in this chapter may be viewed at the OTT Web site http://ott.od.nih.gov/NewPages/RTguide_final.html. Additional information may be found on the general Web site under current issues, see http://ott.od.nih.gov.

CHANNELS FOR TRANSFERRING IP TO INDUSTRY

These case studies explore the transfer of intellectual property to industry in the form of licences and spin-off companies, with special focus on the ICT sector.

Chapter 15

IP-BASED SPIN-OFFS OF PUBLIC RESEARCH ORGANISATIONS IN THE DUTCH LIFE SCIENCES AND ICT SECTORS

by

Rudi Bekkers
Dialogic, the Netherlands

and

Marianne van der Steen
Dutch Ministry of Economic Affairs

Introduction

A basic assumption of publicly financed research is that its results will be used and contribute to social and economic welfare. It is widely recognised that this happens; for the Netherlands it has been established that about 21% of all technological innovations are based on public research (NOWT, 2000, p. 76). However, various obstacles have to be overcome before the results of public research are actually used. A major question therefore is how technology transfer can be best achieved. An effective mechanism must create an optimal balance between knowledge creation, diffusion and utilisation, taking both public and private interests into account.

Two relatively recent phenomena relating to effective technology transfer are intellectual property (IP) protection by public research organisations (PROs)[1] and the establishment of spin-offs. IP protection by PROs (*e.g.* by taking out patents) may lead to the use of inventions that would not otherwise have occurred. Spin-offs are firms that are generally established to develop an invention into an actual product or service, in cases where established firms are unlikely to do so. In addition, the often intensive contacts between spin-off and "parent" PRO may contribute to the further development of the invention.

This chapter focuses on the combination of these two phenomena, *i.e.* IP-based spin-offs of PROs. This combination is at the heart of current discussions about commercialising the results of public research. In a recent study of the European Union, this commercialisation is identified as one of the four key areas of industry-science relations (ISR) (European Commission, 2001). Also, a recent OECD study concludes that commercialisation of scientific research is an important component of ISR, and that research and commercialisation are not only compatible but can also reinforce each other (OECD, 2002). However, this study also notes that many OECD countries lag behind in the modernisation of ISR. The interest in spin-offs is also reflected in a very recent "best practices" study of spin-offs by DG Enterprise of the European Union (European Commission, 2002).

In the Netherlands, PROs increasingly protect their inventions by applying for patents, exercising copyrights and using other forms of intellectual property rights (IPRs).[2] For instance, the annual number of patent applications by Dutch universities grew from four in 1981 to about 80 in 1998 (Bureau Industriële Eigendom, in Ministry of Economic Affairs, 2001), and patenting at other PROs is also growing at a steady pace. Of the various motivations for IP protection at universities and other PROs, one is particularly relevant here: it may facilitate firms' use of publicly funded research results, especially when commercial use requires substantial additional research. Just as some firms will not consider further development of their own innovations if they cannot protect them from being copied, they may also not consider further developing a PRO innovation without suitable protection. Further, IP protection can contribute to the funding of new research and strengthen the position of institutes in light of firms' increasingly ferocious IPR and licensing strategies. It may also reward, retain and recruit staff, induce closer ties to industry and promote economic growth. On the other hand, it may have a negative effect on publication efforts by PRO staff and result in gaps between various fields of science. It may also create a threshold (financial or otherwise) for using research results or allow a firm with an exclusive licence to monopolise the application of a potentially valuable innovation. Finally, from the PRO's perspective, applying for and owning IPR entails substantial costs.

For universities and other PROs, the most important argument for spin-offs is that they improve the effective transfer of technology. Attempts in the late 1980s to promote the commercial use of inventions and research results revealed that technology transfer could be greatly facilitated if the (tacit) knowledge, ideas and enthusiasm of the researchers involved could be transferred along with the codified knowledge (Wintjes *et al.*, 2002). This can be achieved by involving PRO researchers in further development and commercialisation in a spin-off. In addition to effective technology transfer, PROs perceive a number of other advantages associated with spin-offs (Table 1).

Table 1. Reasons for promoting PRO spin-off projects

Contribute to regional development	Jobs (job creation, particularly high-technology jobs; keep graduates in region).
	Better industrial structure (new types of industry; development of knowledge-based companies; new products open new markets outside region; significant research capacity: spin-off potential).
Improve technology transfer to industry	Transfer of technology.
	Stimulate collaboration between PROs and industry.
	Get closer to industry and market.
	Structured approach to enterprise development.
	Possibility of clustering, focus.
Better student performance	Education (help to develop student curriculum; better education; pro-active programme).
	Professional perspective (reduce graduate unemployment; counterpart for multinationals).
Improve PRO culture and image	Culture (alternative career option for researchers; profit from research; innovations by industrial research labs).
	Image (make institutes more acceptable politically and socially; attract better students/staff; increase quality of institute; gain funds for better research).

Source: Based on UNISPIN (1999), reprinted in van der Sijde and van Tilburg (2000).

Policy makers are generally interested in the development of PRO spin-offs because they may generate economic growth and jobs. PRO spin-offs grow much more slowly than corporate spin-offs (*e.g.* Claryse *et al.*, 2001), but it is believed that the indirect effects of PRO spin-offs are larger than the direct effects. In relatively new areas dominated by very complex technologies, PRO spin-offs may be of crucial importance to innovative initiatives. Recent data show, for instance, that spin-offs represent some 44% (29% university spin-offs; 15% corporate spin-offs) of all life-science firms founded in the Netherlands between 1990 and 2002 (Biopartner, 2002). Other reasons why policy makers are interested in PRO spin-offs are that they may:

- Create a field of entrepreneurial activity near the PRO, which may contribute to innovativeness, economic vitality and competitiveness (Senter, 2001, p. 19). As such, they may contribute substantially to the national system of innovation.

- Contribute to the renewal of economic structures.

- Play an intermediate and interactive role between PROs and businesses.

- Improve regional employment and development.

Aim and conceptual framework

IP protection at PROs and PRO spin-offs have attracted considerable attention from policy makers. Individually, they have advantages and drawbacks, and their combination is believed to have special strengths, but may also have particular weaknesses. IP-based spin-offs, as such combinations are referred to, are particularly valuable in specific situations (sectors, type of inventions). Their chances of success are generally believed to be strongly dependent upon the availability of a suitable context, which may differ according to the country, industry and even institute. This aim of this study has been to gain deeper insight into the practical functioning of this technology transfer mechanism and learn about specific features of the Dutch context. It asks how current IP-based spin-offs in the Netherlands are shaped and what conditions affected the establishment and chances of success of such spin-offs. Emphasis is placed on the life sciences and information and communication technology (ICT) sectors. The underlying goal has been to learn about the usefulness of IP-based PRO spin-offs as a method for technology transfer and to understand what measures might be taken at various levels (national policy, PRO policy, firm policy) to improve the use and success of this method.

The definition of an IP-based spin-off of a PRO adopted here has two elements. It is *i)* a new firm whose start-up includes a substantial contribution of knowledge recently developed in a PRO; and *ii)* this knowledge is protected by IPRs that are either licensed or transferred to the firm. This definition does not require the direct involvement in the spin-off firm of staff or former staff of the PRO.[3] This is true of some well-known start-ups (*e.g.* the Belgium speech technology firm Lernout & Hauspie), and some US experience indicates that such firms are especially promising.

In the Netherlands, there are currently 124 PROs, of which 13 universities and 36 institutes for higher professional education. These institutes differ considerably in size and focus. Some have created spin-offs, others have not. They also differ in terms of IP protection. Although the advantages of IP-based spin-offs are increasingly recognised, they are still relatively new and Dutch experience is relatively limited, as illustrated by Tables 2 (for all Dutch PROs) and 3 (Dutch universities).

Table 2. Dutch PROs categories and their identified spin-offs

Category	Number of institutes	Identified spin-offs
Universities	13	499
Academic hospitals	8	0
Large technological institutes	5	11
Institutes of the Netherlands Organisation for Applied Scientific Research (TNO)	20	21
Agricultural Research Service (DLO)	8	3
Netherlands Organisation for Scientific Research (NWO)	9	11
Royal Netherlands Academy of Arts and Sciences (KNAW)	21	0
Top technological institutes	4	0
Institutes for higher professional education	36	1
Totals	124	546

Source: Based on Senter (2001).

Table 3. Spin-offs and patents for Dutch universities

University	Identified spin-offs	Patent applications 1990-99
Technische Universiteit Delft (TUD)	57	90
Rijksuniversiteit Groningen (RUG)	42	26
Rijksuniversiteit Leiden (RUL)	12	24
Universiteit Utrecht (UU)	4	19
Universiteit Twente (UT)[1]	226	18
Technische Universiteit Eindhoven (TUE)	40	17
Universiteit van Amsterdam (UvA)	19	10
Katholieke Universiteit Nijmegen (KUN)	30	8
Vrije Universiteit Amsterdam (VU)		4
Universiteit Maastricht (UM)	39	3[2]
Erasmus Universiteit Rotterdam (EUR)	20	3
Wageningen Universiteit (WU)	10	2
Katholieke Universiteit Brabant (UvT, formerly KUB)		0
Totals	499	224

1. The high score of this university is due to the fact that it actively stimulates spin-offs and that it has been systematically registering spin-offs (see below).
2. The score on IP-based spin-offs suggest that either the patenting of this universality increased substantially between 1999 and 2001 or that some of the data are erroneous.
Source: Spin-offs based on Senter (2001); patent applications based on Onderzoek Nederland, quoted in AWT (2001).

There seems to be a curious paradox between the arguments for IP protection at PROs and those for transferring technology by means of a spin-off. One of the main arguments for IP protection is that many PRO inventions require substantial further investments in research before they result in any practical application. The argument assumes that firms will not make such investments unless they are sure no other firm will do so. As a result, protecting the invention and granting an exclusive licence to a firm is the only road to its use. The issue then is how a spin-off, usually with limited funds, can afford such investments.

This study aims to shed light on this issue. This requires looking closely at the patenting/spin-off behaviour of PROs, at what allows such spin-offs to be established and what might stimulate and support such firms. The behaviour of PROs is strongly embedded in both an institutional and a sector-specific context, *i.e.* national laws and policy as well as sector-specific features influence their behaviour and thus the chances for spin-offs.

Figure 1. Conditions for the establishment and opportunities and barriers for the survival of IP-based spin-offs

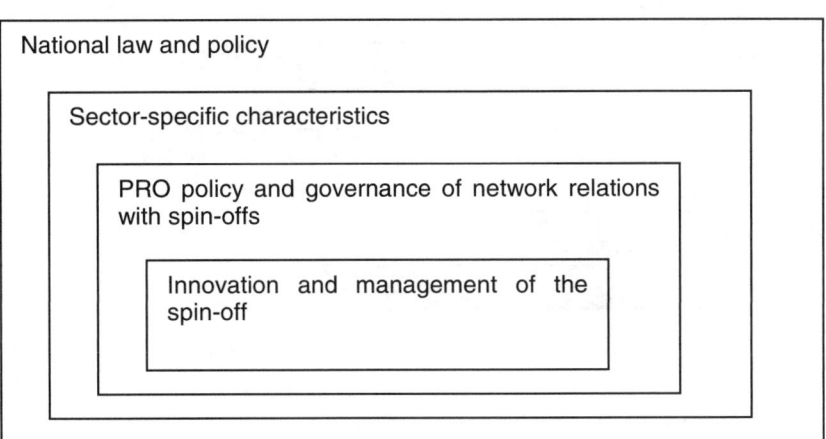

Source: Adapted from Van der Steen (1999).

A conceptual framework that distinguishes four layers of conditions, each at a different level of abstraction, was used to analyse this situation (Figure 1). It is based on a taxonomy of the institutions of a national system of innovation.[4] Using this framework, the literature is analysed and a number of interviews were conducted. US PROs are generally believed to be much more experienced in both patenting and spin-offs. Their level of patenting is convincingly confirmed by the data presented in Figure 2. For the second phenomenon, the figures differ less radically but the average US PRO still surpasses the average Dutch PRO. In the United States, there is a large spread among the institutes; some of the top public research institutes apply for more than 100 patents and create a dozen or more IP-based spin-offs each year. To learn more of their experiences, a number of talks were held with American institutes and spin-off representatives as well.

In all, eight PROs were interviewed (four in the Netherlands, four in the United States), as well as six spin-off firms (four in the Netherlands, two in the United States). Generally, the interviewee was the manager of the technology transfer office (TTO), whose views were not necessarily those of the general management or other entities at the institute. Internationally, spin-offs are most often in the life sciences[5] (including biotechnology, pharmaceuticals, medical technology and agri-food), and ICT,[6] the sectors in which spin-off firms were interviewed. Two are involved in the life sciences: CLEA Technologies (Delft) and Protein Pathways (Woodland Hills, California). Three spin-offs are in the (broad) field of ICT: Bizzdesign (Enschede), Lionix (Enschede) and Nantero (Woburn, Massachusetts). A sixth spin-off interviewed, Advanced Lightweight Engineering (Delft), is in the field of advanced materials. In addition, a support organisation for life science spin-offs (BioPartner) was interviewed. The data gathered in these interviews are used as a basis for analysis. Selected cases are described in text boxes throughout the chapter.

Figure 2. Patent applications and IPR-based spin-offs in the Netherlands and the United States[1]

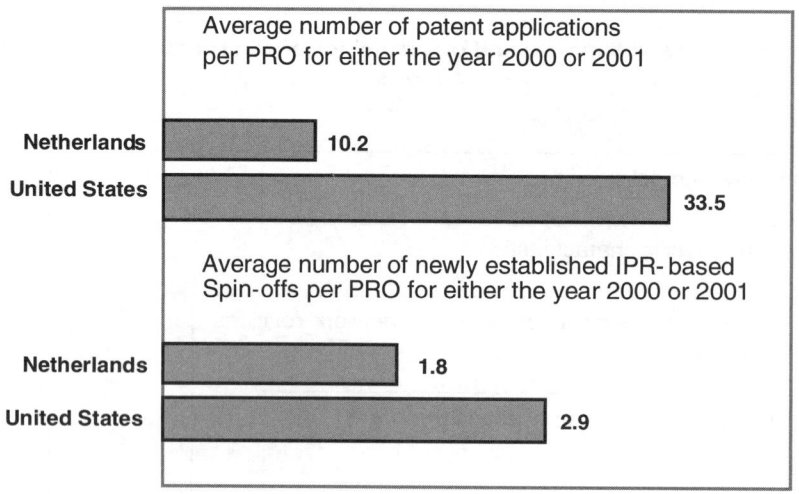

1. Dutch data are based on the OECD Focus Group questionnaire. US data are based on AUTM (2000), p. 1. Some PROs covered by the survey did not supply patent or spin-off data and PROs supplied data for either 2000 or 2001. US data are for 2000.

The following sections are structured along the lines of the four layers of the conceptual model. Each section introduces a layer and discusses the empirical results.

National laws and policies for the protection of IP and the establishment of spin-offs

At national level, laws and regulations govern the ownership and use of IP created by PROs. For instance, the Bayh-Dole Act in the United States influences whether and how universities deal with IP and IP-based spin-offs. Other laws, regulations and policies, such as the general patent and copyright laws (and culture), government research regulations, national spin-off policy and SME and entrepreneurship policies (and culture) may affect the creation and shape of IP-based spin-offs. Two aspects are discussed: national laws and policies regarding IP at PROs and national policy regarding spin-offs.

National patenting law and policy regarding PROs

The Dutch Patent Act grants PROs title for ownership unless agreed otherwise by contract. In general, performers of government research, including universities and commercial contractors, are allowed to patent and license inventions. PROs can own patentable inventions, but this varies from institute to institute. Sometimes the individual inventor owns a patentable invention.

In the Netherlands, the university system is quite autonomous. This may explain in part why IP ownership in Dutch universities differs markedly. In addition, there is no national legal or regulatory obligation or responsibility to use the IP (to foster national economic benefit). Neither is there a legal or funding requirement from the national government for a researcher to report or disclose IP to the PRO (or, for that matter, a requirement for a researcher/PRO to disclose IP to the government). National laws or institutional guidelines for allocating royalties from patents or licences are lacking. The Bayh-Dole Act in the United States stipulates that royalties from licensing should be shared with the inventors and that the remaining income, less payment and expenses, should be used to support research and education within the university. In the Netherlands, the individual PRO decides whether to create incentives to encourage researchers to disclose inventions and determines the requirements for applying for a patent and disclosing patent information.

The fact that the Netherlands lacks the type of regulations discussed above (and does not foresee implementing any in the short term) does not mean, however, that Dutch PROs do not protect their inventions. By now, most Dutch PROs have a TTO that is responsible for tracking inventions that are worth protecting, for patenting or applying for other types of IPR and for licensing. External firms are sometimes involved in these processes. the TTOs are also sometimes involved in stimulating the establishment of spin-off companies.

The Netherlands has no specific national laws, rules or regulations with regard to ownership of IP deriving from research funded by industry. The results of sponsored research are shared between the firm and the PRO. In many cases, it is unclear whether this reflects joint ownership of a patented invention or a contract that requires the PRO to license a patent on an exclusive basis to the sponsoring firm, or inversely the requirement that the university retain a non-exclusive licence to the invention.

In the United States, the role of the federal government has at least three important aspects: *i)* the introduction of the Bayh-Dole Act in the 1980s and amendments to that act;[7] *ii)* the assignment of research funds and the role of the National Institutes of Health (NIH); and *iii)* regulations concerning the grace period. The grace period allows a research institute (or any other party) to apply for a patent even though the invention in question has already been made public. The US patent law allows for a grace period of one year, while patent laws in the various European countries do not contain such a provision. For PROs, a grace period can be important. It can resolve the dilemma between the scientific community's desire for broad discussion and fast publication of research results and the novelty requirement for patenting. Scientists are sometimes not aware of the value of their invention or of the advantages of patenting. They may also doubt the feasibility of patenting and publish, thus destroying the road to what might have been a valuable patent. The empirical data suggest that Dutch universities would benefit from the introduction of a grace period. This is only meaningful, however, when other European countries do the same, as owning only a Dutch patent may be of too little value for many business models. Currently, several European countries are investigating the introduction of a grace period.[8]

National policy with regard to spin-offs

In the Netherlands, the first scheme to stimulate new technology-based firms (NTBFs) was Twinning, introduced in 1998. This scheme aims to stimulate entrepreneurship in the ICT sector by offering affordable housing in four incubator centres (plus one in Silicon Valley in the United States) and encompasses a network of recognised ICT entrepreneurs that provide support and advice. Twinning also grants seed and growth funds to participating firms. Twinning is limited to NTBFs in general and to the ICT sector.[9]

A number of other schemes have been introduced or will be introduced in the short term. The so-called *Technostartersregeling* (technology start-up regulation) is fully focused on PRO spin-offs, while Dreamstart and Biopartner relate to technology-based start-ups in general.[10] All these programmes are initiated (but not necessarily carried out) by the Dutch Ministry of Economic Affairs.

Technostartersregeling aims to raise the number of successful spin-offs by granting subsidies to universities, institutes for higher professional education and other PROs. These subsidies can be used to support and facilitate NTBFs in the form of housing, equipment, counselling, coaching or advice by third parties (*e.g.* on IPR issues). The programme creates a stimulating environment for such new firms at PROs. Subsidies may cover a maximum of 50% of total costs. For the period 2001-03, a budget of EUR 45 million is reserved for this programme.

The Dreamstart programme is aimed at individual NTBFs (including, but not limited to those initiated by a PRO). Transfer of knowledge is key to Dreamstart, and it encourages an exchange of experience among NTBFs via networking. In addition, it offers counselling services in the areas of business plans, financing/subsidies, legal matters (including IPR), entrepreneurial skills and access to or sharing of R&D facilities. Finally, Dreamstart aims to assist existing incubators and NTBF support organisations at the institute or regional level, among other things by mutual sharing of knowledge and experience. As such, it tries to eliminate the drawbacks of the current, rather fragmented support for technostarters.

Biopartner, which began in 2000 for a term of four years, is aimed at the life sciences. Its aim is to stimulate entrepreneurship and responds to an observation of the Ministry of Economic Affairs that while the Netherlands performed well in terms of research in the life sciences, it has considerably less entrepreneurial activity than countries such as Germany. The aim of the programme (with a total budget of EUR 45 million) is the establishment of at least 75 new life sciences companies in the years 2000-04. Biopartner encompasses five programmes, including a grant programme for prospective entrepreneurs to allow them to work on a business plan while employed by a PRO (up to EUR 180 000 per application) and a programme that offers suitable housing for life science start-ups (including shared laboratory facilities) in five cities with major life science research activities. In addition, there is a fund for advanced equipment and other research facilities (an annual total of EUR 1.3 million) and an investment fund for start-ups (a total of about EUR 10 million). Biopartner programmes are aimed at PRO spin-offs as well as start-ups without any link to a PRO.

During the interviews, there were very few spontaneous references to these national programmes by PROs or spin-offs. When the programmes were mentioned, interviewees were often unaware of their features, scope and opportunities. This may indicate that the programmes are not well-known. It may also be that some PROs feel that there is a competence overlap or that newly introduced support programmes are irrelevant for established spin-offs. It was generally felt that supportive measures are more effective at regional than at national level. This is encouraging for programmes that are actually executed at regional or institute level, such as Technostarter. Furthermore, several interviewees mentioned that many regulations/programmes are a burden for institutes and spin-offs because of their long, bureaucratic procedures. This is especially the case for (more general) European programmes. Although some procedures are indeed indispensable to achieve the intended objective and prevent abuse, feelings were that many procedures would benefit from streamlining.

A striking result of the case study is that several spin-offs were quite critical of support for prospective entrepreneurs during the very early phases, *i.e.* before the business plan is written and venture capital is attracted. Several programmes do offer early-phase support, including Biopartner and the TopSpin programme of the University of Twente. Offering subsidies to stimulate researchers to develop business plans, for instance, was believed mainly to benefit unfeasible initiatives. It was felt that an entrepreneur with the right qualities and skills should be able to produce a viable business plan and attract capital. Otherwise, that individual would be unable to succeed in the business world. Although established spin-offs may be inclined to discount such early support, this is an interesting point.

In the United States, the federal government supports a strong spin-off policy because it believes this to be important for the country's economic development. States (and cities), however, have a more important role in terms of technology transfer policy which figures prominently on the agenda of the different states. Universities are (also) seen as instruments for economic development and applied research is strongly encouraged. Many states have programmes that aim to keep the commercialisation of PRO knowledge within the state's borders. They often pursue very active technology transfer programmes and can go further than what is allowed in the European Union. For example, they may include tax reductions or financial incentives for co-operation between universities and companies.

In spite of these activities, US spin-offs and TTOs indicate that such support programmes often take too much time and that their administrative burden is too high. When establishing a spin-off, substantial funding has to be raised very quickly. This requires agreements with parties such as venture capitalists. State programmes are too slow to be effective at this point.

The **State of Utah** offers an example of an active state policy. The state is known for its high-level scientific achievements, the commercialisation of which often took place beyond state borders, especially in the Californian Palo Alto region. The Utah state government saw this as a great economic loss. It has implemented policy to keep commercialisation within Utah's borders, including the Silicon Valley Alliance, which aims to make Utah attractive to firms from the Palo Alto region that seek to expand, by suggesting Salt Lake City as an attractive alternative to San Francisco (with regard to travel time, facilities and real estate costs). Also, firms can submit proposals for subsidies, for instance to develop a prototype. Finally, Utah developed incubator parks and stimulation programmes for PRO spin-offs.

Sector-specific characteristics with relevance to IPRs and spin-offs

Sector-specific characteristics concern the peculiarities of the type of knowledge involved. The shape of knowledge differs substantially in different fields of science and also in the industrial sectors in which the knowledge is applied. In some fields, knowledge is easily codified and transferred by means of publications or patent texts, while in others, tacit knowledge is indispensable. Another difference involves the relative importance of fundamental and applied knowledge and the phase in the technical development process. Such differences influence more practical issues within sectors, such as whether inventions can be protected by IPRs, and what the importance is of various types of IPR. In certain sectors, new types of IPR, such as software patents, may become increasingly important. Furthermore, there may be differences in how IPR relates to alternative mechanisms (including secrecy and lead time). The necessary start-up capital might also be sector-related; in some sectors it may be necessary to own or have access to specific, costly technical facilities. Lastly, it is often believed that the presence of sector-related, geographical clusters and networks between organisations in that cluster are relevant to the functioning and chances of NTBFs such as IPR-based spin-offs.

This section focuses on: *i)* the relevance of various types of IPR and other mechanisms for the protection of knowledge; *ii)* characteristics of the necessary technical facilities; and *iii)* cluster factors. Emphasis is again on the life sciences and ICT.

Relevance of various types of IPR and other mechanisms for the protection of knowledge

The degree to which inventions can be protected by the various types of IPR differs among sectors. The scope of existing IPR can be extended and new types of IPR can be introduced. In spite of the recent attention to issues such as software and business patents, none of those interviewed expected that such changes would be relevant in the short to medium term. Surprisingly, even the ICT spin-offs interviewed did not believe that software patents would be relevant for them. One explanation is that such spin-offs can be protected by regular patents, and that software patents are more relevant to commercial software.

Non-IPR types of protection, in contrast, were considered important. One interviewed spin-off (LioniX, see box) was in fact not based on IPR but on a licensing agreement giving the spin-off exclusive, direct access to new university findings and thus lead time. The same findings become public at a later stage (in regular scientific publications) but then lose part of their value because of continuous technical progress. Another interviewee underlined the importance of other protection mechanisms such as secrecy and lead time, possibly in combination with regular IPR. In fact, one representative of an IP-based spin-off indicated that the IPR it licensed from the PRO was not very important to the firm's operations.

One US university interviewee is now seeing an involvement in IPR other than patents.[11] This university now exercises copyright on software, and there is also one start-up for which a software patent is significant. In the life sciences, owning certain biological materials or test animals can also be very important; however, this is physical not intellectual ownership.

In the life sciences, it was noted that the research agenda was already set, *i.e.* that many research groups knew more or less what they were looking for, and that there was a race to get the results first.

LioniX is a spin-off of Twente University (the Netherlands), which was founded in January 2001. In mid-2002, it employed 14 persons. LioniX develops and produces integrated optics, innovative components and subsystems for applications in telecommunications, industrial process control and the life sciences. Its appealing products include a lab-on-a-chip for water analysis and an optical chip for biochemical experiments.

Technology developed at the university contributed substantially to the creation and operations of this firm. The interesting element is that in this case university knowledge is not protected by patents. Instead, there is an agreement that LioniX has exclusive, early access to university research and inventions. Although the findings are later published through the regular channels, the spin-off has valuable lead time and can develop products while the competition has to wait for the published findings. In addition to this agreement with the TTO, LioniX is rapidly building a firm IPR position in its fields.

LioniX owns several research facilities and also has an agreement that provides access to university-owned facilities. This access is essential, as the investment for a facility such as a clean room exceeds EUR 20 million, an amount which is too much for a start-up company. The access to university facilities is based on market-based compensation.

The biggest challenge LioniX experienced during its establishment phase was obtaining the necessary funding. Venture capitalists require a solid growth plan plus an experienced management team. With the entirely different culture at PROs, culture clashes are inevitable.

The founders of LioniX believe that there are several ways in which the government could stimulate and support the establishment of spin-offs. Peripheral needs such as administration and housing consume much time and energy that could be better spent on core activities. Support for such activities would be very welcome as part of a university or government programme. It is, however, essential that such support should be granted only after the spin-off succeeds in funding its activities. Earlier support interferes with market selection mechanisms. Also, it is important that under such a programme the spin-off must be free to choose where to purchase such support services, as PROs or other institutions are not necessarily the most experienced suppliers.

Characteristics of necessary technical facilities and consequences for start-up capital

A conspicuous finding was the importance of access to technical facilities for life science firms. They require access to expensive laboratory facilities even for relatively standard work. Many Dutch spin-offs in the life sciences are relatively small and dependent on access to external facilities, for example those of their parent PRO. Some Dutch interviewees indicated that if access to laboratory facilities was not part of the arrangement between PRO and spin-off, the spin-off operation would not be viable. However, these spin-offs indicated the need to own certain facilities themselves (possibly housed at the university but in a place not accessible to others). Such facilities are so essential to the core business of the spin-off that fraud, unauthorised access to firm data or accidental damage by other users could severely hurt the spin-off.

Contrary to the Netherlands, commercial firms' access to PRO facilities in the United States is often prohibited by law.[12] As a result, spin-offs have to provide for their own needs, and only those that have received substantial funding are able to do so.

In the ICT sector, many spin-offs do not need such facilities. They can often begin with an office and a set of computers. It is important to recognise, however, that the ICT sector is very broad and some activities may require costly laboratory facilities. For instance, the ICT spin-off LioniX (see box), which produces sensors and components based on micro-system technology, indicated that both their agreement with the PRO for laboratory access as well as their self-owned facilities were essential for their operations.

Obviously, the need for self-owned research facilities (either for strategic reasons or because access to PRO facilities is not allowed) requires spin-offs to raise substantial funds. External funders, such as venture capitalists, are indispensable. This contrasts strongly with the situation in one ICT spin-off interviewed, which was fully financed on the basis of the founders' private capital.

Protein Pathways is a spin-off of the University of California, Los Angeles. This life science firm uses a unique, patented method that can help to discover novel or known proteins that are related to a specific disease. Initially their activities were mainly computer-based and a small office was sufficient. Not long after they started operations, the firm developed a need for more extensive laboratory facilities and moved into other premises.

Cluster factors

There are two main views on technological clusters, one in which regional aspects predominate, and one in which clusters are regarded from the perspective of a sector-based value chain (with actors not necessarily located close to each other). As many PROs perceive regional developments as most relevant, the focus here is on the former view, without prejudice to the importance of the latter. In practice, regional clusters are often sector-related.

It is often claimed that regional factors, such as the availability of high-grade knowledge, experience, capital, talent and housing, lead to highly productive and innovative clusters that are a good breeding ground for start-ups. Clusters, as understood here, are geographical concentrations of related enterprises and institutes. The geographical element is crucial. Although some have expected that developments such as the Internet would make physical proximity irrelevant, current developments indicate that this is not yet the case. Often, a set of related factors explains the development of an innovative cluster in a certain region.

The presence of a knowledge-generating body (university, public research institute) is often essential to a cluster. In this context, PRO-based spin-offs are of particular interest as they can play a pivotal role in spreading knowledge developed at PROs and generating interaction. In relation to spin-offs, three cluster factors may influence the opportunities for spin-offs:[13]

- Availability of start-up capital. To what extent and under what conditions high-tech start-ups can appeal to funds to starts their firms and span the period between establishment of the firm and the first capital investments.

- Level of incubation activities. The availability of services to support starting firms, such as support and advice in the fields of management, financing, infrastructure and technical problems.

- Networking. The degree to which entrepreneurs can learn from each other and how this learning process is organised, as well as interaction between firms and non-firms.

The influence of the entrepreneurial climate and the attractiveness of specific geographic clusters have often been studied in relation to the success of Silicon Valley. Although many of the factors that explain its success have been identified, it has been difficult to copy and implement Silicon Valley's business and network concepts in other regions, new or existing. So-called technopoles are difficult to plan. Here, chance events may be at least as important as policy and business plans (Bouwman and Hulsink, 2000). On a smaller scale, this may also be true for the clustering of the spin-offs studied here.

Advanced Lightweight Engineering (ALE) is a spin-off of the Delft University of Technology. When studying aerospace engineering, ALE's founder Jan-Jaap Koppert and his professor worked on specific materials that offer a unique combination of strength and weight. When a patent application was being prepared, it was recognised that applications might go beyond the aeronautical sector. In particular, the material could be used for fuel containers in cars run on liquid petrol. ALE was founded in 1996 and now employs 11 people. One of its strengths is its ability to translate its innovative lightweight technologies for use in other sectors. Apart from fuel containers for cars, ALE is involved in gas bottles for the home appliances market (for cooking and heating, as used by 60% of all people worldwide) and structural parts of marine vessels. It has also produced satellite antennas for the European Space Agency (ESA). Apart from product design, ALE offers services in the field of testing and research for multinationals like Airbus and Akzo Nobel.

A substantial contribution to the start-up was a patent application that was transferred from the university to the spin-off. About early relations with the university, ALE's founder recalls: "One problem is that the TTO wears two hats. On the one hand, it aims to facilitate a successful start-up; on the other, it has an interest in maximising gains from its intellectual property. Although we did not experience real problems, such a conflict of interest could hamper negotiations."

According to its founder, the real value of spin-offs such as ALE lies in the available tacit knowledge and the motivation and enthusiasm of the people involved. ALE's relation with the university is one in which cross-fertilisation prevails, both in the field of knowledge and market development. Furthermore, the relation with the university offers ALE a valuable recruitment ground and the university opportunities for its students. In ALE's field, access to research facilities (laboratories) is crucially important, as well as access to people and knowledge. In this respect, improvements can be made. However, support by universities for spin-offs should essentially be limited to providing facilities: "In ALE's case, the search for capital went relatively smoothly. Anyway, in my sector, nobody believes in financial subsidies by universities. If a prospective entrepreneur is not able to raise capital by himself, there is something essentially wrong. One should not subsidise such cases."

The Netherlands has a number of geographical clusters. The best-known is the ICT cluster around the city of Eindhoven, which attracts a significant part of the nation-wide R&D budget. This city is the home of the electronics giant Philips. Its research institute Natlab, the Eindhoven University of Technology and the European Design Centre Academy are pivotal knowledge generators in this cluster. The cluster also includes the DAF and Nedcar automobile factories, a number of Philips spin-offs such as ASML Lithography, Origin consultancy and Flat Panel Display Co., as well as some 1 200 smaller ICT companies. Another Dutch geographical cluster is Amsterdam Alley, a multimedia and Internet cluster with some 1 300 multimedia firms. Knowledge generators include the National Research Institute for Mathematics and Computer Science (CWI) and several other parts of the University of Amsterdam. The physical proximity of the Amsterdam Internet Exchange (AIX) is also important. Among these multimedia firms there are many start-ups, and their work is mainly project-based. In a recent study, this cluster was found to be dynamic and fluid. However, it was also found to be in its adolescence: although it is beginning to take form, many do not yet recognise it as a cluster.

In terms of structure and performance, there were still various barriers to be removed (Den Hertog *et al.*, 2000). In some other locations (the Twente area, the city of Emmen), actors are attempting to develop and strengthen geographic clusters. Although all the clusters discussed have their strengths, they also share some weaknesses: the public knowledge infrastructure is not fully exploited (an area where spin-offs can help) and there is a relative lack of interaction (networking) and of market transparency (Bouwman and Hulsink, 2000).

In the life sciences, the Netherlands has several clusters. The largest is around the city of Leiden, which not only has a leading university in this field but also is home to a number of large firms such as Centocor, Pharming (which started as a spin-off), Crucell and Mogen. To illustrate the importance of such clusters, the Leiden cluster plus the eight other, smaller life science clusters account for more than 80% of the total employment of new Dutch life science companies.

Yale University (New Haven, Connecticut) has a very active TTO that is committed to establishing successful spin-offs based on its technology. It has contributed to local economic development and the creation of a successful biotechnology cluster in the New Haven area. Yale's TTO employs a process that covers analysis of the discovery, disclosure and opportunity up to commercialisation. The process includes various feedback loops as well as decision points, such as whether or not to protect the invention and how to commercialise it (licensing to large or small existing firms *vis-à-vis* establishment of a spin-off). The main considerations in opting for a spin-off are: *i)* the chances of success of the technology in question; *ii)* the degree to which the TTO's expertise is necessary; and *iii)* value creation.

In the Yale model, four actors provide the main inputs for the prospective spin-off: the inventor(s), the scientists (non-inventors), the university and the CEO. In return for its input, each receives 25% equity in the firm (before the first round of investments).

The input of the inventor(s) and the scientific team is evident: the invention and its further development make a substantial contribution to the firm. The role of the inventor(s) often includes a position on the scientific board of the start-up. The university's input consists of developing the initial business strategy, applying for and maintaining the IP, recruiting the management and key (science) advisors, and raising money from qualified investors. As a matter of policy, however, the university is not prepared to waive licence fees for equity. Finally, the university finds the CEO. His/her role is to further develop the business strategy and business plans, recruit additional management, manage the formation of the start-up, negotiate licence agreements with the university and negotiate financing with investors. A typical CEO has a successful start-up track record, is acceptable to investors, understands, accepts and manages risk, understands science, has realistic expectations and an entrepreneurial attitude. Although this person initially works at own risk (*i.e.* without salary), the equity received may be very valuable in the longer run. This increases motivation.

As a result of their pro-active patenting and spin-off activities, Yale forms half a dozen to a dozen new spin-offs each year. Four Yale spin-offs have raised well above USD 10 million of public money. Furthermore, Yale-founded spin-offs account for more than 10% of all biotechnology investments in the New England area.

The strong clustering observed in various studies (Clarysse *et al.*, 2001; Biopartner, 2002) is indicates that context – and in particular aspects of the context that are by definition related to physical closeness – is very important. In general, the interviewees underlined the importance of clusters. Especially during the first phase of the spin-off, housing in or very close to the institute's premises (less than a few kilometres) is believed to be very valuable. Access to knowledge, informal contacts with ex-colleagues, possibilities for using laboratory or other facilities (see below) and attracting new talent are essential for such young firms. It was also mentioned that the availability of affordable private housing affected the chances of attracting talent and thus indirectly influenced the spin-off's chances.

PRO policy and governance of network relations with spin-offs

The fourth level of conditions concerns PRO policy and governance of network relations with spin-offs. The policies pursued by PROs concerning protecting their knowledge and the phenomenon of spin-offs obviously influence the extent to which IP-based spin-offs are established. In addition, the stimulation and support (or opposition) that spin-offs receive from their institute are likely to influence their chances of success. The ongoing relation between institute and spin-off appears to be crucial.

It is important to recognise that universities (and other PROs) do not act with one voice. They are made up of a large number of smaller entities (general management, one or more TTOs, faculties, chairs) that may have different responsibilities, competencies, goals, interests and policies.

This section discusses the following issues:

- Susceptibility, stimulation and support of spin-offs by PROs.

- IPR and spin-off policy at PROs.

- Deciding between licensing out and spin-offs.

- Organisation of technology transfer and spin-off support at PROs.

- Arrangements between institute and spin-off.

- Cultural clashes and controversies concerning IPR.

Susceptibility, stimulation and support of spin-offs

Although there are various good reasons for PROs to stimulate the establishment of spin-offs (see Table 1), Wintjes *et al.* (2002, p. 5) recently observed that many do not yet appreciate their own interest in stimulating spin-offs. The case study partly supports this idea: even though the motivation to support spin-offs is high at the TTO level, this is not always the case at other levels (general management, faculty). As a result, universities often hinder the establishment of spin-offs and do not encourage or facilitate their further development. Large regional differences in the number of spin-offs may very well be due to the attitude of the dominant PROs towards spin-offs. In contrast to Wintjes *et al.*, the interviews in this case study did not reveal an unwillingness to stimulate and support spin-offs. The PROs interviewed took a positive view. This does not alter the fact that the entrepreneurial climate at the institute level is usually poor. This is not surprising, as many PRO staff consciously chose to work in an institute rather than in more entrepreneurial commercial firms.

In the United States, all the PROs interviewed greatly appreciated the advantages of spin-offs. Although they all work within the framework of the Bayh-Dole Act, which determines to some degree their obligations to identify, protect and commercialise knowledge, there is still a wide diversity in TTO policies. The differences are due, among other things, to institutional culture (including that of the staff), history, priorities of the administration, regulatory issues (*i.e.* whether the university has the right to participate in a spin-off) and the perceived importance of a contribution to the area's economic development (city, county or state).

IPR and spin-off policy at PROs

Although Dutch institutes were expected to have at least some type of policy regarding IPR and spin-offs, this study found that this was often not the case. Some institutes were working on increasing staff awareness concerning IPRs, so that they understand the opportunities that may arise. Still, the autonomy of faculties, research groups and chairs in many PROs makes it difficult to pursue a consistent policy. Dutch PROs have only produced modest numbers of IP-based spin-offs. Because every proposed spin-off has its own – often unique – nature, most PROs do not have a well-defined policy. Stimulation, support and arrangements with spin-offs are handled on a case-by-case basis.[14] Some indicate, however, that plans are being made for such a policy. One PRO indicated that arguments for introducing such a policy are:

- Spin-offs are an important performance indicator for the PRO.

- Spin-offs are an active form of knowledge transfer.

- Knowledge is generated only once but can be used by a spin-off on a more continuous basis in a commercial context.

- The institute in question does some quite applied research and it would be good to ensure that these results are used.

As noted earlier, patent applications at Dutch PROs grew considerably over the last two decades. In the institutes interviewed, the number of IPR applications varied between one and ten a year. Most indicated that the figure was rising. Dutch PROs generate somewhere between two and five spin-offs each year. Several PROs indicated that most of their spin-offs were based on a patent.[15]

The Dutch case studies show a consensus that the financial gains from patenting/licensing may be modest at best. Discoveries at PROs are often fundamental in nature, making considerable additional research necessary before they can be used. This lowers the commercial value of the patent. Also, a single patent is often of limited value in fields such as biotechnology where complete portfolios of patents are needed. In addition, it is difficult and expensive to monitor systematically whether others use the invention without a licence, and litigation is costly and requires very specific skills, especially if the defendant is a strong firm. In the United States, some universities operate at a much larger scale, and the income generated by TTOs, according to AUTM figures, suggests that larger PROs make good profits. It should be noted, however, that there was a general impression during the interviews that those PROs that profit from licences actually rely on a few IPRs, the "winning numbers" in a lottery.[16] A few US universities own such patents (*e.g.* Taxol, Cardiolite), as does the British Technology Group, the organisation that once held a government-created monopoly on the management of IP across all UK universities.

Almost all parties agreed that there is a relative lack of experience and knowledge in the field of IPRs, spin-offs and the combination of the two. Institutes could clearly learn from each other, and this is probably also true for spin-offs. Government could play a role by organising workshops for TTO managers or by collecting and circulating best practices both nationally and abroad.

Deciding between licensing out and spin-offs

Even though there are several arguments in favour of spin-offs, the choice in particular cases is still rather difficult. In the United States, some well-developed TTOs take a pro-active approach and assess the value of the various options. Several US universities indicated that they are working on a specific, strategic approach. It is crucial to recognise opportunities and to identify the right criteria. It seems that disruptive, unproven technologies are among the most promising candidates. As a general policy, other universities make protected inventions public by sending out an abstract. When existing firms express no interest in a licence, a start-up is considered. This may appear to be a negative choice, and it may be argued that such spin-offs will be based on less promising or "weaker" technologies. However, there may be situations in which IPRs are more valuable to spin-offs than to existing firms.

In both countries, exclusivity of licences is usually determined on a case-by-case basis. Some universities – again notably in the United States – first offer non-exclusive licences. If several parties express interest, multiple, non-exclusive licences are granted. However, if no firm is interested, an exclusive licence is offered. One university noted that although it aims at non-exclusive licences, it most often awards exclusive ones because that is what clients want. Exclusive licences usually include provisions that stipulate actual use (thus preventing defensive licences) and require the licensee to grant sub-licences for application in markets that it does not serve itself.

Organisation of technology transfer and spin-off support

In the course of this study, it became apparent that there are various organisational models for both technology transfer and spin-off support at universities. Most often, both activities are carried out in a single office (with various names, all referred to here as TTOs). In some cases, however, IPR activities were separate from spin-off support activities.

The responsibilities, competencies (in theory and practice), power and budget of TTOs vary considerably. In the Netherlands, they depend entirely on the policy of an institute's administration, while in the United States some are implicitly defined by the Bayh-Dole Act. In both countries, the university administration does not always fully support the protection of inventions and/or entrepreneurial activities. Most often, the TTO is a central body at the same organisational level as, for instance, the legal department. It often purchases specialist services from external sources such as patent attorneys. There are also cases in which the whole TTO activity is outsourced to a separate organisation.[17]

Dutch TTOs are generally small, often with only one or two FTE. The staff are necessarily generalists, and the office's performance will depend in part on the budget for purchasing external services. The TTOs at the large US universities visited often employ 10-25 persons. Traditionally, they were generalists who also had specific knowledge of a particular field of science. Increasingly, however, these offices are becoming organisations that work with teams of high-level experts on patent applications, licensing negotiations or start-up enterprises.

Range of support and arrangements between institute and spin-off

PROs vary widely in the intensity with which they stimulate and support spin-offs. Both in the Netherlands and in the United States, three situations were observed (Figure 3).

In some areas (in the United States, notably Silicon Valley and Palo Alto, the home of Caltech, Stanford and Berkeley), strong clusters are already present. There is strong interaction between PRO staff and businesses, capital providers, entrepreneurs, etc., and spin-offs have a fair chance to succeed on their own. Intensive support for spin-offs may come from specialised venture capital providers or from "business angels". This diminishes the need for specific support from the PRO. In fact, the TTO only acts as a licensing agent. This situation is depicted at the top of the triangle.

Figure 3. Intensity of spin-off stimulation and support and the strength of the regional cluster

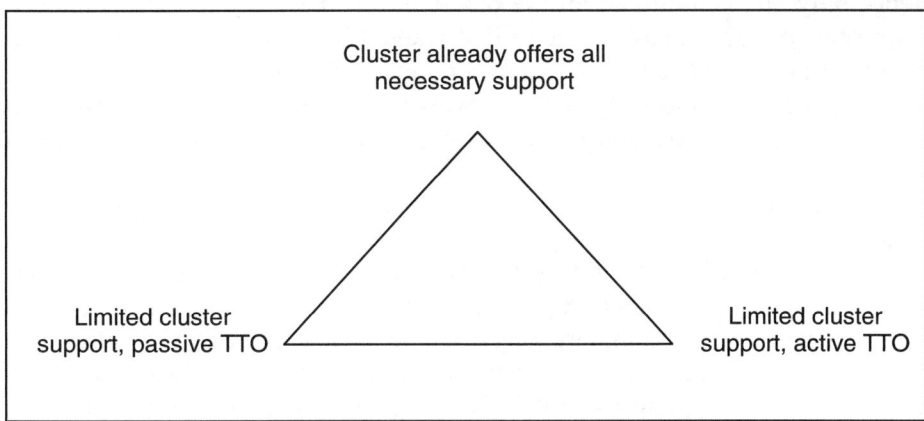

In areas where regional clusters are less strong (or weak), there are two options. One is for the PRO to offer support and facilities. It is thought that a strong focus on certain promising technologies (such as biotechnology or nanotechnology) may even lead to a cluster that will eventually become self-supporting. This situation is depicted in the lower right-hand corner of the triangle. The other option is a PRO that is passive and offers no support even though (or because) strong cluster advantages are lacking (the lower left-hand corner).

PROs' support to spin-offs can take various shapes. The types of support mentioned during the interviews were:

- Financial participation of the PRO (or fund established by the PRO) in the spin-off.

- Secretarial and other facilitative support.

- Options for housing.

- Access to facilities such as laboratories, libraries, etc.

- Help with finding additional sources of funding and facilities.

- Short-term flexibility towards existing appointments so that prospective entrepreneurs can prepare business plans and attract start-up capital without fully giving up their regular work and income.

- Long-term options for the entrepreneur to retain a part-time appointment at the PRO, thus reducing personal risks.

Agreements between PROs and spin-offs, in particular those concerning IPR, differ widely. Some PROs actually transfer ownership of IPR to the spin-off. In return, the institute receives a lump sum or, more often, some equity in the new firm. For the institute, this has the advantage of relieving it of the costs and burden of obtaining and retaining the IPR. Other PROs choose to own the IPR and license it to the spin-off, on either an exclusive or non-exclusive basis. The advantage, again from the perspective of the PRO, is that if the spin-off fails, the IPR is not lost. On the other hand, the consequences in case of a possible liability claim can be tremendous. (In the United States, IP rights are never transferred to firms as this is prohibited by law. However, the law also limits the liability of PROs.)

There were different opinions on the issue of the costs associated with obtaining and retaining IPRs (including all internal and external costs related to that process). Some responded that these costs were substantial and constituted a barrier. One commented, "Taking out IPR is like joining the lottery: out of ten patents, only one is a hit and all the others never make any money." Another interviewee urged the government to make funds available if it wanted PROs to take out more patents. Another PRO representative, however, found these costs to be lower than often claimed and did not feel this was a serious barrier. Also, for most of the US universities, licensing is still regarded essentially as a loss-making activity. As noted above, only a few own money-making "golden eggs" (see above).

In the Netherlands, it is usual for the inventor to have a high management position in the new firm, often as the CEO. Usually, institutes prefer this person to choose between the institute and the firm, in order to prevent conflicts of interest and of commitment (although some Dutch universities decided otherwise in certain cases because of the wish of the faculty member or in a belief that it would increase the chances for the undertaking). In the United States, it is rather unusual for the inventor/faculty member to join the spin-off. Usually the spin-off is run by experienced entrepreneurs that are attracted either by the inventor(s), the TTO or a venture capitalist. Often, the faculty member takes a position as chairman of the spin-off's scientific board, and any possible conflict of interest is well managed. In addition, the Bayh-Dole Act requires institutes to have a compensation scheme for inventors, and many schemes include rather generous payments to these faculty members.[18]

Nantero is a Boston-based spin-off established in 2001. It develops a non-volatile computer memory technology on the basis of a nanotechnology invention developed at Harvard University. The intended memory chips work on the basis of single-wall carbon nanotubes with a wall thickness of 1 atom and a diameter of 0.4-3 nanometres. The chips are non-volatile, very fast and have high density. They may thus replace several existing memory technologies such as Flash (often found in portable devices such as digital cameras, PDAs and mobile phones), DRAM (the main memory of personal computers and laptops) and SRAM (high-speed memory, used in routers, switches and also for certain purposes in personal computers). Interesting possible uses include the enabling of instant-on computers.

The founders of the spin-off, two Harvard inventors and an experienced entrepreneur who had previously established several start-ups, set up the firm without any specific support from Harvard. Although there are many valuable informal contacts with Harvard (as well as MIT), their only formal link is a licence agreement.

It is the conviction of Nantero that existing market players would not have adopted this new technology if they had been offered a licence because: *i)* they had already invested in existing technologies and opt more for incremental improvements; *ii)* the motivation to make such a novel technology succeed might be less strong than that of spin-off employees, whose driver is high reward in case of success; and *iii)* they lack the necessary skills (nanotechnology is a rather different field from that of traditional chips). Also, existing firms might take out a licence only for defensive reasons.

The business model of this spin-off is product-based. It is not a service model. Nevertheless, it is imaginable that final production will be outsourced (despite its novelty, the memory chips can be produced with conventional production techniques) or that Nantero will sub-license its product to existing memory producers. Although existing firms tend to prefer incremental improvements in-house, they are sometimes willing to partner with start-up firms that are pursuing radical improvements. Ideally, the firm would launch an initial public offering (IPO), but given the current market situation this is not the right moment. Selling the firm at a later stage is also an option.

Contrary to what some might expect, spin-offs prefer to pay a fair price to the institute for the use of facilities (*e.g.* laboratory access, secretarial support) or for housing. In this way, they do not owe anything to the institute and cannot be accused of having an unfair advantage. Moreover, others are not discriminated against. It is also important that when they pay for it, the spin-off can indeed reserve and claim laboratory time, minimising the risk that they will be hindered by other rightful users.

In the United States, the "wall" between institutes and firms is much thicker. For this reason, long-term support is more limited. An example is access to facilities such as laboratories. Most universities do not allow such access, and state universities are prohibited from doing so by their status.

Cultural clashes and controversies concerning IPR

Spin-offs can quite easily lead to clashes between two quite different organisational cultures (*e.g.* Jones-Evans, 1998). In the interviews, both PRO representatives and spin-off representatives recognised this. From the day that a prospective entrepreneur decides to start a spin-off, he or she has to stop thinking as a member of the institute and has to start defending the interests of the company-to-be. Especially when negotiating with the institute the value of the IPR and compensation for the use of facilities, this can be difficult. Some spin-offs felt a contradiction in the behaviour of universities that claim they want to stimulate the establishment of spin-offs but require too high a licence fee.

In the PROs, the TTO is not the only organisation able to fulfil the support role. In the United States, several venture capitalists also offer a wide range of support services to start-ups they participate in.

Innovation and management of the spin-off

The fifth and final level in the model concerns the innovation and management of the spin-off. Factors at this level appear to affect the chances of success (the survival rate as well as growth opportunities) for spin-offs and to a lesser degree the number of spin-offs established. The focus is on two important aspects:

- Underlying business model of the spin-off.

- Presence of entrepreneurial skills and management experience.

Underlying business model of the spin-off

A worrying observation, on the basis of empirical data and the literature, is that many spin-offs employ a so-called "tools" or "service" business model.[19] That is, they sell services, technology or research results, provide consulting or focus on contract research or customised services. Although these models have the advantage that they can generate income from the start, margins and profits are relatively low and competition is strong. This contrasts with the production model which covers the whole value chain. With this model, it may take years before a profit is seen, but potential gains are much larger. In particular, the combination of the IPR, R&D results, secrecy and first-mover advantages may lead to a very valuable market position. A possible solution is the hybrid model, in which a tools or service model is used to generate cash and experience during the first years and a unique product is planned for a later stage.

Presence of entrepreneurial skills and management experience

In the Netherlands, it is almost implicitly assumed that in the case of an IPR-based spin-off, the inventor will leave the research institute and become manager of the new firm. (Although a part-time appointment at the institute is not automatically rejected, most TTOs do not like this solution.) There are two potential drawbacks: *i)* inventors, however motivated, do not necessarily have the right qualities and experience for the crucial position of CEO;[20] and *ii)* the institute loses a valuable staff member.

US spin-offs tend to be run by professional managers instead of ex-faculty staff. Two considerations are relevant: *i)* the new management needs to have certain qualities and experience; and *ii)* possible conflicts of interest or of commitment are avoided. For example, Yale University attracts external management for the spin-offs it helps to establish (see box). Often, because of their career choices, university staff have other qualities. In some of the cases examined, the chief executive officers of US spin-offs receive a share in the firm but no initial salary and thus have a strong incentive to make the firm succeed. Nantero (see box) is an example of an American spin-off which is managed by experienced managers. US spin-offs also tend to be larger in terms of personnel and capital. This is likely to affect positively the presence of the right skills at various levels in the firm.

The material used for this study suggests that spin-offs have better chances of success when they take on an external manager. This conclusion is also in line with recent findings of the EC (European Commission, 2002, p. VIII).

Conclusions

This chapter focuses on how current Dutch IP-based spin-offs are shaped and the conditions that affect their establishment and chances for success. All four layers of the analytical model adopted need to be taken into account. The highest and most abstract levels of the model (Figure 4) particularly affect whether such spin-offs are established, while the lower layers mostly influence their chances of success.

Figure 4. The analytical framework related to effects on IPR-based spin-offs

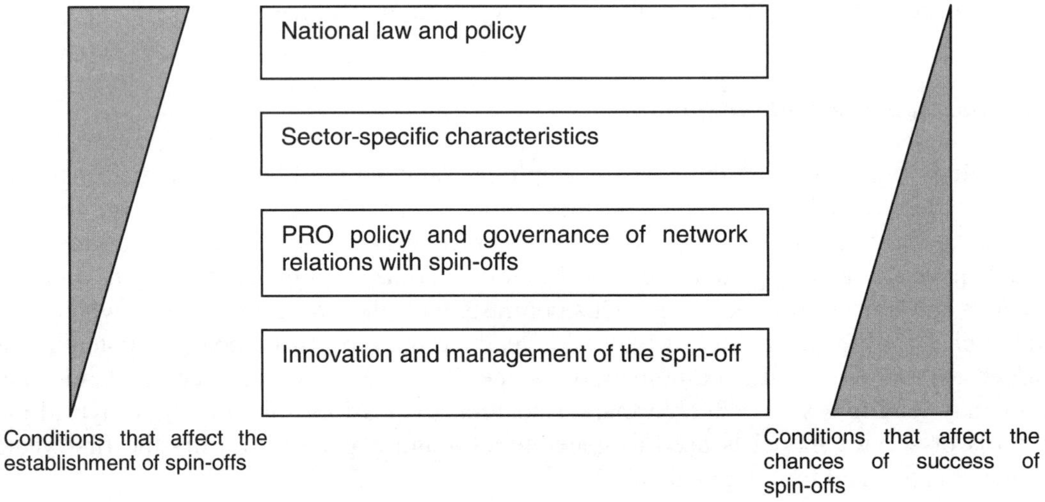

| National law and policy |
| Sector-specific characteristics |
| PRO policy and governance of network relations with spin-offs |
| Innovation and management of the spin-off |

Conditions that affect the establishment of spin-offs

Conditions that affect the chances of success of spin-offs

Before discussing the policy implications of the various layers of the framework, it is useful to return to the paradox of IP-based spin-offs as a means of technology transfer. On the basis of the material used here, it can be concluded that the paradox is only an apparent one. IPR-based spin-offs can be a very efficient means of technology transfer in situations where other methods fail or prove to be less effective. First, transfer of tacit knowledge and involvement of original inventors can help increase the chances of successful utilisation.[21] Second, many inventions concern ways to make (or do) a certain thing more efficiently. However, established firms often have invested substantial sums of money in existing methods or products ("sunk investments"). As a result, they may not embrace new inventions even when they are considerably more efficient (*e.g.* greater price/performance ratio). As a consequence, society does not benefit from the innovation. Establishing a spin-off can ensure the use of such an innovation and force other parties to consider more efficient processes, or at least to lower their prices to the level of more efficiently operating competitors. Third, spin-offs can result in a true two-way exchange of knowledge ("cross-fertilisation") and can create a certain continuity with the institute. In addition to these arguments in favour of spin-offs as a mode of technology transfer, there is also the important argument for spin-offs as a stimulant for regional economic development and employment. This advantage is recognised by both Dutch and US PROs.

In any case, the choice for spin-offs has to be weighed against other technology transfer options (*e.g.* issuing licences to established firms; opting for publication without any protection). While it is difficult to predict in which cases the establishment of spin-offs is most appropriate, this study suggests a number of clues. Spin-offs can realise advantages that exceed those of other technology transfer options when: *i)* the technology in question is disruptive and risks are high; *ii)* chances are that established parties are not willing to adopt the invention because of their vested interests; *iii)* tacit and background knowledge of the inventors is indispensable for successfully transferring the invention into a product or service; and *iv)* the inventors express interest in being involved in the spin-off.

This study shows that there is no single best national and TTO-level policy for successful IPR-based spin-offs. The best national policy should take cultural elements, scale, existing TTO policies/practices and the presence (or absence) of regional clusters into consideration. TTO-level policy should take clusters and sector-specific features of technology into account, among other things. For the Netherlands, this study indicates that there is no single barrier to the establishment of spin-offs. A complex set of factors is involved. What is problematic in one case is of little relevance in others. In specific cases, a set of preconditions has either already been met or must be addressed.

On the basis of this study, a number of policy suggestions can be made. These are structured along the three actor-based levels of the model used.

National law and policy

- The government might establish a policy that stimulates PROs to protect their inventions and be involved in the creation of spin-offs in appropriate situations. Clear, harmonised rules on where the intellectual property of PRO research lies (especially research that involves commercial partners) may help.[22] Although such rules need not go as far as the US Bayh-Dole Act, they should stimulate an active (though not aggressive) attitude at PROs.

- In the Netherlands, the introduction of a grace period could benefit universities by relieving the dilemma between the desire to publish and the opportunities afforded by patents. This must, however, be accompanied by similar moves in other European countries.

- Existing national programmes for new technology-based firms are a useful stimulus, although the general feeling is that these programmes should not be aimed at a very early stage of the prospective firm. Also, the acquaintance of both TTO officers and spin-off representatives with such programmes could be improved.

PRO policy and governance of network relations with spin-offs

- PROs could encourage the development of IP-based spin-offs by adopting a pro-active policy. The policies of some more experienced US universities can serve as examples, although one should not lose sight of context-specific issues.

- Depending on regional or sector-specific needs, PROs can stimulate IP-based spin-offs by offering appropriate types of support. It is important, however, to assess carefully which type of support is most appreciated by spin-offs, as the perception by PROs and (experienced) spin-offs of what constitutes useful support currently differs. One type of support that was found to be of great importance in the life sciences was access to technical facilities, which must, however, be on a non-discriminatory basis.

- PRO support would be best aimed at spin-offs with a product-based business model. In order not to disturb market selection mechanisms, this support would best be given after access to venture capital is assured.

- Given Dutch PROs' relatively limited experience, mutual sharing of knowledge, experience and best practices might be fruitful. This could also stimulate further co-operation and eventually even lead to bundling opportunities.[23] Both PROs and the government could play an active role by establishing an appropriate platform.

Innovation and management of the spin-off

- A product-based business model has clear advantages over other models (*e.g.* "tools" or "service" business models). Because of the nature of many PRO inventions, IP-based spin-offs usually operate in areas where risks are relatively high. A product-based business model can compensate for this, and its inherently higher opportunities will facilitate funding by venture capitalists.

- Experience from the United States suggest advantages for spin-offs that attract experienced management. This not only ensures good entrepreneurial skills and management experience, it also prevents conflicts of interest and of commitment. Original inventors usually retain their faculty position and do not work for the spin-off (though they often hold a position as chairman of the scientific board).

If the highest priority is given to effective technology transfer, then policy – at all levels – should aim at larger spin-offs with a product-based, rather than a "tools" or "service" business model, that have attracted professional management. Such spin-offs should be able to ensure access to sufficient funds on market-compatible conditions (involvement of venture capitalists may be helpful). Alternatively, if higher priority is given to aspects such as local/regional employment or the university's attractiveness to students, a focus on smaller spin-offs would be justified.

Although TTO operations are likely to be cost centres (not profit centres[24]), they can in the longer term have benefits that are in the public interest. This concerns in particular technology spillovers from spin-offs. New technology fields often develop outside established firms because of their relatively high level of risk and because of past investments in technological trajectories. Spin-offs can bridge the gap between generators of revolutionary innovations (PROs) and commercial adoption. From an ethical perspective, some argue that knowledge is developed at PROs with public money and that the results should be freely available to the public. In other words, they argue that universities and other PROs should not patent or otherwise protect their inventions. This chapter concludes, however, that IP-based spin-offs can result in use of innovations that otherwise would have remained unused. It may be argued that that this matches the public interest better than a publication that does not result in any practical application.

Our society is increasingly knowledge-based and the generation and use of scientific knowledge (as well as the innovative efforts of enterprises) are as an important dimension of the performance of national innovation systems. In this context, both the EU and the OECD attribute a large role to industry-science relationships. IP-based spin-offs are a promising way to achieve such relationships. Even though the degree to which such spin-offs can be used should not be overestimated, this study confirms the general feeling that more can be achieved than what is realised today.

NOTES

1. PROs include universities as well as other research institutes that are funded by public money to a substantial degree.

2. Similar trends have been observed and analysed in other countries. Nelson (2000), for instance, indicates that the number of patents granted to universities increased more than eight-fold between 1979 and 2000.

3. This is different from many definitions of spin-offs that do require such involvement. Wintjes *et al.* (2002) devote a chapter to the definitions of spin-offs used in various studies.

4. For an in-depth discussion of the institutional model, see Van der Steen (1999).

5. Defined as a multidisciplinary science in which research is conducted on the building blocks and life processes of plants, micro-organisms, animals and humans.

6. Arguably, this may be because such initiatives are especially suitable for relatively new technology fields with a vacuum in specific areas (see, for instance, Wintjes *et al.*, 2002). Clarysse *et al.* (2001, p. 14) argue that there are also many PRO spin-offs active in the field of consultancy. As such firms seem unlikely to be IP-based, this sector is not explored in this chapter.

7. The Department of Commerce recently evaluated the Act (autumn 2001), and an evaluation by the White House in 2002 may lead to changes.

8. See, for instance, the 2002 European Commission workshops relating to the "patenting dilemma" and the grace period issue; a hearing by the European Commission in 1998: www.european-patent-office.org/epo/pubs/oj99/3-99/3-1559.pdf; and German Federal Ministry of Education and Research (2001).

9. A recent evaluation of Twinning concluded that the Twinning concept worked well, but that the participating firms are increasingly competing with comparable start-ups that did not receive government funding. The Dutch government is now studying ways to decrease its involvement.

10. In addition to the programmes mentioned, there are some general national funds that can be applied for by spin-offs, even though these are not specifically aimed at spin-offs (or, in fact, at NTBFs).

11. Apart from the "traditional" trademark licences for T-shirts and caps, which are not financially irrelevant for some US universities.

12. This may depend, among other things, on the status of the university (public or private).

13. On such factors, see Clarysse *et al.* (2001). More broadly (*i.e.* not only relating to spin-offs), Manuel (2000, p. 93 ff.) distinguishes six factors: "chutzpah" (more or less, the entrepreneurial spirit), centres of opportunities, conditions (*e.g.* talent, venture capital, public and quasi-public facilities, civil and technical infrastructure), co-operation, competition and concentration.

14. The University of Twente gave rise to a considerable number of spin-offs after implementing its so-called TopSpin programme. However, most of these firms are established by alumni and none has been an IP-based spin-off. For this reason, the TopSpin programme is less relevant for this study.

15. This was the case for the spin-offs they were involved with, but not those, for instance, of staff members who left the institute to create a consultancy firm without any help from the institute.

16. Data of visited universities confirm this. For UCLA, more than 30% of the income of all 850 "income-generating licences" is generated by a single patent for the Hepatitis-B vaccine ("UC Technology Transfer Annual Report", 2001). Yale reports that 1% of its inventions represents 70% of its licensing income (1996 data: "From Bench to Bedside", Yale University Office of Cooperative Research).

17. This is the case at Indiana University, for instance, where TTO work is outsourced to the Advanced Research and Technology Institute (ARTI).

18. At one university interviewed, the inventor(s) receive(s) 50% of net income up to USD 100 000, 40% between USD 100 000 and USD 200 000 and 30% of all turnover above USD 200 000. With an unusually valuable invention (a "golden egg"), some faculty members have become multimillionaires.

19. According to Biopartner (2002), this is the case of the large majority of Dutch spin-offs in the life sciences.

20. In fact, in a recent survey of the literature, Wintjes *et al.* (2002) found "entrepreneurial skills and knowledge" and "management experience" to be two of the six most important factors in the success of spin-offs.

21. The transfer of tacit knowledge is guaranteed if the inventor moves to the spin-off. If the inventor only becomes involved as chairman of the scientific board, transfer of such knowledge is facilitated.

22. Partnering commercial organisations often claim possible IPR in advance. This is incompatible, however, with the conditions set by research funding organisations that participate in the same programmes, such as NWO. This issue could be solved by clearer rules, as illustrated by the US example.

23. This could be interesting in light of the value of a bundle of related IPRs compared to that of single licences.

24. Some IPR may nevertheless be very valuable, in which case the TTO would generate significant income. In this case, the revenue can be used to stimulate and support IP activities and spin-off support at universities and other PROs.

REFERENCES

Adviesraad voor het Wetenschaps- en Technologiebeleid (AWT) (2001), Handelen met kennis: Universitair octrooibeleid omwille van kennisbenutting (Trade with knowledge: Universities' patent policies for knowledge utilisation), The Hague.

Association of University Technology Managers (AUTM) (2000), Licensing Survey, FY 2000, Survey Summary, Northbrook, Illinois.

Biopartner (2002), The Netherlands Life Sciences Sector Report 2002, Ede.

Bouwman, H. and W. Hulsink (eds.) (2000), Silicon Valley in de polder: ICT-clusters in de Lage Landen (Silicon Valley in the polder: ICT clusters in the lowlands of Holland), Lemma, Utrecht.

Clarysse, B., A. Heirman and J-J Degroof (2001), Het fenomeen spin-off in België, IWT Observatorium, Brussels

European Commission (2001), *Benchmarking Industry-Science Relations: The Role of Framework Conditions*, Vienna/Mannheim.

European Commission (2002), *University Spin-outs in Europe: Overview and Good Practice*, Luxembourg.

Federal Ministry of Education and Research (2001), "On the Introduction of a Grace Period in Patent Law – a United States–Germany Comparison with Regard to the Higher Education Sector", Düsseldorf.

Hertog, P. den, a. Arundel and H. de Groot (2001), Quick scan ten behoeve van strategische beleidsvisie kennisbescherming (Quick scan for the purpose of strategic policymaking for knowledge protection), study commissioned by the Dutch Ministry of Economic Affairs, Utrecht.

Hertog, P. den *et al.* (2000), "Clustermonitor multimedia", Ministry of Economic Affairs, The Hague.

Jones-Evans, D. (ed.). (s.d.) "Universities, Technology Transfer and Spin-off Activities: Academic Entrepreneurship in Different European Regions, targeted socio-economic research project No.1042, University of Glamorgan.

Manuel, D. (2000), "De regio als incubator: Een analysemodel voor ICT-regio's" (The region as incubator: An analytical model for ICT regions, in Bouwman and Hulsink, 2000, pp. 79-102.

Ministry of Economic Affairs (2001), *Over de rol van intellectueel eigendom in de Nederlandse kenniseconomie* (Concerning the role of intellectual property in the Dutch knowledge society), The Hague.

Nelson, R.N. (2000), "Observations on the Post Bayh-Dole Rise of Patenting at American Universities", paper presented at the Swedish International Symposium on Economics, Law and Intellectual Property, Chalmers University of Technology, Gothenburg, 26-30 June.

NOWT (2000), *Wetenschaps- en technologie indicatoren*, CWTS/Merit, Leiden/Maastricht.

OECD(2002), *Benchmarking Industry-Science Relationships*, OECD, Paris.

Senter (2001), *Geld voor kennisinstelling en spin-offs* (Funds for Knowledge Institutes and Spin-offs), The Hague.

Steen, M. van der (1999), *Evolutionary Systems of Innovations*, Van Gorcum Publishers.

Van der Sijde, P. and J-J van Tilburg (2000), "Support of University Spin-off Companies", *International Journal of Entrepreneurship and Innovation*, Vol. 1.

Wintjes, R., J-J van Tilburg, P. van der Sijde and M. Hocke (2002), "Spin-offs uit kennisinstellingen: Een vergelijkend literatuuronderzoek", report commissioned by the Dutch Ministry of Economic Affairs.

Chapter 16

TRENDS IN ICT AND THE IMPACT ON IPR: THE CASE OF IMEC

by

Johan Van Helleputte
Vice-president, Strategic Development, IMEC

and

Kristin Robeyns, Strategic Development Unit, IMEC

Introduction

As the world prepares to enter the nanotechnology era and meet the associated challenges, new modes of scientific and technological co-operation will be needed, owing to challenges that are complex and cross-disciplinary. At the same time, there is an increasing lack of talent worldwide. Global strategic partnerships will require strong, recognised "networks of excellence", as well as new collaboration and IPR models to encourage successful strategic partnerships.

Strategic partnerships will increasingly (and at best) take place in the embryonic phase of the research, allowing partners to build a strong background IP portfolio and be prepared to grasp the optimum industrial window of opportunity into the market.

This case study describes how IMEC, a major R&D centre in the field of microelectronics, nanotechnology and information and communications technology (ICT), has developed and adapted its business model and its IPR policy in line with the trend towards global strategic partnerships.

IMEC's mission and set-up

In 1982, the Flemish government set up a comprehensive programme to strengthen Flanders' microelectronics industry. The decision was inspired by the strategic importance of microelectronics for industry and by the major investments required to keep up with developments in this field.

The programme included the establishment of a laboratory for advanced research in microelectronics (IMEC) and of a semiconductor company (former Alcatel Microelectronics, now acquired by STMicroelectronics and sold to AMI Semiconductors (United States), and the organisation of a training programme for VLSI design engineers, which is now fully integrated into IMEC activities (INVOMEC & MTC, Microelectronics Training Centre).

In 1984, IMEC was established on the outskirts of Leuven, Belgium, adjacent to the university campus. IMEC's mission was to perform scientific research that runs three to ten years ahead of industry needs in the area of microelectronics, nanotechnology, design methods and technologies for ICT.

IMEC bridges scientific research and industrial needs. Scientists build up knowledge in fundamental as well as applied research that is subsequently transferred to industry. This can be accomplished through knowledge transfer or through a licence for a specific application, but also by transferring IMEC'S trained experts. People from Flemish universities, higher polytechnics and industry can request tailored training from IMEC's microelectronic training centre.

In addition, IMEC wants to create and support new high-technology companies and attract international investment. Collaboration with other research institutes and industrial partners is of the highest importance to attune strategic research to future industrial needs.

Since its foundation in 1984, IMEC has become one of Europe's largest independent research centres in its areas of competence. With a budget of EUR 120 million (2001) and more than 1 200 highly qualified staff, IMEC performs world-class research. In 2001, IMEC co-operated with 467 partners worldwide.

In 2001 IMEC's self-generated income (apart from the government grant) rose by 22% to EUR 91.1 million (Figure 1). Today, IMEC generates 76% of its total budget, the remaining 24% being funded by the Flemish community.

Figure1. Evolution of total income 1985-2001

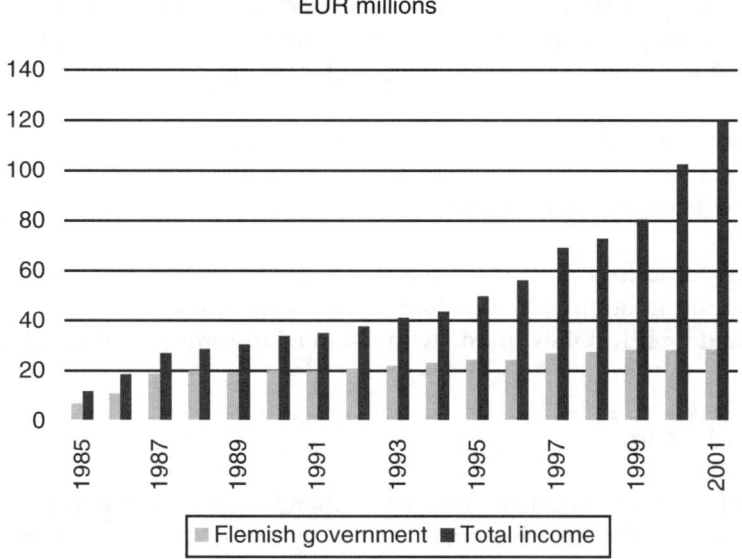

Income from international bilateral contracts amounted to EUR 40 million in 2001, which accounts for 44% of IMEC's self-generated income (Figure 2). Also in 2001, income from bilateral collaboration with 72 Flemish companies grew to EUR 30.27 million or 33% of IMEC's income generated from the market (Figure 3). The increasing importance of Flemish industry fits IMEC's mission, as it was founded by the Flemish government in part to support technology development in the Flanders region.

Figure 2. Total income from contract research, 1984-2001

EUR millions

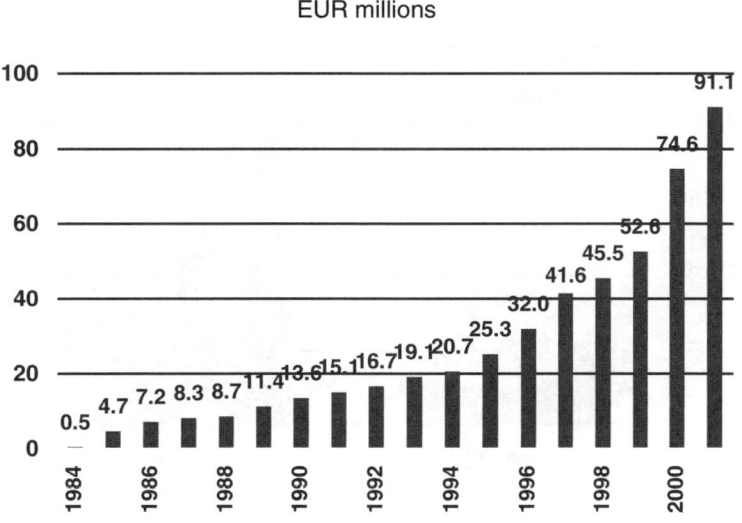

Figure 3. Total income from contract research with Flemish industry 1985-2001

EUR millions

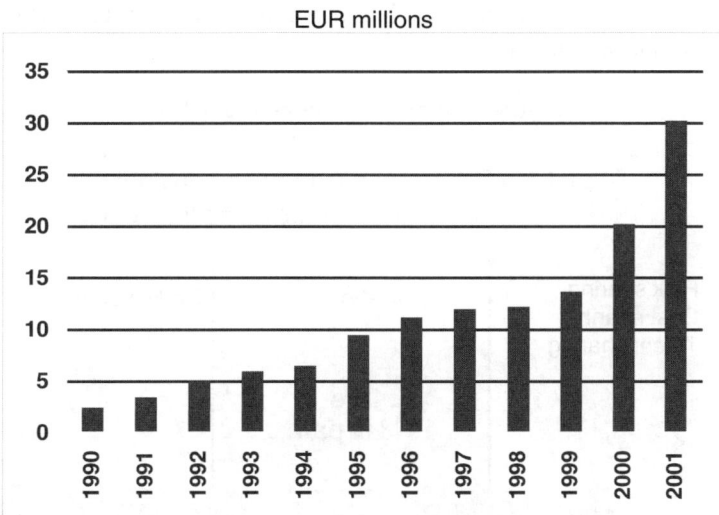

IMEC collaborates with Flemish universities as well as Flemish industry. This collaboration is partly funded by the Flemish government.[1]

Figure 4 illustrates the number of patents filed and patents granted between 1991 and 2000. In 2001, 39 patents were applied for. These applications, together with some applications from previous years, resulted in a total of 41 patents granted in 2001. IMEC's overall patent portfolio exceeds 300 patents at present.

Figure 4. Number of patents filed and granted, 1991-2000

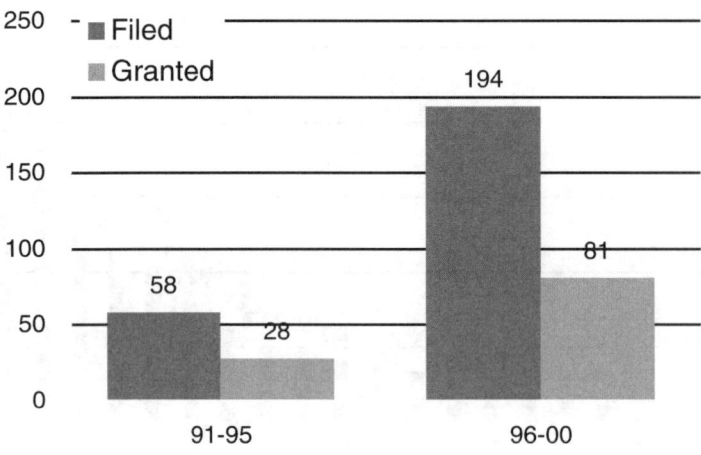

IMEC moves towards a programme-driven organisation

Fairly soon after its creation in 1984, IMEC was confronted with an important strategic issue: as the Flanders region and home market of IMEC was fairly small, it was difficult or even impossible to gain enough critical mass and momentum to be leading-edge and fulfil its mission statement (Figure 5) unless it operated at international level.

Figure 5. Mission statement of IMEC

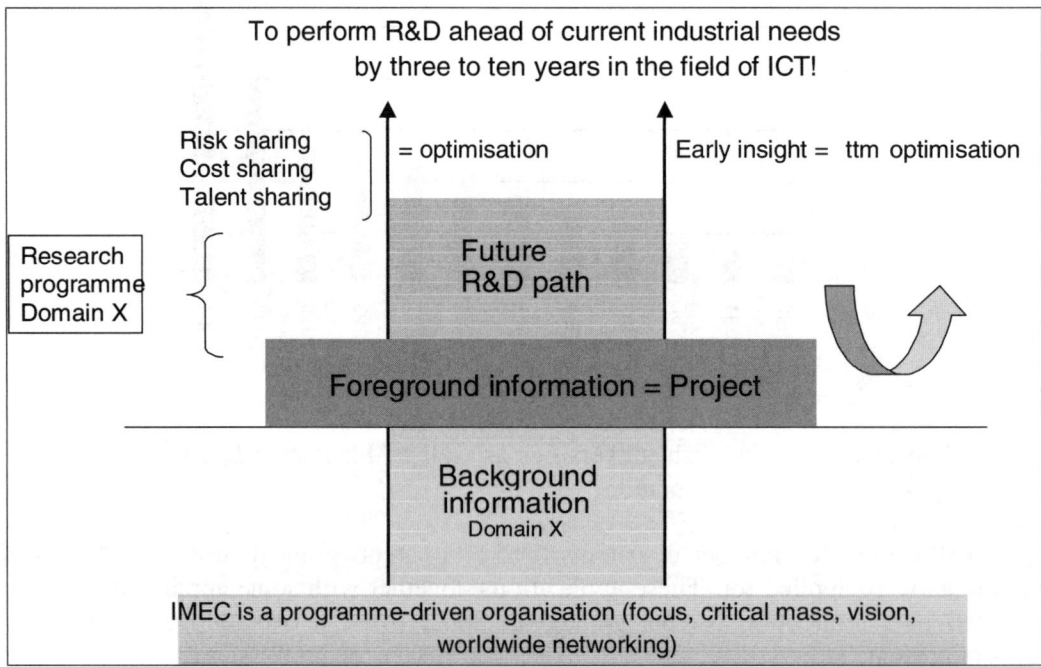

IMEC's mission is to perform R&D in the field of microelectronics[2] and ICT, ahead of current industrial needs by three to ten years. This was only possible if:

- IMEC was capable of good insight into the future needs of industry. The best way to achieve such insight was to build a worldwide network of relationships with top industrial performers.

- IMEC knew when new results should be brought to the market, in order to optimise its efforts in terms of "the window of opportunity". In other words, IMEC had to be aware of the major industrial and technological roadmaps, as the (market) value of knowledge declines rapidly over time.

To be a leading-edge organisation, critical mass was also needed. As the local market (about 6 million inhabitants) was too small to bear all the financial consequences of building critical mass, it was obvious to look to the international level for co-funding.

Moreover, talent was becoming scarce and the trend towards global strategic R&D partnerships was a question of time, so that international recognition and exposure would become necessary to attract international talent to IMEC.[3] From the start, such reasons drove IMEC to build a strong international network, which today encompasses close to 500 partners worldwide.

As part of IMEC's budget was granted by the government of Flanders, IMEC needed an IPR policy that combined international co-operation with regional development targets, in line with market reality and new business models, which would be acceptable to the international industrial community.

As a result, IMEC gradually moved from an organisation based on projects addressing specific problems for single companies, towards a more programme-driven R&D organisation addressing problems for a class of companies based on:

- Visionary R&D programmes.

- Worldwide networking.

- Critical mass.

- The multidisciplinarity of different research teams under the same roof.

- Strong background information in well-focused research programmes.

- Roadmap-driven R&D planning.

- Independence.

In order to implement such an approach, a more international set-up for collaboration was needed.

Figure 6 compares the evolution of the total income from contract research between 1990 and 2001 with the evolution of the income from contracts with the Flemish industry in the same period. It shows the evolution of income from the international community and the positive effect of international growth on the local industry.

Figure 6. Total income and income from contracts with Flemish industry from contract research, 1990-2001

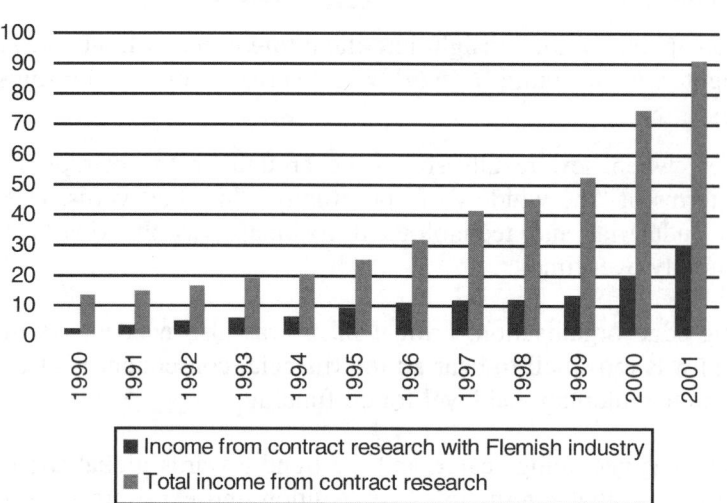

IMEC is judged both by local government and by the (international) market on its output parameters (results). It is not driven by input criteria (definition of research orientation from outside). IMEC's approach is therefore different from many consortium-driven approaches where a number of industrial members jointly define a research programme. The consortium approach requires a consensus[4] of those sponsoring the research programme. Consortia are mostly closed by nature, with research results only accessible to members.[5]

IMEC defines its programmes independently[6] and invites industrial partners to join dedicated research programmes through bilateral contracts. The industrial partner can tap into IMEC's strategic background information and optimise along different lines in terms of cost sharing, risk sharing, cross-fertilisation, talent sharing, early insight and early recognition of time to market.

IPR policies in a changing ICT environment at IMEC

Dynamic model of interaction with the industry

The international industrial community is facing a challenging reality, in which different elements of strategy[7] are being merged to build and maintain a clear "differentiation" with respect to customers, whether business-to-business (B2B) or business-to-consumer (B2C). Such differentiation is closely linked to the way products or services are valued and perceived in the market, but this is clearly a marketing and branding issue and will not be further dealt with here.

As Figure 7 illustrates, industry is gradually shifting to earlier phases of the research cycle to become further differentiated from their competitors.

Industry no longer waits until a strategically important research programme conducted by an outside R&D centre is finished before entering into a contractual relationship to gain access to such results. In the early phase of a more generic research programme, addressing problems interesting a wider group of industrial actors, industry tends to co-finance the research, provided it has access to early insight on a cost-shared basis. At the same time, the industrial partner will wish to participate in teams to be able to steer the programme slightly towards the perceived generic needs and to shorten the learning curve by rapidly absorbing new concepts,[8] new methods and new approaches as quickly and fully as possible.

Figure 7. Dynamic model of interaction between the research institute and industry

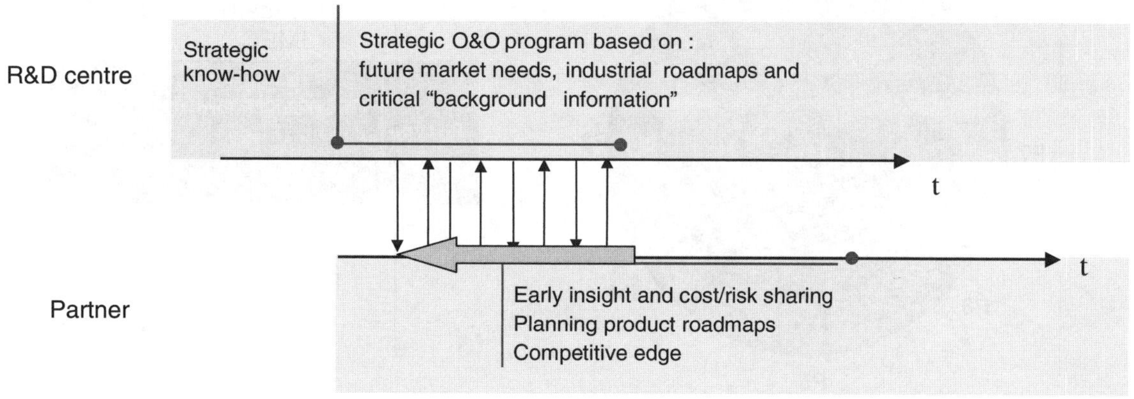

At the same time, many industrial partners realise that it is less useful to acquire exclusive rights to rapidly evolving generic technologies. It is more useful to get early insight into breakthroughs in generic technologies and to translate this into their own, company-specific products, which they own exclusively. This provides the industrial partner with a strong competitive edge at an optimised cost.

A dedicated collaboration model: the IMEC Industrial Affiliation Programme (IIAP)

In 1991, IMEC created its Industrial Affiliation Programme (IIAP) for joint R&D based on sharing of costs, risks, talent and IP. This programme is recognised worldwide as one of the more successful international partnership models for joint research on next-generation technologies, running two to three generations ahead of industrial ramp-up and addressing generic industrial problems.[9]

An IIAP is an R&D partnership that enables industrial researchers to become part of IMEC's research teams in well-defined research programmes. For each industrial partner and within each programme, there is room for customised, as well as jointly shared, R&D results.

Figure 8 illustrates the IPR model linked to this mode of co-operation and its linkage to a collaboration model. The right-hand side represents a research programme set-up by IMEC in domain X, where IMEC has been building up strong background information (BI), composed of tacit knowledge, documented internal research results and patents. Using this information, IMEC defines a focused research programme, based on a certain vision and inputs from IMEC's worldwide network to be executed in the coming years when new foreground information (FI) is to be created. Such FI will be created by a mixed team of IMEC researchers (core team) and industrial residents, as part of bilateral agreements between IMEC and its industrial partners. IMEC concludes bilateral contracts with a number of different industrial partners, each time defining the contract deliverables in line with the overall programme objectives.

Figure 8. IMEC's Industrial Affiliation Programme

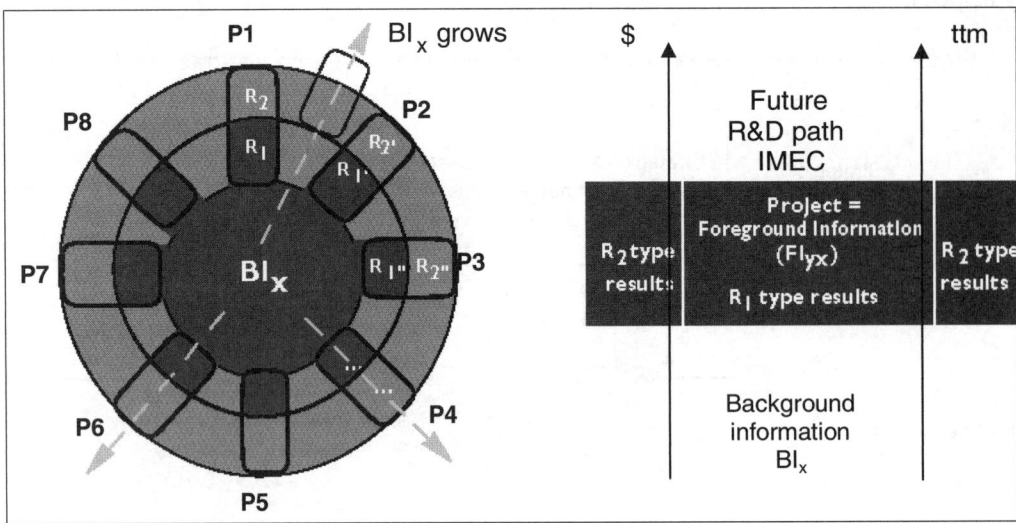

The deliverables (FI) are defined as part of the contract and are labelled into two broad categories of IPR:

- In line with IMEC's mission statement and based upon IMEC's BI, the more generic FI results of IMEC's broader research programme are "co-owned by both parties without any accounting to each other". This means that each party can freely use the results without permission from the other partners. Such results are called R1 results. R1 results can be licensed to third parties.

- Other results are very company-specific and based upon confidential company information. They tend to be more product-oriented and hence closer to the market. As IMEC does not produce products, but develops (generic) technology, such results do not constitute a roadblock for future in-house R&D programmes. Hence, the industrial partner can be granted exclusive rights to such results, called R2 results, in a very flexible way. These results cannot be licensed to third parties.

This labelling is done up front as part of the contract and is very flexible as all contracts are negotiated on a bilateral basis. The more R1 results are obtained, the more IMEC can re-use the results and the more a notion of cost-sharing can be introduced, building a number of leveraging effects, as discussed above.

Furthermore, industrial partners obtain a non-exclusive licence to the BI of IMEC which is needed to perform and exploit the foreground research work. Such rights and their scope are also part of the contract. In principle, such licensing rights do not contain the right to grant sub-licenses.

Increasingly, owing to a shortage of talent, companies are selectively outsourcing strategic R&D (well enough advanced in the life cycle to allow for differentiation before entering the market on a competitive basis) on a cost-shared basis in order to explore different, promising avenues (options) and to tap into promising new breakthroughs at an early stage.

Given that IMEC's mission statement requires it to develop generic technology rather than products, there is a strong complementarity between the research institute and its industrial partners, in terms of the technology life cycle (Figure 9).

Figure 9. Technology life cycle

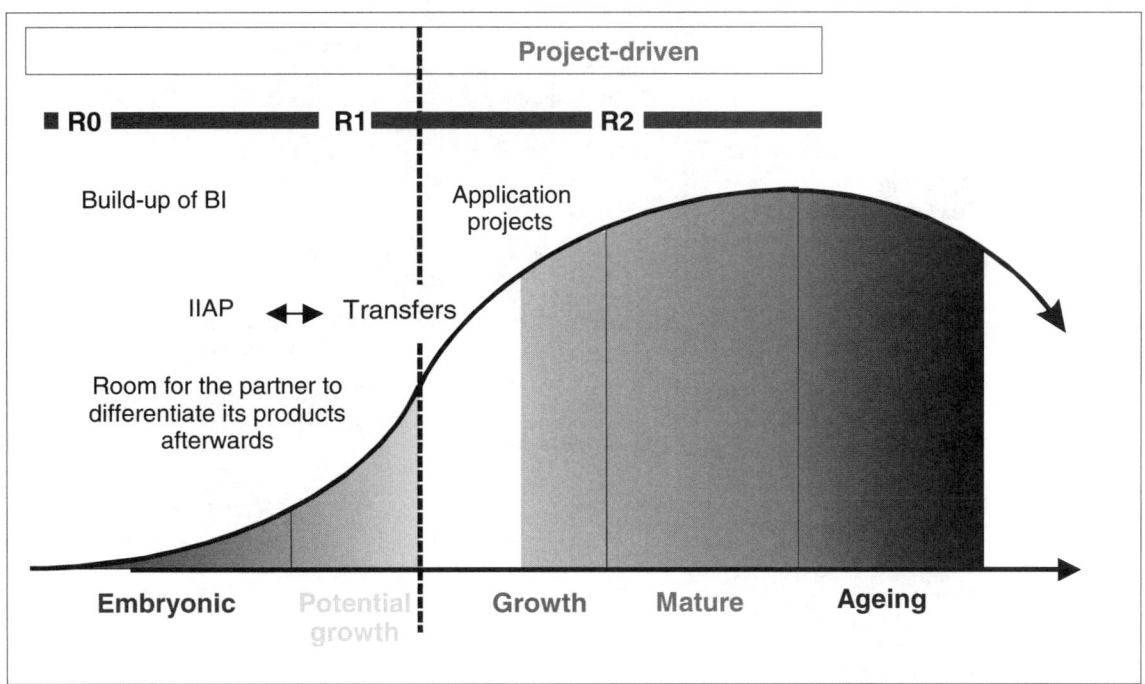

Clearly, the more a research institute such as IMEC moves to the right, the closer it comes to the market, the more the industrial partner will require R2 results, with no re-usability and hence, no sharing of costs or IP. Such co-operation will then be project-driven rather than programme-driven, and hence is generally less interesting for the research institute.[10] A research institute such as IMEC should, naturally and in line with its mission statement, focus largely on the left side of the figure, resulting in a win-win complementarity.

By obtaining R1 results, IMEC can build critical mass and also deploy an industrial policy linked to regional development based on knowledge, internal research and background information, including R1 results from previous contracts. It also will have enough talent to contribute to building a "region of excellence", an essential node in a networked economy of regions of excellence. This becomes even more important as talent becomes scarce and very mobile. Talent will seek talent just as capital attracts capital.

In IMEC's case, its international policy is a natural complement to regional development, provided an appropriate IPR model, as explained above, underpins the business model adopted, which has to be embedded in a win-win model with industrial partners. At the same time, it allows for much flexibility and fits into a trend towards global strategic R&D partnerships based on international recognition and quality labelling.

An example of a successful IIAP collaboration was the development of the 193 nm lithography IIAP, in which IMEC speeded up the development and introduction of 193 nm lithography by worldwide co-operation with more than 35 industrial partners (Figure 10).

Figure 10. IMEC's 193 nm lithography consortium

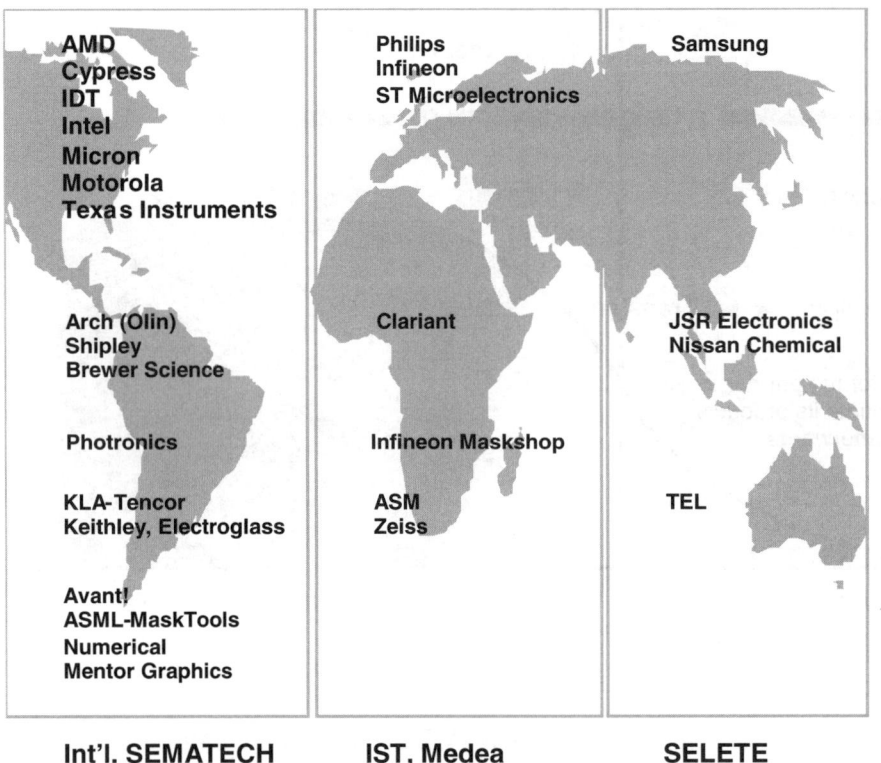

| Int'l. SEMATECH | IST, Medea | SELETE |

IMEC currently has IIAPs running in 14 different areas.[11]

The IMEC IP fingerprint model

Collaboration with an industrial partner

Having obtained generic IP as a result of an IIAP, each industrial partner should be able build its own, unique IP portfolio or IP fingerprint in order to differentiate itself from other companies or competitors that participated in the same R&D programme.

The IP portfolio of an industrial partner can be composed of results from different sources and can contain different types of IPR (Figure 11):

- Non-exclusive IP (R1), from IMEC and co-owned by the different IIAP members, without any accounting to each other. This means that each party can freely use common results, without requiring permission from the other partners. These results are the same for all members and as such are not unique or exclusive to one partner. They are obtained at much lower cost than exclusive IP.

- Exclusive IP (R2), exclusive rights for one industrial partner, resulting from co-operation with IMEC. In general, such IP is an application of R1 results to the partner's industrial context.

- Exclusive IP (R0co) of the company, resulting from the partner's own "internal research", based upon IMEC's generic results. It is mostly product-oriented and realised outside the collaboration with IMEC.

Figure 11. IPR fingerprint model – collaboration with an industrial partner

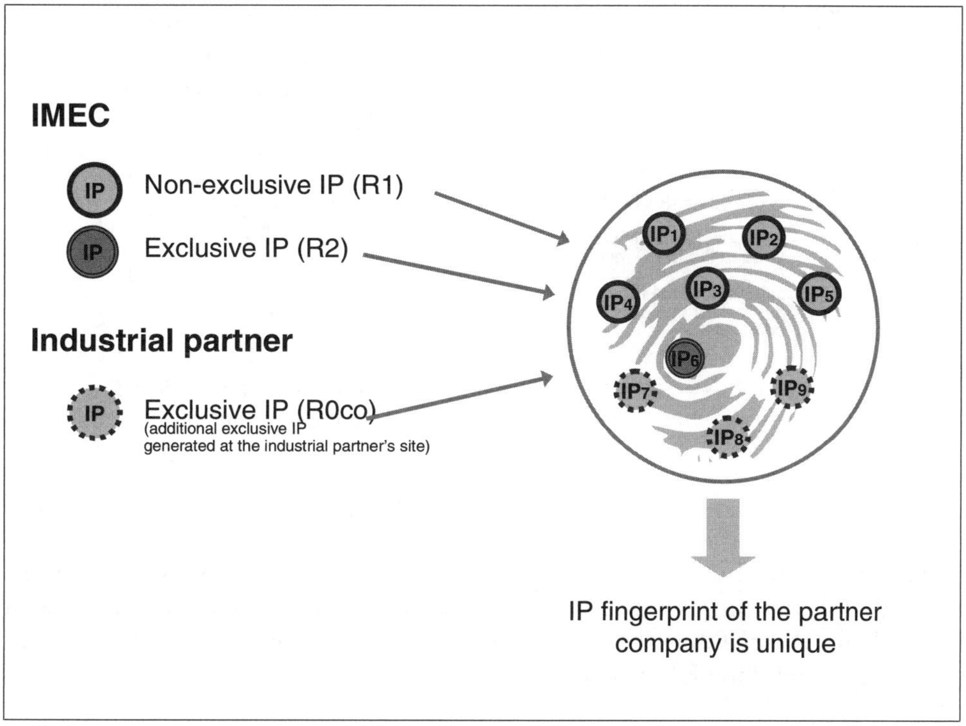

IMEC

IP Non-exclusive IP (R1)

IP Exclusive IP (R2)

Industrial partner

IP Exclusive IP (R0co)
(additional exclusive IP
generated at the industrial partner's site)

IP fingerprint of the partner
company is unique

By combining the R1 and R2 results obtained from collaboration with IMEC and the internal R0co results, the company achieves a unique IP portfolio or IP fingerprint. It thus can gain a unique competitive advantage after having benefited from sharing the costs and risks for the R1 part of results, as well as from access to IMEC background, talent sharing and cross-fertilisation. For the company, the optimal situation is enough R1 IP subsets (cost effectiveness) and yet enough R2 or R0co to provide the "unique fingerprint".

Creation of a spin-off company

In addition to collaboration with industrial partners, IMEC also started using the IP fingerprint model to start up new spin-off companies.

Until now, each spin-off company created by IMEC had its own IP portfolio with exclusive IP (R2) only, as generally requested by venture capital companies. This implied that IMEC had to make a choice, at the very beginning of its research, between performing R&D on its own funding to create exclusive R2 results for the spin-off company and performing research with industrial partners and creating more non-exclusive R1 results. This meant a cheaper cost-shared basis, but no exclusive rights for IMEC (Figure 12).

The exclusive rights requested by venture capital often created a high financial burden for the starting spin-off, while part of the more generic IP was evolving rapidly and too expensive to be owned exclusively by a spin-off.

301

Figure 12. IPR fingerprint model – creation of a spin-off company

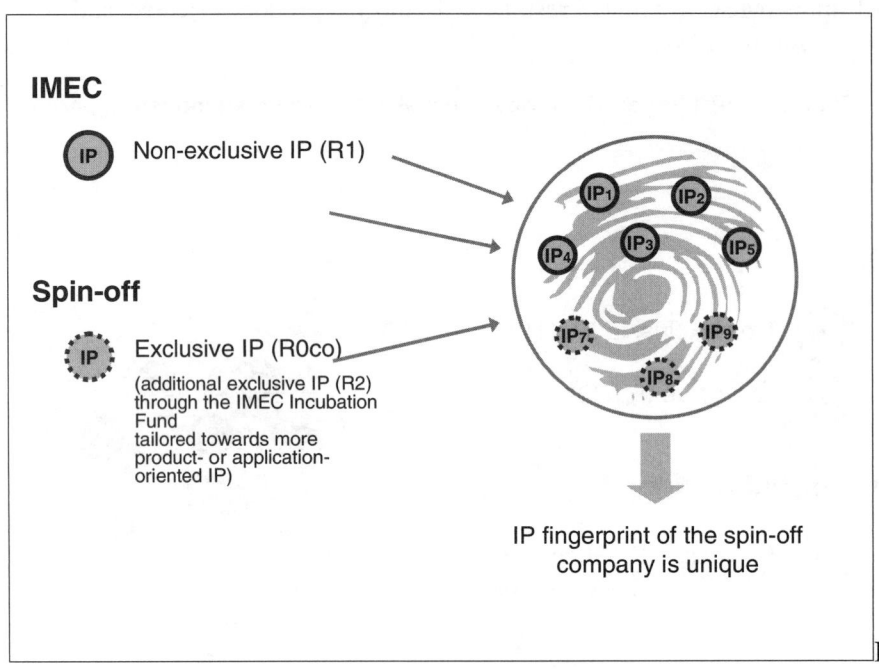

By introducing the IP fingerprint model, IMEC now creates a unique IP portfolio by combining non-exclusive IP (R1 resulting from IIAPs) with exclusive IP (R0co) generated with incubation funding of IMEC, thereby enabling the spin-off to build a unique fingerprint and to differentiate itself from competitors by combining R1 and R0co.

With such a model, the spin-off can create a unique IP fingerprint at much lower cost. The spin-off combines R1 (shared with other industrial partners) with its own, more product-oriented R0co. There is thus no conflict of interest between industrial partners (even competitors) that join IMEC's IIAPs and IMEC spin-offs that have access to the same R1 results.

It may happen, and has happened in the past, that the spin-off company is later taken over. Until now, the activities of the former spin-off company have remained in Flanders owing to the presence of IMEC. Only the ownership changed.

Collaboration between different R&D providers

In future, this model can be used to organise collaboration between different providers of IPR based on R&D. Classic approaches make it difficult for different technology providers to work together, but even here advantages such as the sharing of costs, risks and talent can be gained through the IP fingerprint approach.

If different technology providers collaborate to create joint non-exclusive IP (R1) in the "embryonic" phase of the technology life cycle (Figure 13), they can share costs and risks by joining forces and sharing the resulting IP, according to the rule on IPR for R1 results. Such IP forms the basis of generic, early-phase IP blocks. Each technology partner will, at the end of the collaboration, introduce such IP blocks (co-shared without any accounting to each other, R1) into their own IP portfolio. Then, each party will create own (exclusive) IP on own internal research (R0) or work with third parties to generate new R1 results.

Figure13. IPR fingerprint model – step 1: collaboration with an R&D partner in the embryonic phase of the technology life cycle to create joint IP

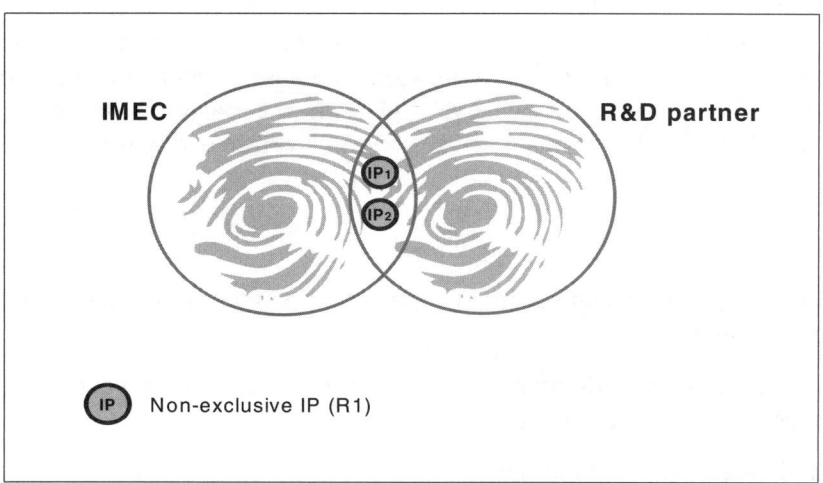

Their respective IP portfolios and hence their IP fingerprints will gradually evolve and become more and more differentiated (and hence unique). By the time they are approaching the market (for industrial collaboration), the IP portfolio of each R&D partner will be so different that they will no longer be direct competitors, although they share some common IP (R1 results, jointly developed in the embryonic phase of the life cycle).

Figure 14. IPR fingerprint model – step 2: collaboration with an R&D partner in the growth phase of the technology life cycle

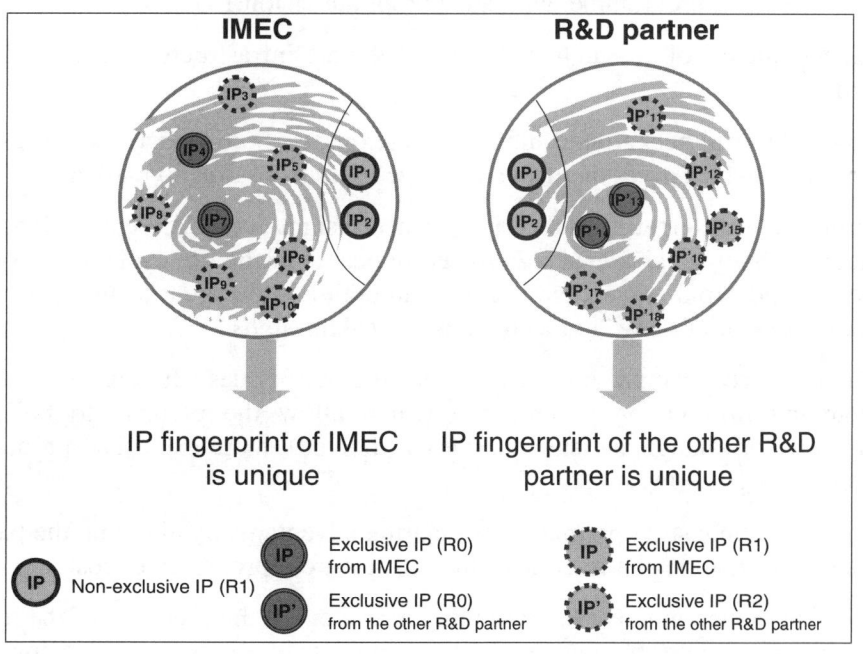

Conclusions

The IMEC case leads to a number of conclusions. In terms of generic technology development, industrial partners seem gradually to move towards broader models of "co-competition".[12] It is becoming less necessary to obtain exclusive rights in the early phase of generic technology development on a project-based relationship with a research centre owing to:

- The high costs of exclusive rights.

- The high risks involved in the early phase.

- The increasing cross-disciplinarity of recent technology developments and the rapid increase in their complexity.

- The lack of talent to study many different options, in-house, especially taking into account the branching out of micro(nano)electronics.

- The rapid evolution of technologies.

- The need for critical mass and rapid deployment of resources to meet time-to-market requirements.

- The opportunity of cross-fertilisation between researchers of different origins.

As a consequence, many industrial partners are willing to consider a more programme-driven approach and co-operation with an independent centre of excellence, provided they have a number of obvious advantages to overcome the lack of exclusive ownership, such as:

- A broad research programme, with an appropriate vision.13

- Excellent quality of research and state-of-the-art infrastructure, proven by a good track record.

- Strong and useful background information (expertise, knowledge, useful results, underlying patents, etc.) which gives them an advantage in terms of time to market.

- Offering the participating industrial partner insight into different options for potentially strategic technological avenues. In the early phases of the life cycle, many options are open. Important industrial players tend to have an option in different technological orientations to lower the risk of missing "hot technology" breakthroughs.

- Providing early insight into critical technology issues through new research results (foreground information programme) which allow the partners to build an additional competitive advantage and start their own (derived), more exclusive, product roadmap in a concurrent engineering mode.

- Providing the industrial partner a cost-sharing advantage, by allowing the partner to tap into strategic information at a fraction of the full research (programme) cost.

- Shortening the learning curve by sending a resident to the premises of the research institute. This also provides extra cross-fertilisation among the various research teams.

A programme-driven approach also provides significant flexibility:

- Unlike a closed consortium approach, the IMEC business model does not require the partners to agree on a research programme all together or at the same moment. All contracts are concluded bilaterally and the programme is in principle open to any partner willing to adhere to the contractual terms and conditions. In practice, once a sufficient core team of partners is gathered in line with marketing planning, the programme can start. The optimal size of the programme team and of the programme, the costs involved, the acceptable unit rates and the window of opportunity (positioning on the life cycle and on the roadmaps) all play a role.

- Partners can join the programme at a moment that is convenient.14. Pricing15 is based on the life cycle of the research programme and takes into account the moment of joining.

- This allows the organising institute (e.g. IMEC) to start very flexibly, taking the optimal window of opportunity, provided it is willing to take the commercial risk of initiating the overall research programme. To minimise the commercial risk, programme road shows are organised to be sure of a minimum of industrial interest and commitment, especially if heavy investment is required to perform the overall research programme.

- The system of bilateral contracting allows for flexible labelling of IPR into R0 results (exclusive right for the organising institute with user rights for the partner), R1 results (co-owned without any accounting to each other) and R2 results (exclusively owned by the industrial partner) on a case-by-case-basis. R2 (which always represents a minority of the contract deliverables and results) allows for bringing into the programme company-specific and confidential materials and specifications, to be tested within the programme, without jeopardising the company's confidential data.

The system requires, however, sufficient independence and sufficient internal research to build continuously new and appealing strategic background information. A minimum level of public grants or public funding is essential to maintain independence. Indeed, the more a research institute is dependent on the market for income, the more the market tends to force it towards the shorter term. A good balance is mandatory.

As public co-funding plays an important role, it is important to place enough emphasis on longer-term or embryonic, hence riskier, research for which the market is not (yet) willing to pay. This becomes more evident, if one considers a model in which different research institutes are asked to work together to perform joint research in a pan-European or even global network of excellence. This will be the case in the near future, owing to the complexity of the technological challenges and the scarcity of talent.

Relations between research institutes (or universities) and industry are more natural, from a financial point of view, than co-operation among research institutes (and/or universities) themselves. The latter type of co-operation will only be successful if:

- Co-operation takes place in the embryonic phase of the technology life cycle and is driven by a complementary visionary research programme.

- There are enough financial incentives (co-funding, grants) from national or supra-national organisations.

- The contracting, co-operating partners contribute in a comparable way to the joint research programme (both in terms of background information16 being made available and in terms of contributions to new joint foreground information).

- A clear IPR policy is worked out. The most feasible, transparent and easy way is to share the programme results (FI) among all participating partners, without any accounting to each other. In other words, partners can, if they wish, re-use the results (FI) in bilateral relationships with industrial partners.

Such co-operation allows for building networks of excellence, even virtual networks to a certain degree. The use of public money is also justified for complex, risky research in the early phase of the life cycle, where the market is not willing to co-fund, or for research programmes where the costs surpass the financial commitments of single nations.

It is important to note that IMEC's IP strategy has contributed to regional development, as expected by the Flemish government[17] and as was concluded by a recent external evaluation panel, and this by:

- Offering the possibility to reuse IP (R1) in Flanders.

- Creating international exposure for the Flemish region.

- Allowing local industry to have insight into international trends.

- Making a critical mass of R&D accessible to regional industry and universities.

- Attraction of foreign talent to Flanders.

NOTES

1.   The Flemish government has signed a framework agreement with IMEC, according to which IMEC receives an annual research grant of EUR 33.3 million The term of the contract is five years. Only 95% of the grant is fixed. The remaining 5%, or EUR 1.7 million, depends on the realisation of 12 key performance indicators.

   The frame agreement engages IMEC to remain a worldwide centre of excellence in the field of microelectronics; collaborate with Flemish universities in an interactive and multidisciplinary way with a focus on joint research objectives with a view to develop technologies for tomorrow's world and to strengthen collaboration with Flemish industry. These challenges have been translated into measurable annual objectives (key performance indicators) that have to be met to get the remaining 5% of the annual research grant.

2.   Which today is evolving towards nanotechnology.

3.   At present, about 30% of IMEC's staff of about 1 200 is not Belgian; they represent more than 40 different nationalities.

4.   Quite often this implies some degree of "power games" among industrial members. Also, the research only starts when consensus is reached. In some cases, this can be a somewhat lengthy process.

5.   In some cases, results can also be licensed to third parties, against payment, after a certain delay (*e.g.* SELETE in Japan).

6.   Based upon information flows among its contacts and partners worldwide.

7.   Technological, commercial, business, organisational, managerial, etc.

8.   Hence, the importance of "industrial residents".

9.   The success of this business model has been proven in the semiconductor industry. To be successful in other domains, the technology has to evolve very quickly and the joint research has to be done on technologies addressing generic industrial problems. A programme-driven business model can only be successful when an organisation invests in the creation of background information, especially in the embryonic phase of the technology life cycle.

10.   A minimum of such contracts can be useful to have enough research feedback from dedicated cases.

11.   More information on these IIAPs can be found in IMEC's Annual Report 2001 and at www.imec.be

12.   Co-operation between competitors. The same trend has been noted in the automotive sector, where competitors developed new engines. The joint results were later translated into different, competing products (car models).

13. Positioned early enough in the life cycle to allow industrial partners to differentiate their products before entering the market as competitors.

14. Within the programme time horizon, which is defined in function of the corresponding technology roadmap (if available) and desired (expected) optimal window of opportunity.

15. Especially related to the available BI (when joining), which is translated into an entrance fee.

16. The more such research takes place in the early phase of the technology life cycle (embryonic research), the less pre-existing background information there will be, which will make collaboration easier. Only new foreground information, as well as the efforts and the risks, will be generated and shared.

17. The Flemish government requests IMEC to remain a world centre of excellence in the field of microelectronics; collaborate with universities in an interactive, multidisciplinary way with a focus on joint research objectives with a view to developing technologies for tomorrow's world and to strengthen collaboration with Flemish industry.

OECD PUBLICATIONS, 2, rue André-Pascal, 75775 PARIS CEDEX 16
PRINTED IN FRANCE
(92 2003 02 1 P) ISBN 92-64-10022-9 – No. 52979 2003